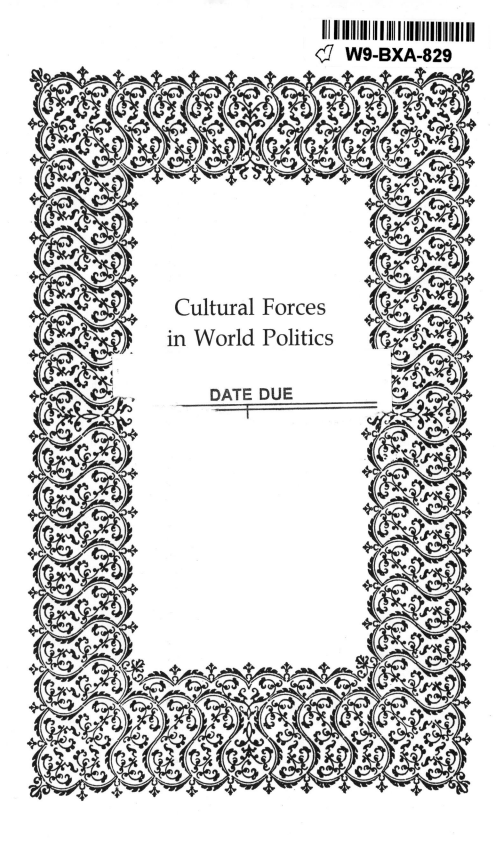

Cultural Forces
in World Politics

DATE DUE

Reviews of

Ali A. Mazrui

Cultural Forces in World Politics

'Mazrui delights in dualism and dichotomy, in pairs and parallels, and the paradoxes thereof. Bringing the south's point of view to the north, the east's to the west, and in return showing how the north and west's standpoint and behaviour have been culturally conditioned may begin to loosen hidebound beliefs. A book that makes one think...' Bob Marshall in *The Bookseller*, London

'... presents an alternative view of the world that does not see Europe or America as the only players in world affairs.' Rosalinde Yarde in *The Times Higher Education Supplement*, London

'... probably his most controversial yet ...' *BBC World Service* , London

'What Ali Mazrui is best at is flying kites' David Maugham Brown in *Social Dynamics*, Durban

'... commands attention and merits respect simply for attempting to construct a full-blown thesis that might illuminate today's politics.' Kevin J. Kelly in *The Daily Nation*, Nairobi

'Many of the arguments which Mazrui advances will infuriate and offend principally because they are so manifestly true... 'Guy Arnold in *The Journal of Southern African Studies*, Oxford

'Himself a cultural mongrel (he is an Afro-Asiatic westerner) Mazrui is, perhaps, better placed than any of us to use Afro-Islamic and Judeo-western prisms to discern the cultural forces that are at work in world politics.' William R. Ochieng' in the *Weekly Review*, Nairobi

'This is an erudite , encyclopedic and provocative essay.' Andrew J. Pierre in *Foreign Affairs* New York

'Of all the academics writing on the Third World and particularly on Africa, Professor Ali Mazrui alone seems to have mastered the art of effortlessly picking out the gems from cavernous mines of history...' Anver Versi in *The New African* and *Al Qalam*, London

'The book will be controversial and will even give offence to some – notably in the comparison between apartheid and Zionism – but it will not and should not be ignored.' Keith Somerville in *International Affairs*, London

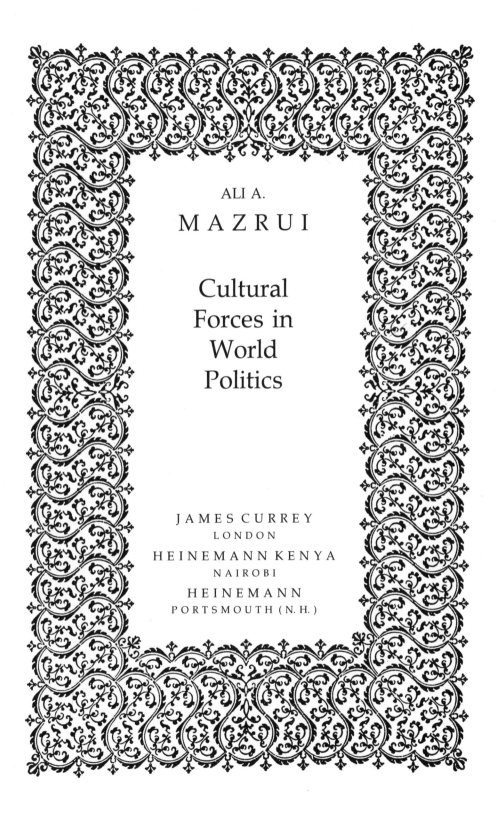

ALI A.
MAZRUI

Cultural
Forces in
World
Politics

JAMES CURREY
LONDON
HEINEMANN KENYA
NAIROBI
HEINEMANN
PORTSMOUTH (N.H.)

James Currey Ltd
54b Thornhill Square, Islington
London N1 1BE

Heinemann Kenya
Kijabe Street, PO Box 45314
Nairobi

Heinemann Educational Books Inc
361 Hanover Street
Portsmouth, New Hampshire 03801

4 5   95

British Library Cataloguing in Publication Data

Mazrui, Ali A. (Ali Al'Amin)
  Cultural forces in world politics
  1. Foreign relations. Political aspects
  I. Title
  327

ISBN 0-85255-321-8
ISBN 0-85255-322-6 Pbk

Library of Congress Cataloging-in-Publication Data

Mazrui, Ali Al'Amin.
  Cultural forces in world politics / Ali A. Mazrui.
    p.   cm.
  Includes bibliographical references.
  1. World politics--1945- 2. Politics and culture.   I. Title.
D849.M387   1990
909.82--dc20   90-4869
                                                   CIP

ISBN 0-435-08047-4

The Arabesque border of fleurons
used on the title page and the part titles
was designed and assembled by Bruce Rogers
for an edition of Sir Thomas More's *Utopia*
(New York, Limited Editions Club, 1934).
The Monotype designs were based on
Arab tooling for book bindings.

Set in 10/11 Parlament
by Opus 43
and printed in Britain by
Villiers Publications, London N6

Contents

Contents

PART II

Ideology & Power   65

Contents

PART III

In Search of Change 193

Acknowledgements

This book was conceived at an international colloquium on 'Nuclear War, Nuclear Proliferation and Their Consequences' held in Geneva in June 1985, and sponsored by Groupe de Bellerive and Prince Sadruddin Aga Khan. It was a star-studded conference, opened by the late Prime Minister Olaf Palme of Sweden and closed by Prince Sadruddin. Superpower participants included Vice-President George Bush (now president), and Senator Edward Kennedy from the United States and Professor Anatoly Gromyko (son of former president Andrei Gromyko) and Dr Georgi Arbatov, Director of the Institute of the USA and Canada of the Academy of Sciences of the USSR.

My own short presentation at the conference linked nuclear proliferation to global cultural issues. It was not long before Fred Praeger approached me and encouraged me to bring together into one volume the varied concerns I had expressed in other contexts about the role of culture in world politics.

Meanwhile, James Currey had separately been urging me to relate once again my global interests with my African commitments. I had worked with James many times before when he was part of the team of Heinemann Educational Books, but this latest book was going to be my first collaboration with his now independent publishing firm. Fred Praeger and James Currey between them were therefore the original instigators of this volume.

Some of the ideas in this collection have been presented in their earlier versions to other audiences. I am greatly indebted to all the journals which have given us the intellectual green light to bring together my work in this manner.

Many of the ideas in these pages evolved out of my involvement in the work of the United Nations and its agencies. Specially relevant has been my participation in the UNESCO General History of Africa.

On legal issues and jurisprudence in these chapters I have often been stimulated by Isaac J. Mowoe of Ohio State University at Columbus. On Pan-African issues I have learnt a lot from Locksley Edmondson at Cornell University, Ithaca, New York.

To Michael Tidy I remain forever grateful for his continuing editorial and research support. He has been invaluable in updating some of my chapters against the background of rapidly changing events in world affairs. Michael has been aided in these research tasks by my friend at the University of Michigan and State University of New York, Omari H. Kokole. I salute their dedication. I am also grateful to the Center for Afroamerican and African Studies (CAAS) at the University of Michigan for making such services possible.

Typing and related secretarial responsibilities for this volume were handled by Judy Baughn and Mary Breijak — two central pillars of my career at Michigan. Without their intervention, order in my life would still be seriously threatened. I am indebted to the Department of Political Science and to CAAS at Michigan for making this secretarial support possible.

The final stages of this book were aided by the Abel Schweitzer Unit at the State University of New York and by the support and stimulation provided by my colleagues on the Binghamton campus.

To Brenda and Maureen Kiberu I owe the strong domestic foundation which my career needed in the period in question. The two women provided that support with liveliness and youthful vigour.

To my three sons — Jamal, Al'Amin and Kim — I owe not only the joys of parenthood but also many hours of intellectual excitement when we argued about world affairs and moral issues until the cockerel proclaimed a new dawn.

As for the faults in this book, Harry Truman said it for all authors as well as all presidents: 'The buck stops here!'

Ali A. Mazrui

INTRODUCTION
The Culture of Power
& the Power of Culture

The Hidden Agenda
of World Politics

The central divide between East and West since World War II has of course been *ideological* — communism versus capitalism. The central divide between the North and South in the same period has been *technological* — the industrialized states *versus* the developing societies. East—West tensions have resulted in *military* rivalries. North—South tensions have been linked to *economic* disparities. The East and the West have competed for new skills of *destruction*. The North and South have been estranged by different levels of *production*. This book seeks to demonstrate that both *ideology* and *technology* are rooted in *culture*.

The ideological divide between East and West may turn out to be much more transient than the technological gap between North and South. A single Northern leader like Mikhail Gorbachev could change the atmosphere in East—West relations and initiate a partial cultural and ideological convergence. But it would take more than the fortunate emergence of a reformist leader in a single country to narrow the *technological* divide between North and South. Cultural change needed for technological progress is more complex than cultural change needed for ideological revisionism.

The International Costs of 'Perestroika'

There is an additional worry facing the 1990s. Will the narrowing ideological gap between East and West widen the technological gap between North and South? Will *perestroika* and the rapprochement between the Soviet 'commonwealth' and the Western alliance deepen the economic disparities between North and South? What are the cultural costs involved?

The issue arises partly because much of foreign aid to the Third World since World War II has been inspired by the ideological and strategic rivalry between East and West. The American concept of 'enlightened self-interest' as a rationalization of American foreign aid was based in the main on a strategic concept of 'self-interest'. It was assumed that foreign aid helped to protect the security interests of the United States in far-flung corners of the world.

Soviet aid to the Third World has often been even more blatantly strategic. Cuba has been by far the biggest beneficiary of Soviet aid. To some extent, Cuba has been to the Soviet Union what Israel has been to the United States. But Cuba's value to the Soviet Union is more purely strategic than is the value of Israel to the United States. While Soviet financial commitment to Cuba is almost certainly likely to decline in the wake of Soviet *perestroika* at home and Soviet rapprochement with the Western world, the American financial commitment to Israel will almost certainly remain resilient. American links to Israel have firmer *cultural* foundations than has the Soviet connection with Cuba.

What seems probable in both Washington and Moscow is the decline of the *urgency* of foreign aid as an international priority. Reduced ideological and strategic competition between East and West will almost certainly mean reduced transfer of resources from North to South. What is more, there may be a sharper drop in Soviet aid to the Third World than in Western aid to the same regions. In any case, the *culture of giving* at the international level is still too weak.

Another reason why East—West rapprochement could mean greater North—South disparities concerns the likely acceleration of civilian and consumer technology within the Soviet alliance as a consequence of *perestroika*. As the focus of industrial emphasis shifts from military equipment to economic needs, the industrialized socialist countries may increase the technological distance between themselves and the Third World. The Northern hemisphere would become even more *advanced* — outstripping the South even further. Some of the pains of restructuring or *perestroika* in the Second World of socialism will be borne by the Third World of underdevelopment.

We define the world of industrialized socialist countries as the Second World — encompassing mainly the Soviet Union and its European allies. We define the First World as industrialized North America, Western Europe and Japan. We define the Third World as encompassing most of Asia, Africa and Latin America. The cultural divide between East and West is much narrower than the cultural divide between North and South. This book will explore the implications.

As the First World of capitalism gets closer to the Second World of industrialized socialism, trade between them may indeed expand. The question which arises is whether this *increased* trade between East and West would result in *reduced* trade between North and South. Will Western businessmen be so tempted and mesmerized by the newly open markets of the Eastern bloc that the flight of Western capital from the Third World towards Northern opportunities will accelerate? That could be one more cost of the rapprochement between East and West.

Yet another cost is the likely atrophy of the public conscience of the superpowers. For much of the second half of the twentieth century the United States and the Soviet Union have served as each other's consciences. When one superpower was guilty of excesses, the other superpower blew the international whistle — and cried out 'Foul!' The United States led the international condemnation of the Soviet invasion of Afghanistan — just as the Soviet Union had once been among the first to blow the whistle against increasing American involvement in Vietnam.

Will the new rapprochement between the superpowers result in a *de facto* conspiracy of silence between the superpowers — sparing each other embarrassment rather than ringing the international alarm?

When the Soviet Union tragically shot down a Korean civilian aircraft (Flight 007) in 1983, it was before the rapprochement between Washington and Moscow. The United States cried foul — and served as the conscience of the world in its outrage. But when the United States in turn shot down an Iranian aircraft in an international

2

air corridor in 1988, the rapprochement between East and West had started. Far from the Soviet Union blowing the whistle and mobilizing international condemnation of Washington, the Soviet reaction was subdued, deliberately calculated not to embarrass the United States. When the Soviets committed their tragic blunder against hundreds of innocent civilian passengers, Moscow paid heavily in public relations. But when the United States destroyed a comparable number of innocent passengers, the cost which the United States paid in public relations was minimal. The Soviet foreign affairs spokesman, Gennadi Gerasimov, revealed to the world one major reason. The Soviets did not want to 'exploit' the American blunder. In reality, this meant that the Soviet Union did not want to serve as the conscience of the world in the old way any longer. Among the losers were the families of the Iranian passengers whom the American ship *U.S. Vincennes* had shot down and killed. Their moral cause had one less international champion — the Soviet voice of outrage.

As the Soviet Union now values good relations with the West more and more, will it value good relations with the Third World less and less? Was that a factor behind Soviet pressure on Cuba and Angola to agree to the link between Namibia's independence and the withdrawal of Cuban troops from Angola? Have the Soviets put undue pressure on the Palestine Liberation Organization to make premature concessions to Israel? Would Soviet support for the newly proclaimed Palestinian state have been more spectacular and ostentatious if the cold war between East and West had still been vigorously waged?

Particularly worrying for Africa is whether Soviet commitment to *armed* struggle against apartheid in South Africa is weakening. It seems most unlikely that white minority rule in South Africa could ever be ended by means other than armed struggle. Nowhere else in Africa has a local white minority, strong enough militarily to defend its privileges, ever given up those privileges without a military fight. This has been true of white privileges in Algeria, Kenya, Zimbabwe, Angola, Mozambique and elsewhere. Until the rapprochement between the Soviet alliance and the West, armed struggle against white minority rule in Africa had relied for military support disproportionately upon socialist countries — especially from the 1960s onwards. And now Africa faces the most intractable of all cases of white minority governments — the case of white rule in the Republic of South Africa. Will the struggle against this last racist bastion be hampered by the global rapprochement between the Soviet commonwealth and the Western alliance? Will the socialist countries so value good relations with the West that they will come close to abandoning the African National Congress and the Pan-African Congress in the struggle against this last citadel of institutionalized racism?

Before the East—West rapprochement Africans used to emphasize that side of their ancestral heritage which affirmed *'when two elephants fight, it is the grass which suffers.'* The rivalry between East and West, the two elephants, sometimes hurt the grass of the Third World. Korea, Vietnam, Afghanistan and Latin America have been hurt even more directly than Africa by the rivalry between the superpowers.

But with the new rapprochement between East and West, the Third World is wondering whether it is not equally true that *when two elephants make love, it is also the grass which suffers.* Another side of Africa's proverbial wisdom is asserting its relevance. The affectionate kicks and embraces of superpowers in amorous mutual discovery can be as costly to the grass of the Third World as the original rivalry of the cold war. Indeed, while the rapprochement is good news in

3

the field of disarmament and reduced danger of conflict between East and West, it may be bad news from the point of view of economic justice and technological fairness between North and South.

The problem of North—South relations has always been *how to close the power gap*. But now it is also how to prevent the gap from widening further.

This power gap takes a number of forms.

The biggest economic gap is perhaps between North America on one side and Africa, on the other. Latest estimates say that thirty of the hungriest nations in the world are in Africa. The World Food Council estimates that population in much of the African continent is growing at 3 or 4 times the rate of growth in food production. And the threat of famine in Africa will persist well into the twenty-first century.

The gap between the Northern hemisphere and much of Asia may not be quite as stark in the years ahead. Famine in Asia may well be abolished before the end of the century. And a number of Asian countries may well have taken off into full developmental orbit. Four gaps have been particularly critical in North—South relations: (1) the gap in skill and technique (technological); (2) the gap in income (financial); (3) the gap in naked power (military); (4) the gap in values and attitudes (cultural). Is the fourth gap in values and attitudes the most fundamental?

Certainly differences in skills and technique are, on the whole, more basic than differences in income. And these skill differences are profoundly affected by *culture*. International stratification is more about know-how than about income. International class formation is more about *who-knows-what* than about *who-earns-what*.

That is why Saudi Arabia, in spite of its enormous income, is more vulnerable than a middle-level Western European power. This book is partly about the dilemmas of skills in relation to culture, and how those dilemmas have affected disparities in power between North and South.

Between Modernization and Westernization

Egypt was the first non-European country to confront the issue of the gap in technique between North and South — even before Japan met the problem eye-ball to eye-ball after the Meiji Restoration.

A central aspect of the gap in technique is the relationship between *culture* and technical modernization. In order to modernize industrially, is it necessary to Westernize culturally?

Japan from 1868 decided that a country could modernize industrially without Westernizing culturally. 'Western technique, Japanese spirit' was Japan's slogan. Japan proceeded on that basic assumption.

Turkey under Mustafa Kemal Ataturk in the 1920s and 1930s decided that in order to modernize industrially a country *had* to Westernize culturally. Turkey even abolished the Fez headgear and substituted the Latin alphabet for the Arabic. Turkey tried to go truly European.

Egypt under Muhammad Ali a century before Ataturk, and half a century before the Meiji Restoration, had faced the same issue. Egypt's reformist ruler, Muhammad Ali, faced the great test.

Were Muhammad Ali's efforts more like Japan's (how to technically modernize *without* culturally Westernizing)? Or was the experiment more like Ataturk's reforms (how to technically modernize *through* culturally Westernizing)?

4

Muhammad Ali's efforts could have established Egypt's take-off into an orbit similar to that of Japan half-a-century later. Muhammad Ali attempted technical modernization without excessive cultural Westernization. Some Western writers have criticized Muhammad Ali for not attempting to change Egyptian Islam a little more. As the American historian, Robert July, put it:

> Perhaps Muhammad Ali's greatest shortcoming was his failure to see need for a modernized, revitalized Islam to accompany and guide technical and economic modernization. . . . Traditional Islamic thought and practice was left to continue, resentful and suspicious, and its reconciliation with Western technical superiority still remains a major problem of Muslim leadership in the Middle East today.[1]

Muhammad Ali's state capitalism — like Japan's later on — enhanced national productivity and increased the revenues of the state. But neither in Egypt nor in Japan did the ordinary people benefit much in the initial phases. And both Muhammad Ali and the Japanese rulers used militarism as an aspect of the earlier phases of modernization.

But the Egyptian experiment (unlike the Japanese Meiji take-off) was aborted.

> In 1838 Britain obtained the right of virtual free trade within the Ottoman dominions, and 3 years later the Treaty of London forced Muhammad Ali to conform — to abolish his protective tariffs and sharply reduce the size of his army. His nascent industrialization thus scuttled and his military force emasculated, the aging viceroy could no longer maintain his interest in economic reform, and most of his programmes, particularly in education and industry, were permitted to lapse during the years preceding his death in 1848.[2]

On balance the neo-Japanese scenario of Egypt's industrial development was aborted by the effective intervention of European imperialism.

From then on Egypt was sentenced to a fate which came to be shared by much of the rest of Africa. Egypt's destiny was not a Japanese fate of technical modernization *without* cultural Westernization, nor was it an Ataturk fate of technical modernization *through* cultural Westernization. It was Africa's painful process of cultural Westernization *without* technical modernization.

Not any cultural baggage will do for the task of economic modernization. Some aspects of culture are more relevant than others; some aspects may even be more destructive.

Closing the gap in skill has everything to do with closing the gap in production — closing the technological gap helps to close the productive gap.

Africa as a whole borrowed the wrong things from the West — even the wrong components of capitalism. We borrowed the profit motive but not the entre-preneurial spirit. We borrowed the acquisitive appetites of capitalism but not the creative risk-taking. We are at home with Western gadgets but are bewildered by Western workshops. We wear the wristwatch but refuse to watch it for the culture of punctuality. We have learnt to parade in display, but not to drill in discipline. The West's consumption patterns have arrived, but not necessarily the West's technique of production.

There are other anomalies arising out of the nature of colonial development in much of the Third World. These distortions include: (1) urbanization without industrialization; (2) verbal education without productive training; (3) secular-ization without scientification (decline of religion without the rise of science); (4) capitalist greed without capitalist discipline.

It is out of such distortions that *dependency relationships* between North and South emerge. Dependency itself involves at least one of two forms of relation-ship. One is a relationship of *surplus need*. Society B is dependent on Society A if B needs A more than A needs B.

The second type of dependency involves *deficit control*. B is dependent on A if B has less control over their relationship than A has. In a colonial relationship proper A is the imperial power and B is each colony. After independence A's control may decline in some spheres.

But which spheres? For analytical purposes we may distinguish between the political sphere of dependency, the economic sphere, the military sphere and the cultural.

In terms of surplus need before B became annexed as a colony, it was A as the metropole that 'needed' B economically. Colonies were perceived by the metropole as potential sources of raw materials, or potential markets, or sources of labour or recipients of surplus population from Europe. Technically therefore England was a dependency of its own Empire in this special sense of England's economic needs, real or imagined.

But in terms of deficit economic control, it was the colonies that were dancing to England's economic commands instead of the other way round.

The factors which made the difference in control at that time were political and military. By definition the colonies were political dependencies on Great Britain, and subject to its monopoly of physical force over their territory.

But while the British and the French were covetous of, say, Africa's economic resources, they had little interest in Africa's cultural resources. Indeed, the French doctrine of assimilation was even prepared to exchange French culture for African economic riches.

This introduces a fundamental difference between economic dependency and cultural dependency. While economic dependency has always included some leverage on the part of the 'colony' upon the metropole (since the centre needs the periphery economically), cultural dependency has been much more of a one-way traffic at the organized level. The imperial power was prepared to dump its cultural goods on the African market, but it was not interested in purposefully importing African culture back into Europe. Whatever African culture has penetrated Europe has been due far less to organized European policies than to the activities of individual scholars, artists and antiquarians, and to the cultural impact of African slaves imported into the western world.

Europe on the whole was prepared to offer its religion, languages and culture to Africans — but only in exchange for land, mines, labour, energy and other economic riches of Africa. Jomo Kenyatta in the old colonial Kenya was more profound than even he may have realized when he observed:

When the white man came to Africa he had the Bible and we had the land. And now? We have the Bible and he has the land.

It was a classic case of offering culture in exchange for material goods — as Europe was exporting arts and ideas and importing economic riches.

By the time African universities were established Africans themselves were all too eager to scramble for Western culture. On the basis of surplus need, there was no doubt at all that Africans felt a need for Western culture far greater than the West felt it needed African culture. On the basis of deficit control, Western institutions exerted disproportionate control over African institutions. Cultural dependency was becoming much more acute, and less reciprocal, than economic dependency.

But what is *culture* anyway? And what role does it play in human society and world politics? It is to this complex theme that we must now turn.

The Seven Functions of Culture

For our purposes in this book, culture serves seven fundamental functions in society. First, it helps to provide *lenses of perception and cognition*. How people view the world is greatly conditioned by one or more cultural paradigms to which they have been exposed. An ayatollah in Iran views the world around him qualitatively differently from how Henry Kissinger has viewed it. Part of that gulf is personal and ideological, and part of it is rooted in a thousand years of differing civilizations.

The second function of culture lies in providing *motives for human behaviour*. What makes a person respond behaviourally in a particular manner is partly cultural in origin. Under the first Reagan administration American marines were taken by surprise in Lebanon because they did not allow for the factor of martyrdom and sacred suicide in Shiite political culture. And so the driver of a car full of explosives was able to smash himself and his car into an American compound — and over 240 marines were killed.

The third function of culture lies in providing criteria of *evaluation*. What is deemed better or worse, ugly or beautiful, moral or immoral, attractive or repulsive, is partly a child of culture. The evaluative function of culture need not always correspond with the behavioural. The USA condemns 'terrorism' when it is committed by Palestinians, but has been known to subsidize it in the case of UNITA in Angola or the Contras in Nicaragua. One man's 'terrorist' is often another's 'freedom fighter' — partly because one culture's hero is another's villain. We shall return to this theme later in the book.

The fourth function of culture is to provide *a basis of identity*. Ethnic nepotism is itself a product of culture in this identity sense. Religion and race are often a basis of solidarity or a cause of hostility. Western culture as transmitted in educational institutions provides rival forms of identification in Africa and Asia — some of them related to the emergence of new elites and new social classes. Are the Jews a 'race' or merely followers of a religion? That is a question of historic cultural proportions. We shall return to it in this book.

Fifthly, culture is a *mode of communication*. The most elaborate system of communication is language itself. In Africa and Asia there has been considerable debate about language policy. Should the local languages be given priority in the new post-colonial era? Should Hindi or Kiswahili be promoted as national languages? Or did the cultural logic of European imperialism imply the continuing promotion of European cultures and languages instead? Culture as communication can take other forms — including music, the performing arts, and the wider world of ideas.

The sixth function of culture is as *a basis of stratification*. Class, rank and status are profoundly conditioned by cultural variables. University education became a major factor in redefining status and gradation in modern African societies. What type of personality is elected President in France or how influential bishops are in another Western country is partly a function of culture.

The seventh function of culture lies in *the system of production and consumption.* In our scheme of analysis — unlike in some Marxist schools — patterns of consumption sometimes affect production as profoundly as production helps to shape consumption. Oil from the Middle East and industrial minerals from Africa cater for Western consumption patterns as they distort the relations of production between North and South. And how much of a *cultural* achievement is the economic success of Japan?

These seven functions of culture have relevance for the new international cultural order. What lies in the way is once again the whole problem of dependency in North—South relations. More fundamentally, culture is at the heart of the nature of *power* in international relations.

Cultural Foundations of Power

In the final section of the book I will suggest ways of moderating disparities in power. But in the meantime let us illustrate the gap in such power between North and South and the cultural foundations which underlie it.

Let us look especially at Israel and the Republic of South Africa as *cultural fragments of the Western world* lodged in the heartland of the Third World.

What do those two Western cultural fragments lodged in the Third World tell us about disparities in technological power between North and South? How does that technological gap relate to the other gaps — skills, income, strategic location? And where does general morality fit into all this?

The cultural and technological inequalities between whites . and blacks in Southern Africa and between Israelis and Arabs in the Middle East, affect other areas of performance. The Republic of South Africa has used its technological superiority to bully its black neighbours into submission and into 'non-aggression' pacts. The sovereignty of Mozambique, Angola, Botswana, Lesotho, and even independent Zimbabwe has been violated from time to time, sometimes with utter impunity. European technological leadership in the last three centuries of the cultural history of the world has been inherited by people of European extraction operating in Africa — and has been used as a decisive military resource against black Africans. South Africa's neighbours have begun to appreciate what it must feel like to be Israel's neighbour — for both South Africa and Israel have seldom hesitated to use blatant military muscle at the expense of the sovereignty of their neighbours.

Again, cultural and technological inequalities have played a part in these politics of intervention. As we shall demonstrate later, Israelis have enjoyed military pre-eminence for so long not because they are Jews but because a large part of their population is Western and European. Had the population of Israel consisted overwhelmingly of Middle Eastern Jews, the Arabs would have won every single war they have fought with their Jewish neighbours. Indeed, there might have been only one war — the 1948 one. Numbers would have counted. Middle Eastern Jews in Israel are often more hawkish and eager to fight the Arabs, but the military capability for assuring Israeli victory has come more from their European compatriots. Again culture has played a decisive role in deciding victory and defeat in military equations.

The danger both in the Middle East and Southern Africa lies in pushing the weak too far. Cultural supremacy has its limits. We shall later show how desperate conditions in the two sub-regions can easily become fertile ground for different forms of terrorism. For the time being, that terrorism in the two geographical areas has not gone nuclear. We shall examine this theme in a separate chapter later on. But if the cultural imbalances between Israeli and Arab, and between white and black, continue to deepen the sense of desperation among the disadvantaged, we cannot rule out the possibility of Arabs and black Africans acquiring those nuclear devices one day from radical friends elsewhere. As we shall later demonstrate, powerlessness also corrupts — and absolute powerlessness can corrupt absolutely.

There is one 'happy' prospect that black Africans can contemplate which the Arabs are denied. Black Africans can contemplate the prospect of inheriting the white bomb of the Republic of South Africa. What white culture has invented black hands will inherit. As we have argued elsewhere in this book, before the end of this century the blacks of South Africa will probably succeed in overthrowing the regime of white supremacy. In the wake of the racial war which has to precede the black victory, half the white population will probably have had to leave the Republic. But it seems almost certain that half the white population of South Africa will in the end also still remain behind. Partly through that other half, South Africa's nuclear capability will be transmitted from white control to black command.

It is therefore a fair question to ask whether the prospect of a nuclearized South Africa today is a blessing or a curse for the rest of Africa. Is it possible that white South Africa's nuclear bomb is a short-term nuisance for black Africa but a long-term advantage? Are South Africa's blacks going to be the legitimate heirs of South Africa's nuclear capability before the end of the century?

There is little doubt that white South Africa's bomb is irrelevant for the survival of apartheid. The main threat to South Africa's racist regime is *internal* to South Africa — and the regime is unlikely to use the nuclear devices in the streets of Soweto. Such a use would, in any case, precipitate a white exodus — at least as serious a crisis for *apartheid* as the rebellion of blacks.

But while nuclear power is of marginal significance in the fortunes of present-date South Africa, it may be more significant in the *post-apartheid* era of the Republic. As the new black rulers inherit the white nuclear bomb, they will be transformed from the status of being the most humiliated blacks of the twentieth century to the status of becoming the most powerful blacks of the twenty-first century. As we have indicated in other chapters in this volume, black-ruled South Africa will of course remain not only one of the richest countries in the world in terms of mineral resources, but also one of the most industrialized in the Southern hemisphere. The nuclear capability will remain part of a wider industrial complex.

Towards a Creative Culture Shock

The nuclear age arrived when black people were at their most technologically backward stage in comparison to others. We shall later discuss vertical nuclear proliferation more fully in terms of the expanding arsenals of those who are already nuclear powers. Horizontal proliferation is the spread of those skills to new countries.

But can such 'horizontal nuclear proliferation' to Third World countries be a cure to vertical proliferation among Big Powers? The underlying hope lies in creating the necessary *culture shock* for a serious commitment to *universal* nuclear disarmament. In any case, black inheritance of South Africa's bomb will not be horizontal nuclear proliferation in the usual sense. No new *country* will have been added to the membership of the nuclear club — only a new *race*. For the first time the nuclear club will have a *new* culture represented, a black member. At the most, the horizontal proliferation will have crossed the racial and cultural divide rather than state boundaries. And since Northern nuclear powers are more afraid of South African blacks handling the bomb than of South African whites doing so, the new black member of the nuclear club may well precipitate an agonizing reappraisal as to whether the club should exist at all. The racial prejudices and cultural distrusts of the white members of the nuclear club may well serve the positive function of disbanding the club — and dismantling the nuclear arsenals in the cellars which had constituted credentials for membership.

But nuclear disarmament is not enough. There is need to reduce the risk of war. After all, once the 'genie' of nuclear know-how is already out of the bottle, it can be re-utilized if war broke out — and a new nuclear arms race be inaugurated. The ultimate evil is man's proclivity towards war — and not merely the weapons with which he has fought it. Africa and its own values will need to play a larger part in that ultimate peace crusade. We shall return to those issues in subsequent chapters of this book, against the background of the primacy of culture in world affairs.

The struggle to close the power gap between North and South must continue. But the most obstinate of all gaps will remain the gap in skills — rooted as skills are in the imponderables of culture and the imperatives of history. This book is about those hidden cultural forces at work in international affairs and global history.

But culture is not only about power. The power of culture is sometimes a protective shield for freedom. There is such a thing as the culture of freedom. In a basic sense this book is therefore also about *freedom*. It may well turn out to be my most controversial ever. One chapter (Chapter 3) was originally a conference paper which was ceremonially burnt by Muslim 'fundamentalists' in Nigeria on charges of 'blasphemy'. Another chapter in this study (Chapter 4) holds Salman Rushdie accountable for his own 'cultural treason'. There is a statement made in this book which was censored by American public television and other statements which were censored by African governments. One chapter (Chapter 7) may please Jews; another may offend Zionists (Chapter 8). I have been criticized in an article in *Pravda* as well as in the columns of the *New York Times* for views now encompassed in this volume. My gratitude is to *freedom* in our own times, in spite of all the censorship which continues to be imposed. In each civilization there is a cultural current which seeks to drown free expression; but in each culture there is a parallel force in defence of liberty. This book is a celebration of the liberating power of culture at its best — both within individual societies and across differing civilizations.

Notes

1. Robert W. July, *A History of the African People*, third edition (New York: Charles Scribner's Sons, 1980), p. 229.
2. Ibid, p. 228.

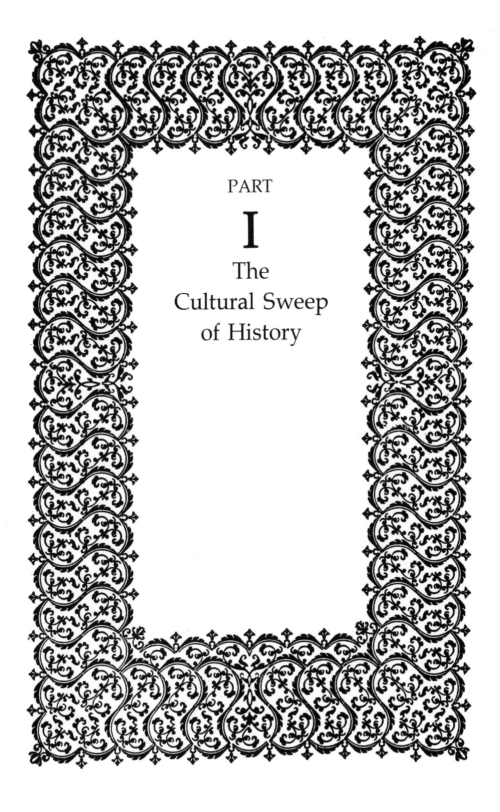

PART

I

The
Cultural Sweep
of History

1

The Moving Frontier of World Culture

The 'us/them' confrontation is the most persistent theme in world order perceptions. To what extent is this dichotomy between 'us' and 'them' a cultural artefact? Problems of security and combat, problems of competition and negotiation, are all caught up in that obstinate dichotomy.

The dichotomy can take a variety of forms — the native versus the foreigner, the friend versus the foe, the familiar versus the strange, the Orient versus the Occident, the East versus the West, the North versus the South, the developed versus the developing countries, and so on. This dichotomous framework of world order perceptions amounts to an iron law of dualism, a persistent conceptualization of the world in terms of 'us' and 'them'. To what extent is this mode of thinking a product of culture? Is it inevitable? Are we prisoners of dualism?

My first proposition is that the culture of politics (though not necessarily of economics) has a strong tendency towards dualism in most parts of the world. The 'us' versus 'them' tendency is, in the political arena, almost universal. It could be friend versus foe, supporter versus opponent, ally versus adversary, conformist versus dissident, loyalist versus rebel. The range of cultural examples is also wide — from Whigs and Tories to the tensions between Confucians and legalists in the Chinese political tradition.

But although a certain level of dualism is inescapable in political thinking, the degree of dualism is culturally relative. Societies vary considerably in how they perceive the wider world, and some paradigms are more dualistic than others.

My more complicated thesis is, paradoxically, that monotheism is particularly dualistic, though not uniquely so. There is a tendency in monotheism to divide the human race between believers and unbelievers, between the virtuous and the sinful, between good and evil, between 'us' and 'them'.

There is only one God, with no rival. He should command all loyalty and all obedience. The lines begin to be drawn precisely because one is either for or against God.

In contrast, polytheistic religions like those of parts of Africa and Asia are tolerant partly because they are ready to accommodate additional gods. So what is an extra god between friends? There were hardly any religious wars in Africa before the intrusion of Islam and Christianity. African traditional religions

13

permitted different ethnic groups to have their own gods, and divine plurality was the order of the day.

But to suggest that all religions are either monotheistic or polytheistic is itself to commit the sin of dualism. Many religions in both India and parts of Africa accommodate both monotheistic and polytheistic elements. And a religion like Zoroastrianism could be regarded as being ditheistic: having more than one god but fewer than three gods.

What is clear is that the Judeo-Christian-Islamic paradigm is more dichotomous than the paradigms normally encountered in polytheistic cultures. The three Middle Eastern religions are also all monotheistic. Is there a causal link between their tendency to dichotomize and their monotheism? Is there a link between the powerful idea of one universal God, on one side, and the dangerous dualism of 'us' versus them'?

My major purpose here is to demonstrate this paradox of monotheistic dualism and its impact on contemporary world politics and international relations.

My second concern is to try to demonstrate that at the international level the class structure of the world is often culturally rather than economically defined.

The third thrust of my analysis is to illustrate how, in the absence of the world government, the idea of 'community' at the transnational level has been defined in terms of shared values and culture rather than shared political authority.

There is indeed a hidden cultural agenda in world-order problems. And from the point of view of this essay, it stems from the monotheistic origins of bipolarity in world politics, the cultural basis of international stratification, and the cultural basis of transnational communities in the absence of shared political authority.

There is indeed a cultural theme at the centre of the history of the international system, complete with a moving frontier of cultural exclusivity. Let us now turn to these theses in greater detail.

The Origins of Sacred Order

We mentioned earlier that the dual paradigm in world-order thinking has been shaped by two factors: the culture of politics, which tends to dichotomize, and the impact of monotheism on world culture. These two factors were fused in the earlier versions of Judaism, Christianity, and Islam. God was conceived in the image of the king, often complete with a throne. Monotheistic thought in these three religions not only anthropomorphized God but also royalized Him. Terms like 'majesty' and 'the kingdom of God' were central to religious discourse. The tendency to emphasize the oneness of God tended to attract the kingly metaphor, a unique throne.

It would seem that the god of these three monotheistic religions also had a royal court of his own. The courtiers were angels, usually committed to continuous adoration of the king. The hymns and prayers emphasized that the king was almighty, omnipotent, omniscient, all-powerful — Glory be to God, Hallelujah!

Like most royal courts, however, God's court was not without its intrigues. It would seem that the only intrigue which had been recorded in human annals in any detail was the one which culminated in Satan's rebellion. Satan, jealous of the creation of Adam, finally found the will to rebel against that culture of constant adoration of the king, constant prayer and devotion, unmitigated submissiveness. If the English poet, John Milton, is to be believed, Satan was driven to conclude that it was 'Better to reign in Hell than serve in Heav'n.'

14

The paradigm of dichotomy, so characteristic of the culture of politics, is captured in that line from *Paradise Lost*. Indeed, the very dichotomy of Heaven and Hell is part of the grand divide between rewards and sanctions as part of political authority. The notion of loyalty to the king, leading on to heavenly rewards, and treason to God leading on to damnation and hellfire, was a stark polarization embedded in those earlier versions of monotheistic divine order.

Of the three religions, Christianity tried to balance the majesty of God with the humbleness of his son. The Prince of Peace was born in a stable, preached among the poor, and praised both poverty and humility. It was a measure of Jesus's sacrifice that He had descended from the ultimate royal house of them all, to mingle with the meek on earth, and to die for them. For God to send his own son to earth was a major act of policy, a political act of momentous importance. It had to be balanced with another major political act here on earth — the sentencing of Jesus to crucifixion. But here Christian dualism gets intermingled with the concept of trinity and poses problems about political authority. The idea of three-in-one and one-in-three provides us with God the Father, God the Son, and God the Holy Ghost. But one momentous Friday, God the Son was crucified. Was there a crisis of authority in the universe?

Islam, a younger religion than Christianity and one which honours Jesus as a prophet, argues that the trinity was an invention of over-enthusiastic followers of Jesus. Islam also asserts that Jesus never claimed to be Son of God. Monotheism in Islam is uncompromising.

Islam is also uncompromising in the majesty it accords Allah. Since there is no equivalent of a prince in rags on earth, descending from Heaven, the majesty of the being is not tempered by the humility of an offspring. Islam, therefore, has a greater propensity for dichotomizing than does Christianity.

Third, the culture of politics has conditioned Islam more directly than it has affected Christian doctrine. This is partly because the founder of Islam, unlike the founders of most great religions, underwent in his lifetime upward political mobility and became a head of state.

Jesus and Buddha were, according to their followers, princes who decided to descend to the level of the common people and teach them uncommon things. Muhammad, on the other hand, was the humble camel driver who lived to become head of state and to lay the foundations of an empire here on earth.

One consequence of this upward political mobility that Muhammad underwent was the need to establish a system of law and judicial order. This was the Shari'a, the Islamic Law. This was clearly in contrast to the role of Jesus as a founder of Christianity. After all, if the main mission of a founder of a religion is self-sacrifice, a crucifixion by way of atonement, there is no need to devise an elaborate system of social and political control for society. On the contrary, Jesus's crucifixion was at best a judgement on the existing laws of a particular society, rather than a blueprint for an alternative judicial order.

The prophet of Islam, on the other hand, had to rule and exercise authority. The innocent had to be protected, the guilty had to be discouraged or punished, and society had to be strengthened. The Shari'a was born — at once one of the glories of Islam and one of its shackles. A system of vice and virtue, crime and punishment, reward and sanction came into being. The trend toward dualism — so characteristic of monotheism and the culture of politics — was consolidated in Islam by the political success of the prophet Muhammad and his immediate successors.

Judaism is, of course, as monotheistic as Islam, and more so than Chrisitianity since Judaism is not encumbered as is Christianity by the doctrine of three-in-one and one-in-three. The tendency towards dichotomizing and dualism is also strong in both Jewish history and Jewish doctrine. It certainly conditions the Jewish paradigm of identity: Jews on one side, Gentiles on the other.

The identity crisis of Jews confronting the rest of the human race has taken a variety of forms over the centuries and was reinforced by the exodus from Palestine, the general Jewish dispersal, and the historical experience of discrimination and martyrdom. Political Zionism was born in its modern manifestation partly as a dichotomy between a Jewish 'us' and a Gentile 'them'. There had to be a Jewish state to protect the Jews against the world. Hitler's holocaust vindicated some of these Jewish fears. Zionism gathered momentum, and Israel was born.

The tragedy of dichotomizing continued. Could not Jews live in Palestine without partitioning the territory? For the Jews, the answer was no: there had to be a separate Jewish state. Of course, the practicalities of creating a separate state were more complicated than the doctrines. On balance, many Zionists believed in a total dichotomy, so that ideally there would be no Arabs at all in the land of Israel. To adapt Rudyard Kipling: 'Jews are Jews and Arabs are Arabs — and never the twain shall meet'!

But in practice there were 'too many' Arabs still in the land of Palestine. And even after partition and the efforts of many Zionist zealots to frighten Arab peasants out of Israel, there remained an Arab presence in the new land of the Jews. The Zionist dichotomists failed to accomplish a complete purification.

Meanwhile, the culture of politics in Israel was influenced also by the theocratic heritage of monotheism. Jehovah was king. Citizenship in the Israeli state was partly religiously defined, and Israel's Law of Return offered the embrace of citizenship to all professing the genuine Jewish faith throughout the world.

Though the general laws of Israel are, on the whole, in the tradition of Western liberal democracy rather than centralized theocracy, the idea that the state is under some kind of divine jurisidiction has influenced the political culture of the society. Such an idea is indeed sometimes taken literally by right-wing parties and movements, and by leaders like Menachem Begin. Once again, the dichotomizing tendency in the culture of politics, combined with the anthropomorphic conception of God as king within a monotheistic framework, have sharpened the dualism of 'us' and 'them'.

But to what extent have these tendencies affected the wider international and world order? It is to this transnational and global level of analysis that we should now turn.

Towards Globalizing the Sacred Order

Of the three monotheistic religions under review in this essay, Judaism has had a less direct impact on the existing world order than have Islam and Christianity. Indirect Jewish influences have been diverse. They range from the impact of Jewish jurists and thinkers upon international law to the repercussions of the creation of the state of Israel, and from Jewish elements in Islamic and Christian doctrines to the suggested role of Karl Marx as one of the last of the Jewish prophets. There can therefore be little doubt that Judaism has been a major contributory force in the world of rules and ideas as we know it today.

Nevertheless, in terms of direct impact on the structure of the world system, Christianity has been a more fundamental force by far, with Islam trailing significantly behind.

The trend towards dichotomizing at the international level took in Islam the form of a division of the world into *Dar el Islam* (the Abode of Islam) and *Dar el Harb* (the Abode of War). The Abode of Islam was, by definition, governed by shared values and principles, shared allegiance to that ultimate of all sovereigns, God. Within the world of Islam, the rules of intersocietal relations assumed the bonds of community. Indeed, Muslims all over the world were supposed to constitute an *Umma*, a community and a people. The culture of Islam was the bond of commonality.

As for the Abode of War, this was almost in the sense which the English philosopher Thomas Hobbes came to articulate many centuries after the founding of Islam. Hobbes argued that where there was no shared sovereign, conditions amounted to a state of war, with every man for himself and with the persistent danger that the life of man might become 'nasty, brutish and short'. Hobbes was interested in civil society rather than in the broader world community. His conception of the state of war has often been internationalized nonetheless. It has indeed been suggested that the world system, in the absence of world government, has conditions which amount to an immanent state of war.

Similarly, *Dar el Harb* in Islam assumed that the lands which were not governed by shared principles, and did not recognize shared allegiance to the one God, were potentially theatres of war.

Future Islamic jurists attempted to modify this strong dichotomy in Islamic international law between *Dar el Harb* and *Dar el Islam*. Intermediate categories were sometimes devised by jurists, partly to allow for special alliances between Islam and friendly non-Muslims, and partly to accommodate the distinctive conditions of places like India where Hindu and Muslim rulers constituted a complex pattern of subcontinental relationships.

The division of the world in this manner may still be a living residual element in the political thinking of rulers like the Ayatollah Khomeini of Iran and Muammar Gaddafi of Libya. In less stark forms the dichotomy underlies even the more peaceful Islamic movements and the global Islamic conference that came into being in recent years. 'Us' and 'them' persists as an aspect of the political culture of Islam.

The dichotomous tendency of Islamic international law has had its equivalent in Western international law. It is worth remembering that the origins of the present international system, including contemporary international law and its usages, go back to Europe and its culture. Originally, the polarized stratification of the world was, at least in part, religious. World order was for a while perceived as an order of Christian faith. International law was for Christendom. There was a time when community in Europe was defined not merely in terms of shared values and culture but also in terms of the supreme power of the Pope and, in a substantial part of Europe, this emperor or that. In other words, communal ties included shared political and religious authority, which went back in part to the conversion to Christianity of the Roman Emperor Constantine the Great in the fourth century.

Much later, the Christian nations of Europe formulated rules of international conduct; but they perceived themselves as *Christian* nations. As B. V. A. Roling once put it:

Those Christian Nations emanated from the spiritual unity prevailing in Western Europe before the Reformation. After the overthrow of the supreme power of Pope and Emperor and the acceptance of the concept of national sovereignty, the monarchs of Europe continued to consider themselves subject to God's commandments and the law of nature. . . . The Christian States considered themselves bound by Christian law. Christianity was the source of their standards. In addition, each determined the circle within which law should prevail: a different law, or none at all, held good for relations with heathens. Finally, Christianity was the justification of the domination of other peoples.'[1]

Roling traces the legalistic dichotomy between Christians and 'heathens' at least to the Lateran Council of 1139. This forbade, *sub anathema*, the use of the cross-bow among Christian knights, *adversos Christianos et Catholicos*. It was accepted that Christian standards did not apply to heathens and heretics.

Roling also refers to an interesting early illustration of germ warfare. In 1649–1650 Christians decided to use 'pestilential vapors' against the Turks in Crete. They sent a certain Dr Michaelangelo. His mission was to infect the Turkish army with his 'quintessence of the pest.' This exercise in biological warfare was rationalized officially at the time by the old crusading argument: 'The usual considerations do not apply to the Turks who are enemies by religion, treacherous by nature and who have betrayed your excellencies.'[2]

Implicit in all this is once again a dichotomy — this time between the Abode of Christianity and the Abode of War, a mirror reflection of *Dar el Islam* and *Dar el Harb*. And underlying that dualism is once again a definition of community based on shared values and faith. In Shakespeare's *Henry the Sixth, Part 1* Gloucester suggests that peace with France is 'the only means to stop effusion of our Christian blood.' The king reflects:

> . . . I always thought
> It was both impious and unnatural
> That such immanity and bloody strife
> Should reign among professors of one faith.[3]

At a less articulate level, this dichotomy between Christian nations and barbarians of other faiths has persisted in different forms in the Western world to more recent times. A former Dutch prime minister is reported to have wondered in Parliament how a Muslim or Hindu could really grasp what the essence of aggression was. This judgement, in his view, required the sensibilities of Christian culture. An American diplomat, engaged in the quest for a solution to the Arab-Israeli conflicts in the 1950s, inadvertently drifted into advising the Jews and Arabs 'to settle the conflict in a true Christian spirit'.[4] And more recently, many Christians in the West have probably discovered that their attitudes to the Ayatollah Khomeini in Iran were very similar to the attitudes of their grandfathers in the nineteenth century towards the abstract 'Turks'.

It is not merely the relevance of culture in international polarization in history that is thus revealed; it is also the relevance of culture in international stratification. Polarization is a horizontal divide, a cleavage and possible confrontation which could be between equals. Stratification, on the other hand, is a vertical divide, a confrontation between the privileged and the underprivileged, the dominant and the oppressed, the higher in status and the lower. In an earlier phase there existed a cultural definition of international stratification which divided communities on the basis of who believes what, rather than on the basis of who owns what. The international class structure was culturally derived rather than economically based, at least in those earlier days when religious solidarity was an explicit foundation of what was to become the Law of Nations.

Secularism and the Hierarchy of Civilization

But the cultural frontier of Western international law had in fact been moving, redefining the class divide. Instead of international law being a law for Christian nations, it became for a while a law for *civilized* nations. This is one of the costs of the secularization of world order. It is arguable that modern race consciousness has its origins in the decline of religion in Europe. To some extent race consciousness was a parallel development to the evolution of the nation-state. Religious tensions in Europe between Catholics and Protestants first culminated in the treaty of Augsburg in 1555. There was a fusion of religion with sovereignty in this treaty as the religion of the prince was deemed to be the religion of the principality, the king's faith was the faith of the kingdom. This famous doctrine was expressed in the words *Cuius Regio Eius Religio.*

In reality, the decision to equate the religion of the king with the religion of the kingdom was a principle of no interference in the different princes' internal religious affairs.

But this *modus vivendi* broke down. Europe underwent the agonies of the Thirty Years War. And out of that war emerged the Peace of Westphalia in 1648, which laid the foundations of the modern state system and the principles of modern conceptions of sovereignty.

This secularization of allegiance (to the State rather than through the Church), which came with Westphalia led to secularization of *identity* — and nations and races became more visible than religious communities.

Out of this parallel development there emerged new theories of racial gradation and ethnic stratification. In the ultimate analysis, however, the great divide was between the civilized and the uncivilized, defined in terms of a scale both of cultures and of skin pigmentations.

Even such a devout Western lover of liberty as John Stuart Mill could argue that 'barbarians' had no rights as nations except the right to be converted into nations as rapidly as possible. As for the application of international law, this once again required not only a horizontal homogeneity of values, but also vertical equality of civilization.

> There is a great difference between the case in which the nations concerned are of the same, or something like the same, degree of civilization, and that in which one of the parties to the situation is of a high, and the other of a very low, grade of social improvement. To suppose that the same international customs, and the same rules of international morality, can obtain between one civilized nation and another and between civilized nations and barbarians is a grave error, and one which no statesman can fall into, however it may be that those who, from a safe and unresponsible position, criticize statesmen. . . . To characterize any conduct towards the barbarous people as a violation of the Law of Nations, only shows that he who so speaks has never considered the subject.[5]

19

But this approach was by no means unique to liberalism. It also characterized the thinking of those founding fathers of modern radicalism, Karl Marx and Friedrich Engels. Engels was delighted by the French conquest of Algeria, which he regarded as an important and fortunate development in the progress of civilization.

> And the conquest of Algeria has already forced the Beys of Tunis and Tripoli, and even the Emperor of Morocco, to enter upon the path of civilization. . . . All these nations of free barbarians look very proud, noble, glorious at a distance, but only come near them and you will find that they, as well as the more civilized nations, are ruled by the lust of Cain, and only employ ruder and more cruel means. And after all, the modern bourgeois, with civilization, industry, order, and at least relative enlightenment following him, is preferable to the feudal lord or to the marauding robber, with the barbarian state of society to which they belong.[6]

Engels's partner, Karl Marx, was even more sophisticated in his defence of British rule in India. Marx saw Western imperialism as an engine of progress in Asia and Africa. On 25 January 1853 Karl Marx made the following observation:

> English interference [in India] . . . produced the greatest and, so to speak the truth, the only social revolution ever heard of in Asia. Now, sickening as it must be to human feeling to witness myriads of industrial, patriarchal and inoffensive social organizations disorganized and dissolved into their units, thrown into a sea of woes, and their individual members losing at the same time their ancient form of civilization and their hereditary means of subsistence, we must not forget that these idyllic village communities, inoffensive though they may appear, had always been the solid foundation of oriental despotism, that they restrained the human mind within the smallest possible compass, making it the unresisting tool of superstition, enslaving it beneath traditional rules, depriving it of all grandeur and historical energies. . . . England, it is true, in causing a social revolution in Hindoostan, was activated by only the vilest of interests, and was stupid in her manner of enforcing them. But that is not the question. The question is: Can mankind fulfil its destiny without a fundamental revolution in the social state of Asia? If not, whatever may have been the crimes of England, she was the unconscious tool of history in bringing about the revolution.
>
> But then whatever bitterness the spectacle of the crumbling of an ancient world may have for our personal feelings, we have the right to exclaim with Goethe:

> Should this torture then torment us?
> Since it brings us great pleasure?
> Were not through the rule of Timur
> Souls devoured without measure?

Karl Marx later formulated his own version of the 'Dual Mandate' in Asia.

> England has to fulfil a double mission in India: one destructive, the other regenerating — the annihilation of all Asiatic societies, and the laying of the material foundations of Western society in Asia.[7]

The major difference between Karl Marx and Rudyard Kipling, the poet of 'The

White Man's Burden', is that Kipling made a virtue out of the unintended constructive consequences of imperialism whereas Marx recognized the developmental effects of British rule in India as primarily amoral and incidental. Rudyard Kipling, in contrast, took this developmental side-effect of imperialism to a level of self-righteousness.

What emerges in this comparison of John Stuart Mill on one side and Marx and Engels on the other is the shared belief in the superiority of Western civilization and the shared conviction that the civilized had a right to dominate and even exploit the barbarians. Once again the dualistic paradigm was in play, articulated by a highly secularized product of monotheistic Westernism (Mill) and a highly secularized product of Hebraic intellectualism (Marx).

This cultural stratification did lay the foundations of imperialism not just in Algeria and India but elsewhere in Asia and Africa. Even as late as World War II, Winston Churchill and Franklin Roosevelt could sign the Atlantic Charter affirming the rights of peoples everywhere to control their own destiny; yet the same Churchill soon after, when questioned in the House of Commons in London, could sharply differentiate between the freedom of the Belgians under the Nazis, a freedom which needed to be encouraged, and freedom of the colonized peoples of the British Empire, which Churchill regarded as an entirely different matter. Not very long after, when confronted with the demand of India to become independent, Winston Churchill, the signatory of the Atlantic Charter with its ringing acknowledgement of the right of self-determination, could nevertheless refuse to 'preside over the liquidation of the British Empire'.

Once again the basic dichotomy between the 'civilized' and the 'uncivilized' was in play even if no longer articulated in those terms. Community and stratification were culturally defined once again.

The Prince of Peace at the United Nations

Because the term 'civilized nations' had been used to justify European imperialism, it began to decline in public usage with the rise of nationalism in Asia and Africa. The new assertiveness of the colonized peoples and their sense of dignity gradually discouraged Europeans from talking about them as 'barbarians' and 'heathens'.

A related factor was the revolution in communications. When in the nineteenth century people like John Stuart Mill and Karl Marx discussed Indians, other Asians, and Africans as 'uncivilized', such conversation was almost exclusively among Westerners. Literacy was still very low in Africa and Asia, and books written in England were not likely to constitute bedtime reading in the Orient. Nor were there news agencies that transmitted public utterances made in London or New York to radio listeners or newspaper readers in Lagos or Bombay. Europeans in the nineteenth century could comfortably speak their minds about non-white people without risking the embarrassment of reaction from them.

By the time the United Nations Organization was formed in 1945, it no longer made sense to think of restricting membership to 'civilized nations'. It was also much too late to return to the old language of 'Christian nations'. And yet, in a sense, there was a partial return to Jesus as the Prince of Peace. And so the Charter of the United Nations designated the membership as 'peace-loving nations'. In this regard the concept was first used in the Moscow Declaration on General

Security on 30 October 1943. But the United Nations' emphasis on peace went beyond the concept of peace-loving nations. Those who framed the United Nations Charter in 1945 first declared their determination to 'save succeeding generations from the scourge of war' and then, only secondarily, to 'reaffirm faith in fundamental human rights, in the dignity and worth of the human person, and the equal rights of men and women, and of nations large and small'.

Whether the framers of the Charter realized it or not, their document revealed a historical Christian tendency to regard peace and 'love' as an answer to the scourge of war. Indeed, the English wording of 'peace-loving' does encompass the two most central concepts in Christian ethics — precisely, peace and love.

Justice, on the other hand, quite often invokes a different framework of reasoning. The ethic of turning the other cheek is consistent with the pursuit of peace and love, but may seldom prove consistent with the pursuit of social justice.

The God of Christianity has been regarded doctrinally as ultimately a god of love; and his Son has been regarded as a Prince of Peace. The God of Islam and Judaism, on the other hand, has been more a god of justice, ready to invoke sanctions against violators, capable of purposeful ruthlessness in defence of divine justice and order.

When the French rose up in arms against their own *ancien régime* in 1789, they wanted to tear down the Church as well. They did tear down the monasteries that had encouraged the poor to turn the other cheek while the rich puffed their own cheeks in luxurious living. The French Revolution was almost as anticlerical as it was antimonarchical.

When the Russians overthrew their own tsarist imperial system in 1917, they were rebelling against their nobility in an idiom which was also profoundly distrustful of religion. In the poetry of Karl Marx: 'Religion is a sigh of the oppressed creature, the sentiment of a heartless world, and the soul of soulless conditions. It is the opium of the people.' Tsarist Russia and pre-revolutionary France were Christian countries. Popular rebellion against injustice encompassed rebellion against religious institutions as well.

Iran, on the other hand, is a Muslim country. Popular rebellion in 1979 against political injustice was far from being simultaneously a rebellion against religious institutions. On the contrary, the call to revolution against the Shah was often couched in fervent religious terms. The god of justice in Islam encouraged at times resort to arms in defence of justice, as perceived by Muslims. The god of love in Christianity, on the other hand, was more comfortable with the doctrine of loving one's enemy and turning the other cheek.

In reality, Christian nations (as distinct from devout individual Christians) have never been all that 'peace-loving'. Many of them used the idiom of Christianity either to disarm their own people or to 'pacify' rebellious natives and promote acceptance of imperial rule. Even the idea of giving to Caesar what is Caesar's and to God what is God's was often a call to obedience and submission to Caesar — in the name of God!

Similarly, when the United Nations came into being, the language of peaceful solutions was often invoked to legitimize a status quo, to enable those who already 'have' to secure their privileges and to encourage the 'have nots' to accept their lot at least for the time being.

The United States also used the concept of 'peace-loving nations' as a basis for excluding the People's Republic of China from the United Nations for more than twenty years. And China's seat on the Security Council, complete with the permanent member veto that went with it, was allowed to be occupied by Taiwan throughout that period. In debate about the credentials of the People's Republic of China for occupying that seat, the United States year in, year out, invoked the argument that the People's Republic was not a peace-loving nation, and was not therefore the right China for the United Nations. After all, so the argument went, Article IV of the United Nations Charter restricted membership to those countries which were 'peace-loving'.

As more and more countries from Africa and Asia became members of the United Nations, a normative change was discernible in both voting pattern and the emphasis given to specific parts of the Charter. For the new nations of Africa and Asia, issues of social justice were more important than issues of peace and war prevention. The Prince of Peace at the United Nations was demoted as the world body became culturally and ideologically more diverse. Instead of trying to keep out the People's Republic of China on the argument that it was not peace-loving, the majority of the members were now more inclined to keep out the Republic of South Africa on the argument that it was guilty of gross injustices. Even Israel has, from time to time, been a target of demands for exclusion — but in the case of Israel, the basis for attack has rested on both issues of peace and issues of social justice. Was Israel peace-loving enough? This question echoed the earlier vocabulary of the Messiah of Peace. Was Israel sufficiently respectful of human rights and social justice? The second question revealed the new concerns of the formerly colonized nations of Africa, Asia, and the rest of the Third World.

Issues of social justice go beyond colonialism, racism, and military occupation. They also have economic dimensions. Yet the tradition of dichotomization has continued. In the new dualism, the world is perceived in terms of developed countries on one side and developing countries on the other. From a world system involving Christians versus non-Christians, civilized versus non-civilized, peace-loving versus not peace-loving, we have now entered a world which recognizes development as the central divide in the configuration of the globe.

Outside the United Nations, issues of war and peace remain, of course, quite fundamental. The then Secretary General of the United Nations, Kurt Waldheim, reminded the world in June 1980 that it was spending a million dollars a minute on armaments and had acquired the capacity to destroy the human race ten times over. The imperative of being 'peace-loving' had in this sense become more vital than in the days of the Prince of Peace. And yet the causes of war were not simply attitudinal; they were also structural.

The most dangerous arena from the point of view of peace is the arena of East-West relations. This is a dichotomy within a dichotomy. The world of communism on one side, and the world of capitalism on the other, continuously accuse each other of being 'war-mongering'. The idiom of peace is characteristic of the rhetoric of both parts of the North — northwest (the capitalist world) and northeast (the Soviet Union and its allies). At the height of the cold war, the United States regarded the Soviet Union as fundamentally expansionist and communism as fundamentally aggressive. At the beginning of the 1950s the United States was sufficiently in control of the United Nations to rally the world body in defence of the independence of South Korea. When the Security Council appeared paralyzed by the Soviet veto, the United States took the issue to the General Assembly and successfully invented the idea of 'uniting for peace'. The world body became the banner of defence for South Korea against the incursion of North Korea and the Chinese. The world body had entered a regional war in the name of world peace.

Since then, the United Nations has taken part in a variety of other conflicts, but not in as directly combatant a role as it had assumed in Korea. Major international assignments for the world body in defence of peace have ranged from its various roles in the Middle East to the efforts to save the Congo (now Zaire) from chaos; from its role in Cyprus to the General Assembly's censure of the Soviet Union's invasion of Afghanistan.

The United States and its allies have not by any means monopolized the language of peace, however. The Soviet Union has managed the unlikely combination of an ideology of revolution with a rhetoric of peace. Various recommendations have emerged from Moscow over the years concerning proposed principles of 'peaceful coexistence'. The Soviet Union also has often paid lip service to the goal of total disarmament, though never with an adequate acceptance of the safeguards needed to carry through such a process. The value of peace remains honoured in words though not always in deeds. The world needs peace as a moral ideal more than ever, since the world's very survival may depend upon it. Despite this fact the stratification system of the globe is no longer conceived in terms of peace-loving nations on one side and war-mongers on the other. The central dichotomy has now become technological, between the technologically advanced countries and the technologically backward, between the developed and the developing countries. It is to this last dichotomy that we must now turn.

Monotheism and Development

If one looks at the history of the international system over the last 600 years, the transition has been from a dualism based on faith to the new dualism based on know-how. The world which distinguished *Dar el Harb* from *Dar el Islam*, which differentiated Christian nations from heathen, still put an emphasis on confessional credentials for participation within a communal system. By contrast, the world which distinguishes between developed and developing countries is invoking credentials of technical know-how and expertise.

The geographical area designated by the term 'civilized world' in the nineteenth century almost coincides with what today is called the developed world. The barbarians and heathens of the nineteenth century are today the developing societies of Africa and Asia.

If one went even further back in time and looked at the word 'Christendom' as conceived in the seventeenth century before the signing of the Peace of Westphalia, one would find that it applied to a considerable fraction of what is today the industrialized world.

We may therefore say that there is a direct transition from the religious dualism through the civilization dualism right up to the development dualism. Approximately the same geographical areas were covered across the centuries by these terms, once we allow for the fact that Europeans populated and 'developed' much of the Western hemisphere and of Australasia.

What lies outside the straight transition through religion and civilization to technology is the dualism of peace. It is as if this particular component was not really a stage in a transition from the seventeenth century but was in fact a continuing sub-theme in global history. Its latest incarnation may be seen in the role of the United Nations in areas of human conflict.

And yet, in another sense, even the latest cleavage based on technology has its

24

origins in those years when the cleavage was based on religion. Modern technology was born out of modern capitalism, and modern capitalism was in part born out of the same causes which gave rise to the religious wars in Europe. The Protestant revolution helped to transform value patterns in the economic domain of behaviour, and not merely in the religious domain. I find the Weberian thesis substantially persuasive — there is a link between the rise of capitalism and the Protestant ethic. Protestantism helped to make what was previously the sin of avarice morally respectable. Indeed, the pursuit of worldly success was now deemed to be a good way of measuring whether one was in good standing with the King of Kings. Piety was not merely in prayer, but also in works and business. The Calvinistic notion of God was particularly monarchical. Human beings were subjects of the Lord, and in need of Grace. Their fates were often already sealed within the doctrine of predestination, but this doctrine was prevented from becoming another version of fatalism by the accompanying duty of struggling to find evidence that one was among the saved, and this evidence could take the form of prosperity and material success. Responding to one's calling was an important part of the quest for salvation.

In addition, the puritanical factor in Calvinism prepared the grounds for economic accumulation. On the one hand, the pious were encouraged to acquire more and more; but they were not encouraged to consume more and more. 'Make money, but do not spend it!' — this seemed to be the ultimate commercial imperative operating within the Protestant ethic. If more money had been made, but life styles were supposed to be austere, the alternatives were either to save the surplus, or to reinvest it. A third strategy was to do a little of both. With this accumulation of capital and entrepreneurial drive, the European was set for a capitalist take-off. And as the capitalist revolution matured, the industrial revolution got under way as part of a cumulative process of developmental change.[8]

It was not only with the rise of capitalism that Protestantism seems to have been linked, but also with the rise of modern science. In England, the Royal Society, overwhelmingly Protestant from its foundation in the late seventeenth century, was also disproportionately Puritan. The men of science in England tended towards Calvinism rather than Anglo-Catholicism and later towards non-conformism. Cambridge University became more scientifically oriented than Oxford perhaps partly because of the prevalence of this tendency.

In the United States too the Puritan influence on the growth of the scientific spirit was considerable. Part of the influence came through Cambridge University in England, which was described in that period as the *alma mater* of the Puritans. Of twenty leading Puritan clergymen in New England, seventeen were graduates of Cambridge, and only three of Oxford. The US educational programme also felt this Puritan influence. The sciences in the United States were certainly upheld better in Protestant than in Catholic institutions; within Protestant circles, the Puritan bias towards science stood out.[9]

If there was a heavy Protestant factor in the scientific revolution and also a disproportionate Protestant factor in the rise of capitalism, the two processes together (the mating of science with the economy) helped to create a technological momentum. The world of faith had interacted with the world of technical know-how and laid the foundations for this latest dichotomy in the global structure: the dichotomy between the developed and the underdeveloped, the technically knowledgeable and the technically pre-literate. Western civilization is still triumphant, but the credentials of supremacy are technological rather than spiritual.

Two major challenges to the West have now emerged, one of which evokes aspects of the old Crusades. One of the challenges to the West is indeed Islam, which has been undergoing a new resurgence on the world scene. The other challenge to Western culture is Marxism, which has been making new converts in the global seminaries of values.

As it happens, Islam is, of course, militantly monotheistic; Marxism is self-consciously atheistic. This new bipolarity captures the contemporary predicament of Western civilization as a whole — which is indeed 'between the sacred and the secular, the monotheistic and the atheistic'.

The Islamic challenge to the West, because of its very nature, is a challenge from the sacred. The Marxist challenge to the West attempts to be a challenge from the secular.

Islam seeks to reintroduce God in international relations, a partial return to a sacred world order. Marxism seeks to subtract capital from international relations, a quest to reverse the Protestant revolution.

Islam's challenge to the West is the Challenge from the South; it is vertical since leaders of Islam are overwhelmingly Southern. Marxism's challenge to the West is a challenge from the East; it is horizontal since leaders of old Marxism are overwhelmingly Northern.

Islam's challenge to the West is born of concern for cultural authenticity; the Marxist challenge is ultimately inspired by economic equity.

In the final analysis, systems of values and ideas of the world of Islam, the world of Marxism and Western civilization are interrelated. Islam's challenge to the West is a challenge from a cousin. After all, both Western values and Islamic ideas were profoundly conditioned and influenced by Judaism. Second, both Western values and Islamic scholarship were conditioned and influenced by the civilization of ancient Greece.

Marxism, on the other hand, is a *child* of the West. Karl Marx and Friedrich Engels were themselves Westerners; and their theories and ideas emerged out of Western intellectual and economic history. In that sense, the confrontation between Marxism and Western civilization is between a parent and its offspring; it is an inter-generational conflict in the realm of ideas and values.

Meanwhile the centre of the economic world is still basically monotheistic in culture. The greatest exporters of oil are Muslims; the greatest importers of oil are Christians. The exporters include Saudi Arabia (the heartland of Sunni Islam) and Iran (the heartland of Shi'a Islam). A majority of the other members of the Organization of Petroleum Exporting Countries are Muslim too. The greatest importers of oil include Western Europe and the United States.

Japan remains the striking exception to the rule that the greatest capitalist countries are also culturally of Christian persuasion. Again apart from Japan, ultimately leadership in technology continues to coincide with cultures that were originally Christian, while their need for energy continues to link them with countries which are self-consciously Islamic.

Technology seems destined to be the last cultural frontier of the first two millennia of the Christian era. Only a few more years are left of the second millennium. Christianity itself has declined in its heartland in the Western world. And yet the cultures of monotheism continue to cast their shadow on world events. The centre of the world economy is Christo-Islamic. Monotheism as a doctrine may no longer condition behaviour and perspectives directly. The heritage of dualism persists nonetheless, and the latest cultural frontier between the haves and the have-nots is, in the ultimate analysis, technological.

Conclusion

I have sought to demonstrate in this essay that there is a hidden cultural agenda in world-order problems which ranges from dogma (both sacred and secular) to international stratification. A particularly important perceptual factor is the tendency towards dualism in modes of identification — the culture of 'us' and 'them'.

In addition, this chapter seeks to demonstrate that dualistic thinking is to some extent culturally relative. Some civilizations show a greater propensity for it than others. Focusing on monotheistic civilizations, I attempted to show that those which anthropomorphized God in monarchical terms, and made him one God for all mankind, had a strong propensity to divide the world between God-fearing people and sinners. This dichotomizing was partly reinforced by what I have termed the culture of politics, which also inclines towards separating the sheep from the goats, differentiating supporters from adversaries.

Bipolarity, the tendency towards two opposing foci, did not begin with the cold war and the division of the world between capitalists and communists, but goes back to that basic dichotomizing tendency which some cultures emphasize more than others. Of special interest is the origin of the present international system in the days when international law was arranged to govern relations among Christian states, leaving the rest of the world to find alternative arrangements. International law in the days of John Stuart Mill and Karl Marx was a system of rules for civilized nations with the rest of the world subject to other rules, if any. This was the world which produced imperialism and legitimized the subjugation of the peoples of Asia and Africa by the peoples of the Western world.

The system of stratification based on degrees of civilization gave way in our own time to one based on development, implying technological know-how. Thus, we witnessed international stratification in the seventeenth century linked partly to credentials of faith, giving way in the nineteenth and the first half of the twentieth century to credentials of civilized behaviour, culminating in our own day in credentials of technical know-how.

Alongside this transition was also a different kind of cleavage, however, between those regarded as peace—loving nations and those regarded as part of the wider wilderness of war. This parallel mode of classification, partly influenced by the Christian moral system with its focus on peace and love, was with us, changing as it evolved, from before the Peace of Westphalia right up to the promulgation of the Charter of the United Nations.

The cultural frontier of our world order has indeed been moving, and monotheism, though now much weakened with the decline of religion generally, continues to cast its shadow over international relations and world affairs. Western civilization has become increasingly secularized, yet its two greatest challenges are, on one side, militantly monotheistic (Islam) and, on the other, self-consciously atheistic (Marxism). But Marxism, Western civilization, and Islam are in any case interrelated. The dialectic in Marxism is dualistic; so is the constant tension between good and evil in both Christianity and Islam. The map of world power today is a map covered by Islam, Western civilization, and

Marxist systems. All three cultural universes betray the historical and normative impact of monotheism and its derivative patterns of cognition. 'In the beginning was the Word, and the Word was with God, and the Word was God.'[10]

Notes

1. B. V. A. Roling, *International Law in an Expanded World* (Amsterdam: Djambatan, 1960), pp. 17—18.
2. Sir George Clark, *War and Society in the 17th Century* (Cambridge: Cambridge University Press, 1958), p. 88. Cited by Roling, ibid., p. 18.
3. *Henry the Sixth, Part 1*, Act V, Scene 1.
4. For the references to the former Dutch prime minister and the American diplomat, see Roling, ibid., pp. 21—22.
5. John Stuart Mill, 'A Few Words on Non-Intervention', in *Dissertations and Discussions*, Volume 3 (London, 1867), pp. 153—158.
6. Friedrich Engels, article for the *Northern Star* (English Chartist newspaper), Volume XI, 22 January 1848.
7. Cf. Karl Marx, 'The Future Results of British Rule in India' (8 August 1853), Shlomo Aveniri (editor), *Marx on Colonialism and Modernization* (New York: Doubleday & Co., Anchor Books, 1969), pp. 94—95, 132—134. I am also greatly indebted to my former student Dr Rovan Locke for stimulation and bibliographical guidance on Marx's theories of cultural stratification.
8. Max Weber, *The Protestant Ethic and the Spirit of Capitalism*. See also R. H. Tawney, *Religion and the Rise of Capitalism* (1926) (New York: New American Library, 1954).
9. Robert K. Merton, *Social Theory and Social Structure* (New York: The Free Press, 1967), pp. 574—605.
10. John, 1:1.

2
Hegemony

From Semites to Anglo-Saxons

'God, gold and glory!' Captured in a slogan, these are in fact the three basic imperatives in the history of cultural diffusion. Why do men burst forth from their boundaries in search of new horizons? They are inspired either by a search for religious fulfilment (the God standard) or by a yearning for economic realization (the gold standard) or by that passion for renown (the quest for glory) that John Milton described as 'that last infirmity of Noble mind'.

Though these three elements have always been present in the history of cultural expansionism, there has also, indeed, been the issue of 'the first among equals'. Which particular force — God, gold or glory — is supreme in the drive for cultural expansion?

This chapter divides world history not into feudal, capitalist, and socialist epochs, but into the three imperatives listed above. Most simply, we might say that the pre-capitalist world upheld a universe of the supremacy of God. The capitalist phase manifested the supremacy of gold. In the post-capitalist world which is governed by the supremacy of glory, the main issue is whether that glory is sectional or planetary, chauvinist or humane.

In the search for the God standard in world culture, especially important have been the Semitic peoples — particularly the Jews and the Arabs. In the search for the gold standard in our special sense, particularly important have been the Europeans and their extensions in the Americas. In the search for glory, there are two ultimate routes — one through outer space and the other through grassroots social movements. Space exploration in the twentieth century is primarily a search neither for God nor gold. The ultimate investment until now has been in national glory. But that glory is sectional rather than global. It may be planetary measured against the Milky Way, but it is not planetary in world-order terms.

The quest for ultimate human glory is at the crossroads. It must emphasize either flight into outer space or putting its own house on earth in order. The former demands cosmonauts and astronauts. The latter requires grassroots social movements. It was Julius Nyerere of Tanzania who once said: 'While they are trying to reach the moon, we are still trying to reach the village.' And yet the most momentous social movement may well turn out to be the women's movement, a theme to which we shall return.

Meanwhile let us view history in its own terms. Those forces which first taught the world that the human race was one were indeed religious forces. The most universalist of all religions were the Semitic religions, especially Christianity and Islam. Precisely because Christianity and Islam wanted to convert every human being to their faiths, they were the most militantly globalist of all cultures. Their ambitions exceeded their powers of communication.

It is still worth following this remarkable story of the impact of the Semites on our consciousness of a single world. Part of that story is religious bigotry, part of it is militarism and conquest, part of it is ethnic exclusivity. It was the semitic belief in the oneness of the human race which led to Christian crusades and Islamic *jihads*. Both represented a commitment to global conversion. This religious dimension should be examined before turning to the imperatives of the gold standard and beyond.

Between God and Gold

'What do you think of Western civilization?' asked the interviewer.

'I didn't know they had any!' replied Mahatma Gandhi.

This reported exchange captures one of the most important debates of the twentieth century: what is the moral worth of the West's contribution to the human condition? Has the West left the human race better off or worse off than it found it?

Gandhi was not disputing the claim that the West had a culture; he was raising the question of whether it had a civilization. Culture may be defined as a system of inter-related values, active enough to condition perception, judgment, communication, and behaviour in a given society. Civilization, in those terms, is a culture which has endured, expanded, innovated, and been elevated to new moral sensibilities. It was presumably the last criterion of 'moral sensibilities' which Mahatma Gandhi was implicitly questioning when he queried whether the West had evolved a civilization.

The two biggest contributors to world culture are the Semites, on one side, and Europeans, on the other. The Semitic peoples (especially Jews and Arabs) helped to change the world through religion, introducing a theocratic approach to cultural universalism. Europeans have helped to change the world through technology and science, the technocratic approach to cultural universalism.

By the nineteenth and twentieth centuries the Arabs had become the biggest exporters of culture in the Southern continents. The Anglo-Saxons of the North have now replaced them. To explore this remarkable impact of the Semites and the Europeans upon the nascent global civilization involves a study in macro-history rather than a general theory of causation. We are not trying to explain why the torch of universalism passed from the Semites to the Anglo-Saxons, but simply to show the transition. Nor are we theorizing as to why the God standard gave way to the gold standard, but simply telling the story of changing human pursuits in a cultural perspective.

The triple ambition of 'God, gold, and glory!' has been at least as important in cultural expansion as the aspiration of '*liberté, egalité, fraternité*' in modern revolutions. The pursuit of religious fulfilment (God), economic gain (gold), and political ambition (glory) have been three of the most decisive factors in cultural diffusion and institutional transfer in world history. These three ambitions have constituted the *ends* of cultural expansion.

What about the *means* of this conquest? Three primary forms of technology have facilitated the spread of cultures: the technology of production (with economic output), the technology of destruction (with military output), and the technology of communication (with the output of messages). So to the three goals of God, gold, and glory, there are three paths, economic, military, and communicative.

The relative weight of the three goals has, of course, varied in different periods and for different societies. Economic determinists would insist that the pursuit of gold and its equivalents is paramount. As a poet once put it when characterizing the Arab *jihads* and conquests of the seventh and eighth centuries A.D.:

No, not for paradise didst thou
the desert life forsake;
Rather, I believe, it was thine
yearning for bread and date.[1]

The primacy of economic gain is a much more recent phenomenon, however, than outright economic determinists would argue. Earlier phases of history did sometimes witness the tilting of the balance in favour of God in preference to 'pure' economic gain. In other words, there was a God standard before there was a gold standard in the history of culture.

Furthermore, and quite simply, the pursuit of gold has reached new global proportions with the rise of Western capitalism. Economic gain has been put on the world stage, with considerable implications for cultural change and diffusion. Western capitalism holds the reins of the technologies of both production and communication.

Third, the pursuit of glory under European leadership has created the sovereign state, which has also been globalized. The sovereign state holds the reins of the technology of destruction.

Our fourth concern is with grassroots movements. In the second half of the twentieth century these are opposed to capitalism, on one side, and the state-system, on the other, and what is at stake is the nature and texture of world civilization itself.

That the God standard was often the dynamo of large-scale cultural expansion can be discerned from the simple fact that religious movements were for so many centuries the major carriers of new values and norms across societal boundaries. The banner of religion was held aloft during the long evolution towards something approaching a world culture.

The largest exporters of culture in history have been India, the Middle East, and Western Europe. India's most important cultural export has been a religion which has not been triumphant within India itself. Buddhism is a religion more successful in exile than at home, thriving in Burma, Thailand, Kampuchea, Laos, Vietnam, China, Korea, and Japan rather than in India itself.

While Buddhism is indeed a major cultural export, it is less central to world culture than are the contributions made by the Semites and the Europeans. We define world culture as a shared heritage which has spread to at least three continents and, in different degrees, affects the lives of at least half the human race. Humanity in the twentieth century has just begun to evolve something approaching a world culture. And within that heritage the contributions made by the Semitic and European peoples is immense and disproportionate.

31

Let us first look at the history of this Semitic and European impact before we examine its contemporary implications.

The Jewish impact on world culture has been through both Judaism and Christianity, both the Old Testament and the New. Judaism itself is more trans-territorial than international. It makes better sense to talk of 'the Jewish nation' scattered in different countries than to talk of 'international Judaism'. The Jewish community world-wide is relatively small (currently some fifteen million) and the Jews can therefore be deemed an ethnic group, as they are to some extent a biological group of shared descent. This is a small group, but one which has had an enormous impact on world history.

The Jews gave birth not just to Judaism but also of course to Christianity. And Christianity is the most international of all religions, a status it has reached through five major stages. There was first the conversion of Paul, with all its consequences. In time this was followed by the conversion of Emperor Constantine I resulting in the Christianization of the Roman Empire. Third, there was the Reformation and the inauguration of competitive proselytization. Fourth, there was the peopling of the Americas under Christian auspices. The fifth stage is the European colonization of the African continent. The two ancient stages (the conversions of Paul and Constantine) should be examined first.

The first stage of Christian internationalism was the de-nationalization of the religion, delinking it from the Jews. After all, Christianity began with a Jewish sect. Early Christians accepted Jewish rituals. The early church in Jerusalem regarded circumcision as obligatory and the Mosaic Laws as binding.

It was the Jews of the Diaspora who initiated the trend toward Christian universalism. An early convert, Stephen, demanded the abrogation of the Mosaic code and was dragged before the Jewish Sanhedrin. He denounced official Judaism as unreceptive to the Holy Spirit. Stephen was stoned to death, becoming perhaps the first Christian martyr.

There followed persecution of liberal Jews, when many fled and sought asylum in Antioch. It seems to have been the Christians of Antioch who began to convert gentiles. What is more, they said that gentiles did not have to be circumcized. A new frontier in the de-nationalization of Christianity had been reached. Before long the Antioch church started to send missionaries elsewhere.

The conversion of Paul helped to start the process of the true internationalization of Christianity. Paul was probably the first to preach a thoroughgoing universalism. As he himself declared in his letter to the Romans: 'there is no distinction between the Jew and the Greek; the same Lord is Lord of all and bestows his riches upon all who call upon him.'[2]

Between AD 48 and 58 Paul covered much of Asia Minor and Greece, travelling and preaching the Gospel to Jews and gentiles alike. Christianity began to penetrate the eastern provinces of the Roman Empire. Before long even Rome itself had a small Christian community.

Meanwhile, tension had developed between Jewish Christians and universalist Christians. The Jewish Christians were under the Jerusalem Church, the universalists under the Church of Antioch. James, Jesus's brother, was the central figure in the Jerusalem Church; Paul presided over the destiny of Antioch. The Jerusalem Church was Jewish orthodox; the universalists were liberal. Jerusalem insisted on circumcision for Christians. On the other hand, Paul denounced those who insisted on 'mutilation of the flesh'. Paul was imprisoned for two years and was probably executed by Emperor Nero.

Paul had fulfilled his historical destiny as the second founder of Christianity. The legacy of the Antioch Church continued while the Jerusalem Church died. Christianity became primarily a gentile and a grassroots movement.

The new Christian religion began to spread further afield. It became internationalized within the Roman Empire in the sense of making converts across ethnic, national, and provincial frontiers. At the same time it was isolationist and separatist because of the tendency for believers to live apart while rejecting the pagan worship of the god-emperor. Christians regarded emperor-worship as idolatry. The Roman government in turn regarded the Christian rejection of the god-emperor as treason punishable by death. The game of throwing Christians to the lions was inaugurated. The followers of Jesus had to pray in secret.

By the fourth century the Christian community had grown to such an extent that recognition seemed politically prudent. Emperor Constantine proclaimed the Edict of Milan in AD 313, extending toleration to Christians alongside followers of other religions of the Empire.

Why did Constantine do this? In one critical battle — so legend goes — the Emperor called upon the god of the Christians. Constantine is supposed to have beheld the sign of the cross in the sky with the words, *In hoc signo vinces* ('In this sign shalt thou conquer').

Constantine procrastinated over his own formal conversion and left it until rather later in his life. Indeed, in the eastern part of his Empire, he never quite abandoned the concept of god-emperor. He did, nevertheless, lay the foundations of the Christianization of the Roman Empire, and indeed also of Europe as a whole. One more step had been taken in the slow evolution of a global political culture.

Thus while the two largest contributors to world culture have been the Semites and the Europeans, when the Roman Empire was converted to Christianity these two universalist contributions were for a while fused. The Greco-Roman heritage and the Judeo-Christian legacy started their joint adventure towards changing the world. The God standard had taken over an Empire and shared the temporal splendour which went with it. European Christianity became less a grassroots movement and more an imperial system. Notwithstanding, the idea that the world was one derived from a merger between the Greco-Roman and the Judeo-Christian legacies.

Islam: A New Semitic Impact

But while Christianity was slowly consolidating itself in Europe, another branch of the Semitic peoples — the Arabs — burst on to the world stage carrying the banner of Islam. The expansion of Islam in its first century was much faster than that of any religion before it. What is more, unlike Christianity and Buddhism — the two other international religions — Islam has remained successful where it was born as well as abroad, in its cradle as well as in exile. This has made the Arabs the most successful exporters of their own religion in human history. Europe has exported a religion it borrowed from others — Christianity. India exported a faith it had basically rejected for itself — Buddhism. Only the Arabs among the cultural exporters stand out continuously as leaders in the religion which they themselves produced and continue to profess.

In the period of human history since the birth of Islam in the seventh century AD, the Arabs were ahead of India in cultural expansionism. Within a brief period following the death of the Prophet Muhammad in AD 632, the Arabs had taken on two mighty empires of the ancient world — those of Byzantium and Persia. Syria fell to the Muslims in AD 636, Iraq in AD 637, Mesopotamia in AD 641, Egypt in AD 642, and Persia itself in AD 651. Two processes of slow acculturation were set in motion: Arabization (through language transfer) and Islamization (through religious conversion). Countries like Egypt underwent both processes, eventually becoming both Arab and Muslim. Persia, on the other hand, underwent mainly Islamization (religious conversion) without becoming an Arab country, by linguistic definition. In subsequent centuries other parts of Asia were also Islamized without becoming Arab countries. The range is from Afghanistan to Indonesia, from Asia Minor to large parts of the Indian subcontinent. In time Islam became the most widespread religion in Asia. The largest Muslim societies are now outside the Middle East, and include Indonesia, Bangladesh, Pakistan and indeed the remaining millions of Muslims in the Republic of India.

Islam's future rival in expansionism was, however, Europe. Centuries before Europe colonized the world of Islam, Islam had attempted to take over Europe. In this ambition Islam was partially and temporarily triumphant. In AD 711, the Muslims crossed with an army from North Africa into Spain and defeated the Visigothic king, Roderick. By 715 Muslims had either captured or indirectly controlled the main cities of Spain. Narbonne in the south of France was also occupied as part of the Visigothic Empire. Spain became a province of the Islamic Empire, controlled for a while from Damascus under the Umayyad Dynasty. Islam, inspired by a new universalism, sought to take over the world in the name of God. Its ambition outstripped both its power and its means of communication, but a global mission was nevertheless attempted.

In AD 750 the capital of Islam moved from Damascus under the Umayyad Dynasty to Baghdad under the Abbasids. A young Umayyad, Abdulrahman I, issued a Unilateral Declaration of Independence and established the Umayyad Dynasty of Cordova.

The height of power and prosperity was reached under Abdulrahman III (912–961) when the Muslims controlled most of the Iberian peninsula. But fragmentation soon began and, with it, the political decline of Islam in Iberia. In 1031 there were some 30 independent rulers. The spirit of universalism was cracking under the strain of political rivalries.

Some of these rulers appealed to the Almoravids, rulers of the Berber Empire in North Africa. The Almoravids defeated a Christian challenge in Spain and then ruled Spain themselves from 1090 to 1145. They were succeeded by fellow Berbers, the Almohads, who ruled Muslim Spain until the year 1223. Under pressure they subsequently withdrew to North Africa as Christian Spain sought to reassert itself. Cordova fell to the Christians in 1236, Seville in 1248.

In 1492 Granada (with the Alhambra) was incorporated into the new United Kingdom of Aragon and Castile. The stage was set for both the expulsion of the Moors and for the dark period of the Inquisition. Both Islamic and Christian universalism were under siege. The desire to convert the world had resulted in a new fragmentation. Universalism wore the frightening mask of sectarianism.

The first Islamic raid on Sicily was in AD 652, but the final occupation was not completed until 902. Parts of mainland Italy were also threatened. The Arabs were at Naples in 837. Indeed, in 846 and 849 Rome itself was threatened, but it was not invaded or captured. There is reason to believe that Pope John VIII (elected 872, died 882) had to pay tribute to the Muslims on his borders for about two years.

Once again competitive universalism was a prescription for strife and dominion.

Before the end of that century Byzantine Greek power began to reassert itself in southern Italy. This resulted in ending the Arab occupation of mainland Italy. As for Sicily, it was recovered from the Muslim conquerors in the year 1091.

The Christian crusading movement of the later eleventh century arose further north in Europe, and failed to reconquer the Holy Land. But at least the bulk of Europe managed to keep Islam at bay. In the year 732 a Muslim raiding expedition had penetrated to the area between Poitiers and Tours. The Muslims were defeated by the Franks led by Charles Martel. This has been acclaimed by European historians as one of the most decisive battles of all history. In a sense, it marked the utmost military expansion of Islam into Western Europe.

But in the intellectual field Islam still continued for a while to outshine Europe. The 'Dark Ages' in Europe coincided with the flourishing of Islamic science and scholarship. The Muslim world reintroduced Europe to the intellectual glories of classical Greece. Geography and the nautical sciences received a new stimulus from Islam. The zero and the metric system entered the world stage. And what we now call Arabic numerals replaced the numerals of Rome, under the mathematical tutorship of both the Muslim world and India. Today words of Arabic derivation in English as a world language include algebra, amalgam, average, atlas, chemistry, cypher, drug, tariff, zenith, and zero. The scientific foundations of all three forms of modern technology (production, destruction, and communication) were slowly being laid.

During this entire period, however, science and scholarship were still primarily theocentric. Islam had expanded the horizons of learning *fi sabil el Allah* (in God's path and in God's name). Cultural expansionism was still animated by a universalist religious fervour. The God standard continued to outshine the gold standard, at least in the field of culture.

Monotheism and the Origins of the State

The most important *political* contributions to world culture that the Semites have made include ideas of centralized government and the principle of patriarchy. Both of these ideas have contributed to the evolution of the modern sovereign state.

People's ideas about God can condition their ideas about government. The Semitic concept of God (whether Judaic, Christian, or Islamic) saw him as royal, masculine, as King, expecting loyalty and obedience. God was also supreme judge. The Hereafter was a centralized and absolutist dominion, divided between the paradise of the obedient pious and the ghetto of the disloyal sinners.

What God decreed was good. The history of theology and philosophy is replete with debates as to whether God could be omnipotent if he could not help being good. Does good define God — or is God the ultimate definition of what is good? The early debates were a precursor of the issue as to whether 'the king could do no wrong'. Echoes of this doctrine influenced Richard Nixon in his paradigm that the president, by definition, could do no wrong. The origins of state sovereignty lie in the conception of royal absolutism, itself greatly influenced by the absolutism of the Semitic kingdom of God.

John Milton, author of *Areopagitica*, one of the most eloquent defences of earthly liberty, at the same time justified divine absolutism in his *Paradise Lost*. Satan in the early phases of the poem rebels against a king who demands absolute obedience and seems to enjoy the constant prayer and hymns in his glory. Satan becomes a freedom fighter, rebelling against the absolutism of the Almighty. And yet by the end of the poem God has triumphed over Satan and absolutist authority is victorious.

Milton's God was the Old Testament God of the Jews — a God who used his power and sat in judgment. Milton was a seventeenth-century Christian but there is little of the gentler Christian God of the New Testament in his great poem.

In reality the New Testament conception of God is more complex than that in the Old Testament. In the New Testament, God is indeed still king in heaven, but he is wretched on earth. The crucifixion is a process by which God humbles himself before men. Was the crucifixion in the service of God, or in the service of man?

It was God who decreed that atonement had to be through the crucifixion. God decided that he had to humble himself before man's sins could be atoned. The humility of God was part of the majesty of God. Jesus declared that his kingdom was not of this world. He advised his followers to give unto Caesar what was Caesar's and unto God what was God's. Jesus's recognition of Caesar as sovereign on earth was part of the background to modern European conceptions of sovereignty. Man was king on earth, and God was king in heaven.

After the conversion of Emperor Constantine I in the fourth century, Christianity became an imperial religion rather than a religion of the underdog. Under Constantine and his successors, God was conceived as supreme on earth as well as in heaven. These became the years of Christian theocracy, a total of twelve centuries from the fourth to the sixteenth centuries. In this period the Christian conception of God (the New Testament) came close to the Judeo-Islamic conception of God (the Old Testament). In those twelve centuries the Old Testament was dominant in Christendom, as well as in Judaism and Islam.

As we have indicated, there are occasions when theology is the mother of political philosophy. Ideas about divine governance are often interlinked with ideas of politics among men.

Under the Semitic impact, what is the relationship between heaven and earth as political entities? In orthodox Judaism and in Islam the pull is towards a kind of divine unitarism linking heaven and earth. In the final analysis, theocracy is triumphant in the Judeo-Islamic tradition. Heaven and earth are together a unitary kingdom under God. Ultra-conservative Israelis have a lot in common with Iranian Ayatollahs.

The modern Christian tradition is more federalist than unitary as between the kingdoms of heaven and earth. The move towards liberal secularism in culture was linked to the move towards federalizing in politics. Separating church from state was like separating the kingdom of heaven from the kingdom of this earth in a cosmic federation.

On the other hand, the origins of separation of powers in politics may partly lie in the doctrine of the Trinity in religion. The Christian God was the source of legislation, the ultimate fountain of law. God's son was the executive branch, needing to transform himself into man in order to close the gap between divine decree and human performance. But help is needed in the interpretation of divine purpose. Could this be from the Holy Spirit? When translated into human equivalents, do we discern the spirit of the laws and judicial review? The Anglo-Saxon doctrine of separation of powers may have a primordial philosophical link with the neo-Semitic concept of the Trinity (three-in-one and one-in-three). Both have been manifested in the evolution of the concept of sovereignty.

Semitic monotheism has influenced the emergence of sovereign absolutism, while at the same time the ideas of shared humanity, derived from Genesis, have encouraged the notions of shared fraternity which cut across the notion of the sovereign state. The balance has been tilted away from the concept of shared humanity and in favour of state sovereignty by a powerful emphasis on a third Semitic principle — that of patriarchy. Earlier polytheistic or pantheistic traditions in world history, including those of ancient Egypt, ancient Greece and Rome, and the 'tribal' religions of the world, allowed considerable room for female deities. Semitic monotheism was the great destroyer of the female factor in the character of the deity. From the Semites onwards the great symbols of fertility became masculine. No more goddesses — only one God, and it is a 'He', with a capital H.

The God standard in politics was in part the cradle of the sovereign state. The Semites were the midwives of the concept of sovereignty. But who were the midwives of the gold standard?

Europe and the Rise of the Gold Standard

As Islam went into decline, the torch of science, technology and scholarship was being passed to a newly awakened Europe. In the fourteenth century of the Christian era the classical poet Petrarch was among the first to interpret the preceding thousand years of European history, including his own day, as an age of darkness. Culture and virtue had declined. Petrarch called for a renewed study not of the Gospel but of Europe's own Greco-Roman antiquity. He set the stage for the Renaissance, based on the twin myths that Europe's antiquity was the zenith of human creativity and that the 'Dark Ages' were the nadir. It was up to Europe to revive the spirit of its own classical past, innovative and dynamic.

Three interrelated European movements were to play a critical role in the emergence of modern Europe — the Renaissance, the Reformation, and the Enlightenment. The Renaissance helped to free European art from excessive service to God and church, and laid the foundations of aesthetic individualism.

The Enlightenment helped to secularize European science and scholarship and gave new prominence to the role of reason as opposed to faith. Great figures of the Enlightenment included Francis Bacon and his method of induction, Descartes and his method of deduction, Galileo Galilei who pushed the Copernican revolution a stage further with telescopic observation, Isaac Newton who formulated new heavenly laws based on gravitation, such empirical philosophers as David Hume, such romantic thinkers as Rousseau, such epistemological innovators as John Locke, and such incorrigible sceptics as Voltaire. They were part of the constellation of stars which constituted the Enlightenment.

The Protestant Reformation was another such constellation. Martin Luther (1483–1546), a miner's son who had become an Augustinian friar, was appalled by the abuses of indulgences under Pope Leo X. Luther posted his 95 theses on the church door at Wittenberg: one of the great gestures of protest of all time. Luther proclaimed that faith was the true salvation, and the truly repentant did not need priestly intercession or the Church's indulgences, but direct communication between the creature and his Maker.

What should be borne in mind is that these three European movements — the Renaissance, the Reformation, and the Enlightenment — were part of the origins of both the sovereign state and European capitalism.

The Renaissance as a period did indeed generate artistic independence and innovative individualism. It was also the period of the New Monarchies and the renewed doctrines of royal absolutism. The years of new individual liberation in the arts were also the years of the new political centralization of the state. The glories of the palace of Versailles as an artistic achievement are inseparable from the politics of Louis XIV, who proclaimed 'I am the state.' Artistic individualism was in the service of royal absolutism at Versailles.

The Protestant Reformation was linked to the origins of the modern sovereign state and of Western capitalism. In the evolution of the state system, the Reformation contributed to the break-up of what remained of the Holy Roman Empire. Quarrels among the different principalities resulted in the Peace of Augsburg of 1555, which set forth a formula of state sovereignty based on the principle of religious non-intervention. Hence the convention or *modus vivendi* agreed upon between European princes, founded on the idea that the religion of the ruler was to be counted as the religion of the society — *Cuius regio eius religio* as quoted above (p. 19). The whole exercise was designed to reduce interference and intervention across the territorial boundaries of each prince's domain. The idea of the sovereign kingdom was directly at stake in the Treaty of Augsburg.

This 1555 treaty did not end the religious wars in Europe which the Protestant Reformation had unleashed. Europe was later to plunge into another thirty years of conflict. Out of this particular period of internecine religious conflagration emerged at long last the Peace of Westphalia of 1648, widely regarded as the true genesis of the modern system of sovereign states on the world scene. The conflicts unleashed in Europe by the Protestant Revolution had set the stage for the whole modern state system, which today governs the destiny of the human race.

The Reformation was not only part of the genesis of modern statecraft and of the dynamics of sovereignty but also of modern Western capitalism. It is to this part of the global equation that we must now turn. A new tilt was beginning to take place from the God standard to the gold standard, in a fundamental but subtle transition.

The story of the Protestant ethic and the spirit of capitalism is familiar enough, thanks largely to the brilliant pioneering work of Max Weber. By eliminating priestly intercession in man's relations with God, Protestantism promoted a new spirit of personal accountability and initiative. The laity could interpret for themselves what was avarice and what was usury without reference to priests or church officials. Acquisitiveness assumed a new legitimacy, and piety was no longer equated with poverty, regardless of the challenge of squeezing a camel through the eye of a needle!

John Calvin (1509–1564) pushed the Protestant ethic even further. It was at the age of twenty that he had his 'conversion' and began to preach for a return to Christian simplicity. In 1536 Calvin published his *Institutes of the Christian Religion*. These stripped the church of pomp, much of the splendour, and much of the ritual. The impact on the new converted bourgeoisie was to discourage ostentation and to discredit elaborate consumption. And so, the new Protestant-ism was, on the one hand, giving acquisitiveness greater legitimacy than ever, and, on the other, denying legitimacy to pomp and ostentation. The implicit and compelling message was 'Acquire, but don't consume! Make money, but don't spend it!' The stage was set for primitive accumulation; the trumpet had sounded for a crusade of savings and reinvestment.

John Calvin also preached predestination and the doctrine of the Elect and the saints. To prosper was regarded as a possible sign of God's favour — a signal that one might be among the Elect. Economic exertion became a form of prayer, and success could be God's pat on the back. The God standard and the gold standard were being merged.

Under Protestantism guilt was generally taken out of the pursuit of wealth. A new economic morality came into being, and Protestant Europe and Protestant North America took the lead in the new capitalist revolution. It was therefore not an accident that from the eighteenth century Protestant England was industrially ahead of Catholic Italy, that Protestant Ulster was industrially ahead of the Irish Republic, that Protestant United States was ahead of Latin America, and Protestant Scandinavia was ahead of Catholic Iberia. Only France remained a seeming exception to this rule: it was Catholic by religious allegiance but basically Protestant in its culture. The French Revolution of 1789, with its massive attack on the church and the monasteries, had been France's equivalent of a Protestant Reformation. French individualism and the liberalism of the legacy of 1789 transformed France into a country which was at once denominationally Catholic and culturally Protestant.

At the centre of it all has been the newly emergent capitalism and the newly triumphant sovereign state. The foundations of the West's hegemony had been set. A new global history was being born.

FIGURE 2.1 THE RISE OF THE WEST

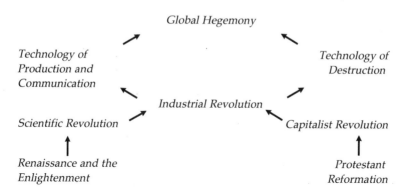

On Race and Communications

It was not Europe's technology of production alone which was stimulated by the Reformation and the scientific revolution; it was also Europe's technology of communication. We have already noted that production helped to consolidate capitalism. We must now also note that communication helped to expand imperialism. The genius of Western capitalism is indeed the sheer capacity to keep on producing. The genius of Western imperialism is its tentacles of communication. At least in a crude way, it can be argued that capitalism is the pursuit of gold through production; whereas imperialism has increasingly become the pursuit of glory through communication. But in Western history the two are welded together almost indissolubly.

Indeed, whether or not Protestantism was the midwife of capitalism, there is little doubt that capitalism was the midwife of Western imperialism. Imperialism was the globalization of the gold standard.

And yet, in a curious manner, imperialism was a marriage between expanding capitalism and expanding communications. Imperialism was a strange intimacy between the technologies of production, communication, and destruction. What is more, imperialism was a fusion between racist ideology and triumphant technology.

The communications revolution in the modern world did not begin with Sputnik or with the invention of the telephone. It began with European explorations and voyages of discovery, especially from the fifteenth century onwards. That is why the revolution has been linked not only to advances in technology but also to stages in imperialism. The stage was being set for European penetration of the rest of the world, with considerable danger to cultural autonomy and global human diversity.

A very curious but still major point to bear in mind is that today, while the communications revolution is indeed bad news for cultural autonomy in the Third World, it is at long last good news for the struggle against racism. Cultural authenticity among non-Westerners has never been in greater danger, with the penetration of Western culture deeper and deeper in much of the Third World. On the other hand, the communications revolution has now become an ally in the struggle against racism. Blatant racial discrimination is on the defensive. The language of racial abuse is looking around for euphemisms. The racists have never been more reluctant to proclaim their prejudices in public. Racism on the world scene is at best declining and is at worst in search of disguise and camouflage.

The decline of cultural autonomy and the retreat of racism are connected. There was a time when racism was itself regarded as an area of cultural autonomy. The southern states of the United States were permitted to invoke the dictum of 'Separate but Equal' and thus 'enjoy' their own Southern authenticity. There was also a time when South Africa could insist on the principle of 'domestic jurisdiction' and get away with apartheid as an ideology of 'cultural authenticity' and 'separate development'. The communications revolution, however, is making it even harder to use cultural autonomy as a justification for a racist ideology.

What should be remembered is that the link between communications and racism has not always been so positive. Indeed, the story of the relationship between these two has been tumultuous and variable across the centuries.

There is, for example, that whole complex story of Europe's interest in finding a sea route to Asia, which posed a major problem in communications. The imperatives of trading with Asia were forcing Europeans into an age of discovery, an era of exploration.

At that time Africa was just a stumbling-block on the way to Asia. Western Europeans had to sail around the landmass called Africa in order to get to Asia. Bartholomew Diaz tried to circumnavigate Africa and gave up after rounding the Cape, calling it the 'Cape of Storms'. Vasco da Gama was more successful and renamed the Cape, 'Good Hope'. The 'hope' was not about what Africa might have to offer but about communicating with Asia by sea.

Indeed, if Africa had not existed or had been a much lesser obstacle, the chances are that the discovery of the Americas by Europeans would probably have been delayed by another century or longer. Christopher Columbus would have had a much harder time raising money for a westward exploration if the sea-route around Africa towards Asia was less strenuous, hazardous, and expensive.

40

And yet history had its cruel revenge upon Africa. Christopher Columbus did not realize what damage he was doing to the African continent by 'discovering' the American hemisphere. In a relatively short time the demand for slaves in the 'New World' played havoc with population patterns and social institutions in Western Africa. A substantial part of Africa was forcibly shipped to the new plantations of the Americas. The maritime and nautical achievements of Europe and the 'discovery' of new worlds to conquer did irreparable damage to black Africa. Today one of every five people of black African ancestry lives in the Americas: a very high proportion indeed. From Africa's point of view Christopher Columbus and his navigational skills have a good deal to answer for. No people in history have been forcibly exported in such large numbers as Africans. And the Americas were the largest recipients of these reluctant immigrants.

The next link between communications and racism came with the industrial revolution proper and its impact on European imperialism in Africa and Asia. On the one hand, the industrial revolution helped to make slavery obsolete and generated support for the abolitionist movement. On the other hand, the industrial revolution created in Europe new demands for raw materials and other commodities, and resulted in Europe's economic and political expansionsm. The subsequent invention of the steam engine and a new wave of interest in building railways strengthened the penetrative capabilities of Europeans in parts of Asia and Africa and created an entirely new and repressive colonial order.

The third link between communications and racism was more positive. The colonized peoples in different continents began to know about each other and to learn about how to confront racism and imperialism. The anti-colonial movement in India under the leadership of Mahatma Gandhi was particularly influential at a certain period. Africans would not have known much about what was going on in India had Gandhi's movement taken place fifty years earlier. After all, very few Africans knew about the Indian Mutiny in the mid-nineteenth century. Communications between Africa and India at that time did not lend themselves to such mutual familiarization. But by the 1930s African nationalists were already able to follow from the radio and from newspapers the whole exciting unfolding of *Satyagraha* and the struggle against British imperialism. Future African historical figures who were inspired by the Indian national movement included Kwame Nkrumah (later founding president of Ghana), Kenneth Kaunda (later founding president of Zambia), and Obafemi Awolowo (later one of the giants of independent Nigeria). The communications' revolution had made it possible for the oppressed to learn from each other.

It is not often remembered that modern war is itself a revolution in communication. Beneficial from a very narrow point of view for the Third World was World War II and its aftermath. The war wounded the European imperial order mortally. France emerged humiliated and to some extent humbled. Britain was impoverished and exhausted. The imperial will, the will to grandeur, had been seriously shaken. It was not long before the British had to give up India. Almost exactly ten years after India's independence came Ghana's independence, and Ghana became the first black African country to attain sovereignty after European colonization. These events took place in the full glare of world publicity.

Part of the whole process of liberation was the experience of expanding political horizons among the colonized. The war had conscripted large numbers of people from the Third World. Africans were fighting in Burma; Gurkhas were fighting in the Middle East. Village lads were seeing the rest of the world. Later on some of these ex-servicemen became part of the vanguard of anti-colonialism in their own countries. A world war is indeed a globalizing experience. It is a brutal way of communicating the fact that we belong to one world. One such war helped to end European territorial imperialism in Africa and Asia.

The best phase in the alliance between communications and the struggle against racism is the present one of global exposure. The communications revolution has militated against racism in a variety of ways.

There is first the instant reporting of racial unrest or racial atrocities thousands of miles away. There now exists a *de facto* monitoring system upon the racial situation in the world as a whole. Major racial convulsions are guaranteed instant publicity from continent to continent.

Second, modern communications are a constant reminder to humanity as to how diverse humankind is. Television news covers events in obviously varied racial situations. Familiarity may sometimes breed contempt, but at least as often it can ameliorate a pre-existent disdain. Half of prejudice arises out of ignorance. Modern communications help to remind the world that humankind is, like love, a many-splendoured thing.

The globalization of communications has also helped to give more meaning to the concept of world opinion. There is more participation of the weak in the global system than there has ever been. Ambassadors of tiny countries have never been given greater formal respect by the mightiest. And so, even the governments of the mighty have learned to watch their language on some issues affecting the weak.

Further to be considered is the phenomenon of the spread of European languages in the rest of the world. The West has less linguistic privacy than it once had — precisely because it has made so much of the rest of the world learn European languages. Ethnic jokes about non-Westerners are now easily understood by the victims. It is now much easier for the Chinese to indulge in ethnic jokes against other races than it is for the Americans, since fewer non-Chinese understand Chinese than non-Americans understand English. American officials have to watch their language more closely than Chinese officials.

Finally, there is the language of the interconnected world economy, the language of economic rationality and economic interest. Racism has been over-taken by events. Just as international capitalism once discovered that slave labour was less efficient than wage labour, so international capitalism has now discovered that restricted racial exploitation is less profitable than a free labour market. Western capitalism is more genuinely opposed to apartheid than might at first appear. Apartheid has indeed become an anachronism in capitalist terms, just as slavery had become. Expanding communications help to reveal and dramatize that basic incompatibility.

Although, as has already been said, these new communications are good news for the struggle against racism and bad news for the quest for cultural autonomy, it would be naïve to consider this question independently of power more generally. Communication is not something independent of other forms of power. Indeed, power itself is, or can be, a medium of communication.

Since the Protestant Reformation, capitalism has become a whole new language of economic discourse, based on the West's technology of production. The sovereign state system has become a whole new language of diplomatic discourse, based on the West's technology of destruction. And Western civilization has become a whole new language of cultural discourse, based on the West's technology of communication.

Since the Industrial Revolution there has developed a focus of power within the Western world: the ultimate focus has now become Anglo-Saxon hegemony. A central feature of this phase of world cultural history is that white Anglo-Saxon Protestants (WASPs) have presided over the two most momentous centuries of all time, the nineteenth and twentieth. The Anglo-Saxons have been the most effective in using the language of capitalism and the technology of production. They have mobilized the symbols of the state system and the technology of destruction. And they have exploited the medium of their own culture through their technology of communication. The Anglo-Saxons are the new Semites of the technocratic era.

The Language of State Power

Who are the Anglo-Saxons? Our sense of 'Anglo-Saxon' is almost purely Gaullist, rather than genealogical. Like Charles de Gaulle, we mean by 'Anglo-Saxon' in this period those white nations whose mother tongue is the English language. The criteria are skin pigment and language. Jamaicans are not Anglo-Saxons, although their mother tongue is English. Cypriots are not Anglo-Saxons, although their skin is white. The people of the Falklands are indeed Anglo-Saxon because they are both white and native speakers of English.

What Charles de Gaulle called Anglo-Saxons, Winston Churchill called the English-speaking peoples. Both de Gaulle and Churchill excluded, on the whole, non-white native speakers of the English language, who may already outnumber the population of the United Kingdom.

In this part of the chapter we are concentrating on the political and state manifestations of Anglo-Saxon supremacy in these two centuries. In the next we shall focus on Anglo-Saxon hegemony in the language of capitalism. In the third section our concern will be with the Anglo-Saxon role in world culture.

An underlying motif in all three sections is the dialectic between Anglo-Saxon insularity and Anglo-Saxon expansionism, the political culture of one and the political economy of the other.

In the history of the Anglo-Saxons insularity has itself taken two forms. England has represented the insularity of an island people. The United States has signified the isolationism of a continental nation.

Western expansionism has also taken more than one form. Territorially, the United States expanded as a state but not as an empire. Territorially, Britain expanded as an empire but not as a state. The doctrine of Manifest Destiny inspired the United States to swallow neighbouring territory from the purchase of Louisiana to the conquest of California (contiguous expansionism). The doctrine of *Pax Britannica* inspired Britain to annex distant territory, from the creation of an Indian Empire to the establishment of a protectorate of Zanzibar. Territorially the United Kingdom will be smaller at the end of the twentieth century than it was at the beginning of the nineteenth. By contrast, the United States will be larger at the end of the twentieth century than it was at the beginning of the nineteenth.

The geographical region that the British state was least able to dominate or colonize in these two centuries was its own region — Europe. The geographical region that the United States was most able to dominate was its own hemisphere, the Americas. Britain was a balancing state in Europe, restoring equilibrium rather than asserting supremacy. The United States was a hegemonic power in the

Americas, asserting supremacy and averting equilibrium. The Monroe Doctrine in the Americas became a doctrine of American imperial hegemony. The doctrine of balance of power in Europe was a doctrine of Britain's balancing act.

In these two centuries, the Anglo-Saxons communicated with the world in three forms of political language: the power of intimidation (mainly military), the power of persuasion (mainly diplomatic), and the power of control (basically imperial). These three forms of power are closely interrelated.

The means of intimidation in the period have ranged from the Maxim gun to nuclear weapons, from British naval pre-eminence in the nineteenth century to Reagan's grand design of militarizing outer space before the end of the twentieth century. The Anglo-Saxons were the first to produce nuclear weapons. They were the first to use nuclear weapons (with Hiroshima and Nagasaki in August 1945 as the first targets). They were the first to take the world to the brink of a nuclear war (in the Cuban missile crisis of 1962). And they are the foremost in refusing to outlaw nuclear first strike.

On the other hand, the Anglo-Saxons have also led in seeking to control nuclear testing. In July 1963 British negotiators led by Lord Hailsham and American negotiators led by Averell Harriman arrived in Moscow. After five days of negotiations, tentative agreement was reached and a copy of the draft treaty was publicized on 24 July banning all tests in the atmosphere, under water, and in space, but not underground.

On 5 August 1963, Soviet Foreign Minister Andrei Gromyko, US Secretary of State Dean Rusk, and British Foreign Secretary Lord Home put their signatures to the document. The United States Senate ratified it on 24 September after a lengthy debate (the vote was 80 to 19).

A large majority of the world's nations followed suit and signed. France and China remained militantly opposed to the treaty.[3]

By this time the Americans were already the senior Anglo-Saxons. The transition from British global pre-eminence to American global hegemony was sometimes subtle and sometimes dramatic. The drama of the transition was partly a result of World War II, American leadership having consolidated itself in the course of the war. It was not until the Suez War of 1956, however, that the torch seemed clearly to have passed from London to Washington. Anthony Eden was decisively humbled by Dwight Eisenhower and Secretary of State John Foster Dulles. Britain's power of intimidation in world politics was now decisively overshadowed by American power. The British Lion was forced to withdraw from Suez, some would say with its tail between its legs! Both the gold and the glory of the empire were disappearing.

In the era of the balance of power in the preceding three centuries, Britain had been the queen of changing alliances. It could side with Austria against France and Prussia in one decade; and side with Prussia against France and Austria in the next decade. The balance of power in a world of conventional weapons had given way to a balance of terror in a world of nuclear weapons and Britain was no longer ahead in this new Anglo-Saxon roulette, having recourse only to its 'special relationship' with the senior Anglo-Saxons across the Atlantic.

The global political role of the Anglo-Saxons did not rely simply on instruments of intimidation, through military power, but also on means of persuasion. The Anglo-Saxon nations took the lead in the creation of both the League of Nations and the United Nations, but Britain and the United States were not consistent in supporting these institutions. Woodrow Wilson inspired the formation of the League of Nations but his country did not ratify its own membership. Britain was lukewarm in supporting the League's sanctions against Mussolini for his invasion of Ethiopia.

The United States played midwife to the birth of the United Nations at the formative conference in San Francisco in 1945. New York became the head-quarters of the new world body. Many Anglo-Saxon ideas influenced the text of the Charter. The Security Council became the equivalent of the House of Lords, 'war lords' with veto power. The General Assembly was the House of Commons, based on democratic ideas of representation. The history of the United Nations has witnessed the greater democratization of the General Assembly. But in the Security Council two out of the five 'war lords' are Anglo-Saxon. The Council has two English-speaking vetoes out of five.

In addition to the means of intimidation and persuasion, the Anglo-Saxons have utilized instruments of control. The British, as we know, created the largest political empire in human history. The Americans created the largest economic empire ever. Their means of intimidation and their techniques of persuasion helped to consolidate their capacity for control.

In terms of territorial control, the United Kingdom was virtually the architect of modern imperialism. Curiously enough, the Americans became the pioneers of modern anti-imperialism. The American Declaration of Independence remains one of the landmarks of the history of decolonization in the modern world.

The two Anglo-Saxon powers have also played fascinating roles in the history of politicized hereditary status in world affairs. Even before the French Revolution the American revolution attacked the principle of monarchy and a hereditary aristocracy. Britain, on the other hand, took the lead in attacking the principle of slavery and hereditary servitude. The Americans were pioneers in ending the hereditary privileges of the super-class, or nobility. The British were pioneers in ending the hereditary subjection of the under-class, or slaves.

By the twentieth century, however, neither the Americans nor the British were prepared to tackle the new equivalents of the old heredity: ecological privilege and ecological servitude. The people of the northern continents have become the Brahmins of affluence and geo-historical advantage. The people of the Southern continents (the Third World) have become the untouchables of servitude and geo-historical poverty.

The Anglo-Saxons have been among the foremost opponents of the New International Economic Order and the New World Information Order. The budgets of the UN and of a number of other world organizations are one third Anglo-Saxon. Alas, that one third is opposed to fundamental change in favour of the underprivileged.

What is more, the Anglo-Saxons can sometimes decide to switch off and not listen. They can use power to break off communication, rather than promote it. One example is America's technique of withdrawing from such bodies as the International Labour Organization (ILO) or the United Nations Educational, Scientific and Cultural Organization (UNESCO). This is a combined power of silence and the purse. Anglo-Saxon threats of withdrawal have been, in part, a mechanism of censorship, a brutal leverage to change the agenda of international discourse. The sovereign state system is manipulated as a method of silencing certain voices of the South, certain messages from the dispossessed. The state is not only a medium of communication. It is also a guillotine for cutting off further dialogue.

The Anglo-Saxons have not only dominated the state system. They have also presided over the fortunes of capitalism. And for good reason. The Anglo-Saxons have provided the greatest stability to both liberalism and capitalism. It is to this area of hegemonic capitalism that we must now turn.

The Language of Capitalist Power

What is the link between liberalism as a political system and capitalism as a mode of production? Part of the answer lies again in the history of the Anglo-Saxon states, especially Britain and the United States. We define liberalism in this chapter as a pluralistic system of government which puts a special premium on political choice and individual freedom. We define capitalism as an industrial system in which the means of production, distribution, and exchange are under mainly private control and operate in the context of unequal class relations.

Of all the people of the world, the Anglo-Saxons have perhaps been the most successful in stabilizing liberal democracy in their own countries. The Anglo-Saxons have also been the leaders in stabilizing capitalism as a global system. In other words, they have presided over the interconnected fate of liberalism domestically and capitalism globally.

All countries with liberal political systems are capitalist in their economic organization. Is this a historical accident or a logical causal necessity? From the seventeenth century onwards England was a laboratory of modern capitalism. In the same period England was evolving into a laboratory of liberal ideas. How causally connected were these trends?

Modern liberalism was born out of three revolutions, two of them Anglo-Saxon. These were the 1688 Glorious Revolution in England, the American Revolution from 1776 onwards, and the 1789 Revolution in France. The Anglo-Saxon revolutions were decidedly different from the French, and the difference goes towards explaining Anglo-Saxon stability. The English and American revolutions were from above, led by members of the disgruntled establishment. The French Revolution, on the other hand, was an explosion from below, symbolized by the mob onslaught on the Bastille.

The Anglo-Saxon revolutions engaged in selective transformation, upholding the Burkean principle that a people should 'neither entirely nor at once depart from antiquity'. The French revolution, on the other hand, was an exercise in comprehensive transformation, aspiring to wipe the historical slate clean.

The American revolution especially was more liberal than democratic, as it sought to protect the people from the power of the government. The French revolution was more democratic than liberal, as it sought to increase the power of the underprivileged. In other words, the American revolution was preoccupied with checking the power of the mighty; the French were obsessed with enhancing the power of the meek.

Checks and balances, separation of powers, and federalism were America's answer to despotism. Mass involvement, referenda, and Bonapartism were France's prescription for popular participation. The ethos of American liberalism was decentralization, the ethos of the French version was centralization. The English and American revolutions were basically elitist; the French revolution was mass-oriented.

It is precisely these contrasting factors which helped to make Anglo-Saxon liberalism so stable and French liberalism so changeable. The French have had many constitutions since 1789. The Americans have had only cne since the late 1790s.

Particularly relevant for the link with capitalism was the convergence between stability of government and stability of property. The French revolution was no respecter of property. The Anglo-Saxon revolutions, on the other hand, were preoccupied with property rights. John Locke was the philosopher-prophet of both Anglo-Saxon revolutions. He stood for 'Life, Liberty, and Estate'. And when Thomas Jefferson amended Locke's phrase into 'Life, Liberty, and the Pursuit of Happiness', Jefferson might still have meant 'the pursuit of property'.

Locke was the forerunner of a long list of Anglo-Saxon communicators who helped to rationalize capitalism and thereby helped to stabilize it internationally. Adam Smith is regarded as the founder of the classical school of economics. Born in Scotland in June 1723, he lived to become the first systematic economist. His message was brilliantly communicated. His impact demolished feudal economics, the medieval guilds and mercantilism. The capitalism of the division of labour in production prepared the way for today's capitalism of mass production.

Another British communicator who helped to rationalize and stabilize capitalism was, of course, David Ricardo. Born in London in 1772, he lived to develop influential theories of rent and of labour which had a considerable impact on the evolution of modern economics. Karl Marx's theory of surplus value owed a good deal to Ricardo. He wrote on money and trade, and helped to develop the iron law of wages based on the doctrine of scarcity of economic goods.

And when capitalism faced its worst crisis in the twentieth century, it was once again a British thinker and communicator who rationalized the necessary reforms and helped to rescue the global system. Born in Cambridge, England, in June 1883, John Maynard Keynes became the most influential economist of the first half of the twentieth century. He was the founder of the expansionist school of economics, promoters of a strategy for overcoming unemployment and deflation through public works. He helped to rescue that other Anglo-Saxon power across the Atlantic when his ideas influenced President Franklin D. Roosevelt's New Deal strategy against the Great Depression.

From the eighteenth century onwards the English-speaking peoples have communicated to the world by far the most brilliant theories in defence of capitalism, from Smith to Friedman, from Malthus to John Kenneth Galbraith. These intellectual foundations have helped to give capitalism as a global system both durability and resilience.

Not surprisingly, the very paradigmatic quality of Anglo-Saxon capitalism also provided the setting for the most brilliant critiques of capitalism. After all, where would Marxism be without Marx's close study of the workings of capitalism in England?

Similarly, the paradigmatic quality of Anglo-Saxon imperialism provided the ammunition for the most brilliant attacks against imperialism. Where would Lenin's theory of imperialism be without Hobson's prior theory? Where would theories of *dependencia* be without a study of American economic imperialism?

But the Anglo-Saxon impact on the world economy has not been merely in terms of brilliant rationalizations or critiques of capitalism. The impact has taken more direct forms as well. First there was England's leadership in the industrial revolution and its emergence as a 'workshop of the world'. There was also England's role in stabilizing for many decades the principle of free trade, which was so important in the evolution of western capitalism. England's role in stabilizing the principle of the 'gold standard' as a basis of international exchange was also an important factor in the development of a capitalist world economy.

The economic torch was once again passed from the British to the Americans. In time the United States became the most important national economy in the global system. The collapse of Wall Street in 1929 sentenced the rest of the world to the deprivations of the Great Depression. From then on the health of the world economy as a whole was indissolubly linked to the health of the American economy. Before long the gold standard was, to all intents and purposes, replaced by the dollar standard.

After World War II western Europe's reconstruction depended on the enlightened self-interest of the United States and its Marshall Plan. And the Bretton Woods Conference in New Hampshire in July 1944 laid the foundations of the post-war international monetary and banking system dominated by the United States. Symbolically, the president of the World Bank is always an American. And the International Monetary Fund and International Development Association need the good mood of the American Congress to keep them in business.

The Anglo-Saxon factor in the world economy continues to be pronounced and critical. For better or worse, the English-speaking nations continue to be both the most stable liberal democracies in the world and the greatest stabilizers of international capitalism. They have been more successful in exporting capitalism to others than exporting democracy.

In this leadership of the world of capitalism, do the Anglo-Saxons now see a potential rival on the horizon? If Japan is emerging as a super-industrial state, will its importance for the health of the world economy ever approximate the importance of the Anglo-Saxons?

There was a time when Japan appeared to be another England. Britain led Europe in the industrial revolution; Japan led Asia. Both were island nations which managed to combine attachment to tradition with a spirit of modernization. Both were monarchies with elaborate class structures which combined feudal and bourgeois elements. Both became expansionist imperial powers. In many ways Japan appeared to be the England of the Far East. But while England helped to demonstrate that liberalism without capitalism was not possible, Japan demonstrated that capitalism could exist without liberalism. It is indeed true that all liberal democracies have capitalist economies; but it is not true that all capitalist economies are within liberal democracies. All liberal donkeys are capitalist animals, but not all capitalist animals are donkeys. Before World War II Japan demonstrated convincingly that the growth and maturation of capitalism need not be accomplished by the evolution of a democratic political system.

Apart from that major difference, Japan before the war did appear to be another England in its political economy. But since World War II, has Japan been developing into another United States? In industrial might, Japan has certainly left England far behind, and it has narrowed the industrial gap between itself and the United States. Japan is now the second industrial giant of the capitalist world, and its share of international trade is now a critical factor in the world economy.

While Japanese industrial expertise is catching up with that of the United States, however, Japanese natural resources are almost non-existent when compared with the natural endowment of America. Japan has, moreover, less than half the population of the United States. It seems unlikely, therefore, that Japan will ever overshadow the Anglo-Saxon factor in world capitalism, no matter how large its industrial output becomes.

Will the Anglo-Saxons remain capitalist? Marx was wrong in having ever expected a communist revolution in either Britain or the United States. There is probably a level of capitalist development below which a socialist revolution is indeed feasible, but above which a proletarian revolution becomes impossible. Almost all the Anglo-Saxon countries in our sense of the term (Britain, the United States, Australia, Canada, New Zealand, etc.) may have reached and passed that stage. Among the white English-speaking countries perhaps only Ireland is still at a stage of capitalist development at which a socialist revolution is conceivable.

Elsewhere in the white English-speaking world, internal liberal stability and external capitalist equilibrium have already produced a different result. The Anglo-Saxon nations are the least likely to vindicate Marx's prediction that advanced capitalism inevitably leads on to a proletarian socialist revolution.

Liberal Anglo-Saxons have presided over the destiny of capitalism for two centuries, and their nations seem to be further away from a Marxist revolution today than they were during Marx's lifetime. The Anglo-Saxons have switched on their amplifiers to convey their capitalist message to the rest of the world. But they have switched off their hearing aid and turned a deaf ear to the global call for social justice.

The Language of Cultural Power

As indicated earlier, a special dialectic between insularity and expansionism is discernible in the history of the Anglo-Saxon peoples. This dialectic has operated in both the political economy and the political culture of the Anglo-Saxon experience.

In this section, particular emphasis is placed on political culture. Let us now examine the interplay between Anglo-Saxon history and global culture transfers, especially trends in religion, race, language, and leisure.

The interplay in religion goes back to the Tudors. There is first the Anglo-Saxon impact on the relationship between church and state, a major aspect of the recurrent contradictions of world culture. The Protestant Reformation had, in retrospect, three major founders, two theologians and one king. The theologians we mentioned before were the German Martin Luther and the French John Calvin. The king was Henry VIII of England (1509–1547). Luther and Calvin challenged the church on matters of theology and doctrine. Henry challenged the Pope on issues of authority. In the ultimate analysis, Henry's protest was political rather than spiritual. While Luther and Calvin were re-defining the relationship between the individual and the priest, Henry was re-defining the relationship between church and state.

The history of the world would have been very different if Henry VIII had had a marriage counsellor or a good psychiatrist. The story is all too familiar. The second Tudor king had had problems with his marriage to Katherine of Aragon, widow of Henry's brother, Arthur. Henry wanted the marriage annulled on the grounds that the law forbade a man to marry his brother's widow (advance shades of Hamlet's self-torment over his mother's marriage to his uncle).

Pope Julius II had granted the original dispensation authorizing the marriage, but Henry was now disputing the Pope's authority. Pope Clement VII procrastinated. Henry decided to catch the 'Papal Bull' by the horns. In 1531, he forced an assembly of clergy to recognize him as the supreme head of the English Church.

He forced Parliament to stop payments to Rome and to appoint bishops without the permission of the Pope. Henry's marriage to Catherine was declared null and void by the Archbishop of Canterbury, Thomas Cranmer, and Henry's marriage to Ann Boleyn was declared valid.

In 1534 Henry forced Parliament to pass the Act of Supremacy declaring the English monarch to be 'the only supreme head on earth of the church of England'.

Theologically, Henry did not depart from the Catholic creed except on this issue of papal authority. He retained the articles of faith of the Catholic church, distant indeed from both Lutherism and Calvinism. It was Edward VI (1547–1553) who presided over the true transition to Protestantism, when altars and images were brought down and the Mass gave way to Holy Communion. The right of the king to marry (which had obsessed Henry) was now followed by the right of the priest to marry. In their pragmatic way, the Anglo-Saxons were forging their own version of Protestantism.

How did all this relate to the dialectic between insularity and expansionism among the Anglo-Saxons? The birth of Anglicanism signified the nationalization of Christianity, for it inaugurated the principle of creating an established church within the state, fusing a national monarchy with a universal church. The Church of England was born, and Christianity was nationalized, four centuries before British politicians started debating the nationalization of the economy.

Protestantism as a whole came to signify a movement for greater liberation of the individual from the centralized church. But Anglicanism in its origins seemed more concerned with the greater liberation of the nation-state from the universal church. The King of England was standing up against the Roman Pope. For quite a while Anglo-Saxon Protestantism was more preoccupied with the rights of the state against the church than with the rights of the individual against priestly power. The Anglo-Saxons were confined to religious insularity in this phase of their history.

As Anglo-Saxon culture and thought became more diverse, however, and the people migrated and populated other areas, striking differences developed. The two leading Anglo-Saxon powers signified drastically different relationships between church and state. The United States became a model of the principle of separating church and state constitutionally. Even today the issue of prayer in a public school is a matter of heated constitutional debate in the United States.

England, on the other hand, is a model of constitutional integration of church with state. The Queen is both head of state and governor of the Church of England. Major doctrinal changes in the Church of England need the implicit approval of the British parliament, though theoretically delegated to the synod. And the Archbishop of Canterbury is technically appointed by the Prime Minister. The two largest Anglo-Saxon nations thus provide contrasting paradigms for the rest of the world on the issue of church and state. It is the American ethos of separation rather than the British model of integration which is gaining ground in contemporary world culture.

There are, of course, Anglo-Saxon religious denominations with differing doctrinal content. The spread of these sects has been less dramatic than might have been expected. The Anglo-Saxons have been more effective in spreading their language than their religion. They have beaten the Latin countries linguistically, making the English language a greater global force than French, Spanish, Portuguese, or Italian. Protestantism, however, failed to become a bigger religious force in the world than Roman Catholicism.

The explanation may lie partly with the pluralistic nature of Protestantism, by contrast with the monolithic nature of Roman Catholicism. British imperial policy was more tolerant of competitive evangelization and proselytization than was the imperial policy of France, let alone Spain and Portugal. There was even an ecumenical principle in British immigration policies into the American colonies: Catholics to Maryland, Congregationalists to New England, Quakers to Pennsylvania, Anglicans to Virginia, and Dutch Reformed colonists to old New York (New Amsterdam) and New Jersey.

Partly because of the expansionist pragmatism of the Anglo-Saxons, they have had a role in the destiny of other faiths as well. We have already referred to their innovation in nationalizing Christianity during the days of Henry VIII. Four centuries later the Anglo-Saxons presided over the nationalization of Judaism as well, by playing midwife to the birth of the state of Israel and later committing themselves to the survival of that state. Britain's role in the history of Israel has of course been different from that of the United States, but both Anglo-Saxon roles have been fundamental to the destiny of Zionism and the Jewish state.

Britain was the power entrusted with the Mandate over Palestine after World War I. The Balfour Declaration of 1917 — issued even before the end of the war — is widely interpreted as a landmark in the legitimation of Zionism as a force and in the validation of the principle of a Jewish homeland. With typical British equivocation and ambivalence, the Balfour Declaration affirmed:

> His Majesty's Government view with favour the establishment in Palestine of a national home for the Jewish people, and will use their best endeavours to facilitate the achievement of this object, it being clearly understood that nothing shall be done which may prejudice the civil and religious rights of existing non-Jewish communities in Palestine or the rights and political status enjoyed by Jews in any other country.[4]

The Declaration was very influential. President Woodrow Wilson had approved it before publication and it was subsequently endorsed by France, Italy and other allied governments. Many international instruments incorporated the words of the Balfour Declaration, including the League of Nations Mandate for Palestine in 1922 and the US—British Palestine Mandate convention in 1924.

Later on it was the United States rather than Britain that presided over the destiny of Zionism and the dream of the Jewish state. President Truman's role was critical in determining the vote in the United Nations in favour of the partition of Palestine. From then on the United States has remained the patron of the state of Israel, providing moral, military, and economic means of survival.

The Anglo-Saxon factor in the history of the Jews in the twentieth century is second only to the role of the Jews themselves. It is not for nothing that the English language is now second only to Hebrew in the state of Israel.

What about the impact of the Anglo-Saxons on Islam? Has there also been a nationalization of Islam? There has, indeed, been a similar tendency in the Anglo-Saxon impact. The British ruled India and presided over its partition which was in many ways similar to that of Palestine. Pakistan nationalized Islam. Lawrence of Arabia (T. E. Lawrence) played a role in causing the Arabs to rebel against Turkish imperialism. In so doing, the Arabs replaced Ottoman overlords with European overlords. They exchanged fellow Muslims for Christians as masters. But out of British and French imperialism in the Middle East, Islamic nations were created.

The Gulf States, from Kuwait to Oman, and including Saudi Arabia, share an Anglo-American fascination. Both the British and the Americans continue to play a historic role. The compartmentalization of the Ottoman Empire was part of the trend towards the nationalization of Islam. And the Anglo-Saxons have been central to the process.

Where does the Iranian revolution fit into this interplay between Islam and the Anglo-Saxons? The Iranian revolution is, in a way, an effort to resurrect an Islamic Empire, an attempt seeking to revive a kind of Ottoman Empire in a more radical incarnation. Once again the Anglo-Saxons are quite central to Iranian sensibilities, as the crisis of the American hostages in Teheran in 1979—1981 dramatically illustrated.

The heartland of Sunni Islam is Saudi Arabia, and the Sunnis are in alliance with the Anglo-Saxons. The heartland of Shiite Islam is Iran, and the Shiites are at daggers drawn with the Anglo-Saxons. The Shiites are out to internationalize Islam in its radical form, rather than bow to Anglo-Saxon preference for national churches.

Finally, the role of the Anglo-Saxons in relation to Hinduism must be considered. The heartland of Hinduism was India, and India was ruled by the British. India borrowed from the Americans the principle of the secular state and of federalism, however modified or even distorted to suit local conditions. India borrowed from Britain more profound components of political culture. Thanks to the Anglo-Saxon impact, Hinduism has changed internally and found a new relationship with Western civilization. And even figures like Mahatma Gandhi were themselves products of the interplay between Hindu nationalism, the Yogi tradition, and Anglo-Saxon liberalism. India's greatest prime ministers — Jawaharlal Nehru, his daughter Indira Gandhi, and Nehru's grandson, Rajiv Gandhi — have been three of the most anglicized Indians that the British Raj ever produced. In short, the Anglo-Saxons had once again presided, for better or worse, over the modernization of yet another great religious civilization, Hinduism.

Anglo-Saxon influence in the colonies included racial issues, of course, as well as religions. When he was US Ambassador to the United Nations, Andrew Young (himself black) once accused the British of having 'invented modern racism'. If that was an exaggeration, there is nevertheless a sense in which Anglo-Saxon peoples have taken a major lead in the 'modernization of racism', and in its application to historical conditions in the last three centuries.

A major product of racism before the twentieth century was of course the trade in black slaves, especially across the Atlantic. In time the British became the biggest carriers of slaves from Africa to the Americas, selling slaves not only to their own colonies but also to Spanish and Portuguese America. In time, the southern states of North America evolved what was probably the most race-conscious form of plantation slavery in the western hemisphere. 'Miscegenation' between masters and slaves was not a way of liberating the offspring, as was often the case in Latin and Islamic forms of slavery. In the United States children of slaves were indeed slaves even if the father was the master himself. Chicken George, of innumerable examples, was sold by his own father to a Scottish slave-owner in Alex Haley's *Roots*.

Although the Anglo-Saxons played a major role in commercializing racism and making money out of the humiliation of Africa, history also gave the Anglo-Saxons a leading role in the fight to abolish slavery. British ships rescued many a slave on the high seas. It was indeed the Anglo-Saxons who helped promote black Zionism — the return of former black slaves to their ancestral Africa. That is how Liberia, the oldest African republic, was born. In 1816, the American Colonization Society created a government of repatriated black Americans (Americo-Liberians) over the indigenous African population. The society handed over political control more fully to the immigrant blacks in 1847. Sierra Leone was similarly a British settlement for emancipated slaves, from whom the Creoles, some of the leading citizens of Sierra Leone, are mainly descended. Nowhere else in the world is descent from ex-slaves as much a matter of pride as it is in Liberia and Sierra Leone. The Anglo-Saxons had a good deal to do with creating such a sense of privilege for the imported blacks as opposed to the indigenes.

This itself was part of Anglo-Saxon racism. Semi-westernized ex-slaves were superior to the non-westernized 'natives'. Indeed, the leading abolitionist nation in the world — England — was at precisely the same period the biggest empire-builder. England helped to end the sale of blacks but increased the conquest of black lands. Abolitionist England was simultaneously imperialist, the biggest territorial imperialist in human history. Americans, on the other hand, built the biggest economic empire.

As part of the modernization of racism, the Anglo-Saxons also played a leading role in two interrelated processes — the application of science and poetry to racism. The influence of Charles Darwin on racial theories symbolized the former process and of Rudyard Kipling the latter.

Darwin's biological theory of natural selection and the survival of the fittest was applied by others to racial gradation. 'Social Darwinism' became, in part, a theory to justify white supremacy.

Kipling turned racism into an imperialist crusade for the white man. Kipling's poem 'The White Man's Burden' (referred to on p. 20), remains the most imperialist poem in the English language. The poetry of racism is captured in such images of the 'native' as 'half-devil, half-child'. And white patriotism is stirred by such lines as:

Take up the White Man's burden
— The savage wars of peace
Fill full the mouth of famine
And bid the sickness cease.

The ports ye shall not enter,
The roads ye shall not tread,
Go make them with your living,
And mark them with your dead.[5]

This brings us to the linguistic impact of the Anglo-Saxons upon world culture. Some would say the English language is by far the most important contribution that the Anglo-Saxons have made to world culture, since it has become the most widely spoken language in human history, in terms of distribution. Sometimes the linguistic contribution is linked to such other Anglo-Saxon roles as international trade and imperialism. Until the second half of the twentieth century, the greatest disseminator of the English language was Britain, especially in relation to its territorial empire. Since World War II the greatest promoter of the English language has been the United States and its economic empire.

The English language is also tied to racism. Shakespeare was probably more anti-Semitic than anti-black. Certainly the *Merchant of Venice* (with its Shylock) is a more racist play than *Othello*. Subsequent Anglo-Saxons became more anti-Negro than anti-Jewish. Indeed, England was often ambivalent about teaching colonial natives the English language. It was a neo-Germanic distrust. England was somewhere between Germany and France in its attitude to language and race. The Germans in the colonies tended to believe that no native was good enough to speak German. The French tended to believe that no native was good enough *unless* he spoke French. The British fluctuated between these two forms of arrogance.

Although there are still more Chinese speakers than English speakers in the world, the chances are that the Chinese will have to learn English rather than the English learning Chinese. In the raging battle of two exclusive civilizations (Chinese and Anglo-Saxon), it is the linguistic expansionism of the Anglo-Saxons that is likely to prevail.

French is a bi-continental language. Almost all Francophone nations are either in Europe or in Africa. Europe has the majority of Francophone individuals; Africa has the majority of Francophone states. But English is a truly multi-continental language, and its expansion seems to be, on the whole, irreversible, although it is encountering some setbacks in linguistically nationalistic countries in Asia and Africa.

Other areas of culture with Anglo-Saxon leadership include some fields of leisure. Pop music (from jazz to rock) has been disproportionately influenced by Anglo-Saxons and 'Afro-Saxons' (blacks whose mother tongue is English). World tennis is usually dominated by Anglo-Saxons, and heavyweight boxing by 'Afro-Saxons'.

The United States' impact on world cinema and television has been enormous. American pop culture as a whole has been expansionist, coca-colanization of the world is under way. Popular American culture ranges from jeans to hamburgers.

American high culture, on the other hand, tends to be derivative and influenced by Europe. It has been less successful on the world scene.

American soft drinks have taken over the world, especially Coca-Cola and Pepsi-Cola. But American alcoholic drinks (like Bourbon whiskey) are far less successful.

American magazines have triumphed globally (especially *Time* and *Newsweek*) but American newspapers are far less successful (except for the peculiar case of the *Herald Tribune* which is not read in the United States itself).

The dialectic between insular newspapers and expansionist magazines becomes symbolic of a wider Anglo-Saxon predisposition. And cultural autonomy elsewhere has continued to be on the defensive as a result of the conquering power of Anglo-Saxon culture.

The State Triumphant

As we approach the twenty-first century, yet another curious trend can be seen. Two legacies from vastly different Semitic figures have been challenging Western hegemony and its Anglo-Saxon vanguard. One legacy is once again Islam and its restlessness whenever threatened by the West. The other legacy is that of Karl Marx, sometimes regarded as the last of the great Semitic prophets. A new battle is joined between the exported cultures of the Semitic and Anglo-Saxon peoples.

There is little doubt that Marxism and Islam are the most universalist of all the challenges to Anglo-Saxon hegemony. Marxism is especially concerned with the triumph of Western culture and seeks to arrest it. What neither Marxism nor Islam in the twentieth century is particularly worried about is the triumph of the sovereign state system.

Two types of revolution have arisen as a result of these concerns: revivalist revolutions, animated by a nostalgia for the past, and innovative revolutions, which aspire to an idealized future. Islam has provided a stimulus for revivalist revolutionary movements; Marxism has inspired innovative revolutionary trends. The revivalist movements are culturally defensive; the innovative movements are structurally transformative. The revivalist movements are usually nationalist; the innovative ones are usually socialist.

The revivalist movements are born out of a crisis of identity; the innovative ones come out of a crisis of inequality. The revivalists tend to be focused on the nation and its sanctity; the innovative ones are concerned with the state and its powers. In reality, however, neither revivalist Islam nor innovative Marxism has challenged the victorious status of the sovereign state.

Two Third World revolutions provide some of the most striking contrasts between these two trends. Iran under the Shah Pahlavi was one of the richest of Third World countries; Ethiopia under Emperor Haile Selassie was one of the poorest. The Iranian revolution was out to reverse the modernizing autocracy of the Shah; the Ethiopian revolution was out to accelerate the modernizing autocracy of the Emperor. The revolution in Iran was in search of a new Islamic theocracy. The revolution in Ethiopia was engaged in terminating an ancient Christian theocracy. The Iranian revolution in 1979 was a spontaneous revolution of unarmed civilians; the Ethiopian revolution in 1974 was a creeping coup by armed soldiers.

The Iranian revolution was opposed to Anglo-Saxon cultural imperialism. The Ethiopian revolution was opposed to Anglo-Saxon economic imperialism.

What neither Islam in Iran nor Marxism in Ethiopia was dedicated against is, once again, the state system. The legitimacy of the sovereign state seems to be the least endangered of all the concepts by which the West and the Anglo-Saxons have come to control the modern world.

The three most universalist movements founded by Semitic prophets are Christianity, Islam, and Marxism. All of them started as grassroots movements. Of the three only Islam captured the state during the Prophet's own lifetime. Christianity had to wait until three centuries after the death of Jesus before capturing the Roman Empire. Marxism had to wait from Marx's death in 1883 until the Russian Revolution of 1917 before capturing the Russian state.

But what is clear is that whenever grassroots movements have captured the state, it is not the state which has changed. It has been the grassroots movements. There is compelling evidence that whoever captures the state is in mortal danger of being captured by it.

When liberation movements succeed in capturing the state, the leaders become converted to the state system itself, sometimes almost fanatically. When workers capture the state in the name of socialism, they too soon develop state consciousness rather than class consciousness. They seek to protect the interests of the state which they now control, rather than continue to struggle to realize the interests of the workers in whose name they captured the state in the first place. The bizarre example of the socialist state in Poland pitched against the workers (before August 1989) is only the most open of the illustrations available in the Second World of advanced socialist countries.

Classical Marxism and orthodox Leninism have always envisaged 'the withering away of the state' as the last stage before ultimate utopia. Since the state has been seen ideologically as the instrument of the ruling class, it has been theoretically taken for granted that it is the withering away of classes that would inevitably result in the withering away of the state.

It is our contention in this chapter that any capture of the state by the proletariat would be a Sisyphean exercise: a stone is taken to the top of the hill, only to roll down the hill, then to be laboriously pushed back to the top of the hill for another rolling down, and so on *ad infinitum*.

Should any section of the working class ever capture the state, its class consciousness is rapidly transformed into state consciousness. The conqueror's orientation changes. The survival of the state becomes the paramount aim, even if this means repressing fellow workers or fellow nationals. When workers capture the state, they commit class suicide. The Sisyphean absurdity arises because we first witness a section of the workers capturing the state in order to roll it down to its doom and redundancy. Before long those same workers are concerned about the 'need' to preserve the state. They roll the stone of the state back upwards to the top of the hill. They may indeed be overcome later on by another set of workers or socialists or nationals bent on the same objective. They in turn wish to roll the state downwards to its doom, only to attempt a renewed ascendancy. Whoever controls the state is compulsively tempted to preserve it. If the controller was originally class conscious, he or she becomes state conscious.

Where does this leave the Marxist-Leninist expectation concerning the withering away of the state? When socialist workers capture the state, it is not the state which begins to wither away, it is socialism itself! The state corrodes socialism, rather than socialism corroding the state. The state tends to corrupt: the absolute state corrupts absolutely. A functional equivalent of the absolute state is the garrison state, a state geared towards militaristic self-preservation.

History has played a cruel game against the Semites. Arabs and Jews are now cast against each other in a devastating game of competitive sovereignty. A striking illustration of the corrupting power of the garrison state is in fact the 'Semitic' state of Israel. Israel was born out of the womb of a social movement, the Zionist movement going back to Theodor Herzl and beyond. The ideals were rooted in compassion and a longing for national dignity and human worth. The Zionist political and social movement felt that it could best realize Jewish dignity and human worth through the creation of a Jewish state.

At first the obstacles in the way of this Zionist movement were immense. Where would the movement find land without a people for use by a people without land? Though a return to Palestine was always the favourite aspiration of the Zionist movement, alternative homes were considered, including the famous offer of parts of Uganda and Kenya to the Zionist movement by Joseph Chamberlain, Britain's Colonial Secretary at the turn of the century.

Curiously enough, it was the excesses of the Nazi absolute state which helped to assure the ultimate political victory of the Zionist movement. Hitler's policy of genocide against the Jews created what many Westerners regarded as a compelling moral case for the establishment of a Jewish state after the war. The excesses of Hitler's absolute state resulted in what was to become a Jewish garrison state. And just as Nazi absolutism corrupted the German state, so did Israeli militarism come to corrupt the Jewish state.

Israel was born out of the marriage between Judaism and the ethos of the Peace of Westphalia of 1648, which helped to inaugurate the modern system of the sovereign state. The legacy of Judaism had contributed enormously to the finer moral sensibilities in the new Jewish state. By the time Israel invaded Lebanon in June 1982, it had already become the most arrogant sovereign state on the world scene since Nazi Germany. Undeniably, the state corrupts, and either absolutism or militarism can make it corrupt absolutely.

Nazi Germany was of course both absolutist and militaristic; but the state of Israel is only militaristic. Within its own borders it is the most open society in the Middle East, though the openness has been shrinking. But in relation to its neighbours, Israel has permitted itself to become the bully of the Near East.

In time, the establishment of the state of Israel created a counter social movement in the other Semitic tradition, the Arab world, especially from the 1960s onwards when Arab Palestinians converted themselves into an independent nationalist movement in their own right. The Palestinians gradually evolved a dream of either recreating a unified Palestine encompassing both Arabs and Jews (the two nations—one state solution) or creating a separate Palestinian state of their own (the two nations—two states solution). A Palestinian diaspora had been created as a result of the establishment of Israel, and those dispersed Palestinians evolved the same kind of longing for a return to their homeland that the Jews had previously manifested in their own Zionism. Again the solution was widely seen in terms of creating yet another state. If the Palestinian state, when it is established, becomes either absolutist or militaristic, it will display the same symptoms of spiritual and moral decay that the state of Israel has manifested in recent years. It is as if the Semites were being punished by fate for having contributed to the evolution of European concepts of the sovereign state.

Once again those who capture the state will discover that they are captured by it. Those who seek to purify the world through the state system continue to discover that they are themselves polluted by the state system.

Social movements are held hostage not simply by the system of sovereign states, however, but also by the machinery of capitalism world-wide. Indeed the future of social movements in the world is subject to dual hegemony, a condominium being exercised by capitalism on one side and the state system on the other. The capitalist world economy and the state system are two distinct prison houses in which our era finds itself, and the Anglo-Saxons are still presiding over both. The most ambitious global reform for the future may have to include a search for alternatives not only to capitalism but also to the state. Partly because of the state system, the world has evolved the most destructive arsenals ever accumulated in history. Partly because of the state system, the resources of this planet (including the sea bed) are still disproportionately controlled by principles of state sovereignty and national jurisdiction. Partly because of the state system governments are prepared to go to war for the sake of inches of barren territory. Impossible as the task may be at the present time, there is a compelling case for exploring both alternative state systems and alternatives to the state. For the time being, however, we are prisoners behind the bars of Westphalia.

If the struggle for cultural and class utopias has not left any dent on the prison walls of these capitalist and state systems, is the situation then hopeless?

We have sought to demonstrate that the underprivileged races and cultures have attempted to capture the state, and were captured by it. Nationalists of Asia and Africa sounded the knock of entry into the world system and then became high priests of the state system itself.

The underprivileged classes have also sought to capture the state — and when they did, were captured by it. The socialists and workers sounded the knock of exit from the capitalist system and at the same time sounded the knock of entry into the state system. Domestically, countries of the Second World have achieved some kind of socialist structure, but externally the prison walls of the global capitalist system surround socialist countries as well as non-socialist ones. The state system is at the present time triumphant in the Second and Third as well as the First World. The underprivileged races and underprivileged classes have not as yet made a difference to the fate of the two global systems.

The question now arises whether the underprivileged sex or gender could hold the secret to global transformation. Women are for the time being fellow prisoners behind the bars of capitalism and Westphalia, but do women hold the key to an eventual escape? Can women guide us away from both the excesses of the Semites and extremities of the Anglo-Saxons?

God, Gold — and Gender

There is one fundamental difference between oppressed races and oppressed classes on one side and the oppressed gender on the other. While an oppressed race or oppressed class might aspire to capture the state for itself, there is no question of women capturing the state instead of men. Indigenous liberation fighters may want to capture the state and replace the privileged classes of the previous era. The balance of probability, however, is that there is no question of women capturing the state instead of men. The feminist case is in reality not substitution but balance, never replacement of men but parity with men. Given the need of men and women for each other, women can never really seek to capture the state as their own monopoly, but only to share it equally. This is in stark contrast with the objectives of other underprivileged groups. National liberation fighters never seek to share equally with foreigners after they have emerged triumphant in their liberation war. Socialist workers never seek to share equally with the bourgeoisie after they have emerged triumphant from the revolution. Women, on the other hand, can never ask for more than equality. Women are prisoners of egalitarianism in their ultimate ambitions. This dilutes absolutism and is therefore a step away from both Semitic and Anglo-Saxon legacies.

When the state becomes androgynous will its nature change? We cannot be sure. All we know is that until now the state has been tied to patriarchy, including its central primordial principle of male dominance.

If the state is an institutionalized monopoly of the legitimate use of physical force, and if women are less physically violent than men, the very concept of legitimate use of physical force may change when the state becomes androgynous.

The state's ultimate instruments of coercion have so far been disproportionately men. The great majority of members of the armed forces in one state after another have been men, the great majority even of the police in most states have been overwhelmingly men. The great majority of prison warders have been men. Those entrusted with the duties of execution, or the guillotine, have been almost exclusively men. The navies of the world and their air forces have been disproportionately men. In other words, all the security forces and security services on which the power of the state has been based have themselves been predominantly masculine.

Who in any case is likely to challenge the state's monopoly of the legitimate use of physical force? Once again, the ratio has been disproportionately male oriented. The overwhelming majority of those who commit crimes of violence in societies which are otherwise vastly different from each other have been men. The Mafia has been a deeply and disproportionately masculine presence in the world of crime. The jails of the world are, especially in their maximum security sections, populated disproportionately by men.

As for the world of political rebellion, military coups, and sheer terrorism, once again masculinity is, on the whole, the order of the day. There are indeed female guerrilla fighters and female 'terrorists'. But when all allowances have been made for great heroines and great female villains, the fact nevertheless defiantly remains that the game of physical violence involving direct spilling of blood has been more a heritage of the male of the human species than of the female. To that extent the inner gender of the state has been basically masculine, for better or worse.

Ironically, both Anglo-Saxons and Semites have experimented with female leaders of the state, but what has happened in those situations where a woman has been at the pinnacle of the state, seemingly in control of its destiny? What has happened when there has been an Anglo-Saxon Queen Elizabeth I, or a Semitic Golda Meir, or another Anglo-Saxon, Margaret Thatcher? In political systems which are primarily male-dominated, a single female at the top does not change the fundamental masculine dynamic of the structure. The women who succeed in a male-dominated world have themselves to display male-derived perceptions of strength. Margaret Thatcher had to out-macho the Tory patriarchs over the Falklands issue if she was to survive the apparent national humiliation, perceived as the outcome of the Argentinian invasion of the islands. The female prime minister in London had to display all the toughness of masculinity if she was to remain credible in a male-dominated political system.

It remains one of the ironies of the last third of the twentieth century that the people who played such a major role in consolidating patriarchy (the Semites and the Anglo-Saxons) should now be among the pioneers of diluting it. Britain for the first time combines a female monarch with a female prime minister. Israel has gone further than any other state in 'militarizing' women. American women have taken the lead in challenging the male domination of Christian churches and in reducing the patriarchy of capitalism. In other words, the Anglo-Saxons and at least the Jewish wing of the Semites are beginning to undo the patriarchal legacy they helped to consolidate in the evolving world system.

The question for the future is whether a real feminization of the state would reduce its propensity for violence. And is the female predicament one which is unlikely to result in a mere substitution of controllers of the state?

On the whole, it is arguable that the feminist movement has been seeking mechanisms for sharing rather than monopolizing power. It is also arguable that feminism, given that men and women need each other more than races or classes do, might result in reducing polarization in the struggle for equity. Further, because femininity is less militaristic than masculinity, the feminist struggle might help to minimize the militarization of ultimate utopias. And given those previous considerations, feminist styles and aspirations should help to minimize this game of post-liberation violence.

The concepts for describing the different struggles have also to be differentiated. The struggle for national or racial utopia is indeed national liberation; the quest for a class utopia is usually class struggle; the new movement for a gender utopia is women's liberation.

National liberation tends sooner or later in this period to be militarized; revolutionary class struggle tends to be armed; but women's liberation can be campaigned for by means of agitation and mobilization, without becoming militarized.

To repeat, national liberation is obsessed with the state, seeking to capture it on behalf of the indigenous population. The quest for a class utopia is in turn also enticed by the state and can subsequently become entrapped by it. But the struggle for a gender utopia can be state neutral, seeking to realize the rights of women without monopolizing the power of the state.

For those who seek to create the right conditions for a nationalist struggle, one of the first phases of liberation lies in cultivating national consciousness. For those who seek to realize a dictatorship of the proletariat, a first phase in the class struggle is the cultivation of class consciousness. But for those who seek to realize a gender utopia, the basic aim lies in conquering gender consciousness rather than cultivating it. National liberation emphasizes the distinction between the alien and the indigenous; class struggle emphasizes the distinction between the alienated and the integrated; the struggle of the sexes transcends such distinctions. The gender of the state has so far been overwhelmingly masculine. Will its androgynization transform its nature? That is the tantalizing question for the future.

But if the state has always been masculine so far, what about capitalism? What has been the gender of the capitalist animal in the world arena?

On the whole, capitalism has become more masculine as it became more internationalized; it also became more masculine as it became more mechanized. The Semites almost invented the process of universalization; the Anglo-Saxons mechanized it. In the earlier years of the pursuit of the profit motive, women were almost as active in producing as men. Certainly in rural production in many societies women were in control of basic cultivation, and sometimes in control of at least part of animal husbandry.

In West Africa women have been conspicuous in trade and marketing, sometimes overshadowing men's commercial activities. But all this was in relation to small-scale economic activities. As the economic activities of West Africa assumed a greater international dimension, and as the transnational corporations themselves entered the scene, the ratio of men to women in economic activity has changed. The greater internationalization of West African economies has meant more men taking decisions on boards of directors or assuming control in factories, overshadowing the 'market ladies' of yesteryear. Greater internationalization of African economies has on the whole meant greater masculine control.

Similarly, greater mechanization of African economies has resulted in a diminishing feminine share in them. Where the technology of cultivation is that of the hoe, women are omnipresent in African agriculture. When the technology of cultivation becomes the tractor, the driver behind the wheel in African situations becomes primarily the male. As industries move from soft to hard, the masculine share increases. The textile industry is more likely to consist of men and women than the steel mill. And certainly industries like mining in Southern Africa are almost entirely masculine in composition of personnel.

To summarize the argument so far, the state has always been basically masculine in its inner dynamic, but the gender of capitalism has been less constant. Capitalism at a primitive stage is androgynous, involving both men and women in comparable productive capacities. As capitalism became more international it also became more male-dominated. Similarly, as it became more mechanized and industrialized, male domination increased. The gender of capitalism is still more androgynous than the gender of the state system, but this is only a relative measurement. On the whole, both the state system and the capitalist global economy are major universes of the male of the human species. They await fundamental reform through partial feminization. God and gold have never provided adequate foundations for social justice. The missing 'g' is no longer 'glory' in Milton's sense of the applause of one's peers. The missing 'g' is gender. By moderating the excesses of both the God standard and the gold standard, women may hold the secret map of escape from the dominion of Semitic absolutes and the Anglo-Saxon versions of compromise.

Conclusion

We have sought to demonstrate in this essay that the history of world culture is, at least in part, a transition from Semitic ideas to European techniques, from the spread of Semitic religions to the triumphs of Anglo-Saxon technology.

This grand cultural transition in our world order has created two mighty forces in the past few hundred years: the power of the sovereign state and the force of capitalism. The modern sovereign state can be traced back to a marriage between Semitic ideas and European experience. The transition was, at one level, from God as king to the king as God's annointed. And then the absolute monarchy became the absolute state. In the words of Louis XIV, 'I am the state!'

The other Semitic tradition, Islam, was also evolving towards a concept of the absolute state. Indeed, the Prophet Muhammad lived to preside over a nascent Islamic state and thereby helped to bequeath a tradition of theocracy to future generations of his followers. On the whole, however, Islam produced either city states or empire states. It was Christian Europeans who were destined to evolve the nation-state. The idea of sovereignty emerged out of the principle of absolutism, which in turn was for a while an earthly translation of the kingdom of God. Semitic monotheism influenced the history of European monarchies and must be seen as part of the intellectual and normative origins of the sovereign state. Europe evolved from a culture of the absolute deity to a culture of the absolute monarch and then onwards to a culture of the absolute state.

As for capitalism, this too was partly a case of Europeanizing the Semitic heritage; subjecting a Semitic legacy to the changing material realities of European existence. As has been indicated, this is the economic face of the Protestant Reformation.

In Islamic history, there was for a while a strong possibility of a parallel evolution of a capitalist tradition. The Prophet Muhammad had himself been a merchant, and some of the verses of the Qur'an praise trade as a calling. Islam is distrustful of interest but not of the profit motive. The early Islamic empires, especially under the Abbasids, displayed signs of vigorous enterprise as a way of life. It appeared as if the foundations were being laid for what we were later to label as 'capitalism'. Islam did contribute to the early stages of the technological and capitalist revolution in Europe, but fell short of evolving its own industrial revolution.

On the whole, it was revised Christianity rather than revised Islam which culminated in what Max Weber later described as 'the spirit of capitalism'.

In the evolution of the gold standard, the Europeans have been the senior partner within the coalition of Semitic ideas and European experience. But in the earlier evolution of the God standard, the Semites were the senior partners and original inventors.

In the last two hundred years, however, the torch of leadership in the world system has been passed to the Anglo-Saxons. Great Britain presided over the fate of capitalism and Empire in the nineteenth century. The United States has increasingly assumed a dominant role in the twentieth century. The Anglo-Saxons have become the 'Semites' of the technocratic era. The Jews and the Arabs had once forged a theocratic approach to universalism through the God standard. The Anglo-Saxons have attempted to chart a technocratic approach to universalism through the gold standard.

The world has since discovered that it is within the prison walls of two new absolutes — the state system and capitalism. Those who have wanted to abolish capitalism by capturing the state found themselves captured by the state. When socialists capture the state, it is not the state which withers away; it is in fact socialism.

What is the way out of this maze interconnecting the absolutes of capitalism and the state-system? The most promising solution lies neither in a new God standard nor in a revised gold standard. It lies in the androgynization of both and in the partial feminization of the state. It seems probable that the androgynization of church, state, and economy will substantially moderate the tendency of each to become absolutist. By the very nature of their predicament, women cannot seek to replace men. Women are condemned to a quest for political and economic equality rather than political and economic monopoly.

The retreat from the excesses of the Semitic heritage and the abuses of the Anglo-Saxon legacy may require the equal status of women as both guides and commanders.

Let us conclude with the imagery of three ships in history: the *Bounty*, the *Titanic* and the *Californian*. They are symbols of a world in partial communication. On his Britannic Majesty's ship *Bounty* there had in fact been tyranny under the rule of Captain William Bligh. In desperation the men ultimately rebelled in the same year that the French people did — 1789. The mutineers on the ship overcame the captain and his supporters, put them in lifeboats, let them loose on the sea, and took charge of the ship themselves. The *Bounty* attempted to disengage from the international nautical system, and to keep its distance from Britain's laws, after the mutiny. The mutineers retired to an island, an exercise in primordial delinking, a severance of communication.

Today the world itself is an island — no mutiny on the *Bounty* can be an escape in its own right. No mutineers from the *Bounty* could find refuge in such stark terms. The world is now faced with *omni-communication* — if it only cared to listen. The tragedy is that of expanded communication and diminishing dialogue.

Our other image of a ship is that of the *Titanic*, the supposedly unsinkable vessel which sank on its maiden voyage when it hit an iceberg on 15 April 1912. There was another ship nearby, the Leyland Liner the *Californian*, less than 20 miles away from the stricken *Titanic*. The radio of the *Californian* was switched off that momentous night, and its crew could not hear the distress signals from less than 32 km away. Once again human beings failed to rescue each other because they had switched off avenues of communication.

You may have noticed that all three ships, the *Bounty*, *Titanic*, and *Californian*, were 'Anglo-Saxon'. But none of the captains or the radio operators were women. So what? If I were a Semitic prophet in the grand tradition, I would describe all this as 'a parable'.

The fate of humanity may indeed depend upon creative communication and androgynization of the command structure. Those social movements which enhance contact and communication and those which seek to expand the role of women may turn out to be the most critical of them all. A greater role for women is needed in the struggle to tame the sovereign state, civilize capitalism, and humanize communication.

To the question 'What is civilization?' it may one day be possible to answer, 'humane communication in a truly androgynized world'.

But that is a message which has yet to find a prophet of Semitic proportions. It cannot even find Anglo-Saxon 'packaging' at present. Perhaps 'civilization' is a word ahead of its time. Perhaps it has always been.

Notes

1. Traditional.
2. Romans, 10: 12, Revised Standard Version.
3. See John G. Stoessinger, *The Might of Nations* (New York: Random House, 1965), 1981 ed., pp. 352–353.
4. J. C. Hurewitz, *Documents of Near East Diplomatic History* (New York: Columbia University Press, 1951), pp. 25–26.
5. Reproduced in Louis L. Snyder (ed.), *The Imperialism Reader: Documents and Readings in Modern Expansionism* (Princeton, N.J.: D. Van Nostrand, 1962), pp. 87–88.

Bibliography

Bronowski, J., *The Ascent of Man* (London: BBC, 1973).
Bull, Hedley, and Adam Watson (eds), *The Expansion of International Society* (Oxford: Clarendon Press, 1984).
Curtin, Philip D. (ed.), *Imperialism* (Documentary History of Western Civilization) (New York: Harper and Row, 1971).
Cutrufelli, Maria Rosa, *Women of Africa: Roots of Oppression* (London: Zed Press, 1983).
De Fleur, Melvin L., *Theories of Mass Communication* (New York: David McKay Co., 1970).
Epstein, Isidore, *Judaism: A Historical Presentation* (New York: Penguin Books, 1977 edition).
Fann, K. T., and Donald C. Hodges (eds), *Readings in US Imperialism* (Boston: Porter Sargent, 1971).
Friedman, Georges, *The End of the Jewish People* (London: Hutchinson, 1965).
Hafkin, Nancy J., and Edna C. Bay (eds) *Women in Africa: Studies in Social and Economic Change* (Stanford: Stanford University Press, 1976).
Institute of Jewish Affairs in Association with the World Jewish Congress, *The Jewish Communities of the World*, Third Revised Edition (London: Andre Deutsch, 1971).
Al-Maamiry, Hamoud Ahmed, *Islamism and Economic Prosperity in Third World Countries* (New Delhi: Lancers Books, 1983).
Mazrui, Ali A., *A World Federation of Cultures* (New York: The Free Press, Series on Preferred World for the 1990s, 1976).
Mba, Nina Emma, *Nigerian Women Mobilized* (Berkeley: Institute of International Studies, 1982).
Oye, Kenneth, Robert Lieber, and Donald Rothschild, *Eagle Defiant: United States Foreign Policy in the 1980s* (Boston: Little, Brown and Co., 1983).
Page, William (ed.), *Future of Politics* (London: Frances Pinter Publishers in association with the World Futures Studies Federation, 1983).
Palmer, R.R., and Joel Colton, *A History of the Modern World* (New York: Alfred A. Knopf, Inc., 1956).
Pipes, Daniel, *In the Path of God: Islam and Political Power* (New York: Basic Books, Inc., 1983).

Radhakrishnan, S., *Eastern Religions and Western Thought* (London, Oxford and New York: University Press, 1969).

Rothermund, Indira, *The Philosophy of Restraint* (Bombay: G. R. Bhatkal, 1963).

Said, Edward W., *Orientalism* (New York: Pantheon Books, 1978).

Singer, Charles, *A Short History of Scientific Ideas to 1900* (Oxford: Clarendon Press, 1959).

Walker, R. B. J. (ed.), *Culture, Ideology and World Order: Studies on a Just World Order* (Boulder and London: Westview Press, 1984).

Wallbank, T. Walter, Alastair Taylor, and Nelson M. Bailkey, *Civilization Past and Present* (Chicago: Scott, Foresman and Co., 1962).

Watt, W. Montgomery, *The Influence of Islam on Medieval Europe: Islamic Surveys* (Edinburgh: Edinburgh University Press, 1972).

Weber, Max, *The Protestant Ethic and the Spirit of Capitalism* (translated by Talcott Parsons) (New York: Charles Scribner's Sons, 1958 edition).

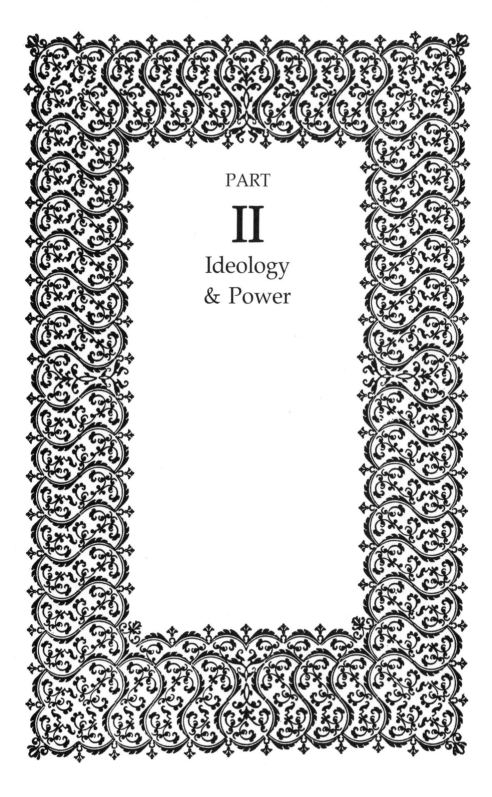

PART

II

Ideology
& Power

3
Muhammad, Marx
& Market Forces

This chapter rests on seven theses, or seven pillars of analysis, basically inter-connected. First, we hope to demonstrate that Islamic economics is a science based more on the rules of consumption than on the laws of production, while Marxian economics is the reverse.

Second, we hope to establish that an economic science based on consumption can be at least as intellectually coherent and empirically valid as a science based on the primacy of production.

Third, we shall indicate in what sense Islam was the first Protestant Revolution, rebelling against distorted versions of Christianity and espousing a new economic morality. In other words, we shall show in what sense the Prophet Muhammad was a precursor of Martin Luther (1483–1546), John Calvin (1509–1564), and Henry VIII of England (reigned 1509–1547). To the extent to which the Protestant Reformation in Europe helped to create a new phase in the history of capitalism, one major antecedent of that European phenomenon was the Protestant revolution under Muhammad in Arabia some eight centuries earlier.

Islamic law is in favour of the profit motive but against interest on loans. This paradox has wide ideological implications. Under the guidance of the Prophet Muhammad himself the Islamic state in Arabia had shown indications of evolving into a mixed economy encompassing both socialist and neo-capitalist tendencies, but within a pre-industrial context. This mixed economy thesis under Muhammad's rule is the fourth pillar of our analysis in this chapter. The anti-Shylock factor in Islam (opposition to interest) constituted opposition to exploitation. But the pro-profit element in Islam favoured capitalism.

We assert, as our fifth thesis, that the expansion of Islam into an empire after the Prophet's death transformed it into a special area of what Karl Marx was later to call 'the Asiatic mode of production'. To that extent, the history of Islam contradicts those unilinear Marxists who insist that the Asiatic mode historically preceded and structurally could not follow either capitalism or socialism. Muhammad's Islam showed signs of evolving into a synthesis of capitalist and socialist tendencies, but the Islam of the Islamic Empire later evolved into the Asiatic mode nonetheless.

Our sixth thesis is that the Asiatic mode of production could indeed be economically regressive and yet still flower into a culturally glorious achievement. The Islamic Empire which followed the Muslim conquests of the seventh century created more economic injustices than occurred under the Prophet Muhammad's own rule. They were, notwithstanding, often more sophisticated and culturally more impressive than Arabia had been in the first half of the first century of the Islamic era (the Hijjra).

Our seventh thesis is that Islam strongly militates against the consolidation of feudalism. This is especially because the Islamic law of inheritance makes it difficult, if not impossible, for large estates to remain intact for any length of time. Lords of the manor with large estates under their control, cultivated by serfs, found it hard to survive for long in the face of the *Shari'a*. Islamic law demands that the heirs should share the estate after the death of the original owner. This was often a prescription for fragmentation of the land into smaller and smaller units.

In short, although Islam has shown signs of being congenial to both capitalism and socialism, the *Shari'a* militates against those aspects of feudalism which are based on large aristocratic estates.

We recognize that to prove each of these seven theses is a formidable intellectual ambition. Each may need a separate chapter, if not a book, in its own right. All we can hope to achieve in this single chapter is to raise the salient issues, some of which have probably never been raised in this manner before. If the chapter succeeds in stimulating comments and criticisms, some of our formulations may later have to be revised in the light of those critiques.

Let us begin with the first thesis about the laws of consumption as the basis of Islamic economics. Does such a thesis trivialize Islamic economics? Or is consumption at least as solid a basis for the science of economics as production?

The Primacy of Consumption

In an attempt to prove the primacy of economics in human affairs and demonstrate the validity of economic determinism, Marx started from the first premise: 'Man must eat in order to live.' It was Marx's equivalent of Descartes' first principle: 'I think, therefore I am.'

To say that man must eat in order to live is to demonstrate the primacy not of production but of consumption. Eating, after all, is an act of consuming.

Second, while every man, woman, and child is a consumer, only some men and women are producers. Consumption is more universal than production. All living beings consume, but only some produce. Indeed, in cultures based on hunting and gathering, 'production' is at best a relative term. People just help themselves to what nature has 'produced' without their help.

In more modern societies, there is an expansion of the non-productive generations. Highly industrialized societies have more and more retired old people. Less industrialized societies have more and more children. Both children and old-age pensioners are essentially consumers rather than producers. In some Third World countries pure consumers outnumber producers, with chronic or expanding unemployment and a majority of the population below 15 years of age.

In these circumstances, a science of economics based on the laws of consumption makes at least as much sense as a science based on the forces of production. Men, after all, produce in order to consume; they do not consume in order to produce. To put it another way, consumption makes life itself possible; but production is a more distant link in the chain of survival than is basic consumption.

Moreover, the forces of history in industrial society seem to be moving towards a consumer society with expanding leisure and diminishing labour. The hours of work are going down in industrial society, the level of consumption is going up, and the hours of leisure are increasing. It is still too early to talk of a post-proletarian society, but it is conceivable that the working class will start shrinking in size. With increasingly mechanized production, the concept of 'worker' may one day become anachronistic, a hangover from the nineteenth and twentieth centuries. One day a few push-button technocrats and skilled technologists may be able to feed the whole of society.

To summarize, while the forces of industrial history have indeed been moving towards greater production, they have not necessarily been involving more producers. Human beings in the North are spending less time working and more time consuming.

Is There an Islamic Mode of Production?

But where does Islam come into this? Here we must distinguish laws of consumption, rooted in natural or social forces, from the rules of consumption, rooted in moral precepts. That men must eat in order to live is a law of basic consumption. That a whole society should try to be self-sufficient in food is a rule of solidarity in consumption.

Islamic morality has rules of consumption. Islamic economics is partly predicated on those rules and seems to assume the support of natural and social laws of consumption. It is to these Islamic implications of the phenomenon of consumption that we must shortly return.

But it is important first to relate this whole discussion of consumption to our second thesis, that the sequence of epochs in Marx's theory of historical materialism (the Asiatic, feudal, bourgeois, and socialist order of historical stages) does not apply to the history of Islam. We propose to demonstrate that in the last years of Prophet Muhammad's life the nascent Islamic state showed all the signs of evolving into a mixed economy of both socialist and capitalist tendencies. It was the territorial expansion of Islam after Muhammad's death that transformed the new Islamic state, limited mainly to Mecca and Medina, into a Muslim empire traversing three continents. With this territorial expansion the initial mixed economy tendency of Islam, part socialist and part capitalist, was aborted, and Islam approximated more closely to what Marx called the Asiatic mode of production.

If the Asiatic mode of production is retrograde as compared with the socio-capitalist mode, then the history of Islam did witness a regression when the Muslim world became an empire. Here another contradiction occurs, however. Imperial Islam was more intellectually diverse and sophisticated than the original Muslim state of Mecca and Medina. In other words, while the transition from the original Islamic state to the Muslim empire may have been socially regressive in Marxian terms (i.e., a relapse from socio-capitalism to the Asiatic mode of production), that same transition was intellectually progressive when judged in terms of civilization. Marx had no real answer to this kind of problem. Intellectual and artistic sophistication should be part of the superstructure. Why should an intellectually superior superstructure rest on an economically inferior sub-structure? No wonder an Italian Marxologist once exclaimed:

> If the Asiatic mode of production really had been 'inferior' — and not merely 'different', or at least not greatly inferior — to the classical modes, it is hard to understand how there could have been such a flowering of religion, art, science and philosophy in the Asiatic framework in India, China, Egypt, Mesopotamia, Persia, Arabia and elsewhere. . . . Since remotest antiquity . . . societies based on that [Asiatic] mode have given rise to some of the most splendid civilizations there have been anywhere.[1]

But which societies did Marx regard as 'Asiatic'? Umberto Melotti reminds us that of the countries Marx specifically mentioned when discussing this Asiatic mode of production, India and China could be cited in the forefront, followed by what we now call the Middle East. To Marx in relation to the Asiatic mode of production, this was particularly applicable to 'Egypt, Mesopotomia, Persia, Arabia and Turkey'.[2]

What was distinctive about this Asiatic mode of production? Especially significant was the dialectic between high and often despotic political centralization, on the one hand, and highly localized methods of production, on the other. In other words, the Asiatic mode of production existed in the face of a startling contradiction between a centralized political superstructure and a decentralized base of village and related industries. The status of landownership was often ambivalent, tending to negate a completely freehold private ownership of land. In Islam this made land subject to rules about usury and regulated consumption, and the produce of land became subject also to the concerns of *zakat*, the Islamic tax. Land was also precluded in Islam from the principle of primogeniture and Islamic law regulated the 'owner's' freedom in determining succession to the estate.

Many of these legal principles survived from the Islamic state of Muhammad to the Islamic Empire of his successors. But imperial Islam moved more and more towards despotic tendencies, control of alien populations, and slavery as a mode of production.

It took a Marxist-inspired Muslim sociologist to point out that slavery was not merely a form of labour preceding serfdom in chronological order, as unilinear Marxists had assumed. Slavery had been combined with different modes of production right into the nineteenth century and beyond. After all, the earlier stages of capitalism in both Europe and North America had depended heavily on slave labour and not merely on the proletariat.

> There is no question of a stage in which serfdom is particularly dominant succeeding one in which slavery is predominant. . . . What we see is a multiform evolution starting from types which are themselves already different.[3]

It is against this background that the unilinear interpretation of Marxism comes into question. For a long time there have been debates in Marxism as to whether stages in the historical process could be skipped. Could Tsarist Russia move from feudalism to socialism without passing through the distinctive trauma of capitalism? This issue was debated while Marx was still alive.

More recently, a related issue has been debated as to whether black Africa could move from primitive communism to modern industrial socialism without passing through the agonies of either European-style feudalism or Western-style capitalism.

The skipping of any stage in the unilinear progression was debated, but scarcely at all the sequence of the progression itself. Must capitalism come after feudalism? And where did the Asiatic mode of production fit in?

The Asiatic mode of production has sometimes been an embarrassment to twentieth century Marxists. Was the concept a racial aberration or lapse by Marx? Was it a way of covering up his ignorance of the non-Western world? Or was it a genuine mode of production?

Most Marxists until recently pushed the Asiatic mode into the mists of antiquity. It was some approach to economic survival which occurred before modern historical times and before the emergence of Europe on the world stage.

In the last decade or two there have been new refinements in Marxist thought. The neo-unilinear viewpoint of historical epochs includes such Africanists as Jean Suret-Canale, such structuralists as Maurice Godelier, such orientalists as Jean Chesneaux, and such American Indologists (specialists on native Americans) as Daniel Thorner. This particular tendency is inclined to insert the Asiatic stage somewhere between the primitive ancient community and the classical slave society. The sequence of the epochs under this paradigm is shown in Figure 3.1.

FIGURE 3.1

Primitive Ancient Community

↓

Asiatic Society

↓

Classical Slave Society

↓

Feudal Serf Society

↓

Bourgeois Society

↓

Proletarian Socialist Society

↓

Classless Communist Society

Perhaps a more stimulating refinement of the Marxist historical sequences of epochs is that put forward by Georgy Plekhanov. Plekhanov recognized the problem of cultural relativism in history, the constraints of different historical experiences for economic evolution. The world of Plekhanov's day tended to be conceptualized in terms of the Orient and the Occident. So was the world of Karl Marx. From this dualism Plekhanov drew the conclusion that Marx's primitive community in world history split into two distinct lines of social development. In the Western world the ancient primitive mode of production gave way to the classical (slave), feudal (serf), and capitalist (proletariat) stages of historical development. However, in the Orient, the ancient primitive mode of production gave way to the distinctive features of the Asiatic model, with its own push towards eventual socialism probably different from Europe's own historical destiny.[4]

FIGURE 3.2

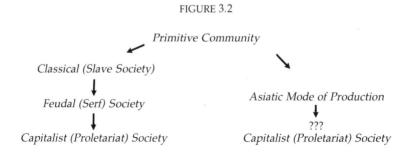

In Plekhanov, the dialectic bows to a division of the world between Europe and Asia. Other continents bow to this basic bi-continental bipolarity. What is more, it is possible to suggest persuasively that the division between Europe and Asia in Marxism, the division between the Occident and the Orient, is the most fundamental of all contradictions after the class struggle itself.

In relation to that division between the Orient and the Occident, Islam was caught in the middle. For a while Islam was the great bridge between the Occident and the Orient. Imperial Islam may ultimately have been reduced by Marx to an Asiatic mode of production, but its intellectual civilization was a supreme synthesis of the Occident (including ancient Greece) and the Orient (including Ancient India). It is not for nothing that the Western numerals today are called 'Arabic numerals' and one of the branches of Western mathematics is called algebra after an Arabian concept. India was involved in this mathematical revolution. It is not for nothing that Western Europe rediscovered Plato and Aristotle through the Arabs. Once again socio-economic backwardness was nevertheless capable of producing a socio-cultural civilization.

Does all this add up to an Islamic mode of production? If we limited ourselves to the Arabian peninsula, the most fundamental of all transitions is the move in the twentieth century from a date-and-camel economy to a petroleum economy. The camel may indeed be the most Muslim of all animals, and the date may well be the most Muslim of all fruit. Precisely because of that, the transition from a camel-and-date economy to a petroleum economy captured a fundamental twentieth century contradiction. Camels and dates were traditional. Petroleum was modern. Camels and dates were a measure of self-sufficiency. Petroleum was a measure of reliance on the external world. The transition was the twentieth century contradiction between the Orient and the Occident, between tradition and modernity, between self-reliance and dependency. Islam was once again caught in between.

And yet the initial tension in Islam was not geographical. It was not a tension between East and West, between the Orient and the Occident, a dialectic between East and West. The most basic of all Islamic principles was no less than the Islamic Trialectic — the relationship between Man, God, and Nature. It was weaker than the indigenous African fusion. But it was stronger than the Western trinity in thought.

Islam: The First Protestant Revolution

There is a second trialectic in Islam. This is the dynamic interplay between Judaism, Christianity, and what this chapter calls 'Muhammadanism' in our special sense. Our definition of Muhammadanism restricts itself to those elements of Islam which are unique to the message of Muhammad and are not shared by either Judaism or Christianity. In other words, the religion of Islam as a whole consists of three legacies — the legacy of the Bible's Old Testament (duly amended), the legacy of the New Testament (duly amended), and the unique message which came with Muhammad himself. The Prophet Muhammad saw himself as successor to Abraham, Moses, and Jesus, carrying the message of God to higher levels of perfection. This message that was unique to Muhammad is what this chapter calls 'Muhammadanism'.

Precisely because Islam conceived of itself in part as a restoration of the message of Jesus after it had been distorted, Muhammad's revolution was the first Protestant assertion in history. Like Luther and Calvin nine hundred years later, Muhammad felt that the message of Jesus had been perverted by his successors in the leadership of the flock.

In keeping with Calvinist reforms centuries later, Muhammad declared himself against a highly structured and hierarchical priesthood. Consistent with the lessons of both Luther and Calvin, Muhammad distrusted intercession between man and God and insisted in direct communication between the worshipper and his or her maker. Like Calvin much later, Muhammad proclaimed the message of predestination and divine planning in human affairs.

Luther and Calvin later denounced the Catholic church for having become too monarchical and too inclined towards pomp and splendour. Muhammad's Protestant Revolution had occurred early enough to challenge this monarchical tendency at its source. The source was the very conception of Jesus as a prince and as a son of the almighty God. Muhammad insisted that Jesus had claimed no more than the role of being messenger of God. All the alleged majesty of Jesus as a prince descended from the Throne of God only led to the pomp of the church itself. The church struggled to do justice to a monarchical conception of its founder. Muhammad had gone further than either Luther or Calvin were to do in challenging the royal and aristocratic tendencies of the legacy of Jesus in the hands of his successors.

What has all this to do with the Islamic mode of production? To some extent we have to look at the later Protestant revolutions of Luther and Calvin in order to understand the earlier Protestant revolution of Muhammad. A whole body of literature has grown about 'the Protestant ethic' and the origins and underlying 'spirit' of capitalism. Our understanding of the Islamic mode of production may have to consult some of the insights not only of Karl Marx but also of analysts like Max Weber and his own paradigm of the Protestant origins of the capitalist revolution.[5]

Before we explore these dimensions more fully, however, it is worth bearing in mind that other founder of European Protestantism after Luther and Calvin, Henry VIII of England. His country later on was to lead the world in industrial capitalism, but Henry's own initial moves against the Pope had little in common with either Martin Luther or John Calvin. Henry was responding to his own matrimonial problems.

This is what makes Henry VIII's links with Muhammad less doctrinal and more

73

personal than Muhammad's links with Luther and Calvin. The historic connection between the Prophet of Islam and the founder of the Anglican church concerns their respective first wives, Muhammad's Khadija and Henry's Katherine of Aragon.

Unlike a Moghul Emperor in another century, Muhammad did not build a Taj Mahal in memory of his beloved wife, Khadija, when she died. The Prophet of Islam did, perhaps, help to build an entire economic mode of production in her memory. Of course as a prophet after Khadija's death, Muhammad felt himself to be divinely inspired. Yet Islam continues to insist that Muhammad was a mere man among men: that in the final analysis, he was a human being. One factor in his humanity was his love for his first wife. As she was a merchant, did she help to shape the future economic world view of the Prophet-to-be?

That a religion should be influenced by the matrimonial relationships of its founder is not unique to Islam. How indeed was the Anglican church born? It was Henry VIII's matrimonial problems with Katherine of Aragon and his desire for a divorce which created a crisis between the King of England and the Papacy. Because of that crisis the Church of England broke away from the Church of Rome.

Of course, the wife that influenced Muhammad the most was not one he wanted to get rid of. It was love for Khadija which may have helped to shape the mind of the Prophet of Islam. The main point that the origins of Islam have in common with the origins of the Church of England is the fact that the founders were themselves deeply influenced by their first marriages and the matrimonial aftermath. Twice it had been demonstrated that the mystery of divinity was inseparable from the intimacy of humanity.

More important as a link between the origins of European Protestantism and the origins of Islam were doctrinal issues. On the economic front, Muhammad's ideas might indeed have been influenced by more personal factors. The ideas which led to the rise of capitalism in the wake of the Protestant revolution in Europe could have had their ancestry in the Islamic mode of production. The Islamic economic mode could, in turn, have been profoundly influenced by the psychological responses of its prophet.

That is why this chapter must begin with Muhammad's personal experiences before prophethood. We know that in his childhood he was poor enough for his condition to warrant a Koranic verse — a condition which he shared with many others in centres of trade like Mecca. In his youth he entered into a relationship with the affluent merchant woman, Khadija, who probably owed her wealth to her two former husbands. Muhammad was first an entrusted manager of her trade enterprises and later a husband whose love for his wife could not have been anything less than passionate. How extensive Muhammad's trade experience was, we are not sure, but it was certainly extensive enough for him to have developed a special fondness for the profession, as a number of his statements — *hadiths* — would seem to indicate.

It is against this background, within the context of the then-prevalent mercantile economy with its market-oriented production which came under the regulation of customary commercial laws, that we may be able to understand Muhammad's ambivalence towards the Arabian merchant class. Partly as a product of his childhood experience he was sympathetic enough towards the 'wretched of the earth' to render him critical, sometimes vehemently so, of the merchant class, especially during the early period of his prophethood. On the other hand, his personal link with Khadija and her trade engagements, and later with influential merchant convertees to Islam, like Umar, produced sentiments which regarded trade as, perhaps, the most honourable profession and merchants as its honourable vanguard. From this duality one could probably infer a desire, on Muhammad's part, for an economic 'arrangement' that would be just to both the rich and the poor.

Of course, Muhammad's favourable views towards the merchants were not unqualified: the merchant had to be honest; only then could he expect to retain his privileged position hereafter. There is evidence of a couple of *hadiths* in which Muhammad suggested that the honest merchant would sit on the right-hand side of Allah. On the other hand, he regarded the acquisition of wealth through dishonest means as tantamount to inviting the worst of punishments in the world to come. One can say, then, if religion allows such a distinction, that Muhammad was sensitive to the interests of the consumer, but instead of making this an issue of economic programming, he accorded it a moral form.

It can of course be suggested that Muhammad's seeming ambivalence towards the merchant class was more of a tactical than a substantive issue: that it had less to do with his own sentiments about trade than with his wish to remould the probably corrupt and morally degenerate merchant class. Under this proposition Muhammad would be said to have realized the strength of the merchants and, therefore, his inability to liquidate them as a class. Consequently he adopted a strategy of winning and confining them to certain moral boundaries. There is a Pakistani scholar who has argued along these lines in order to make a case that Islam is anti-capitalist. Muhammad's own pronouncements would seem to suggest, however, that his views were more than tactical. His favourable portrayal of trade and merchants tends to betray an emotional attachment to trade, but with reservations.

What were the factors in the European Protestant revolution which have been interpreted as aspects of the rise of capitalism? One was the rise of individualism. Because priestly intercession and confession in church were no longer necessary for salvation under Protestantism, man was held more directly accountable for his fate. Islam too had insisted beforehand that no intermediary was needed between the believer and his Maker. In the religious sphere there was emerging, as a liberal doctrine, the image of a man as being ultimately his own advocate before the Almighty. This could become a principle of man being responsible for his own destiny. Such a concept was one day to become part and parcel of economic individualism and private enterprise.

Yet both Islam and Calvinism espoused a principle of predestination. If the fate of every human being was sealed in advance, why should people exert themselves?

Islam had one answer, Calvinism another. Islam, in a tradition of the Prophet, advised each believer to behave, on the one hand, as if he or she were going to die tomorrow, and on the other, as if he or she were going to live forever. A believer was expected to strike a balance between the temporal and the spiritual, between the religious and the secular.

Calvinism's answer was different. John Calvin called upon each believer to seek a sign from God as to whether he or she was among the saved and was endowed with grace. One of the many signs could indeed be legitimate prosperity on earth. Material success in this life could be a signal of possible salvation in the next.

Calvinism also tended to proclaim the principle of prospering without pampering. The idea was to achieve great production without great consumption: ingenuity without indulgence. In capitalist terms, this was the mission of making money without spending it. The result was primitive accumulation and the imperative of reinvestment as a basis of capitalist accumulation.

Islam goes a stage further and regulates explicitly not only production and consumption, but also distribution and exchange. Muhammad stood at the first crossroads of the history of capitalism.

Islam and Exchange

So, in general, we can conclude that, the moral injunction against dishonesty notwithstanding, Muhammad believed in a free-trade, or mercantile, economy in which commodities and money would experience unimpeded interaction in a free market. There are two types of qualifications to be made, however: one has to do with the manner of business transaction and the other with its objects, its commodities.

As a seemingly staunch believer in a free-trade economy, Muhammad is said to have been opposed to price control of any sort. Setting a price maximum was deemed unfair to the merchant. He seems to have trusted the forces of supply and demand to act as the only barometer on the basis of which price was to determine its rightful level. Nonetheless there was the institution of the *hisba* — something akin to a comprehensive ombudsmanship — which was charged with the responsibility of checking foul play, of ensuring that no merchant was being dishonest by charging above the average price range at any one point.

The prophet Muhammad's understanding of price as a supply-demand phenomenon his further attested by his prohibition of hoarding. This practice was not seldom a subject of his verbal wrath. Condemned too were other forms of speculation, especially in foods and the sale of things that had no market value. This could have been aimed specifically at the Jewish community which was believed to have been engaged in activities of economic sabotage against the Muslim community. However, given that the *hisba*, whose jurisdiction was limited to the Muslim community, was also expected to oversee fair play with respect to speculation, it is more likely that Muhammad meant it to be trans-communal as a direct realization of its exploitative character rather than as a product of Arab-Jewish politics. (This is what seems to be Imam Ibn Taymiya's treatise on the *hisba*.)

Two media of exchange existed side by side. They were money in the form of silver and, we believe, gold — the dirham and the dinar — and barter. Dealings in either of the two media, however, came under two types of control. The first type was *riba*, which, by extension, could be broadly defined as any known 'advantage' accruing to any of the parties in a business transaction. This is what can be inferred from the couple of specific instances that Muhammad is supposed to have commented on. But later theologians who had to contend with new and complex developments seem to have come up with a more restricted definition of the term that closely coincides with the notion of interest. The broad definition could, in fact, even apply to surplus value as appropriated by the capitalist employer, something which Muhammad could not have meant. Hence the factors of quantifiability and, more important, sameness were introduced: objects of exchange must be 'weighable' or 'measureable' and must belong to the same species to qualify for the injunction against *riba*.

The foregoing would seem to suggest, then, that Muhammad was of course quite aware of the difference between profit and interest, and whereas he was in favour of the former he was opposed to the latter. The Arab merchants, however, could not accept this position. They probably felt that the injunction against *riba* was somewhat arbitrary, to the extent that anything, including money, could in principle be treated as a commodity. The 'abstract' division between sale for profit and *riba* was quite unacceptable in the context of a growing mercantile economy.

The Prophet Muhammad, however, regarded the *riba* transaction as merely an exchange in prices, one price for another, which is quite different from sale for profit. So, someone who supplies corn seed, which is then 'invested' in an acre of land for greater productivity, would be engaging in *riba* if he claims a larger amount of corn from the harvest: such a transaction is not sale for profit! By extension this was made to apply to interests accruing to bank savings and bank loans.[6]

What was the basis of the injunction against *riba*? Four or more possible explanations can be advanced here: First, the Prophet had a vision of just how capitalist — in the broadest sense of the word — he would like the Islamic economic system to be. The *riba* transaction could thus have been regarded as an expression of (capitalist) economic crudity which was pitted against the moral principles of Islam. If one accepts this argument then interest in any form would be unacceptable. (To what extent can it be argued that the injunction against *riba* was a factor against the early development of capitalism — now in the narrow sense of the word — in the Muslim world, given what is known about the history of banking and its role in economic development?) Second, Muhammad could have meant to promote a spirit of concern for the welfare of individual Muslims within the Muslim community. The Muslim *umma* was economically weak and yet to be economically consolidated. Allowing certain forms of 'exploitation' within the Muslim community was therefore regarded as contrary to the con-solidation efforts of the growing religious organism. This argument would seem to favour the abolition of *riba* in Muslim states with Muslim banks. In other words *riba* transaction between Muslims on one side and non-Muslim banks on the other or *vice versa* would not be illegal.

Third, alternatively, Muhammad could simply have had in mind the welfare of the borrower who, in the majority of cases, was probably from the poorer classes. This would then militate against interest on bank loans but not interest on savings.

Finally, the injunction could again have been aimed at the Jews. The Jews in Medina were economically superior to the pagan Arabs, and while *riba* was common to all the inhabitants of that region, Arabs and Jews, the Jews were certainly its forerunners. In fact, the injunction came at a time when the Prophet Muhammad was particularly vexed with the Jews for their unresponsiveness to his call, for their attempts to discredit and ridicule him and the Muslims at large, and probably for their refusal to give Muhammad and the Muslims interest-free financial support at a time when he and they needed it most. Such adversaries of the Muslims could not, therefore, be allowed to exploit the economically weaker position of the Muslims. In this instance the legality of interest would depend on the bank (local and foreign — and what sense of foreign). If this is so, could it be said that Muhammad was opposed to economic imperialism? Of course, the in-junction against the *riba* could have been motivated by a combination of any of the above factors.

Then there is *maysir* which is usually defined as a game of chance but which, nonetheless, seems to have had some economic applications: in this latter case it is called *gharar* and implies that there must be no element of doubt concerning the obligations that bind each of the parties in a business transaction. Some scholars believe that the injunction against *maysir* or *gharar* includes broking and sales by auction since the seller cannot determine in advance the price he will obtain.

Under the category of manner of business transaction one may also include advertising. Again, there are some weak *hadiths* which suggest that Muhammad also put certain restrictions on advertising: a seller should not praise his commodities. On the contrary, he should make known their faults to the consumers; that is considered the mark of a truly honest businessman. Here too we can see consumer protection being given a moral form. One may also regard this Muhammadan view of advertising as intended to ensure greater fair play in the 'capitalist' competition among the merchants in the sense that only the quality of the commodities would determine their marketability.

Welfare Socialism and the Crescent

While the Islamic mode of production did show many signs of evolving into a kind of pre-industrial model of capitalism, there was the concurrent restraining factor of nascent Islamic socialism. It must not be forgotten that socialism even under Marxism has not really been a mode of production at all. It has been a basis of distribution. According to Lenin himself the lower phase of socialism is, after all, based on the principle, 'From each according to his ability. To each according to his work.' This is a principle of distributive justice in imperfect social conditions. At least the criterion of work as a basis of reward is still linked with the process of production itself. Work is potentially a productive process.

Yet Lenin regards this principle of distribution as being still primitive. At best it defines conditions at a lower phase of socialism — the phase of the dictatorship of the proletariat, well before a truly classless society.

When do we arrive at perfect justice? Lenin tells us. We do so when the basis of distributive justice is the following principle: 'From each according to his ability. To each according to his need.'[7] What is often not realized is that the shift from 'work' as a criterion of distribution to 'need' is in fact a shift from the principle of production (work) to a principle of consumption (need). Yet the criterion of 'need' is ideologically regarded by Lenin as a higher phase of socialist justice than the criterion of 'work'. It is partly in this sense that socialism has not really been a quest for a mode of production. It has been a search for a principle of distribution and a criterion of consumption.

If socialism were a mode of production, the jet engine in the Soviet Union would be produced in a different way from the jet engine in the United States. And yet we know that the modes of production in the United States and the USSR, one socialist and the other capitalist, are closer together than the modes of production of either the United States and Zaire, both capitalist, or the USSR and Mozambique, both socialist. Technology is a more relevant difference between the USSR and Mozambique than ideology is between the United States and Mozambique. And technology is what a mode of production is all about.

If, then, socialism is a quest for distributive justive partly based on the needs of consumption, Islamic preoccupations are not too far removed from a similar effort in socialism. Two of the five pillars of Islam are concerned with distribution and consumption. The Islamic tax of *Zakat* is among the earliest forms of structured personal taxation in human history, modest as it is in percentage terms. The existence of the tax encouraged early Islamic scholarship to devote a good deal of thought to the ethics and principles of distribution. The 'trialectic' of God, man, and nature plays its part in the taxing of flocks of animals in kind, as well as the taxing of other forms of wealth.

Islamic rules of consumption begin with one of the other pillars of the faith, the fast of Ramadhan. From dawn to dusk believers are called upon to abstain from eating, drinking, sexuality, smoking, and the like. One month every year is devoted to the discipline of abstinence, training in restraint and moderation.

In practice, the discipline of Ramadhan in much of the Muslim world has often been honoured in the breach by excessive indulgence in the evenings after the sunset prayer. Many families spend more money on food during the month of Ramadhan than during any other month in the year. On the other hand, genuine hunger and thirst under the sun does cause discomfort and fatigue in daytime. Therefore output goes down in most Muslim societies during a fast. A paradoxical result is that a month which was intended to cut down consumption has ended in cutting down production instead, much to the consternation of such reformist Muslim political leaders as Habib Bourguiba of Tunisia who has often championed other forms of discipline to replace the traditional abstinence from food and drink.

The traditional way of observing Ramadhan continues, nevertheless, including traditional sanctions for those who cannot fast or who break related rules of Ramadhan. The sanctions are themselves exercises in economic re-distribution: enforced charity to compensate for any breach of the rules of the fast. Those who can afford to eat in broad daylight during Ramadhan (for reasons of, say, sickness) are called upon to help the poor eat at night. Once again Islam has tended to work out elaborate rules of consumption, partly based on what are presumed to be natural laws of consumption.

Islamic rules of consumption have wider economic consequences in society. They affect again distribution and exchange. Here we now come to another type of qualification on trade, i.e., restrictions imposed on transaction in certain items. These are of three kinds.

First, items whose consumption or use is prohibited in Islam. These items include alcohol and pork. Second, items which, by their very nature, are considered communal, since Muhammad was essentially in favour of state or communal ownership of natural resources. Third, land, and especially agricultural land. Islam allows the lease of land as long as the transaction does not involve the exchange of one agricultural property for another. An element of *maysir/gharar* is believed to exist in such a transaction to the extent that the productivity of the exchanged plots cannot be predetermined. (This, one supposes, may also be a case of *riba*.) On the basis of this one would have thought that Islam would allow only the type of land lease in which rent fluctuates in proportion to the amount that the land has actually been able to produce, e.g., rent in the form of percentage of the produce. In fact, it also allows land leases of fixed rents, despite any disadvantage to the small farmer when productivity is low. (Imam Malik seemed opposed to the *corvée* system in general.) The laws seem to offer inadequate protection to the *fellaheen*. In addition, does not the law against land exchange serve to neutralize intra-class merchant exploitation? A transaction of this nature is possible only between people who are landed, and its regulation is in effect a regulation of intra-class relationships.

The question of land transactions brings us to the question of ownership and inheritance. It is quite clear that Islam sanctions and protects private property, including ownership of the means of production, of which agricultural land was primary in Muhammad's time. Some people have argued that to the extent that Islam is not in favour of the private ownership of natural resources, it is not in favour of private ownership of agricultural land. However, documentary evidence as well as actual practice in Muhammad's own time would strongly militate against this view. It has been argued too that Islam is opposed to any excessive accumulation of wealth, to monopoly, on the basis of a Koranic verse which urges the distribution of spoils of war to the needy to the exclusion of the rich.

Islamic law of inheritance also operates against the ownership of large estates. There is no Islamic principle of primogeniture — inheritance by the eldest son alone. On the contrary, the estate of a deceased Muslim has to be meticulously shared among the heirs. This has militated against keeping large estates intact and against the rise of a landed gentry in the Muslim world. The feudal lord of the manor was up against the Shari'a and its tendency to fragment the large estate.

Pre-Islamic Arabia had its own system of inheritance, which was under pressure from the dynamics and effects of emerging pre-industrial capitalism. Islam offered an alternative. As head of the new Islamic city states, Muhammad could have desired to establish a more just distribution arrangement. The Islamic inheritance system is definitely an advance over that of pre-Islamic Arabia in which few men and even fewer women were accorded anything at all. Despite this, it is a fact that the Islamic inheritance system is disproportionately in favour of the man. What then is the basis of this unequal distribution of heritable wealth between sexes? It would appear to be the unequal distribution of financial responsibilities: the Muslim man is legally required to be the breadwinner. However, to the extent that before, during and some years after the time of Muhammad, Arab women of the Khadija type, with an obvious ability to be breadwinners in their homes, were quite common, we would suggest that initially Muhammad merely meant to improve the lot of women in matters of inheritance.

Finally, wage labour was quite acceptable to the Prophet Muhammad. Notions of surplus value and exploitation in specific regard to wage labour do not appear to have occurred to him. The kind of labour that existed during the Prophet Muhammad's time was either slave or artisan (skilled) labour, neither of which could be equated with proletarian labour. One could say, then, that the conditions were not quite ripe for the emergence of a labour notion of value. We are not quite sure what was happening in the agricultural sector. One form of agricultural land lease that existed definitely amounted to the appropriation of part of labour of the *fellah*, but we are not certain of the extent to which the produce of this appropriated labour found its way to the market. With regard to the manufacturing sector, the labour-input into many of the commodities that came to be exchanged in places like Mecca took place outside south Arabia and was thus quite removed from the Prophet Muhammad's immediate experiences.

In general, then, it would seem that Islam was more concerned about the needs of the poor than the rights of the workers. The problems of the poor are in the field of consumption; the problems of workers are ultimately in the field of production. Welfare socialism in Islam is designed to meet the consumer needs of the poor more than the producing rights of the emerging pre-industrial labouring classes.

Conclusion

What we witnessed in the early Islamic system was indeed a version of mercant-ilism. But it amounted to a pre-industrial approximation of capitalism, tempered by moral sensitivity to the needs of 'the wretched of the earth'. Islamic welfarism in this early period was a kind of welfare state struggling to be born. It is in that sense that the Islamic cities of Mecca and Medina were evolving into a mixed economy of socialist and capitalist tendencies in a pre-industrial context.

Under the Caliph Umar bin Khatab, Islam at last expanded beyond the boun-daries of Arabia. The Islamic Empire was born and control was extended to larger populations, greater wealth, and vaster opportunities. If Islam in the Prophet Muhammad's own time was an emerging fusion of mercantilist, capitalist, and socialist tendencies, Islam in succeeding centuries evolved into the Marxian Asiatic mode of production.

In terms of economic justice, the Islamic Empire declined and regressed from the Prophet's high standards in his own Islamic state. In terms of culture, the arts, and scholarship, however, Islam moved forward to greater and more glittering achievements in the centuries which followed. If Islam had remained the national religion of the Arabs only, it might well have evolved into one of the earliest forms of sophisticated welfare socialism in the modern era. The cost to the wider heritage of the human race would have been high. A parochial Islam limited to the Arabian peninsula would have produced a more just society but a less scintillating human legacy. The first Protestant Revolution in the history of Semitic religions would not have evolved into a major scientific civilization.

The king of all history decreed otherwise in any case. Islam stepped on to the world stage in all its own resplendent regalia. Was it Allah's *kadr*? Was it Calvin's predestination? Or was it Marx's dialectic at work? Perhaps each is an alias for the same irresistible force, inscrutable and yet strangely purposeful, at once human and divine.

Even when Islam became an empire, there was one obligation which remained perenially egalitarian. This was the pilgrimage to Mecca, the Hajj, which remained a supreme equalizing experience for every pilgrim from whatever part of the Islamic Empire he came. The equality was down to the very type of dress worn during the pilgrimage. Every year there was this dual reminder — absolute obedience to God and absolute equality among his human creatures. Islamic socialism is captured in that dual principle.

It is no wonder that Islam recognizes no dictatorship of the proletariat. It recognizes only the dictatorship of the pious. All men are created equal, but some men become more equal than others in their obedience to God. The latest twentieth century dictatorship of the pious is that of Iran since the fall of the Shah. It remains Islam's closest approximation to the concept of the dictatorship of the proletariat. In Islam socialism is interlocked with salvation and paradise is the supreme classless society.

Islam had its own changing dialectic. At first Islam was a tale of two cities, Mecca and Medina. For a while it became a tale of two dynasties, the Abbasids and the Umayyads. More fundamentally Islam became a tale of two denominations — the Sunnis and the Shiites. In time Islam became a tale of two continents, Asia and Africa, as the two main regions of the Muslim world. In its origins was Islam also a tale of two economic paradigms, capitalism and socialism, struggling to be fused? Did Islam later become the most compelling of all crossroads between the

Occident and the Orient? In distribution, Islam has indeed been an Afro-Asian religion. But in concept is it still a Euro-Asian phenomenon?

We have noted Islam's ideological ambivalence, its capacity to lie astride different modes of production, its quality of intermediacy between the scientific legacy of the West and the spiritual heritage of the East. There is an underlying paradox in Islam, a tendency towards syncretism. Across the ages militant Islam has responded not to the trumpet call of revolution but to the muezzin of reaffirmation. Human civilization itself has heard its own eternal echo from the minarets of Islamic history.

Notes

I am indebted to Al-Amin M. Mazrui, of Ohio State University, for providing stimulation and data about certain concepts in comparative theology expressed in this chapter.

1. Umberto Melotti, *Marx and the Third World* (translated by Pat Ransford) (London: The Macmillan Press, 1977 edition), p. 16.
2. Ibid., p.77.
3. Maxime Rodinson, *Islam et capitalisme*, editions du Seuil, Paris, 1966. English translation, *Islam and Capitalism*, translated by Brian Pearce, Allen Lane (Harmondsworth: Penguin Books, 1974), pp. 58, 64.
4. Plekhanov, *Introduction a l'historie sociale de la Russie* (1914) (Editions Bossards, Paris, 1926), p. 4.
5. See Max Weber, *The Protestant Ethic and the Spirit of Capitalism.*
6. For the general context consult Ali Hassan Abdel Kader, *Study on Islamic Economy and Contemporary Transactions* (Jeddah: Dar el Maal Al-Islamia, 1401 A.H.).
7. V.I. Lenin, *State and Revolution* (1916).

4
Cultural Treason
& Comparative Censorship

The Satanic Verses

In the autumn of 1988 a debate started in Britain. It concerned Salman Rushdie's novel *The Satanic Verses*. Muslims in the British city of Bradford exploded in indignation. The novel was declared blasphemous — and copies were ceremonially burnt.

In November 1988 I visited Lahore and Islamabad in Pakistan. Discussions about Rushdie's novel had already started there. One analogy particularly struck me. 'It is as if Rushdie had composed a brilliant poem about the private parts of his parents, and then recited the poem in the market place to the cheers and laughter of strangers! These strangers then paid him money for all the jokes about his parents' genitalia.' This charge that I heard levelled against Rushdie in Pakistan was of pornographic betrayal of ancestry. It was a concept of *treason* in a special sense.

In February 1989 the Ayatollah Ruhollah Khomeini, the spiritual leader of Iran, passed the death sentence on Salman Rushdie. Other leaders in Teheran offered a reward to anybody who killed Rushdie. Before long the reward had risen beyond $5 million — and diplomatic relations between Britain and Iran rapidly deteriorated. Britain was supported by its partners in the European Community, and the President of the United States expressed concern.

At least for a while the debate was a classic case of the dialogue of the deaf between the West and the world of Islam. The West was bewildered by the depth of Muslim anger. The Muslims were bewildered by Western insensitivity. Was this yet another problem of conflict of cultures?

In the debate concerning Rushdie's *Satanic Verses*, I have had a number of conflicting emotions of my own. I have been torn between being a believer in Islam and a believer in the open society, between being myself a writer and being a religious worshipper, between being a believer in the *Shari'a* and an opponent of all forms of capital punishment in the modern age. This is not the place to resolve all those issues. If I am wrong in my opposition to capital punishment in the twentieth century, I seek the forgiveness of the Almighty and the tolerance of society and the *Umma*.

I also have strong reservations about censorship. This is partly because I have myself been censored over the years. I have been censored in the Republic of

South Africa, in parts of the Muslim world, in my own native Kenya, in Uganda under President Idi Amin, in the United Kingdom and in the United States of America. I have therefore had to argue with my very soul whether the banning of Salman Rushdie's *Satanic Verses* is any more legitimate than the censorship to which I have been subjected in different parts of the world from time to time.

This chapter is only partly a response to such questions. Much more pressing is the need for a translation of values between civilizations — the need to make some of the emotions of the Muslim world more intelligible to the West, even if still fundamentally different from the dominant paradigms of Western thought.

Treason: Political and Cultural

Central to the crisis of mutual incomprehension is indeed the concept of treason. The Western world understands the concept of treason to the state. Indeed, the West understands capital punishment imposed on a traitor to the state. What the West does not understand is the idea of treason to what Islam calls the *Umma*, the religious community, treason to the faith.

If Islam does not always distinguish between the church and state, English law does not always distinguish between the state and the Royal Family. Treason in England has included violating the King's consort, or raping the monarch's eldest daughter, as well as the sexual violation of the wife of the eldest son and heir. To the present day treason under English law includes 'polluting' the royal bloodline or obscuring it. In addition, English law does of course regard as treasonable the act of 'giving aid and comfort to the King's enemies'.

The basic law of the United States defines treason more narrowly in terms of war and military defence. The American founding fathers were aware that the concept of 'treason' could be used by tyrants as an excuse for suppressing liberty, stifling dissent, or preventing legitimate rebellion. The founding fathers' own revolt against George III of England was 'treason' against the English monarch.

And so the American Constitution defined treason to the United States as consisting 'only in levying war against them, and in adhering to their enemies, giving them aid and comfort'.

In the twentieth century defending the United States came to mean defending its ideology of liberal capitalism against the threat of communism, real or perceived. The hysteria of the McCarthy era soon after the Second World War created the pastime of hunting for traitors.

As for actual execution, this hit Julius and Ethel Rosenberg in June 1953. Julius had once been an active member of the Communist Party. We shall never know for certain whether the excesses of the McCarthy era pushed Julius Rosenberg from being merely an American dissenter to being a Soviet spy. He and his wife, Ethel, were executed as spies at the ages of 35 and 32, respectively.

Britain executed after World War II a Briton who had broadcast propaganda on the radio on behalf of Nazi Germany. And in the middle of World War I Sir Roger Casement — an Irish patriot who had served Britain well for a long time and then turned against Britain for the sake of Irish freedom — was executed for treason. Strangely enough, last-minute evidence of Casement's alleged homosexuality sealed his fate. Treason to his King was confused with treason to his gender.

In Islam there is no sharp distinction between church and state. The concept of treason is often indistinguishable from apostasy. The supreme penalty for treason to the *Umma*, or the religious community, was indeed often death.

For his novel *The Satanic Verses* Salman Rushdie was perceived by many Muslims as being guilty of cultural treason. Rushdie had not merely rejected Islam; nor had he merely disagreed with it. Almost unanimously Muslims who had read the book concluded that Rushdie had abused Islam. What is more, he had been lionized, praised, and lavishly rewarded and financed by outright enemies and hostile critics of Islam.

Islam is not unique in regarding attack on religion as a threat to the state. Scottish law until the eighteenth century made blasphemy not only a crime but a capital offence. The Scottish heritage went back at least to the Mosaic Law on one side and the legacy of Roman Emperor Justinian I, on the other. Mosaic law decreed death by stoning as the penalty for the blasphemer. Emperor Justinian — who reigned from 527 to 565 AD — reinforced the death penalty for blasphemy.

In Britain today blasphemy is no longer a capital crime — but it is still both a statutory and common law offence. It has been recognized as an offence under the common law from the seventeenth century. But blasphemy in Britain is only applicable to Christianity. On 20 February 1989, sections of the British press raised the question of whether it was not time that blasphemy in Britain was also defined in reference to Judaism, Hinduism, and Islam, all of which are well represented in the British population. Immanuel Jakobovits, the Chief Rabbi of the United Hebrew Congregation of the (British) Commonwealth, later wrote to *The Times* to call for legislation that would prohibit 'the publication of anything likely to inflame, through obscene defamation, the feelings or beliefs of any section of society'.[1]

Perhaps the most fundamental blasphemy in Salman Rushdie's novel concerns the very title of his novel, *The Satanic Verses*. To explain the issues to people in the Western world let us first place the *Qur'an*, the holy book of Islam, in the context of world literature. It is not just Rushdie's book which should concern Western historians of literature. It is also the *Qur'an* itself as a work of art — the book which Rushdie virtually abuses by calling it 'the Satanic Verses'.

The Qur'an as World Literature

The *Qur'an* is the most widely read book in its original language in human history. The Bible is the most widely read book in translation. The Bible is also a multi-authored work. But the *Qur'an* is in a class by itself as a book which is recited by millions of believers, five times a day, in the very language in which it was first written.

If Salman Rushdie had simply said that the *Qur'an* was the work of the Prophet Muhammad and not the word of God, he would have been repeating the normal interpretation of non-Muslims. Making the *Qur'an* the work of human genius, rather than divine inspiration, would still put the Prophet Muhammad alongside William Shakespeare as the two most influential literary figures of all time — with one vital difference. The *Qur'an* is read by a hundred thousand times more people than are the plays of Shakespeare.

Yet, as ordinary human beings, there are similarities between the Prophet and the Bard. Both were of relatively limited formal education, and yet their names are associated with literary works of immense influence. The plays of Shakespeare have greatly enriched the idiomatic heritage of the English language. The Qur'an has had an even greater impact on the Arabic language — stabilizing its pace of change and diversifying its rhythms, images and power. There is a religious doctrine in Islam to the effect that the Qur'an is impossible to imitate. And yet no book in history has been subjected to more attempts at imitation.

Neither Shakespeare nor, of course, the Prophet Muhammad ever went to a university or its equivalent. And yet, in the case of Shakespeare's plays, there is impressive familiarity with history, law, foreign literatures, high politics and the manners and speech of royalty and nobility. Was all this knowledge conceivable in the son of a provincial tradesman and a common actor?

> This range of knowledge, it is said, is to be expected at that period only in a man of extensive education, one who was familiar with such royal and noble personages as figure largely in Shakespeare's plays. And the dearth of contemporary records has been regarded as incompatible with Shakespeare's eminence and as therefore suggestive of mystery. That none of his manuscripts has survived has been taken as evidence that they were destroyed to conceal the identity of their author.[2]

The Qur'an is also a work of immense learning and versatility — obviously sensitized to the legacies of both the Christian Bible and the Jewish Torah. In addition it shows a capacity for direct legislative change, moral reform, refinement of rules of etiquette, and the power of poetry. Could such a book have been written by a camel herder and travelling salesman?

In the case of Shakespeare, the source of all doubts about the authorship of the plays lies in:

> the disparity between the greatness of Shakespeare's achievement and his comparatively humble origin, the supposed inadequacy of his education, and the obscurity of his life.[3]

In a bid to solve these problems, there have been theories of alternative authors with more obvious learning and social status that Shakespeare had. Such alternative candidates have included Francis Bacon (Viscount St Albans), Edward de Vere (17th Earl of Oxford), William Stanley (6th Earl of Derby) and the dramatist Christopher Marlowe who was supposed to have been killed in a tavern brawl in 1593. But was he really killed? Or was the brawl staged so that he could disappear — and later write anonymously from France and Italy?

For Muslims the literary and spiritual genius of the Qur'an could more easily be explained. No other Arab of Muhammad's day has been put forward as the 'real' author of the Qur'an. To Muslims, the secret of the miracle is, quite simply, that it is the word of God.

Salman Rushdie's blasphemy does not lie in his saying that the Qur'an is the work of Muhammad. The blasphemy lies more in Rushdie's suggestion that it is the work of the Devil. By the term 'Satanic Verses' he refers to more than an alleged incident in the history of Islamic revelation. Rushdie suggests that Muhammad is incapable of distinguishing between inspiration from an angel and inspiration from a devil. Indeed, Rushdie gives the Prophet a name which Rushdie himself describes as 'the Devil's synonym: *Mahound*'.

In the English language the second greatest poet after Shakespeare is widely regarded to be John Milton. One thing which Milton's *Paradise Lost* has in common with the Qur'an is that both great works were recited orally before they were written. Milton dictated much of *Paradise Lost* because he was blind; the Prophet Muhammad dictated much of the Qur'an because he could not himself read or write.

Rushdie suggests that Muhammad was not only incapable of distinguishing between what had been inspired by the Devil and what had come from the Archangel. Muhammad could not even tell between what he himself had dictated to the scribe and what the scribe had mischievously substituted. The Persian scribe in Rushdie's book tells us how he first changed little things in what the Prophet had dictated to see if Muhammad would notice:

> Little things at first. If Mahound recited a verse in which God was described as *all-hearing, all-knowing,* I would write *all-knowing, all wise.* Here's the point: Mahound did not notice the alterations. . . . So the next time I change a bigger thing. He said *Christian,* I wrote down *Jew.* He'd notice that, surely; how could he not? But when I read him the chapter he nodded and thanked me politely, and I went out of the tent with tears in my eyes. . . .[4]

In the end the scribe carried it too far, and Mahound's suspicion was aroused. But the novelist Rushdie has already done his mischief in creating doubt about the authenticity of the Qur'an as Muhammad's own work, let alone as the word of God.

But is this any different from suggesting that parts of *Paradise Lost* were not Milton's genius but mischievous substitutions by the person who was taking down the dictation?

One central difference is that *Paradise Lost* is not the equivalent of a constitution of a country, whereas the Qur'an is the ultimate constitution of the community of believers. American political morality expects its citizens to be ready to 'uphold, protect and defend the Constitution of the United States'. Muslims expect all believers to be ready to defend the Qur'an as their own ultimate fundamental law.

Rushdie not only casts doubt on the authenticity of the source of that fundamental law. He satirizes its rules and attributes fictitious dicta to it:

> . . . rules about every damn thing, if a man farts let him turn his face to the wind, a rule about which hand to use for the purpose of cleaning one's behind . . . sodomy and the missionary position were approved of by the archangel, whereas the forbidden postures included all those in which the female was on top. . . .[5]

This is more than suggesting that John Milton did not write *Paradise Lost.* It is worse than alleging that what Americans take to be their Constitution consists of bastardized passages inserted by mischievous scribes still loyal to King George III of England. If American patriotism consists of upholding, protecting and defending the Constitution of the United States, does not undermining and casting doubt on the authenticity of the Constitution come close to being a form of treason?

Americans regard deliberate stepping on their flag, or purposefully urinating on the star-spangled banner, as sacrilege. Each verse of the Qur'an is like a flag to a Muslim. Has Salman Rushdie deliberately urinated on the Holy Book? Has he defiantly defecated on the equivalent of a thousand crescent-spangled banners?

Milton's *Paradise Lost* is partly about Satan as a fallen angel. It is also about the sin of pride and its consequences. In the immortal words of Milton's Lucifer: 'Better to reign in hell than serve in heaven.' Many Muslims believe that Salman Rushdie has shared aspirations with Lucifer in his own 'Satanic Novel'.

The Defamation of the Dead

Another issue of conflict of cultures at the centre of the Rushdie debate is the question of comparative defamation. Western law of libel and slander tends to focus on the individual, and seldom on a whole class of people. American law is more sensitive to 'class action' than British law is, but on the whole it is individuals and institutions rather than groups of people who sue under libel or slander in Western societies.

In Salman Rushdie's novel the question arises whether he has libelled whole classes of Muslims — ranging from Shiite believers (as symbolized by Rushdie's character 'the Imam') to the wives of the Prophet Muhammad.

A related difficulty concerns the fact that Western law provides very little protection against libel for those who are dead. If twelve women alive today were portrayed in a novel — under their own names — as the equivalent of prostitutes, they would have some kind of legal recourse. But Rushdie is libelling women who have been dead some fourteen hundred years — the wives of Prophet Muhammad. Reputations of people who have been dead for so long have very little protection under Western concepts of libel and slander.

It is true that Rushdie does not say it was the Prophet's real wives who were prostitutes. He creates prostitutes who adopt the names of the Prophet's wives — whores who play at being the spouses of Mahound. Rushdie uses the trick of a play within a play — like Shakespeare's Hamlet staging a play in order to find out if his uncle killed his father before marrying his mother.

Rushdie suggests that the customers of the prostitutes get additional sexual excitement out of pretending to make love to the Prophet's wives:

> The fifteen-year-old whore 'Ayesha' was the most popular with the paying public, just as her namesake was with Mahound. . . . The fifteen-year-old whispered something in the grocer's ear. At once a light began to shine in his eyes . . . she told him . . . about her deflowering at the age of twelve . . . and afterwards he paid double the normal fee because 'it's been the best time of my life.' 'We'll have to be careful about heart conditions,' the Madam said.[6]

Rushdie goes on to say that the prostitutes who were pretending to be Mahound's wives became:

> so skilful in their roles that their previous selves began to fade away . . . and the day came when the prostitutes went together to the Madam to announce that now that they had begun to think of themselves as the wives of the prophet they required a better grade of husband than some spurting stone. . . . The Madam then married them all off herself, and in that den of degeneracy, that anti-mosque, that labyrinth of profanity, Baal became the husband of the wives of the former businessman, Mahound.[7]

In other words all the prostitutes were 'married' to the character called Baal who pretended to be a eunuch at the brothel. Why did the whores bother to get married? Rushdie explains:

> In that age it was customary for a whore, on entering her profession, to take the kind of husband who wouldn't give her any trouble . . . so that she could adopt, for form's sake, the title of a married woman.[8]

Baal, as the 'husband' of twelve whores, pretended to be the Prophet Mahound. He even fell in love with 'Ayesha', the prostitute named after the Prophet's favourite wife:

In short, [Baal] had fallen prey to the seductions of becoming the secret, profane mirror of Mahound.[9]

Rushdie's game of 'a play within a play' is nevertheless a prostitution of the reputations of twelve innocent and respectable women. Had these women been alive Western laws would have protected their reputations. But being deceased for so long, Western law offers no sanctuary.

Is *Satanic Verses* the equivalent to *The Last Temptation of Christ*? In the film Jesus is portrayed as dreaming out his sexual fantasies. The hypothesis is offensive to both Christians and Muslims (since Jesus is a revered Prophet in Islam). But while *The Last Temptation of Christ* is indeed un-Christian, it is not abusive. Jesus is portrayed as essentially good, even divine. But his goodness is struggling with his humanity as he approaches death. It is almost like the human anguish which made him cry out 'Father, why have you forsaken me?' On the whole, therefore, *The Last Temptation of Christ* is far less abusive of Jesus than Rushdie has been of the Prophet Muhammad and his wives.

The real equivalent of comparative blasphemy would be in portraying the Virgin Mary as a prostitute, and Jesus as the son of one of her sexual clients. Also comparable would be any novel based on the thesis that the twelve apostles were Jesus's homosexual lovers, and the Last Supper their last sexual orgy together. It would be interesting to speculate which leading Western writers would march in a procession in defence of the 'rights' of such a novelist.

What is clear is that neither the Virgin Mary, in the first hypothesis of prostitution, nor Jesus and the Twelve Apostles, in the second hypothesis of a homosexual orgy, would receive much legal protection under Western law of libel, slander or defamation.

Comparative Censorship

To turn to a secondary theme of this chapter, is the banning of the *Satanic Verses* any more (or less) legitimate than the forms of censorship exercised in Western democracies? If some of the emotions of the Muslim world are not easily intelligible in the West, is not censorship in the Western world a contradiction of Western liberalism and not readily intelligible to Islamic observers of Western freedoms? Throughout the Western world there is one medium which would almost certainly censor any artistic work based on the thesis that Mary was a prostitute or Jesus a homosexual. That medium is television — precisely the medium which in the West can reach the largest number of people. All Western protestations of freedom of speech are contradicted daily by censorship (official and unofficial) on Western mass media. It is to this problem of comparative censorship that we must now turn. To a certain extent censorship in the industrialized world has moved from the printed word to the electronic media.

In Britain elaborate efforts have been made by the Thatcher government to stop or discourage journalists interviewing the so-called Northern Ireland 'terrorists'. Margaret Thatcher has argued that publicity is the oxygen of terrorism. Is that different from saying democracy is the oxygen of terrorism?

In parts of the United Kingdom you can quote a so-called militant of the Irish Republican Army — but you may not let his own voice say those words. Nor may you show him visibly on TV making his case.

Sinn Féin, as a political arm of the Irish Republican Army, is also subject to severe censorship in parts of the United Kingdom — especially on the electronic media. Even elected parliamentarians for that particular political party are subject to those constraints.

Peter Wright's book *Spycatcher* was chased by Margaret Thatcher's government to different parts of the 'white' Commonwealth — in a bid to have the book banned. The Thatcher government did not always have its way as it traversed the world to get the book suppressed. But the very fact that the government of Britain had criteria of censorship of its own (however secular) belies its protestations in defence of Rushdie's 'freedom of expression'. Margaret Thatcher was on firmer moral ground in defending Rushdie's life.

I personally have also been censored in Britain and the United States, as well as in South Africa and my own native Kenya. In Programme 3 ('New Gods') of my BBC/PBS television series *The Africans: A Triple Heritage*, I start with a bust of Karl Marx. The viewer is supposed to hear my voice saying:

> 'Religion is the sigh of the oppressed creature and the soul of soul-less conditions.' So said Karl Marx, the last of the great Jewish Prophets.

The Public Broadcasting System was afraid of offending Jewish viewers. The potentially offending phrase was 'the last of the great Jewish prophets'.

Nevertheless, the British viewer heard it. Australian viewers heard it. Nigerian viewers heard it. Viewers in Finland heard it. Viewers in Jordan heard it. Even viewers in Israel heard it.

But viewers in the United States did not hear me say 'the last of the great Jewish prophets'. It was censored, in spite of the fact that it made it difficult for me to make my case about 'the Semitic impact on Africa' (Jesus, Muhammad and Marx).

But since the series had already been shown in Britain, many American journalists knew about the deletion. I was interviewed nationwide in the United States in 1986 by newspapers and TV programmes — including on the issue of 'the last of the great Jewish prophets'. The President of the Washington Educational Television Association (WETA) was attacked at the National Press Club in Washington DC, for showing a TV series which had *previously* included the statement 'the last of the great Jewish prophets'.

No journalist anywhere in the USA took up the cudgels on my behalf on the issue of my being able to say that Marx was the last of the great Jewish prophets. Originally I expected criticism from my Marxist friends. Marxists might not want to concede that Marx was a 'prophet' when he personally saw himself as a 'scientist'. Marx had repudiated his Jewish heritage — so the Marxists might object to my referring to it. But in America it was not my Marxist friends who were offended — it was my Jewish friends.

WETA and the PBS decided to delete the phrase, 'the last of the great Jewish prophets' — the most direct form of censorship exercised on *The Africans*. WETA believed that a hostile alliance of right-wing gentiles and irate Jewish liberals was more than the series could cope with in the USA. So the phrase was well and truly excised. But even this was not enough to put an end to the 'Jewish question'. The TV critic of the *New York Times*, John Corry, complained that there was not enough reference to the Jews in *The Africans*. He also complained that there was virtually no reference to Israel. In reality there were references to Jews in five out of the nine programmes — including the most moving Afro-Jewish comparison of all, made in a slave dungeon in Ghana in Programme 4:

As an African visiting a place like this, seeing all this, I began to have some kind of idea as to what the Jew might feel if he visits Auschwitz or some other Nazi Germany concentration camp and sense those powerful emotions of bewilderment, of anger, of infinite sadness.

Moreover, *The Africans* showed only four non-African countries on the screen as part of the story — Britain (a former colonial power), France (also a former colonial power), the United States (a superpower) and Israel (the Knesset and all). Programme 3 covered Sadat's historic visit to Jerusalem.

It is not clear how much more about Israel and the Jews John Corry of the *New York Times* wanted in a television series about Africa before he would accept that the 'balance' was right! It is ironic that in a review of the companion book to the TV series, a British reviewer in the Royal African Society's journal, *African Affairs* (January 1987), complained that I devoted too much space in the book to the Jews. This reviewer was convinced that I was exaggerating the relevance of 'the Jewish question' to the African condition. By contrast, John Corry was outraged that in the TV series I had not devoted more time to Israel and the Jews.[10]

What was the reaction of the Jews themselves (as distinct from the response of over-protective gentiles)? Israel saw *The Africans* when it was shown across the border in Jordan. The *Jerusalem Post* reviewed the companion book and referred to the Jordanian showing of the series. The *Post*'s review was sympathetic and emphasized my treatment of the Jews in the book. An Israeli Fellow of an Oxford College in Britain wrote enthusiastically to me about the TV series. President Harold Shapiro, my boss at the University of Michigan at the time, and his wife Vivian held a major reception in honour of my TV series and also hosted a distinguished dinner in my honour. All this in the midst of the controversy. (Since then President Shapiro has left Michigan and become Princeton University's first Jewish President ever.) But the fact remains that American gentiles censored me in order to protect the presumed sensitivities of the Jews.

Every day of the week something is being censored in the American media. Programmes are denied funding for fear of offending advertisers, subscribers, mainstream patriots, mainstream religious zealots, powerful Jews, powerful gentiles. Otherwise reputable publishers turn down manuscripts, edit out ideas, or surgically remove chapters likely to offend powerful groups in the nation. Censorship in the United States is basically privatized — as befits a private enterprise system. The state leaves censorship to the market place, to the forces of supply and demand. Freelance censors abound.

Comparative Incitement to Violence

What about the Ayatollah Khomeini's death sentence on Salman Rushdie? Surely that was completely outside Western standards of legitimate behaviour? What was new about the Ayatollah Khomeini's death sentence was not the idea of murder by remote control — it was the openness with which it was declared. It was worthy of Agatha Christie's famous title *A Murder is Announced*. If Western countries want to kill somebody in some other country, it becomes part of a covert operation. The Central Intelligence Agency or MI5 may take the initiative. The Israelis may fly all the way to Tunis and kill somebody in his bed. Western cinema-goers enjoy James Bond, 007. He is simply an exaggeration of something utterly believable. As for *Mission Impossible* for American TV viewers, it emphasizes the principle of deniability

Should you or your associate ever get caught, the Secretary will totally disavow any link with you. This tape will self-destruct in five seconds. Good luck, Jim.

As for attempted assassination by bombing, there seems little doubt that the Reagan administration wanted to kill Muammar Gaddafi from the air in the course of the bombing of Tripoli in 1986. The planes had instructions to bomb what they thought was his residence. In a bid to kill Gaddafi, the Americans killed a lot of other people — and missed their primary target. They did kill Gaddafi's adopted child, though. Was that a consolation prize? In the 1960s the Americans also conspired to kill Fidel Castro. The American attempt to kill Castro may have contributed to the subsequent assassination of John F. Kennedy. Then there was President Reagan's declaration to alleged terrorists: 'You can run, but you cannot hide.' This was a declaration that the sovereignty of other countries was no asylum for enemies of America. The United States skyjacked an Egyptian civilian airplane in international skies because there was a suspect on board. The United States also deliberately violated Italian sovereignty in the course of the same operation.

As for the European Community's collective outrage against the Ayatollah's proclamation of violence by remote control, no such collective outrage was evident when one of the European Community's own members sent agents to blow up *The Rainbow Warrior* in a peaceful New Zealand port. The ship belonged to the environmentalist activist group, Greenpeace, which was protesting against France's repeated nuclear tests in the South Pacific. The French authorities decided to teach both New Zealand and the Greenpeace protesters a lesson by sending agents to plant explosives on board the unarmed ship. A Greenpeace member on board was killed as a result of the French sabotage. The whole French exercise was directly intended to silence legitimate protest through an act of state terrorism.

Was the threat of economic sanctions by the European Community ever invoked in connection with the sinking of the *Rainbow Warrior* and the resulting killing of a cameraman? Yes, there was a threat of economic sanctions — but against New Zealand, whose sovereignty had been violated, rather than against France, which had violated it.

New Zealand had caught two of the French agents responsible for the outrage. The agents were tried according to Western concepts of fair trial and due process. The accused were sentenced to long terms of imprisonment. But France secretly threatened economic sanctions against New Zealand if the agents were not handed over for imprisonment under French sovereignty in nearby French colonial islands. And then France blatantly violated the agreement, returned the guilty agents to France and released them. New Zealand's indignation was kept in check out of fear of losing access to the markets of the European Community as a whole.

The same Community which waxed lyrical in defence of Salman Rushdie and against the Ayatollah's proclaimed 'terrorism' stood silently by when one of its own members organized an act of terrorism against a small and friendly country linked to the Western fraternity itself. Nor did the Community show any evidence of outrage when France threatened to deny New Zealand economic access to the Community as a whole if New Zealand refused to bend its own judicial procedures over the convicted French agents.

Four years later the twelve members of the European Community temporarily withdrew their ambassadors from Teheran in the wake of the Ayatollah's threat against Rushdie. Yet they had not threatened even to disgrace France when Paris declared war on a lobbying group called Greenpeace a little earlier.

When the members of the European Community started returning their ambassadors to Iran in March 1989, the Ayatollah Khomeini accused the countries concerned of hypocrisy and opportunism. In view of their contrasting attitudes towards the defence of Salman Rushdie's freedom of expression, on one side, and towards the violation of the freedom of Greenpeace to protest, on the other, the European Community did indeed exhibit both hypocrisy and opportunism. The Ayatollah had seen right through their pseudo-moral gestures.

A dual way in which the West contrives to catch suspects is either by direct kidnapping or by enticing the victim just beyond a particular country's territorial waters. Observing the formalities by enticing the victim beyond the territorial waters is particularly necessary if the country in which the victim is located is friendly to the potential kidnapping country. A particularly interesting illustration is that of the Israeli nuclear scientist, Vanunu. To many Israelis, Mordechai Vanunu was guilty of double treason. He was a traitor to his own state of Israel because he published intimate nuclear secrets in a British newspaper (September 1986). He was also a traitor to his Jewish faith because he became a Christian at about the same time.[11]

The Israeli Secret Service kidnapped him abroad — and then subjected him to a secret trial for treason. He was enticed to Rome by a woman calling herself Cindy. He was offered sex at her sister's apartment. Cindy presented herself as an American student. Vanunu was given an injection and then kidnapped to Israel. He was sentenced to 18 years for treason, espionage and revealing state secrets. If the Iranians had been as sophisticated as the Israelis, they would have enticed Salman Rushdie to international waters — and then kidnapped him for a secret trial in Teheran. It is unlikely that Revolutionary Iran would have offered Mr Rushdie sex in the Mediterranean. But Rushdie could have been tempted with a large lecturing fee. If word leaked out that a British citizen was being tried in Teheran, the Iranians could either have added the charge of cultural espionage against Mr Rushdie or have charged him with incitement to violence.

The United States has also invoked the legalistic strategy of enticing a possible kidnap victim outside a friendly country's territorial waters — before seizing him. The fate of the Lebanese called Yunis, accused of hijacking a plane in 1985, is a case in point. Yunis was abducted and spent 17 months in relative isolation before being brought to trial in the United States.

On Literature and Chaos

In imposing the death sentence on Rushdie *in absentia* the Ayatollah Khomeini has understandably been seen as inciting violence against a citizen of another country. And yet Mr Rushdie is still alive — while twenty other people in the subcontinent in which he was born are dead. Who is inciting whom to violence? Did Mr Rushdie really fail to see that what he had written was the sort of stuff which could provoke violent demonstrations in the Indian subcontinent? Or did he not care? When India prudently decided to ban the book, Rushdie appealed to Rajiv Gandhi to lift the ban.

But Salman Rushdie and his publishers had been warned about the explosive nature of *The Satanic Verses* by Indian advisers before the book was published.

Mr Khushwant Singh, a non-Muslim adviser to Penguin publishers, warned Penguin about the book before publication. He warned that the book could disturb law and order in India. Zamir Ansari, Penguin's representative in India, is reported to have confirmed that such a warning was given. As for Rushdie himself, he was born in India and wrote about the partition of the subcontinent. In a previous book he has shown sensitivity to how easily ordinary folks in India can kill each other for religious reasons. Rushdie was probably perfectly aware that a misunderstood short story published in *The Deccan Herald*, mistaken as portraying the Prophet Muhammad as an idiot, resulted in riots and the death of 50 people.[12]

Even without being published in India, *The Satanic Verses* has already killed more than a dozen people in Rushdie's country of birth. It has also caused deaths in Pakistan. Had it been published in India, casualty numbers would have gone up ten times. Part of the price of having the world transformed into a global village is that incitement can become transterritorial.

The Indian government's ban on *Satanic Verses* has been supported by a large number of distinguished intellectuals — Hindu, Sikh, and Christian as well as Muslim — in that country. A letter to *The Indian Post* was signed by J. P. Dixit, Nissim Ezekiel, Jean Kalgutker, Vrinda Nabar, Vaskar Nandy, V. Raman, Ashim Roy. Was India's ban on the book a case of building a repressive society? *The Times of India* answers:

> No, dear Rushdie, we do not wish to build a repressive India. On the contrary, we are trying our best to build a liberal India where we can all breathe freely. But in order to build such an India, we have to preserve the India that exists. That may not be a pretty India. But this is the only India we possess.[13]

The Written Word and the Global Village

At the centre of the debate about Salman Rushdie's *The Satanic Verses* are two cultural forces which have helped to create 'the global village'. The globalizing forces have included *language* and *religion*. The emergence of world languages has certainly created new opportunities for writers writing in those tongues. When the authors are successful the returns could be immense. The question which arises is whether authors writing in world languages also have very special responsibilities.

We define a world language as one which has at least three hundred million speakers, has been adopted as a national language by at least ten countries, and has spread across more than one continent.

Hindi is spoken by more people than French but Hindi is not a world language in terms of spread. Chinese is spoken by more people than English but Chinese falls short of global status for the same reason.

If Rushdie was an inspired writer in Hindi, no publisher would have given him even a quarter of a million American dollar advance royalties. If Rushdie had been a genius in Kashmiri or Gujerati, he would have been fortunate to get advance royalties in hard Western currencies in five digits at all.

What made Rushdie's manuscript an investment worth a million was not its intrinsic merit as a work of art; it was more that the author had already been successful in the English language. The commercial scale depended in part on the size of the linguistic market. If rights imply duties, and rewards carry obligations, users of world languages are not just more fortunate than their fellow human beings. We are also duty-bound to be more sensitive to the consequences of globalism.

English is ahead of Third World languages even more in terms of the written word than as spoken tongue. Hindi is not too far behind English in total number of fluent speakers but it is much further behind English in terms of sophisticated readers. The difference between Hindi and English in terms of the book market is more than triple the margin in terms of speakers.

What follows from these factors is that the concept of best-seller means something quite different when applied to books written in world languages. The sense of achievement can be something special. The question again arises whether the measure of concern should not also be proportionate.

The Bible became a best-seller long after Mark, Luke, Matthew and John. It was originally written in relatively parochial tongues. Curiously enough the religion had to be globalized before the Bible could be a global best-seller. In every decade — especially in the twentieth century — the Bible is translated into entirely new additional languages.

Ironically it is the Bible itself which proclaimed, 'In the beginning was the word!' But is there any end to the word? Not if 'the word' means God Himself. But if 'the word' means the Gospel, it continues to traverse languages decade after decade. The Gospel of Jesus is a miracle in translation.

But the target of Salman Rushdie's invective was not the Christian Bible. It was that other great book which has helped to turn the world into a global village — the Qur'an. If the Bible is a miracle in translation, the Qur'an is a triumph of durability. It is history's most widely read book in its original language. Every single day millions of believers read it or recite it across the globe. Every single second its words are on somebody's lips — somewhere on earth.

But while the Bible and the Qur'an required prior religious conversions before they became best-sellers, Rushdie's book required mainly a world language. And Rushdie hit it rich even before the melodrama of the death sentence sensationalized his novel.

If such fortunate writers can derive such benefits from the global village, should they not also recognize those special global responsibilities? If a novel published in London or New York can kill people in Karachi or Bombay, should international law attempt to deal with new concepts of transnational incitement to violence? Should writers stop emphasizing their rights and liberties for a moment — and examine their obligations to the world community for a change?

The Rushdie affair has dramatized that issue in a new way. A book can be a lethal weapon. A pen writing three provocative paragraphs in London could let loose a flood of dangerous consequences half a world away. When is a writer guilty of manslaughter? Could it conceivably be at the moment of writing itself? Is that part of the price we have to pay for the global village?

On Religion and Race

The Satanic Verses: Is it the most divisive book in world politics since Hitler's *Mein Kampf*? Of course Hitler's book was anti-Jewish while *The Satanic Verses* is anti-Muslim. Hitler had political aspirations — while Rushdie's ambitions seem to be basically literary and mercenary. But fundamentally the two books are works of alienation and basically divisive in intent and in impact.

As late as 1989 a Hebrew translation of Hitler's book had a hard time finding a publisher in Israel. In the mid-1920s Hitler described himself as a writer. Royalties from his book and fees for newspaper articles were his principal source of income. His tax returns from 1925 to 1929 give figures which approximated closely his income from *Mein Kampf*.

Alan Bullock, in his book *Hitler: A Study in Tyranny*, said, '. . . *Mein Kampf* is a remarkably interesting book for anyone trying to understand Hitler. . . .'[14]

Is *Satanic Verses* also remarkably interesting for anyone trying to understand Salman Rushdie? But *Mein Kampf* did not become a political best-seller until after Hitler came to power. Hitler's original title was *Four and a Half Years of Struggle Against Lies, Stupidity and Cowardice*. I am not sure if Rushdie sees himself as engaged in many years of struggle against Muslim 'Lies, Stupidity and Cowardice'. Amy Max Amann — who was to publish Hitler's book — summarized his title to *Mein Kampf — My Struggle*. Rushdie and his publishers compressed their title to *The Satanic Verses*.

If Hitler hurt the Jews, and Rushdie hurt the Muslims, did both dislike the blacks as well? There is no doubt about Hitler's Negrophobia. But are there elements of Negrophobia in Salman Rushdie's *Satanic Verses* as well?

Here we need to deal with the point of convergence between religion and racism. In Medieval Europe the ultimate religious symbol of the devil on earth was Muhammad. The ultimate racial symbol of the devil on earth was the black man. Islam was the ultimate religious distance away from godliness. Blackness was the ultimate racial distance away from humanness.

Much later Rudyard Kipling portrayed the black colonial as 'half devil, half child'. For a long time Muhammad was regarded as full devil. The white man later had a name of scorn for the black man. The name was 'nigger'. The white man in medieval times also had a scornful name for the Prophet of Islam — the word was 'Mahound'.

Rushdie claims that just as 'Blacks all chose to wear with pride the names they were given in scorn, likewise, our mountain-climbing, prophet-motivated solitary is to be the medieval baby-frightener the Devil's synonym: Mahound.'[15] Rushdie adds:

> That's him. Mahound the businessman, climbing his hot mountain in the Hijaz. The mirage of a city shines below him in the sun.[16]

Rushdie also turns his torch-light on Bilal — the first Black Muslim in history. Rushdie reminds us that the Prophet had seen Bilal being punished for believing in one God. It was like Kunta Kinte being whipped to give up his African name, Toby vs Kunta Kinte.

Bilal was asked outside the pagan Temple of Lat to enumerate the Gods:

> 'One' he answered in that huge musical voice. *Blasphemy, punishable by death.* They stretched him out in the fairground with a boulder on his chest. How many did you say? One, he repeated one. A second boulder was added to the first. *One on one.* Mahound paid his owner a large price and set him free.

Bilal became the first great voice of Islam. The beginning of a black vocal tradition in world history — from Bilal to Paul Robeson and beyond. Black vocal power in world history began with Seyyidna Bilal.

Rushdie seems to give Bilal credit for his uncompromising monotheism — allegedly more uncompromising than even Prophet Mahound himself. After all, according to Rushdie, Mahound temporarily accepted a Pagan Trinity (three pre-Islamic goddesses — below the Supreme God). Bilal was dismayed. He exclaimed, 'God cannot be four' (p. 107). Mahound later reneged on this compromise — regarding these verses as Satanic. Rushdie does not give either Bilal or Islam explicit credit for being a multi-racial religion from so early a stage. Bilal set the grand precedent of Islamic multi-racialism — fourteen centuries before President Jimmy Carter tried to persuade his own church in Georgia to go multi-racial. Rushdie cannot resist certain epithets against the black man, Bilal. He makes a character think of the black man, Bilal, as

> scum . . . the slave Bilal, the one Mahound freed, an enormous black monster, this one, with a voice to match his size.[17]

Baal in the novel is the poet and satirist. Probably Rushdie sees himself in the character Baal (not to be confused with Bilal!) And what does the poet Baal say to the black man Bilal? 'If Mahound's ideas were worth anything, do you think they'd be popular with trash like you?' (p. 104). Bilal reacts but the Persian Salman restrains him. Salman says to the black man, 'We should be honoured that the mighty Baal has chosen to attack us,' he smiles, and Bilal relaxes, subsides (p. 104).

Rushdie gives Bilal a reincarnation as a black American convert to Islam. This time Bilal is called Bilal X — like Malcolm X. Bilal X seems to follow the leadership of a Shiite Imam in rebellion against a reincarnation of the Prophet's wife Ayesha — this time Empress Ayesha. Bilal X has the same old vocal power of the original Bilal. Under the influence of the Imam the black American not only wants to rewrite history. He has been taught to rebel against history — to regard it as 'the intoxicant, the creation and possession of the Devil, of the great Shaitan, the greatest of the lies — progress, science, right. . . .'

The black American's beautiful voice is mobilized against history. Bilal X declaims to the listening night (on the radio):

> We will unmake history, and when it is unravelled, we will see Paradise standing there, in all its glory and light (p. 210).[18]

The Imam has taught the black American that 'history is a deviation from the path, knowledge is a delusion. . . .' Rushdie tells us:

> The Imam chose Bilal for this [propaganda] task on account of the beauty of his voice, which in its previous incarnation succeeded in climbing Everest of the hit parade, not once but a dozen times, to the very top. The voice is rich and authoritative, a voice in the habit of being listened to; well nourished, highly trained, the voice of American confidence, a weapon of the West turned against its makers, whose might upholds the Empress and her tyranny.[19]

When Bilal X, the black American, protested at such a description of his voice, and insisted that it was unjust to equate him with Yankee imperialism, Rushdie puts the following words in the mouth of the Imam:

> Bilal, your suffering is ours as well. But to be raised in the house of power is to learn its ways, to soak them up, through that very skin that is the cause of your oppression. The habit of power, its timbre, its posture, its way of being with others. It is a disease, Bilal, infecting all who come too near to it. If the powerful trample over you, you are infected by the soles of their feet (p. 211).[20]

Is Rushdie making fun of African Americans generally? Or is he satirizing Afroamerican Muslims? Or is he ridiculing the significance of Malcolm X? But since many Afroamerican Muslims regard Islam as one route back towards re-Africanization, and therefore a point of return to *Roots*, is Salman Rushdie simply continuing his basic contempt for his own roots?

Kunta Kinte — if Alex Haley is right — was a Muslim. Alex Haley went looking for his roots. Salman Rushdie turned his back on his. To the question whether *The Satanic Verses* is as racist as *Mein Kampf* was, the answer is definitely not. But there is an undercurrent of Negrophobia in both books. The two books are also both anti-Semitic — but directed at different sections of the Semitic peoples. While Hitler was primarily anti-Jewish, there is an undercurrent of Anti-Arabism in Rushdie. Rushdie cannot believe that Muslim Pakistanis can be pro-Palestinian without prostituting themselves to Arab governments.

In his earlier book, *Shame*, Rushdie says:

> ... about anti-Semitism, an interesting phenomenon, under whose influence people who have never met a Jew vilify all Jews for the sake of maintaining solidarity with the Arab states which offer Pakistani workers, these days, employment and much-needed foreign exchange. . . .[21]

There is a school of thought on the Cornell University campus which says that the case for banning *The Satanic Verses* is implicitly a case for banning the *Qur'an* also. This is like telling Israelis that if they banned *Mein Kampf* they might as well ban the Bible and the Torah. *Mein Kampf* and *The Satanic Verses* are surely hate literature — the Qur'an and the Torah are not.

Conclusion

In 1971, I published a novel in which I put a dead poet on trial in the Hereafter. The charge was that the poet had subordinated his art to his ethnic loyalties — the accused had decided that he was an Igbo first and a poet second. He gave his life in defence of his ancestry — and Christopher Okigbo's Muse died with him.[22]

If Salman Rushdie were to be killed because of *The Satanic Verses*, the charge in the Hereafter could be exactly the opposite to that against the Igbo poet. If Christopher Okigbo before his death had decided that he was an Igbo first and an artist second, Salman Rushdie decided he was an artist first and an Indian Muslim second. If Okigbo had put ancestry before art in sacredness, Rushdie put art before ancestral community in commitment.

But surely *The Satanic Verses* is not a case of art for art's sake? Surely the novel is a work of social and cultural concern? This novel elevates the pleasure of art above the pain of society. Rushdie subordinates the real anguish of Muslim believers to the titillation of his Western readers.

Salman Rushdie should have known that no great culture can be reformed by abusing it. The best approach towards reform is a re-ordering of values within the existing paradigm. In order to get Americans to vote for equal rights for women, it would be counter-productive to tell them that their founding fathers — from Washington to Jefferson and beyond — were just male chauvinist pigs (even if they were). It is better to tell Americans that equal rights for women is the logical conclusion of the wisdom and heritage of the founding fathers ('All *men* are created equal' re-interpreted).

Rushdie says that his novel is not about Islam but about migration. But Islam is partly about migration and asylum. The Muslim calendar does not begin with the birth of Muhammad. It does not begin with the death of Muhammad. It does not begin with the first revelation of the Qur'an — the day he became a Prophet. The Islamic calendar begins with the day Muhammad migrated from Mecca to Medina. The principle of asylum is celebrated in the concept of the *Hijra.*

Is Islam against writers? Rushdie makes his prophet Mahound say that there is no difference between writers and whores. It is true that some writers prostitute themselves. Rushdie himself has been accused of that, as he enriched himself at the expense of the dignity of others. Could Rushdie have written a novel more respectful of Islam while still critical of that heritage? Of course he could. Rushdie himself says in another book, *Shame*: '. . . every story one chooses to tell is a kind of censorship, it prevents the telling of other tales'.[23]

Yet Rushdie makes fun of the *Hijra.* He makes his poet Baal compose a valedictory ode after Mahound's departure from Jahiliya (i.e. Mecca). *'What kind of idea does 'Submission' [Islam] seem today? One full of fear. An idea that runs away.'* [24] Of course, Rushdie did not know that within a few months of publishing those lines, he himself would go into hiding — and issue a Satanic verse of apology from his hiding place. *An idea that runs away.*

Westerners have been busy looking for motives behind the reaction of Muslims.

— Was Iran's reaction due to a battle between moderates and hardliners?
— Was Rajiv Gandhi courting the Muslim vote in India?
— Was Benazir Bhutto in Pakistan being undermined through Rushdie?

The motives of writer Salman Rushdie hardly interest Western political speculators. On the other hand, Muslims are more mystified by the author's motives than by the motives of the demonstrators in the streets of Dacca or Karachi. Westerners find it hard to understand the anger of the demonstrators and of the governmental bans. Muslims find it hard to understand what they regard as the author's cultural treachery. And yet was it motive enough for cultural treason that the author was reportedly paid advance royalties of over $800,000 to parody Islam? Other reports refer to £800,000 (sterling) as the real sum, which would raise the advance royalties to 1.5 million American dollars well before the book was sensationalized by the death sentence from Iran.

As for the assertion that one cannot be indignant about a book unless one has read it himself or herself, since when? There are millions of believing Christians who have read only a few pages of the Bible. There are also Muslims who can read the Qur'an without understanding it. There are also believing Jews who know only a few quotes from the Torah. Many of those who have theories about the Ayatollah Khomeini do not speak a word of Farsi. How many know from direct experience that Khomeini has really passed that death sentence on Rushdie? What about those indignant Muslims who *have* read the book? There is the assumption that all Muslim critics of Rushdie must be ignorant of the English language or incapable of understanding great literature.

A religion with the most sacralized of all books in history is sensitized to the possibility of profane books. Why is the Qur'an the most sacralized of all books?

(a) It is used five times every day in formal worship — by the bus stop in Indonesia, at the market place in Karachi, in the grain fields in Nigeria, at school in Turkey, as well as in the mosque in Syria.
(b) It is viewed by a billion human beings as the direct word of God. (Not the gospel 'according to' Mark, Matthew, etc.).

(c) The Qur'an is a miracle of the non-literate person articulating the most widely read book in its original language in history.

(d) The Qur'an has had a stabilizing effect on the Arabic language. It has combined the doctrine of inimitability with the magnet of attempted imitation.

But when all is said and done, Muslims should appeal to the Islamic leaders of Iran to lift the death sentence — and substitute at worst a curse instead. *La-ana-Mal-un. Maghdhub Alayhi.*

Dr Zaki Badawi, the Egyptian-born chairman of the Imams and Mosques Council and of the Islamic Law Council in Britain, has condemned both Rushdie's apostasy and the Ayatollah's death sentence on the author. Dr Badawi has pronounced:

> Yes, Khomeini reflects the entire Muslim religious view that Rushdie is on the face of it an apostate, a heretic. But neither he nor any Muslim authority has the power to sentence Rushdie to death. I must state with all the authority under my command that anyone who seeks or incites anyone to kill Rushdie is committing a crime against God and the Islamic Sharia.
>
> Even if he were legitimately sentenced to death, Islamic punishment cannot be carried out by anyone other than the Islamic appointed authorities and you cannot in Islam pass any sentence, let alone the death penalty, without a proper trial. It is unacceptable in Islam to try someone in his absence. Teachings both of the minority Shi'a branch of Islam and the majority Sunni, to which I belong, are identical on this.
>
> And even were Rushdie to be tried, it is by no means certain that he would be sentenced to death. The Prophet himself tolerated many people who left Islamic beliefs but were not considered dangerous to the fabric of the state. Those who were put to death were killed because of rebellion, not because of their beliefs.

Badawi stressed that, even if convicted of apostasy, Rushdie would have an opportunity to repent, and according to some scholars he could be given his whole life to re-think. Rushdie's book was 'a very deep wound', 'but the remedy was not to read it'.[25]

If really necessary, a spiritual sentence of a curse rather than a physical sentence of death would be more appropriate. Better still, leave Salman Rushdie to Heaven! Yes, ban the hate literature if need be, but love the author as a fellow human being. After all, the first word ever revealed in the Qur'an was 'Read' ('Iqra'):

Iqra bi-smi rabbika ladhi Khalaq
Khalaqal Insana min alak.
Iqra' wa Rabbukal Akkram
Alladhi Allama bil Qalam
Allamal Insana ma lam yaalam.

Read in the name of your Lord who creates men from a clot
Read, for your Lord is most gracious,
It is He who teaches by means of the pen,
Teaches man what he does not know.
However, man acts as arrogant, for he considers he is self-sufficient.
Yet to your Lord will be the return.

Islam is a religion born out of the imperative to read! In the spirit of that first verse, Muslims should respond by celebrating the written word. Amen.

Notes

1. Reported in *New York Times*, 20 March 1989.
2. See *Encyclopedia Britannica*, 1979, Vol. 16, p. 630. Consult also Arnold Kettle (editor), *Shakespeare in a Changing World* (New York: International Publishers, 1964).
3. Ibid., pp. 629—630. For a similarly sceptical approach to Muhammad and the Qur'an consult Patricia Crone and Michael Cooke, *Haggarism* (Cambridge University Press, 1977).
4. Rushdie, *The Satanic Verses* (London: Jonathan Cape, 1988), p. 368.
5. Ibid., pp. 363—364.
6. Ibid., pp. 381, 380.
7. Ibid., p. 383.
8. Ibid., p. 382.
9. Ibid., p. 382.
10. *New York Times*, 26 October 1986.
11. *Time* magazine, Vol. 131, 11 April 1989; and *Newsweek*, Vol. 110, 7 Septemberr 1987, p. 41.
12. See letter by H. V. Ravinder, *New York Times*, 26 February 1989. 'The Week in Review', p. 22.
13. Quoted by Rafiq Zakaria, *Al-Qalam*, November—December 1988.
14. Bullock, *Hitler* (New York: Harper and Row, 1964), p. 122.
15. *The Satanic Verses*, p. 93.
16. Ibid., p. 93.
17. Ibid., p. 101.
18. Ibid., p. 210.
19. Ibid., p. 211.
20. Ibid., p. 211.
21. Rushdie, *Shame* (London: Jonathan Cape, 1983), p. 72.
22. Mazrui, *The Trial of Christopher Okigbo* (London: Heinemann Educational Books, 1971).
23. *Shame*, p. 73.
24. *The Satanic Verses*, p. 126.
25. *Guardian*, 2 February 1989.

5

The Moral Paradigms
of the Superpowers

From an ethical point of view, one of the most disturbing things about the super-powers is that there are only two of them for the time being. Their physical duality has fed on the theme of ethical dualism.

After all, two lends itself to the notion of *opposites* and to the condition of *dichotomy* in political affairs. It lends itself to the obstinacy of believers against unbelievers, Jews against Gentiles, slave against freeman, and friend against foe. Out of dualism has emerged the whole moral paradigm of evil at war with good. The two superpowers of the contemporary world are caught up in the history of dualism.

It is in the face of this dualism that the Third World has had to deal with the superpowers. Ideological preferences are of course part and parcel of superpower ethics. *Socialism* is supposed to be a redistribution of economic power in favour of the dispossessed. Liberalism is a redistribution of *political* power in favour of the marginalized.

The United States is a liberal polity domestically. But at the global level does American policy favour the redistribution of political power to benefit mar-ginalized nations? The Soviet Union is a socialist system. But at the global level does Soviet policy favour the redistribution of economic power to benefit the dispossessed nations?

Although doctrinally an economic determinist, the Soviet Union's impact on economic change in the Third World is negligible. Although doctrinally liberal, the United States' impact on the liberation of the Third World is worse than negligible — it is negative. There are solid reasons for these doctrinal contradictions. Let us examine them more closely.

The Superpowers and Economic Redistribution

Even in the post-colonial era the Soviet Union and its allies have played a much smaller role in the economic development of, say, Africa than the West has done. There are a number of reasons as to why the capitalist world has been more relevant economically for Africa and other developing areas than the Soviet bloc.

In the first place the world's economic system is dominated by international capitalism in any case. The rules of international exchange are capitalist-derived — including a strong international leaning towards the principle of supply and demand as well as autonomy of market forces. The international conventions of economic behaviour are part of the Western lexicon — including the rules of the General Agreement on Tariffs and Trade (GATT).

The major international currencies of exchange are Western currencies — the pivot of which is the American dollar itself. The major commercial banks of the world are — almost by definition — capitalist, casting out chains of indebtedness to one Third World country after another. Also Western dominated are the major developmental banks of the world — with a pinnacle consisting of the World Bank under an eternal American presidency and the International Monetary Fund under a continuing Western European director-generalship. In confrontations with the IMF, Third World countries have sometimes defied the Fund's conditionality.[1] But in the end, most have recognized the mirage of 'butter' on the wrong side of the bread — and capitulated to the tempting illusion.

Ghana under the second Rawlings government (since the end of 1981) is a classic example of a country taking the IMF medicine and discovering that there was not only no jam tomorrow but no butter either. Two years of continuing economic collapse, and even starvation, forced Rawlings to turn to the IMF in 1983. Ghana's Economic Recovery Programme, bowing to the dictates of the Fund, has applied devaluation of the currency and reduction of expenditure on social services and education, a medicine which has almost killed the patient.

In Tanzania, President Nyerere could not reconcile himself to his country taking the IMF medicine as a remedy for its chronic economic problems. In 1985 Nyerere rejected the terms of a proposed loan agreement with the Fund and resigned later that year. The new president, Ali Hassan Mwinyi, accepted a deal with the IMF in July 1986 to abolish import controls, liberalize internal trade, devalue the currency, and cut public expenditure. The deal forced Tanzania to pay more for imports at a time when prices for agricultural goods on the world market were declining.

President Mobutu Sese Seko announced Zaire's rejection of a long-standing agreement with the IMF in a speech on 29 October 1986, in which he said: 'A young country cannot go on indefinitely sacrificing everything merely for the sake of servicing external debt.' Like Peru two months earlier, Zaire decided to limit debt payments to no more than 10 per cent of export receipts and drafted its own economic programme. The Fund and the World Bank responded to Mobutu's defiance by suspending disbursement of programmed credits to Zaire.

In Zambia, a country suffering from the steady fall of world copper prices, President Kenneth Kaunda accepted IMF support from 1975 to 1985. But in 1985 the Fund insisted on Zambia adopting a full austerity programme, including an end to price controls and lifting of subsidies on food and petrol. As a result, prices of basic foodstuffs in the towns doubled and there were bloody riots and deaths on the Copperbelt in 1987. Kaunda reacted in May 1987 by restoring government food subsidies and abandoning the IMF plan, and limiting Zambia's debt servicing to 10 per cent of foreign exchange earnings. The IMF retaliated, and in September 1987 Zambia was declared 'ineligible' for further financial assistance. Kaunda has launched an indigenous recovery programme based on 'growth from our own sources', but some years later the Zambian economy shows few signs of progress. The worsening foreign exchange shortage may force Zambia to go back to the IMF.

Latin America has had more success than Africa in defying the IMF, or at least in moderating the conditions the Fund imposes on its clients. Mexico has benefited since 1982 from various agreements with the IMF, Western central banks, and the US government to stave off bankruptcy and reschedule debt repayments. Argentina in 1984 gave way to IMF pressure for an economic austerity programme which puts a tight squeeze on public spending. But in 1987 the Fund approved a long-term debt rescheduling agreement, giving Argentina 'relief' from most capital repayments until 1992. However, this agreement has provided little help even in the short term, as in 1988 Argentina owed creditor banks 4.8 billion dollars in interest payments — more than twice the country's expected export earnings.[2]

Peru is the most notable example of a Third World country ready to defy the IMF. In 1985 newly elected President Alan Garcia told Peru's Western creditor banks and governments that Peru would pay its 14 billion dollar foreign debt in its own time. In August, Peru limited payments to foreign creditors to 10 per cent of export earnings — an example, as we have seen, that was followed by Zaire and Zambia. Garcia justified this by saying that the debt is 'the product of the unequal exchange of our raw materials for the industrial products of the rich countries'.[3] He pointed out that Peru's foreign debt burden had become intolerable because of protectionist restrictions in the developed world on Peru's exports, over-valuation of the US dollar, and what he called an 'arbitrary and unjust' rise in interest rates 'just to solve the national deficits of the big creditors'.

At his debut at the UN General Assembly in New York in September 1985, Garcia claimed that Latin America faced a choice of 'debt or democracy'. He said: 'The foreign debt can never be paid off by any of our countries because the effort to service it on time will keep our democracies trapped in misery and violence.'[4]

Garcia's government has consistently rejected IMF-inspired economic adjustment policies. Instead, Peru has launched its own economic recovery programme of price freezes to reduce inflation and wage increases, temporary income support to stimulate demand, guaranteed prices and subsidized credit to promote agricultural growth, and interest rate cuts and protectionist measures to bolster industrial production. This programme led to economic growth of almost 9 per cent in 1986.

But the Western-dominated international financial institutions have hit back at Peru. In September 1986 the IMF declared Peru 'ineligible' for further loans after failing to clear its arrears with them. In 1987 the World Bank suspended disbursements to Peru. Concerted efforts have been made to stifle Peru's trading opportunities with the developed countries, and the resulting failure to increase exports led to a severe slump in foreign exchange earnings in 1987 and 1988. With inflation rising again, Peru's economic difficulties are, once more, very severe.

As for the markets of Third World products, these are again primarily in the Western world. The colonial structure of African, Latin American, and South Asian economies especially has ignored the opportunities of trade with immediate neighbours — and sharpened the North—South and South—North flows of trade instead.

Then there is the whole dialectic of global production. While the genius of socialism may indeed be distribution, it is capitalism which has demonstrated a genius for production. No system in human history has shown a greater capacity for economic expansion than capitalism.

One result is that the West produces far more of what the Third World 'needs' than does the Soviet bloc. And the quality of Western products is usually superior to comparably priced products from the Eastern world. Western civilian technology tends to be more sophisticated — and Western mass production and unit-cost efficiency ensures more competitive prices in commercial sales to the Third World.

Also relevant as part of the explanation for the Western impact on Third World development is the role of foreign aid and international charity. Charity has often been capitalism's classical answer to problems of maldistribution. In the history of capitalism within the Western world itself, charity has sometimes been capitalism's gesture of penance to the Christian conscience. In more pragmatic terms, charity has sought to diffuse not only the suffering of the poor but also their *anger*. Within the class structure of a capitalist society charity has also been a strategy of cooptation and of consolidating allegiance. The poor are made more loyal — and their leaders could respond to the lure of upward social mobility.

Of the four major reasons for extending foreign aid (charity, solidarity, cooptation, and self-interest), the West operates on all four, depending upon the particular case. The Scandinavian countries and the Netherlands score high on aid for reasons of pure charity. So do the many private humanitarian groups from the Christian world generally. The Soviet bloc has no comparable private effort in aid and humanitarianism.[5] For one thing, Soviet official atheism has eliminated missionary church organizations which might otherwise have operated in the Third World. Nor must it be forgotten that the focus of Western missionary work has shifted from saving souls for the Hereafter to saving lives in the here-and-now. There has been a shift from a focus on salvation to an emphasis on service.

The Soviet system also lacks such private secular charities as the Ford and Rockefeller Foundations and such crisis-oriented organizations as OXFAM and other famine relief bodies. Nor is the Soviet tax system geared towards providing tax incentives for those who want to be charitable. The system does not even acknowledge that it has millionaires of its own.

Then there is the Soviet Union's policy posture that underdevelopment in the Third World was caused by Western imperialism — and has to be corrected by Western compensation. It is indeed true that most of the flaws in African, Latin American and South Asian economies especially are directly due to the whole legacy of Western imperialism. These flaws include such economic distortions as undue emphasis on cash crops, a leaning towards monoculturalism, the North–South orientation, the urban bias in development, and the elite bias in priorities. Third World problems of balance of payments, balance of trade, unstable export earnings and the accumulation of debts are substantially derived from those underlying colonial causes.[6] The Soviet Union feels that it is not up to the socialist countries to bail out the West in the face of these post-colonial responsibilities. Nor do the socialist countries have the capacity — even if they had the will — to amend the international system in favour of the dispossessed. The West is in charge of the global economy.

Nor does the Soviet Union have the equivalent of the Western world's private investment in developing countries. By definition the Soviet system has no multinational corporations to balance out the activities of Western entrepreneurs. This whole area of Western private initiative in the Third World has no mirror-image in the Soviet experience.

Finally, there is the persistent Soviet belief that conditions of underdevelopment are fertile ground for a social revolution. Karl Marx himself argued that it was development — rather than underdevelopment — which created a revolutionary situation. It was because of this thesis that Marx expected the first socialist revolutions to occur in such advanced capitalist countries of his era as England and France. But Soviet policy makers today know better — partly from the experience of their own revolution of 1917 but also from the history of Third World recruits to the ranks of the socialist community. Contrary to Marx, it is the weakest not the strongest links of the capitalist chain which have been prone to breaking after all.

In the light of these ideological calculations, the Soviet Union can be forgiven for regarding underdevelopment in the Third World as at worst a mixed curse. If underdevelopment is a potential breeding grund for revolution, Soviet intervention in favour of development may turn out to be a thrust *against* revolution.

Which comes first — development or revolution? Karl Marx thought development came first in each epoch. In the light of the historical experience of the Soviet Union since 1917, Soviet policy makers have been tempted to reverse the order — revolution as the mother of development rather than its offspring. The history of other socialist states, such as China since 1949 and Cuba from 1959, confirms that under-development encourages revolution.

It is against this background that although socialism is ultimately an ethic of distribution, the Union of Soviet Socialist Republics is not a major practitioner of that ethic in its relations with the Third World.

The Superpowers and Liberation

On the other hand, the United States is doctrinally liberal — and liberalism is an ethic of the redistribution of *political* power in favour of the marginalized.

And yet the United States — though a child of revolution late in the eighteenth century — has become the father of imperialism late in the twentieth. Why? In a sense, America was once revolutionary and has now become imperialist for the same reason. And the reason is because the American founding fathers were right in their distrust of concentrated power. Because those founding fathers distrusted such political concentration within the body politic, they ensured decentralization at home. They worked out a system of checks and balances, a doctrine of separation of powers, a principle of separating church from state, a whole constitutional apparatus of federal division of authority between the local and the national levels, and an economic ideology insulating government from the economy, an ideology of unrestrained capitalism which led to massive economic growth.

But the same America which distrusted concentrated power domestically acquired it internationally. The concentration of economic power made the United States exploitative of other societies abroad. The concentration of military power made America overly sensitive to strategic calculations — sometimes at the expense of the independence and territory of small countries elsewhere.

The most disastrous strategic miscalculation was the American military involvement in Vietnam. The miscalculation cost the United States fifty thousand lives and Vietnam more than a million and a half. But American administrations — unlike the American Congress — have refused to learn the full lessons of the catastrophe of Vietnam. The latest strategic experiment is Reagan's policy in Central America — another case of abuse of military might. Fortunately, the constitutional checks and balances of the founding fathers domestically have helped to restrain even the international intervention of Uncle Sam in Central America — at least for the time being.

Two factors influenced President Reagan's policy towards Central America: his confusion of Nicaraguan socialism with Communism and his consequent fear of Nicaragua becoming a Communist state, and, second, his fear of Nicaraguan aid helping left-wing guerrillas to seize power in El Salvador and Guatemala. In 1981 Reagan's administration backed the earliest military operations of the 'Contras', guerrilla rebels opposed to the socialist policies of Nicaragua's Sandinista government. The Contras were then an alliance of liberal democrats who had defected from the Sandinista coalition and extreme right-wing supporters of ex-President Somoza. By 1984 the liberals in the Contra movement, led by Eden Pastora, had effectively abandoned the rebellion, but the Reagan administration continued to support the Contras. In 1984 the United States became involved in direct running of operations by the Contras on the Nicaragua—Honduras border and by government troops against guerrillas in El Salvador. The United States developed a whole new network of bases in Honduras, with 5,000 US troops, to train and assist the Contras. US naval patrols appeared on Nicaragua's Pacific and Atlantic coasts. The CIA mined Nicaragua's ports. Nicaragua, in turn, began to draw heavily on Cuban and Soviet logistical support. Soviet-supplied helicopter gunships in particular began to turn the war against the Contras firmly in the Sandinistas' favour. And in November 1984 the Sandinistas strengthened their position by winning decisively the first free elections held in Nicaragua for fifty years.

Reagan's response to the strengthening of the Sandinistas' position was to impose a total embargo on trade between the United States and Nicaragua (April 1985) and to increase military aid to the Contras.

How did the US Congress react to its president's war in Central America? Even such a renowned right-winger as Senator Barry Goldwater condemned the mining of the ports (April 1984) as 'an act violating international law' and the Speaker of the House of Representatives, 'Tip' O'Neill, called it 'an act of barbarism'. The Senate condemned the operation by 84 votes to 12, and the House did so by 281 votes to 111. In June 1984 the Senate knocked 21 million dollars off the aid to the Contras. In April 1985 both Houses of Congress, shocked by Contra atrocities, blocked the president's plan for further massive aid to them. On 26 June 1986, the House of Representatives did finally, and narrowly, approve Reagan's request for 100 million dollars in aid to the Contras. Two days later, however, the International Court of Justice in the Hague upheld Nicaragua's suit against the United States, ruling that the latter had violated international law by training, equipping, and financing the Contras and by mining Nicaragua's harbours.

It was the Central Americans themselves who took the decisive step towards peace in their region. This was the Arias Plan, as it came to be known, drawn up by President Oscar Arias of Costa Rica and approved by five Central American presidents in August 1987. The Arias Plan provided for ceasefires in Nicaragua, El Salvador, and Guatemala, an end to foreign military aid, arms reduction, and democratization (political dialogue between governments and unarmed opposition groups, and elections). In October 1987 Arias was awarded the Nobel Peace Prize.

The US Congress made it easier for the Arias Plan to work by cutting off all US aid to the Contras in February 1988. The checks and balances of the US Constitution were working smoothly at this stage.

Behind the latest exercises in Central America is a whole history of the growth of the United States into an imperialist power. It did indeed begin with the expansion of the domestic base itself. To that extent the growth of the Soviet Union into a superpower has a lot in common with the growth of the United States into the same rank. Both countries needed to extend their territorial size earlier in their histories before they could acquire superpower credentials by the second half of the twentieth century.

The czars did most of the territorial expansion before the October Revolution of 1917. Russia conquered one principality after another — across two continents. By the time the October Revolution occurred, Russian sovereignty extended across a territory larger than any assembled in the Old World since the Roman Empire.

Soviet Communism's own expansionist thrust has since added to that territorial vastness — as the Baltic states and World War II acquisitions have been absorbed into the body politic of the Soviet Union itself.

The United States' own territorial expansion reveals a similar sense of 'Manifest Destiny'. Sometimes it took the form of 'buying' territory — including of course its inhabitants, without their consent. The purchases of Louisiana from France and Alaska from Russia were not simply transactions in real estate; they were also purchases of people, without regard for their preference.

Then there was the United States' war with Mexico — one of the earliest confrontations with post-colonial Latin America. Again American territorial appetite and imperial self-aggrandizement sought new levels of satisfaction. Areas like California and New Mexico were forever absorbed into the body politic of the United States.

Texas was yet another large territory. A Trojan horse strategy of annexation served the United States well. In time, the Lone Star became part of the American Union — destined to become one of the richest of the member-states, as well as the largest territory after Alaska within the union.

The beginning of superpower ethics is *sheer size* — for without a basic massive size, there can be no superpower status. Both the Soviet Union and the United States were served well by the older territorial ambitions in their respective histories.

The United States had also a relatively modest intermediate role as a colonialist power — in the sense of ruling other societies without incorporating them into the body politic. American rule in the Philippines was, in a sense, the most important of the United States' colonialist experiments. Residual roles of that kind include Puerto Rico, the American Virgin Islands, and a number of other oceanic 'territories' and 'possessions' currently under the American flag.

It was not until after World War II that the United States entered the stage of global imperialism, becoming a sort of global sheriff. Yes, America — the incarnation of liberal decentralization of power at the domestic level — became the incarnation of the most concentrated international power in history. The United States embodied power far greater than the strength of Rome at its most glorious, greater than the leverage of England at its most imperial.

There must have been occasions when the American founding fathers turned in their graves — as they witnessed their child grow into dangerous might. If they were in communication with Lord Acton, all of them together might have jointly reaffirmed: 'Yes, power does corrupt. Absolute power is in danger of corrupting absolutely.' The United States had lost its credentials of revolution — and acquired the fangs of imperialism.

The Moral Paradigms of the Superpowers

But if power has corrupted the United States, has it also corrupted the Soviet Union? If the United States is a bad influence on Third World liberation, why is not the Soviet Union a similarly adverse influence on developing countries?

Needless to say, the Soviet Union has also been corrupted by power. But in the case of the USSR it is not the Third World which is primarily paying the price. Somebody else is doing so.

What has happened is that the Soviet Union is an imperialist power in Europe, a liberating force in Africa and Latin America, and a power with a mixed record in Asia. In Europe the USSR has been heir to both the tsarist and the Nazi empires. What the tsars incorporated into the Russian Empire, the communists retained. What the Nazis had subjugated in World War II, the Russian liberators retained under a new Communist rule. It is in this sense that the Soviet Union has inherited the mantle from both the tsars and the Nazis. It is in this sense that the Soviet Union is an imperial power within Europe.

On the other hand, the Soviet Union has been a liberating force in Africa and Latin America. Southern Africa especially has been a major beneficiary of the military help of Communist countries. Without that help the liberation of Southern Africa — from the Portuguese Empire to Rhodesia — would have been delayed by at least a generation. The Communist world's hardware for Southern African liberation fighters has ranged from the sten gun to the surface-to-air missile. There seems little doubt that the emancipation of Namibia and the Republic of South Africa itself will also have to rely disproportionately on the military favours of the Communist world. This already includes the unique role of Cuban troops in consolidating such liberated areas as Angola.

As for the Soviet role in the liberation of Latin America, the Cuban model is of course a special case. Ideally, Cuba should have been the Western hemisphere's Yugoslavia — a nation which has successfully escaped from the regional superpower without having to sell too much of its sovereignty to the opposite camp. When all is said and done, perhaps Cuba is indeed another Yugoslavia — but forced by the United States to be more dependent on the Soviet Union than Fidel Castro would have preferred.

In recompense, Cuba is more of a revolutionary catalyst in the Western hemisphere than Yugoslavia has proved to be a catalyst of dissent in the Soviet bloc. Cuba is more activist in the West than Yugoslavia has been in the Russian empire. To that extent, Cuba has been a greater force for Latin American liberation from the United States than Yugoslavia has been for Eastern European liberation from the Soviet Union.

The latest confrontations with American imperialism are of course in Central America — especially in Nicaragua, where pro-Cuban forces are in power, and in El Salvador, where pro-Castro forces are in rebellion against a pro-American regime. Grenada in the Caribbean under Maurice Bishop was a case of pro-Cuban forces in power, and so was Michael Manley's Jamaica. Behind all the elements is the basic superpower rivalry. On balance, the Soviet Union has been as liberating a force in Latin America as it has been in Africa, though the manifestations of the struggle have been dramatically different.

It is in Asia that the Soviet role is at its most ambiguous — neither decidedly imperialist as it is in Europe, nor convincingly liberating as it has been in Africa and Latin America. Soviet hardware support for Vietnam helped Hanoi defeat the United States and its allies in the struggle for controlling South Vietnam. The Soviet factor has continued to be a major pillar for the independence of a unified

Vietnam in the face of a basically hostile international environment.

On the other hand, Soviet support for Hanoi has indirectly subsidized Vietnam's occupation of Kampuchea — a negation of the latter's independence. But the most imperialist Soviet action in Asia in the last quarter of the twentieth century was the Soviet invasion of Afghanistan in 1979 and its aftermath. A superpower violated the sovereignty and territorial integrity of one of its small neighbours.

But when all is said and done, the Soviet Union has, on the whole, been an ally of decolonization in the Third World — in spite of the glaring exception of Afghanistan. The Soviet role as a champion of decolonization has been aided by the following factors in recent world history.

First, imperialism in much of Asia and Africa in the nineteenth and twentieth centuries arrived with Western capitalism. In reality capitalist imperialism is only one form of foreign domination — but for most people of Asia and Africa it is the most pervasive form of alien exploitation that they have experienced. Third World resentment of imperialism generally has therefore spilled over into a resentment of capitalism.

Because of this link between Western private enterprise and Western colonization, there has evolved a link between nationalism and socialism in the Third World. Since socialism is the enemy of capitalism, and nationalism the adversary of imperialism, and given that capitalism and imperialism were linked in the first instance, it stands to reason that nationalism and socialism should in turn also enter into an alliance.

Soviet policy towards the Third World has also gained from V. I. Lenin's impact on ideologies and political theorizing in the developing regions — ranging from Kwame Nkrumah's book, *Neo-Colonialism: The Last Stage of Imperialism*, to Latin American theories of *dependencia*. In other words, the Third World's favourable ideological predisposition towards the Soviet Union was greatly aided by the prior popularity of aspects of Leninist thought.

Soviet motivation for supporting Third World liberation has been strengthened by the apparent Soviet grand design to make significant inroads into the lives and politics of post-colonial societies. Supporting decolonization in Western-dominated areas is one way of winning friends and influencing people in the post-colonial era.

Soviet need for foreign exchange is another powerful motive for Soviet sales of armaments to Third World liberation movements and to post-colonial leftist governments. Pure military aid from the Soviet Union is, from all appearances, more the exception than the rule. Southern African liberation movements have often to raise funds from elsewhere (often from Western private sympathizers) in order to be able to buy military hardware from the Soviet Union and other socialist countries. Some arms have been supplied on credit by the Soviets. On balance, ideological solidarity has not had to clash with commercial self-interest from the Soviet perspective.

But that need not mean that the Soviet Union is hypocritical. Even among hardened Soviet policy makers there may remain a sincere conviction that human destiny is ultimately in the hands of the dispossessed — and the masses of Asia, Africa, and Latin America are the majority of the dispossessed of the world. Soviet support for Third World causes cannot but be affected by that wider ethical concern.

Yet the contradiction persists. The *socialist* superpower is the champion of the *liberal* cause of freedom and self-determination, with minimum participation in the more socialist mission of global economic redistribution. In global politics the United States has been more of an economic determinist than the USSR, while the Soviet Union has been more of a liberator.

We have so far focused on political liberation and economic redistribution as two ethical themes between the Third World and the superpowers. But what about the ethics of military security? It is to this third area of moral concern that we must now turn.

The Superpowers and the Ethics of Violence

Both superpowers regard Third World states as fair markets for the sale of conventional armaments — subject to wider political allegiances. The United States' sales are more subject to domestic restraint within the United States than the Soviet sales are within the USSR. For example, the pro-Israeli lobby in Washington has considerable say as to which arms are sold to which Middle Eastern governments.

But while American arms are more subject to private political lobbies at home, Soviet arms are more available to private political movements abroad. Certainly the liberation of Southern Africa would have been delayed by at least a generation if Soviet arms were not available for sale to such movements as ZANLA in colonial Rhodesia and MPLA in colonial Angola.

Yet both superpowers are particularly hypocritical in the field of militarism and the ethics of political violence. And within this military domain two areas are particularly subject to double moral standards — terrorism and nuclear weapons. Let us take up each of these themes in turn.

The first factor to note about terrorism is that it is just another form of warfare — no worse than conventional or nuclear war, and considerably less destructive in scale. Some may argue that terrorism leaves civilians particularly vulnerable. But that is a peculiarity of virtually all forms of warfare in the twentieth century. No one on the side of the Allies worried about how many German civilians were killed in Dresden or Berlin as the two cities were pulverized in the closing stages of World War II. As Thomas C. Schelling once put it, 'in the Second World War non-combatants were deliberately chosen as targets by both Axis and Allied forces.'[7] Harry Truman did not lose much sleep about Japanese civilians when he ordered that atomic bombs be dropped on Hiroshima and Nagasaki. And what sane person genuinely worries about civilian casualties and at the same time arms himself for a nuclear confrontation — as the United States and the Soviet Union are constantly doing? Civilian casualties ceased to be a major worry of twentieth century warfare decades ago. It is an anachronism to proclaim the concern only in the case of terrorism — which kills far fewer civilians than conventional warfare of this era. Compared with nuclear catastrophe, terrorist casualties are less than a drop in an ocean of blood.

Non-governmental terrorism is normally the warfare of the weak. The other side of Lord Acton's coin is that *powerlessness, too, corrupts and absolute powerlessness can corrupt completely.* After all, who took the Palestinians seriously before they became a terrorist nuisance? Not even their fellow Arabs treated them as much more than refugees. The world was prepared to continue treating them as just another refugee problem. It took their own call to arms to make them a constant item on the world's agenda. 'Lest we forget; lest we forget!'

111

More protected from moral scrutiny is state terrorism. Israeli reprisal raids are often a case of counter-terrorism — as insensitive to the lives of innocent civilians and often far more destructive. The anti-personnel cluster bombs that Israel used in its 1982 invasion of Lebanon were a particularly brutal response to Palestinian pinpricks.[8]

The United States also reportedly used cluster bombs in the attack on Benghazi, Libya, in April 1988. President Ronald Reagan had previously asserted that he would have no truck with killers of children. Yet American bombs dropped from the air do kill children as readily as terrorist bombs left at an airport.

Similar state terrorism has been committed by the Soviet Union in Afghanistan. Whole villages have sometimes been wiped out as retaliation against the Afghan *mujahiddeen*. Bombardment of so-called terrorist-infested areas has often been as indifferent to innocent casualties as was Menachem Begin's adventure into Lebanon in 1982.

Apart from direct state terrorism, there is state-supported terrorism by private movements. Both Libya and the United States subsidize movements of violence which often resort to terrorist methods. The Congress has voted funds in support of the Contras in Nicaragua and Jonas Savimbi's United Front for the Liberation of Angola (UNITA). Neither the Contras nor UNITA are morally fastidious about their methods of struggle. Contras place bombs in civilian buses and UNITA places mines near villages — decimating life and limb indiscriminately.

Libya also has subsidized movements of violence — ranging from the Irish Republican Army (IRA) to radical Palestinians, from Basque separatists in Spain to dissident movements in some black African countries. In supporting 'rebel' movements within the Western world itself (like the IRA and the Basques), Libya has helped to teach the West a version of the Christian Golden Rule: 'Do not do unto others what you would not that they do unto you'!

The fourth category of terrorism (after non-governmental terrorism, state terrorism, and state-supported terrorism) is state-tolerated terrorism. The United States has been quite lenient to members of the Irish Republican Army on the run from British justice on charges of terrorist murder and other 'atrocities'. Until 1986 it was extremely difficult for Britain to get suspects extradited from the United States. Both the judges and the Irish lobby on Capitol Hill continue to favour this particular class of 'terrorists' as candidates for asylum.

France also has been a haven of Basque separatists for a long time. From time to time Paris makes an isolated gesture to Madrid by extraditing a terrorist suspect. But this is rare. And yet there is far less disapproval in Washington of French 'protection' of European 'terrorists' than of her granting refuge to Middle Eastern ones.

The Republic of Ireland (Eire) has had a major dilemma about what to do with the Irish Republican Army (Provisionals). Most of the time Dublin tolerates terrorists rather than hunt them down — though Dublin has genuinely agonized over the dilemma.

It is against this background that the politics of international terrorism reveal such a profound moral duplicity. Double standards are at work — and the super-powers and their allies are often at the heart of that duplicity.

Even more fundamental is the duplicity of nuclear ethics. The whole ethos of the Nuclear Weapons Non-Proliferation Treaty (NPT) was based on a principle of *nuclear monopoly*. Those who had the weapons were insufficiently motivated to give them up; those who did not have them were to be decidedly discouraged from acquiring them. A nuclear caste-system was sanctified — a division of the world between nuclear Brahmins and nuclear untouchables. A kind of technological imperialism was in the making. Military nuclear technology is still regarded as something not for Africans, Asians, and children under sixteen.

More sophisticated defenders of the doctrine of the nuclear deterrent have argued that human societies have a right to take risks — even nuclear risks. But risks on whose behalf? Does country *X* have a right to risk the survival of countries *A, B, C,* and *D*? Does either the United States or the Soviet Union have a right to risk the lives of Indians, Nigerians, Swiss and Mexicans? Does anybody short of a world-wide referendum have a right to risk the survival of the human species itself?

In the absence of a global human referendum on nuclear weapons, there may be a case for extending the nuclear franchise itself — for breaking the nuclear monopoly. The extension of the nuclear franchise will require deliberate nuclear proliferation — upward nuclear mobility for the global untouchables. This would be an expansion of the ranks of nuclear Brahmins. One purpose of nuclear pro-liferation horizontally is simply to alarm the superpowers into recognizing that the nuclear world is getting too dangerous and that speedy action needs to be taken towards universal nuclear disarmament.

Of course, horizontal nuclear proliferation has its risks; but are those risks really more dangerous than the risks of vertical proliferation in the arsenals of the superpowers themselves?

Moreover, the underlying ethical priorities are different. The Soviet Union and the United States are risking human survival for the sake of national freedom. But would it not make better moral sense to risk national freedom for the sake of the survival of the human race?

We are beginning to be alarmed by accidents in civilian uses of nuclear energy — like those at Chernobyl in the Soviet Union and at Three-Mile Island in the United States. Perhaps we need also to be alarmed into constructive action by the spectre of horizontal nuclear proliferation in the Third World. Perhaps until now the major powers have worried only about 'the wrong weapons in the right hands', deadly devices in *stable* hands. This has not been alarming enough to force the major powers into genuine disarmament.

When nuclear devices pass into Arab or black African hands, a new nightmare will have arrived — 'the wrong weapons in the wrong hands' — deadly weapons held by *unstable* hands. Perhaps that culture shock, that consternation, will at last create the necessary political will among the great powers to move towards genuine universal nuclear disarmament.

Conclusion

The one thing the Third World remembers very distinctly is that empires do not last forever. The lifespan of my own country's founding father, Jomo Kenyatta, testifies to that. When he was born, Kenya was not yet a British crown colony. Suppose that when the British first arrived, we East Africans and the British had the nuclear bomb. Suppose we said: 'Rather than be colonized, we shall fight a nuclear war which will destroy the population of Kenya — and our neighbours at the same time.'

Fortunately we did not have a nuclear arsenal with which to defend our freedom. It just so happened that Jomo Kenyatta lived right through the colonial period — and survived British rule for fifteen years, ruling Kenya himself. Today Kenyatta's children and grandchildren are alive and well. Our lack of a nuclear deterrent at the end of the last century denied us the option of nuclear self-destruction as a defence against foreign colonization.

Suppose the Soviet Union today conquered the whole world. How long would such a vast empire last? 'Backward' Afghanistan alone has been keeping thousands of Soviet troops busy and to some extent even scared since 1979. Even if all countries were reduced to little Afghanistans — or indeed to Polands — would that really be worse than a nuclear winter? Asia and Africa know only too graphically that empires do not last forever.

Out in the infinite cosmos we live on an island called Earth. A British poet once affirmed: 'No man is an island entire unto itself. And therefore never send to know for whom the bell tolls; it tolls for thee.'

John Donne has acquired a supreme relevance in the nuclear age. No man is an island — *but every man lives on one*. There is no other island we know in the cosmic sea. Believe me, there are no *two* islands to justify the ethics of dualism. In the face of our cosmic isolation, we must end the dualism — and concentrate on our human singularity. Even a liberal who insists 'give me freedom or give me death' must surely realize that he cannot decide for the rest of the human species. For liberals there must surely be one imperative more important than freedom, for socialists one principle more fundamental than economic justice. The two ethical worlds can have no human meaning unless they jointly agree on one thing — that the survival of the human species is a precondition for both freedom and economic justice.

Bibliography

Aronson, Jonathan D. (ed.), *Debt and the Less Developed Countries* (Boulder, Colorado: Westview Press, 1979).

Blackburn, Peter, 'Nigeria: The Year of the IMF', *Africa Report*, Vol. 31, No. 6 (Nov./Dec. 1986), pp. 18—20.

Bull, Hedley, and Adam Watson (eds), *The Expansion of International Society* (Oxford: Clarendon Press, 1984).

Campbell, Kurt M., *Soviet Policy Towards South Africa* (New York: St Martin's Press, 1986).

Chauhan, S. K., *Who Puts Water in the Taps? Community Participation in Third World Drinking Water, Sanitation and Health* (London: Earthscan, 1983).

Chomsky, Noam, *The Fateful Triangle: The United States, Israel and the Palestinians* (Boston: South End Press, 1983).

Chuta E., and S.V. Setheraman (eds), *Rural Small-Scale Industries and Employment in Africa and Asia: A Review of Programmes and Policies* (Geneva: International Labour Office, 1984).

Coates, Redmon, *Come as You Are: The Peace Corps Story* (New York: Harcourt Brace Jovanovich, 1986).

Fanon, Frantz, *The Wretched of the Earth* (New York: Grove Press, 1983).

Kennan, George F., 'The Only Way Out of a Nuclear Nightmare', *Manchester Guardian Weekly*, 31 May 1981.

Khan, Khushi M., *Multinationals of the South* (New York: St Martin's Press, 1986).

Khan, Sadruddin Aga, *Nuclear War, Nuclear Proliferation and Their Consequences* (Oxford: Clarendon Press, 1986).

Mazrui, Ali A., *The African Condition: A Political Diagnosis* (New York: Cambridge University Press, 1980).

Mazrui, Ali A., *The Africans: A Triple Heritage* (New York: Little, Brown, 1986).

Netanyahu, Benjamin, *Terrorism: How the West Can Win* (New York: Farrar, Straus, Giroux, 1986).

Nye, Joseph S., Jr., *Nuclear Ethics* (New York: The Free Press, 1986).

Onwuka, Ralph I., and Olajide Aluko, *The Future of Africa and the New International Economic Order* (New York: St Martin's Press, 1986).

Payer, Cheryl, *The Debt Trap: The International Monetary Fund and the Third World* (New York: Monthly Review, 1974).

Schelling, Thomas C., *Arms and Influence* (Westport, Connecticut: Greenwood, 1966), 1976 ed.

Spector, Leonard S., *Nuclear Proliferation Today* (New York: Vintage, 1984).

Survey: A Journal of East and West Studies (London).

Ungar, Sanford J., *Estrangement: America and the World* (New York: Oxford University Press, 1985).

Weiss, T.G., and A. Jennings, *More for the Least: Prospects for Poorest Countries in the Eighties* (Lexington, Massachussetts: Lexington Books, 1983).

Wionczek, M. S., *Some Key Issues for the World Periphery: Selected Essays* (Oxford: Pergamon, 1982).

Wood, Robert E., 'The Debt Crisis in North—South Relations', *Third World Quarterly*, Vol. 6, No. 3 (July 1984), pp. 703—716.

115

6

America
& the Third World

A Dialogue
of the Deaf

The first thesis of this chapter is that Americans are brilliant communicators but bad listeners. Out of this follows a second thesis. Because Americans can communicate effectively, humanity is becoming Americanized to some extent. Conversely, because Americans are bad listeners, their external relations are refusing to be humanized. In other words, the world is becoming Americanized culturally, but America is refusing to be humanized morally. Let us explore these propositions more fully.

The Iranian Revolution was an excellent illustration of this one-way traffic. It was as if American culture had switched on the amplifiers and loudspeakers towards Iran while Uncle Sam switched off his own hearing aid and turned a deaf ear to Islam. Iran was becoming Americanized and Westernized, but under protest. Uncle Sam did not hear the protest until it was too late.

We shall return to the issue of Islam and American foreign policy, but first let us examine the nature of American effectiveness in communication before we examine Uncle Sam's deaf ear.

Six Languages of American Policy

The means of communication at the disposal of the United States have to be distinguished from the actual messages transmitted. The United States uses a number of different languages in communicating with the world. One is the language of production. Because the American economy is the largest in the world, the United States can use producer power as a medium of protest or disapprobation. This is what President Jimmy Carter did when he imposed an embargo on grain sales to the Soviet Union over the issue of the Soviet invasion of Afghanistan. The moral message of such an embargo was neutralized when the United States invaded Grenada four years later (1983) and intimidated Nicaragua (see Chapter 5). Once again the United States was thorough in communicating its own message of disapproval to the Soviet Union, but Uncle Sam fell far short of attentiveness in listening to the moral implications of US disapproval of the Soviet invasion of a small neighbour.

Another medium available to the United States for international communication is the language of the consumer. Because the United States is, for a wide range of goods, the largest market in the world, Uncle Sam has considerable consumer power. When Idi Amin was in power in Uganda, the United States was sufficiently aroused morally to impose an embargo on the purchase of Ugandan coffee. But successive US governments have consistently refused to impose economic sanctions on the Republic of South Africa, a tyrannical system of far longer duration than the dictatorship of Idi Amin. Once again Uncle Sam was loud and clear in acting against a black tyrant, but seemed to be turning a deaf ear to demands for action against a white tyrant in Africa.

The third form of language available to the United States is the language of currency rather than goods, liquidity rather than commodity. Uncle Sam has immense power over the World Bank, the International Monetary Fund, and the commercial banks of the Western world more generally. Because the Reagan administration has not really been listening attentively to the groans of the world's poor, the budget of the International Development Association has had to sustain a cut. The IDA often helps the poorest of the poor. Reducing its effectiveness is a singular instance of insensitivity. The purse power is being used against the destitute.

On the other hand, the United States has been known to authorize a large loan to the Republic of South Africa while resenting a loan to one of the world's largest concentrations of poor people, India. Once again the purse power is used as a medium of communicating American ideological messages while remaining supremely insensitive to the moral messages of the rest of the world.

The fourth form of language available to Uncle Sam is skill power, which relates to the genius of American technology. On the whole this language has been used more against the Second World (advanced socialist countries) than against the Third World (developing countries). Poland under martial law and the Soviet Union's gas pipeline, as well as periodic embargoes on the export of electronic technology, have been among the examples of technological sanctions by the United States.

With regard to the Third World, the United States tends to impose an embargo on the export of nuclear technology. A conspiracy of nuclear silence has been decided upon. In this case the United States has decided not to communicate with the Third World, although this silence is itself a loud vote of no confidence.

In the face of this conspiracy of nuclear secrecy, Pakistan, for one, seems to have embarked on a strategy of industrial espionage. The world cannot be divided between nuclear Brahmins and non-nuclear untouchables. Nuclear disarmament has to be universal or it is not tenable for long. The United States is busy proclaiming the message of nuclear monopoly by those who are already there, but Uncle Sam is not listening to the grievances of the nuclear have-nots. The United States does not even seem to be aware that a nuclear caste-system of the kind we have is intrinsically unstable. Nuclear proliferation cannot be stopped for much longer, if superpower nuclear disarmament is not achieved soon. Is Uncle Sam listening at all?

We have in fact already made the transition from skill power to weapon power. The latter is yet another language available to the United States. Central America — especially Nicaragua — is the latest arena where the United States has been flexing its military muscles as a mode of militant communication. Again Uncle Sam seems to be turning a deaf ear to the search for autonomy and social justice in the Third World. All that Uncle Sam is seeking to communicate is his own , predictable anti-Sovietism and anti-Castroism, while he switches off the hearing aid on Third World concerns.

The sixth language available to the United States is of course the English language — the most widely understood tongue in human history. English does not, of course, have the largest number of speakers in the world — Chinese outperforms English in number of individual speakers.

It was Great Britain, as we have seen, which helped to decide how many countries of the world adopted English as the main language of national business. But it is now mainly the United States which helps to decide how many more individuals choose to learn the English language. Once again the United States is better at using the available English language for transmitting the American message to the rest of the world than at using the language to listen to the whispers of the rest of humanity.

If the medium is the message, it is certainly difficult to disentangle American means of communication from American messages. We should at least attempt to be more explicit about some of the messages that the United States has been trying to communicate to the rest of the world.

Messages from America

One competing claim is between American capitalism and American democracy. On the whole, the United States has been much more successful in transmitting capitalism than in transmitting democracy. Capitalism is the doctrine of competitive economics, resulting in market forces. Liberal democracy is the doctrine of competitive politics, resulting in political pluralism.

The Carter administration decided to place emphasis on the export of liberal democracy, hence the special premium Carter put on human rights as an aspect of foreign policy. The Reagan administration has emphasized the export of capitalism, with a special premium on private enterprise and fair prices for farmers in American foreign policy.

When the United States consistently emphasizes the sanctity of human rights, that is probably good news for humanity. It could mean that US foreign policy is beginning to be humanized. When the United States stresses the sanctity of the profit motive, however, that is probably bad news for humanity, for it means the Americanization of the human race rather than the humanization of America.

When the United States genuinely tries to promote human rights, there is less American consolidation of repressive regimes in the Third World, though even Carter was insensitive to the oppressiveness of the Shah of Iran. When the United States is out to consolidate capitalism in the world, however, democracy and social justice are seldom priorities in Uncle Sam's calculations. Uncle Sam's hearing aid to the world is more firmly switched off when the main mission is exporting American capitalism than when the main goal is the spread of American democracy.

Capitalism and liberal democracy have not been the only messages that the US communication infrastructure has attempted to transmit to the rest of the world. Less deliberate but even more effective has been the transmission of American life-styles to the four corners of the globe. It is to these aspects that we must now turn.

In the Third World, the competition is partly within the Western tradition itself, with two forces struggling for international advantage. The rivalry is between ancestral European culture and American cultural revisionism. Western Europe and the United States are in the grip of cultural competition for the soul of the Third World.

In terms of formal dress, Western Europe is winning. Indeed the European suit has become the most compelling symbol of Western cultural supremacy in the world. Every man has two dress cultures — his own and Western (the Western man has the two traditions fused into one). No one regards a Japanese in a Western suit, or an Arab in a Western tie, as a cultural incongruity. It is only when we see a Japanese in Arab regalia, or an Arab in Japanese dress, that we are shocked. The European suit, especially, has become truly universalized.

But in terms of casual dress, the picture is very different. The American genius for casual attire is prevailing. Casual bush shirts, t-shirts, denim jackets and trousers, and the like are capturing the imagination of the Third World. Time and again I receive requests from Africa for jeans and t-shirts as special gifts, especially from the new generation of Africans. African youth yearn for American jeans as Christmas gifts.

What is more, American tourists are helping to informalize the dress rules of tourist hotels and restaurants throughout the world. I have known restaurants which in European colonial days used to insist on jacket and tie for dinner, relax the rule in order to attract American tourists in the post-colonial era.

On the issue of food, the American genius is in fast food — while Western Europe continues to prevail in formal cuisine and formal dinner in the Western tradition. The hamburger revolution has begun to penetrate Africa. Some African cities already have at least one Kentucky Fried Chicken and one American-style pizzeria. American impatience and preoccupation with speed are part of this triumph of quick food. 'Let's cruise, baby! Time is up!' When you do not have time to spare, eat American! But when you have a whole evening for indulgence, by all means eat French!

Then there is the rivalry of drinks between Western Europe and the United States. At least in the Third World, Europe still rules supreme in alcoholic drinks. French wine, Scotch whisky, and Czech and German beer are truly triumphant. Their American equivalents are decidedly poor seconds or thirds in popularity.

But where America has communicated effectively is in the field of soft drinks. I personally was selling Coca-Cola at the Mombasa Institute of Muslim Education in Kenya back in the 1950s. There is no real European equivalent to either Coke or Pepsi. We have been witnessing the coca-colanization of the world, symbolic of a much wider process of the Americanization of humanity.

Another field of competition is the printed word. In the world of fiction and art, Europe is still triumphant. In the field of science and society, however, the United States has been establishing a lead. Great American novels and plays are almost unknown in, say, Africa. But in the natural sciences, the applied sciences, and the social sciences, the American impact is clear and unmistakable.

At the more popular level, there is the triumph of American news magazines — especially *Time* and *Newsweek*. This triumph extends to imitation. Several news magazines about the Third World based in London were modelled on *Time* and *Newsweek* in format. These American magazines have become the most imitated in the history of journalism.

On the other hand, American newspapers have less influence among African and Asian elites than do European newspapers. There are a number of reasons for this. First, American newspapers are less national even in their own countries than are European papers at home. Second, the best American papers (like the *New York Times* and the *Washington Post*) are much more bulky and difficult to export than are their European equivalents. Third, American newspapers have a reputation for being more insular and parochial in their news coverage than are their European counterparts. Fourth, a high proportion of Asian and African students studying in, say, Britain are more likely to be reading *The Times* or *The Guardian* regularly than their counterparts studying in the United States are likely to be reading the *New York Times* or the *Washington Post*. British papers cost the same all over Britain. *Le Monde* costs the same all over France. But the *New York Times* is too expensive for students in most of 'these United States'. The presumptive Third World elites studying in the United States are therefore less likely to cultivate a taste for American newspapers than are their equivalents in Britain and France for British or French national newspapers, a taste which can become an abiding interest.

In the field of education in Asia and Africa, the American impact is greater on the tertiary level (colleges and universities) than on the secondary and primary levels. In English-speaking Africa the American idea of semester-long courses is beginning to catch on. Term papers are beginning to count towards the final grade, instead of the grade being based entirely on the final examination. And the American title of Associate Professor has replaced the old British rank of Reader in most former British colonies.

In music, the American impact is restricted to the popular variety of Western sounds, while Europeans continue to lead in classical Western strands. Michael Jackson has already become a world figure and not just an American legend. Third World lovers of Western classical music, on the other hand, are unlikely to know much about either American composers or American performers in this field.

In technology the United States is particularly victorious. Both American varieties of domesticated technology and American successes in high technology have exerted considerable influence on the rest of the world. American home gadgets — from dishwashers to air conditioners — have become part of the elite life-style of the world. And American experience in space and satellite, and indeed in civil aviation, have given the United States an edge in the competition for advanced technology in the global market-place.

In the field of computers the United States seems to be ahead of parts of Europe. The rest of the world, apart from Japan, is only just beginning to be computerized, and American salesmen appear to be stealing a march over the Europeans.

In film and television the United States continues to maintain high international visibility in spite of the decline of Hollywood. American soap operas like *Dynasty* and *Dallas* have wide audiences from Mombasa to Munich, from Singapore to San Juan (*any* San Juan!). Asians, Africans, and Latin Americans await next week's exploits of J.R. in *Dallas* with great interest. But J.R. himself epitomizes America — for J.R. is a great communicator but a bad listener!

American television programmes feature on the screens of the world, but the world's television programmes seldom feature on American screens, except on the highly specialized channels of what Americans call 'public' broadcasting. By the measurement of number of viewers, these are the least public of the channels except for those purveying pornography!

American high art in painting is much more obscure than European high culture of the brush. In much of the world, names like Rembrandt, Michelangelo and Picasso have no American equivalents.

120

On the other hand, is there a European equivalent of Walt Disney? American genius is revealed more starkly in cartoons than in an art gallery. Once again the United States is Europe's follower in the high art of painting, but the United States is absolute leader in the popular art of cartoon.

In most areas of life, American genius lies in the popular art form rather than the elite speciality, in mass involvement rather than aristocratic cultivation. As we indicated, American jazz is better known than classical music, American news magazines better known than novels, American casual dress more appreciated than European formal dress, American fast food more admired than formal cuisine, American soft drinks more toasted than American alcoholic beverages, American soap operas more appreciated than American television documentaries, and so on down the line. Alexis de Tocqueville would feel abundantly vindicated. After all, America was the West's first mass democracy. Why should its popular culture not be its main claim to global immortality?

The only flaw in the argument is that America is insensitive to the popular culture of the rest of the world. This collective genius of popular communication is retarded as a collective listener. The world has learned to dance to the music of the United States. But America has yet to listen to the concert of the world.

What are the underlying forces behind this paradox of the American condition? Why is America effective as a communicator but inattentive as a listener? Why is the world getting Americanized while America is refusing to be humanized?

Part of the answer lies in a third paradox. American democracy was born out of religious toleration coupled with racial intolerance. It is to this third paradox that we must now turn.

Religious Freedom and Racial Bigotry

While it is indeed true that the Pilgrim Fathers turned out to be greater zealots than the religious persecutors they had escaped from in Europe, the longer term trend in American history has indeed been towards greater religious toleration. By the time the American constitution was being drawn up, the United States was already ahead of Europe in seeking to divorce the state from the church. The new constitution dissuaded its legislature from making laws which would infringe on freedom of worship or enhance the political status of one denomination over others. The secular state in Western history was at hand.

That same America which was learning to be more religiously tolerant than Europe was at the same time learning to be less racially tolerant than Europe. In one way, Europe had locked America into precisely that racial situation. It was Europe's trans-Atlantic slave trade, destined for its American colonies, which had set the stage for racism in the Western hemisphere.

By the time America was engaged in creating a non-religious state, it had lost its capacity for creating a non-racial society. The principle of 'separate but equal' was a licence for a racist society; the principle of 'separating church from state' was a confirmation of a secular state. It was a contest between God and genes. American democracy sought to keep God out of politics but to retain genes within the political process. American democracy was both more secular and less racial than its European counterparts.

American democracy itself was born out of at least two forces: American secularism and the American frontier. Secularism taught Americans the virtues of tolerance and the frontier taught them the virtues of individualism. Liberal democracy in America is a fusion of social toleration and rugged individualism. Social toleration was an extension of secularism, rugged individualism an extension of the frontier. American political culture may indeed rest on this basic duality across time and space.

Among American political figures Abraham Lincoln continues to be widely regarded as a symbol of Christian compassion and democratic sensibilities. His religious piety turned him against slavery, but Lincoln's racial prejudices turned him also against anything approaching equality between whites and blacks. Abraham Lincoln was himself a dramatic fusion of America's spiritual vision and racial blinkers, of America's religious virtue and ethnic vice. In that very contradiction Lincoln was once again a symbol of his country's torment.

In his speech on 18 September 1858, in Charleston, Illinois, Abraham Lincoln made it abundantly clear that he was for emancipating 'the Negro' but not for embracing him. Lincoln said 'yes' to Negro freedom but 'No' to Negro equality:

> I do not understand that because I do not want a negro woman for a slave I must necessarily want her for a wife [cheers and laughter]. . . . I will to the very last stand by the law of this state, which forbids the marrying of white people with negroes. . . . I will say then that I am not, nor ever have been, in favour of bringing about in any way the social and political equality of the white and black races [applause] — that I am not nor ever have been in favour of making voters or jurors of negroes; nor of qualifying them to hold office, nor to intermarry with white people.[1]

The American dilemma continues to be the contradiction between high moral purpose and racial prejudice, between democratic ideals and ethnic exclusivity. The dilemma has been part of America's incapacity to respond to the wider world, part of the phenomenon of Uncle Sam's deaf ear.

If America is religiously liberal but racially bigoted, how does the contradiction manifest itself in foreign policy? An answer might be sought in comparing a country with which mainstream America shares religion with another with which it shares race.

In reality there are no neat examples, but from a black point of view, a comparison between the status of Liberia and the status of Israel in American foreign policy can be moderately suggestive. With the Liberian political and social establishment, mainstream America shares the Christian religion but differs in race. With the Ashkenazim Israeli political and social establishment, mainstream America shares a European ancestry but differs in religion. It can be argued that Israel is closer to America racially than religiously; arguably also, Liberia is closer to America religiously than racially. Which type of closeness to America counts for more? In short, is religion or race the salient issue in American foreign policy?

Comparing Israel with Liberia

At one level the comparison of Liberia and Israel is simplistic. Are the Jews really a race or are they a multiracial religious community? We know that Hitler regarded the Jews as a race — with appalling consequences. Surely Hitler was hardly the best judge on either racial or religious issues.

Shakespeare before Hitler also regarded the Jews as, in part, a race. Shakespeare gave Shylock racial as well as religious traits. And yet more important is whether the Jews themselves in the twentieth century regard themselves as a race. Do Israelis regard themselves as racially superior to their Arab neighbours?

The evidence is very inconclusive. If the Jews were indeed a race, they at least contradict the assumption that race is the same thing as colour. The Jews are, at the most, a multi-pigmented race, a rainbow race. The range is from black Jews, the Falasha of Africa, and brown Jews, the Sephardim of Asia and North Africa, to white Jews, the Ashkenazim of Europe. Historical studies suggest that the Jews were, in ancient times, a mixture of peoples of various ethnic origins united by a common religion, Judaism, and that in the Jewish diaspora over the past two thousand years, the Jews have intermixed with local peoples wherever they settled. Arthur Koestler, in his book *The Thirteenth Tribe* (1976), even went as far as to claim that many of the Jews of eastern Europe were descended from the Khazars, a people of Turkish stock, who became converted to Judaism in about AD 740. Most of the evidence indicates that the Jews are a *people*, not a *race*.

From the point of view of this essay, it is not the facts about Israelis which matter; it is the image of Israel in the United States. It is arguable that the only Jews that white America has directly known are white Jews. Do the great majority of Americans assume that all Jews are white? That is more than just possible and may be a factor in white America's favourable attitude to Israel.

It is because of these considerations that one litmus test of the contrast between the racial factor and the religious factor in US foreign policy may lie in a comparison between US policy towards Israel and US policy towards Liberia.

Liberia was a child of the aftermath of slavery, a resettlement of some of the survivors of the Trans-Atlantic slave trade. Israel was a child of the aftermath of the Nazi holocaust, a resettlement of the survivors of European persecution and gas chambers.

Liberia was born out of the spirit of black Zionism, a hunger for a return to the ancestral Holy Land. Liberia is, in part, inhabited by descendants of those who were emancipated from Western slavery. Israel is partially inhabited by those who were emancipated from Western racism.

Liberia was for more than a century regarded as black Africa's only republic. Israel has for less than half a century been regarded as the Middle East's only liberal democracy.

The American conscience has reluctantly been bothered about Liberia. After all, the first rulers of Africa's 'first republic' were themselves ex-slaves liberated from American bondage. Even Abraham Lincoln was convinced that blacks and whites did not really 'belong' to the same Republic, and he supported the American Colonization Society in its efforts to repatriate blacks back to Africa. Lincoln argued:

> I will say in addition to this that there is a physical difference between the white and the black races which I believe will forever forbid the two races living together on terms of social and political equality.[2]

Lincoln was saying this after the creation of Liberia in his own lifetime and after its independence. American conscience over the Jewish condition under the Nazis was less direct than American conscience over Americo-Liberians had been, or should have been, a century earlier.

Why is it then that in less than 60 years the United States has spent many times more dollars on the state of Israel than the United States has spent on the Republic of Liberia in more than 140 years of Liberia's independence?

The answer cannot be because Israel is a longer-standing obligation! Liberia as an American obligation is more than a century older than Israel as an American duty.

The answer to the disproportion in American generosity cannot be because Israel has been more hospitable to American private investment than Liberia. On the contrary, we know that American investment in Liberian rubber and partial American investment in Liberian ore is greater than any American investment *in proportion* in Israeli industry.

The answer to the disproportion in American generosity between Israel and Liberia could not really be because of comparative proximity to the American system of government. Until the Master Sergeant Doe revolution in Liberia as recently as the 1980s, Liberia's problem was that it was too much of an imitation of the American political system, an aping of the American ethos. Liberia was imitating the United States a whole century before Israel was even born. Liberia was a vanguard of American republicanism in the 'dark continent'.

Surely the answer to the disproportion in American generosity towards Israel and Liberia could not lie in the fact that a close American alliance with Liberia was likely to be more damaging to American interests in Africa than a close American alliance with Israel could be to American concerns in the Middle East. Quite the contrary. US links with Liberia have been regionally cost-free whereas the links between the United States and Israel militarily have always included an element of uncertainty and risk with regard to American interests in the Arab world.

Certainly the answer to the comparative disproportion in American generosity towards Israel and Liberia could not be that Israel was necessarily closer to the United States linguistically than Liberia. It is true that English is virtually the second language of Israel. But English is the first language of Liberia's business.

The rationale for the difference in generosity towards Israel and Liberia cannot be because Israel is already more closely integrated with the American economy than is Liberia. The role of Firestone Rubber in Liberia is only one aspect. While the Israelis have been debating whether or not to dollarize their own currency, Liberia's only currency is the US dollar. That may seem generous enough on the part of the United States. And yet there is no Liberian equivalent for the present US–Israeli plans to integrate their economies much more deeply within the coming decade. From an economic point of view Liberia is out in the cold while Israel is being beckoned further into the US economy.

Why then has this difference in generosity persisted? Two residual reasons remain as to why the United States continues to pour billions of dollars into Israel and contributes only a pittance to Liberia. One factor is strategy, and the other is race. The first is the fact that US strategic interests in the Middle East are much more important than in West Africa. On the other hand, the United States has always had client Arab states in the region and has never given them the scale of economic support given to Israel even before Arab petro-wealth. Second, United States uncritical support for Israel has sometimes endangered rather than protected its vital interests in the region. Third, American strategic interests in the Middle East are less vital than those of the NATO allies in Western Europe who depend even more on Middle East oil and on trade east of Suez. Yet Western Europe has turned an ear to the Middle East which has been less deaf than Uncle Sam's. Western Europe has been prepared to entertain the idea of an independent Palestinian state under certain conditions, while the United States remains part of the Rejectionist Front on that issue, alongside Israel itself and Libya.[3]

The mystery persists. Could the issue of race be at all relevant? Is it at least conceivable that white Americans feel closer to Israelis than they do to Liberians because when all is said and done, Israel is European-led while Liberians are totally black? Could it also be that the lobbying group in defence of Israel's interests in America are overwhelmingly white and influential while the lobbying groups for African countries like Liberia are either non-existent or black, with little influence?

Is it conceivable that, when all is said and done, racial solidarity between the ruling establishments of Israel and America is more politically salient than religious solidarity has been between the rulers of Liberia and Uncle Sam for the last hundred and forty years?

The Marshall Plan and the Hiroshima Legacy

This is part of a wider pattern in American history. The most generous things white Americans have done have been to fellow white people. The meanest things white Americans have done have been to non-whites. American generosity reached its apex with the Marshall Plan. American meanness has ranged from genocide against native Americans to the dropping of the atomic bombs on Hiroshima and Nagasaki, from lynching 'Niggers' to the war in Vietnam.

Strictly confining the argument to the twentieth century, Hiroshima, Nagasaki, and Vietnam amount to the worst episodes in American policy. The victims were Asians. The most glorious episode in American policy this century was Marshall Aid. The beneficiaries were Europeans.

Race-consciousness in the United States has sometimes affected American strategists' choice of military guinea-pigs, the nuclear and chemical victims of American strategy. Race-consciousness has also affected America's choice of the white economic beneficiaries of the Marshall Plan.

Harry S. Truman was the American president who presided over both the dropping of the bombs on Hiroshima and Nagasaki and the launching of the Marshall Plan. It was in June 1947 that General George Marshall, Secretary of State, proposed a European Recovery Plan which came to play a fundamental role in the rejuvenation and reconstruction of a Europe devastated by World War II.

The United States spent nearly 20 billion dollars as part of the European reconstruction. Would the United States Congress ever vote for anything near such sums of money, bearing in mind the alteration in the value of the dollar today, to rescue non-white societies? Africa in the 1990s needs a rescue operation at least the size of the Marshall Plan. Yet in 1983 the United States forced the International Development Association of the World Bank to cut down its budget for the poorest of the poor, rather than increase it.

And was the Israeli assault on Beirut in 1982 an Arab equivalent of Hiroshima, another experimental ground for new American weapons? In the words of an American reporter, 'The arsenal of weapons, unleashed in a way that has not been seen since the Vietnam war, clearly horrified those who saw the results first hand. . . . The use of cluster bombs and white phosphorous shells, a vicious weapon, was widespread.'[4]

Bombs were dropped over Chatila and Boirj el Brajneh, 'bombs never previously seen over such heavily residential districts, projectiles that streaked from the aircraft and exploded at 50 foot intervals in the skies in clouds of smoke, apparently spraying smaller bombs in a wider arc around.'[5]

Once again Israel becomes one of the meeting points between the honourable American legacy of the Marshall Plan and the dishonourable American legacy of Hiroshima. The Jewish state has become the *de facto* continuation of the Marshall Programme. Like Western Europe, the Jews were devastated by the horrors of Nazism and World War II. The United States has already spent more on the State of Israel than it spent on the whole of the entire Marshall Programme. American foreign aid to Israel has become the perpetual Marshall Plan.

No one outside the Arab world would begrudge the Jewish state such sums — but for the stark contrast between support for Israel and Uncle Sam's lack of interest in either domestic blacks or the wider world of non-whites. While the Reagan administration has been cutting down support for welfare programmes with black beneficiaries within the United States, the same administration has been increasing support for a Jewish community outside the United States. A foreign country with a population of less than four million has been getting more of Uncle Sam's attention than an American minority of 30 million people.

Does Uncle Sam want to hear any of this? Is the issue of racism still 'radical nonsense' in some American circles? Is a critical examination of Israel one of the most taboo of all subjects in New York? In short, is Uncle Sam about to switch off his hearing aid once again to avoid unpleasant subjects? Some forms of censorship try to prevent unwelcome opinions from being uttered. Uncle Sam has perfected a special censorship of his own to prevent himself from hearing world voices which would make him uncomfortable. Some are born deaf, some become deaf, and others inflict deafness upon themselves.

On Marx and Muhammad

The messages that the United States has been least prepared to listen to are those of Marxism, on one side, and Islam, on the other. In the Third World the Marxist opposition to the United States concerns the issue of America's economic imperialism; Islam's reservations about the United States concern the issue of America's cultural imperialism. Third World Marxists do not want their economies to be controlled or exploited by the West. Third World Muslims do not want their culture to be 'prostituted' by the West. To Third World Marxists, Marx is pitched against Uncle Sam in a struggle for economic resources. To Third World Muslims, Muhammad confronts Uncle Sam in a struggle for human salvation.

If you put on Uncle Sam's spectacles, the two struggles may appear different. The struggle against Marxism is strategic and religious. The struggle against Islam is racial and religious. The struggle against Marxism is an East—West divide; the struggle against 'Islamic fundamentalism' is a North—South divide. The struggle against Marxism is primarily a civil war of white against white. The struggle against 'Islamic fundamentalism' is a racial war of white against non-white.

In other words, Uncle Sam sees all manifestations of Marxism in the Third World as being mere extensions of America's confrontation with the Soviet Union, East against West and white against white. There is an assumption of sanity and stability in East—West relations, but an assumption of fanaticism and instability in relations with the world of Islam.

Islam is basically an Afro-Asian religion. Virtually all Muslim countries are either African or Asian. To that extent Islam is a religion of non-white people. Indeed, that is precisely why Islam has sometimes fascinated black Americans, from Malcolm X to the boxer Muhammad Ali. From the white side, the crusade against Islamic fundamentalism is partly a struggle against the forces of non-white assertiveness and challenge.

Uncle Sam refuses to hear that Marxism in the Third World, far from being an extension of East—West tensions, is in fact a manifestation of North—South unease. People in the Southern hemisphere go Marxist not because they are anti-Christian or even anti-capitalist but because they are primarily anti-imperialist. Scratch a Third World Marxist and you will find a Third World nationalist. The ultimate hostility is not to capitalism as a method of production but to imperialism as a method of domination. Certainly in Africa, the local bourgeoisie are much less threatening than American workers. The cleavages are not really between classes nationally but between power blocs internationally. Third World Marxists are anti-American more because America is a world power controlling their economies than because America has a capitalist mode of production.

America has to be similarly discriminating in listening to messages from the world of Islam. Clearly the Iranian revolution was not anti-Christian but anti-Western. The chief focus of hostility was not against the Vatican but against Washington, not against .the crucifix but against the star-spangled banner. The Iranian emotions were religious, but the target was secular. This was no ancient crusade involving Saladin and Richard the Lion Heart. It was a modern crusade involving the muezzin from the minaret and the disc jockey, involving the Ayatollah and the pop singer.

In a curious way, Marxism and Islam have been in alliance in trying to prevent the Americanization of the world, but they have parted company in any effort to humanize America. Marxism has attempted to prevent further American penetration into the world economy by raising the clarion call of resistance by the workers and the underprivileged. Islam has tried to rally resistance to America's cultural imperialism by citing the vision of Third World authenticity and cultural dignity.

Marxism and Islam have made more progress in preventing the Americanization of humanity than in fostering the humanization of America. No one has yet found out how to operate Uncle Sam's hearing aid.

Conclusion

This chapter started with the thesis that Americans were brilliant communicators but bad listeners. We moved on to the related thesis that the world is closer to the Americanization of humanity than to the humanization of America. These theses are somewhat exaggerated, but there is enough in them to demand Uncle Sam's attentiveness.

We have used the image of Uncle Sam's hearing aid to emphasize the issue of volition in communication. Hearing aids can be switched on or off, worn or not worn. In the case of the United States it has been a case of readiness to listen or not. We have put forward the proposition that in the twentieth century America has been much more prepared to proclaim than to respond, much more prepared to articulate than to listen.

We have put forward part of the explanation. The United States has been religiously liberal but racially bigoted. This has affected American reaction to Marxism and Islam as Uncle Sam's biggest challenges. What should be remembered is that Uncle Sam regards Marxism as an East—West divide involving relations between white and white, while Islam emerges as a North—South confrontation between whites and non-whites.

Underlying it all is the continuing tension between religion and race in the complex and tormented nature of the American soul. *Quo vadis*, America? We hear you, America! Do you hear us?

Notes

1. See Benjamin Quartes, *Lincoln and the Negro* (New York, 1962), and Louis Ruchames (ed.), *Racial Thought in America: From the Puritans to Abraham Lincoln* (New York: The Universal Library, Grosset and Dunlap, 1969), pp. 380—382. Cf. Lerone Bennett, Jr., 'Was Abe Lincoln a White Supremacist?' *Ebony*, February 198 , pp. 35—42, and Herbert Mitgang, 'Was Lincoln Just a Honkie?' *The New York Times Magazine*, 11 February 1968, pp. 35, 100—107.
2. See Louis Ruchames, *Racial Thought in America*, p. 381.
3. For a stimulating new definition of 'Rejectionism' consult Noam Chomsky, *The Fateful Triangle: The United States, Israel and the Palestinians* (Boston: South End Press, 1983), especially pp. 39—53.
4. Charles Power, *Los Angeles Times*, 29 August 1982.
5. Robert Fisk, *The Times* (London), 31 August 1982.

7

On Race
& Performance

Negritude &
the Talmudic Tradition

'Emotion is black — reason is Greek!' This quotation from Leopold Senghor has become one of the central epigrams of negritude. Senghor has argued that the genius of Africa is not in the realm of intellectual abstraction; it is in the domain of emotive sensibility.

As we shall indicate later, some of the assumptions of negritude underlie the whole Black Studies movement in the United States. We shall pay special attention to Black Studies as an effort to intellectualize negritude. But precisely because Black Studies has a major intellectual component in its *raison d'être*, it diverges from Senghor's dictum.

When under attack Senghor reformulates his views on this dictum. His interpretation of original Africa has sometimes exposed him to the charge of having deprived the traditional African of the gift of rationality. Senghor defends himself with his usual ingenuity. But ultimately he still insists on regarding the African as basically intuitive, rather than analytical. He has said:

> Young people have criticized me for reducing Negro-African knowledge to pure emotion, for denying that there is an African 'reason'. . . . I should like to explain myself once again. . . . European reasoning is analytical, discursive by utilization; Negro-African reasoning is intuitive by participation.[1]

Elsewhere Senghor emphasizes that this 'analytic and discursive reason' was part of the Graeco-Roman heritage of Europe at large. 'One could even trace the descent of Marxism from Aristotle!' Senghor asserts.

Descartes had asserted that the ultimate proof that I exist is that I *think*. In his own famous words, 'I think, therefore I am.' According to Senghor, however, African epistemology starts from a different basic postulate. For the black African the world exists by the fact of its reflection upon his emotive self. 'He does not realize that he thinks; he feels that he feels, he feels his *existence*, he feels himself.'[2] In short, black-African epistemology starts from the premise, 'I *feel*, therefore I am.'

What about the genius of the Jews? If emotion is black and reason is Greek, the secret of the Jewish miracle in history is the fusion of emotion with reason. The Talmudic tradition is at the heart of this miracle.

To a certain extent the Talmudic tradition is a fusion of religion, ethnicity, and intellectual pursuits. Through the Talmudic tradition the national consciousness of the Jewish people was both intellectualized and sacralized.

The Black Studies movement in the United States, weak and uncertain as it is, was also born out of the national consciousness of a people. Like the Talmudic tradition, the Black Studies movement also seeks to intellectualize the national consciousness of its people. But among the questions which remain is whether Black Studies is also an effort to sacralize black identity. Is 'blackness' in the United States evolving into a religious as well as a racial experience? In that regard is blackness ever likely to become a neat equivalent of Jewishness, combining sacred and ethnic symbols of identification?

For the time being only members of the Nation of Islam, the Black Muslims of America, have attempted to combine religious with ethnic modes of identification in a manner reminiscent of the Jews. But while Judaism over the centuries has emphasized the nearness of Jews to God, the Nation of Islam tended for a while to emphasize the distance of whites from God.

Judaism was autocentric, emphasizing the self in the face of a hostile environment. The Nation of Islam was for a while eco-centric, emphasizing the hostility of the (white) environment even more than the self. The Nation of Islam was more preoccupied with denouncing the racial 'gentiles', the white people, than with praising the black people. To the Nation of Islam it was more fundamental that whites be exposed as devils than that blacks be accepted as the chosen people. For a while the dominant emotion among black Muslims was anger against the enemy rather than pride in one's self.

But the Nation of Islam has been changing. The challenge which came from Malcolm X before he broke off from the movement was a major stage in this evolution of the black religion. After going on a pilgrimage to Mecca and discovering how multiracial Islam abroad was, Malcolm was no longer convinced that white people were irredeemably devils. He was shifting the emphasis away from hostility against whites to pride in one's self. Shortly afterwards Malcolm was assassinated.

In 1975 Elijah Muhammed, the leader of the Nation of Islam, himself died of natural causes. The shift from eco-centrism (in rebellion against the environment) to autocentrism (inspired by self-confidence) has continued in the movement. To that extent the similarity with at least early Judaism has become somewhat greater, including a number of rituals affecting diet and sexual behaviour.

What has been lacking in the Nation of Islam is a vigorous intellectual tradition, in spite of the relative success of some of their religious publications.

On the one hand, America has witnessed the Black Studies movement as an effort to intellectualize blackness. On the other hand, the Nation of Islam has emerged as an effort to sacralize blackness. What is missing is a viable movement which combines both intellectual and religious strengths. If the Talmudic tradition is a fusion of religion, ethnicity, and analytical power, there is as yet no black equivalent. There is as yet no pooling of resources between the Black Studies movement as an intellectual effort and the Nation of Islam as a religious endeavour in black America. Only a combination of the strengths of the two movements could produce a black equivalent to a tradition which takes pride in the history of the Jews, seeks to understand and analyze the heritage of codified morality, studies the implications of covenant with sacred origins, finds solace and strength in the collective martyrdom of its members over the centuries, and constantly reexamines the historic role of its people in human affairs generally.

How relevant has the Talmudic tradition been for Jewish specialization in intellectual pursuits? How do Jews compare with blacks in such pursuits?

Black Brain, Jewish Intellect

Comparisons of intellectual performance between races and ethnocultural groups have been part of the history of racism itself. Yet there is little doubt that in the modern period of his history the black man has been scientifically marginal, in the sense of being on the outer periphery of scientific and technological achievement.

By contrast the Jewish impact on the intellectual heritage of mankind has been immense. The great Jewish figures who have influenced the evolution of ideas and morals ranged from Jesus Christ to Karl Marx. The ethical component of modern civilization includes a disproportionate contribution from the ideas of Jewish thinkers and prophets. Even if we restricted ourselves to recent times, it is possible to argue that of the five people who have done the most to determine the shape of the modern mind, three are Jews. The five names are those of Isaac Newton, Charles Darwin, Karl Marx, Sigmund Freud and Albert Einstein. Of these five only Newton and Darwin were non-Jewish by descent, although Newton may have been converted secretly to Maimonide Judaism. This is in fact one of the most remarkable things about Jewish history — the Jewish propensity for producing intellectual geniuses. To the present day a disproportionate number of the towering figures in the academic world in the United States are Jews.

What explanation can be advanced for this remarkable intellectual phenomenon? Do the Jews bring into question the old debate about genetic differences in intelligence between one race and another? If we claim that all races are endowed with an equal distribution of intelligence, how then can we explain the Jewish miracle? If we used the number of towering minds as a measure of distribution of intelligence in a given race, and we concluded that the Jews were extra-endowed with intellectual gifts, would not the same reasoning force us to conclude that the blacks were deficient in such gifts? Is Jewish mental superiority the ultimate proof of black inferiority?

The debate is not as antiquated as it might at first sound. Arguments about genetic differences in relation to intelligence have re-entered academic discussions in the Western world.

One memorable day when I was still at Makerere University in Uganda my secretary buzzed my telephone to announce a long distance call from Durban in South Africa. 'Durban?' I asked in surprise, as I had no special connections there. When the call was put through it turned out to be an editor of a South African magazine. The editor wanted me to review a particular book. Considering the trouble he took to make a rather expensive long distance call, I became curious about the whole assignment. The book he referred to was one by a man called Barnett Potter. The title of the book was *The Fault, Black Man*, a phrase adapted from Shakespeare's *Julius Caesar*. 'The fault, dear Brutus, is not in our stars, But in ourselves, that we are underlings.' The South African editor said that the book had created a stir in southern Africa, and he wanted me to write a rebuttal. The central assertion of the book was 'The fault, black man, is not in your stars but in yourself that you are an underling.' The argument was that the black man had been ruled and dominated by others not because of bad luck but because of something inherently within himself. I agreed to write the rebutting review of the book, and arrangements were made for me to receive it from London.

The book itself did not pretend to be scholarly or even sophisticated, but the white man who had written it used the evidence of greater scholars than he could pretend to be. He used in part Arthur Jensen's article in the *Harvard Educational Review* asserting that research among American schoolchildren had indicated that blacks performed less well than whites intellectually for reasons which were partly genetic. Jensen's article had reactivated a long-standing debate concerning the question of whether races differed genetically in intellectual competence.[3]

Barnett Potter linked the findings of Jensen's research to the tribute paid to the Jewish community by C. P. Snow, the British physicist and novelist. C. P. Snow had drawn attention to the remarkable achievements of the Jews in the sciences and the arts. A crude measure like examining the names of Nobel Prize winners would indicate that up to a quarter of those winners bore Jewish names. Why should a population of little more than 15 million Jewish people in the world produce one quarter of the best scientific and scholarly performance in a world of approximately 3,000 million people?

> Or is there something in the Jewish gene-pool which produces talent on quite a different scale from, say, the Anglo-Saxon gene-pool? I am prepared to believe that may be so. . . . One would like to know more about the Jewish gene-pools. In various places — certainly in Eastern Europe — it must have stayed pretty undiluted, or unaltered for hundreds of years.[4]

Lord Snow did not seem aware of the partial contradiction of his statement. The Jews who performed particularly impressively in recent times, and won Nobel Prizes, were not in fact primarily from Eastern Europe where Snow regarded the Jewish gene-pool to be particularly pure and 'unaltered for hundreds of years'. On the contrary, the best Jewish intellectual achievements in recent times have been overwhelmingly from Western Jews, in many ways the least pure in 'gene-pool' among all the Jews of the world.

Whatever the partial contradiction in C. P. Snow's analysis, there is indeed a phenomenon to be explained in the Jewish intellectual edge in Western history. Barnett Potter, as a white gentile, used the Jewish intellectual edge as proof that blacks were genetically inferior. But he too fell short of the logic of his own position. If Jewish intellects in the Western world itself have performed disproportionately in relation to white gentiles, are we also to conclude that white gentiles are genetically inferior intellectually to their Jewish neighbours? Certainly Barnett Potter would regard that conclusion as too high a price to pay for the comfort of proving that the fate of the black man was not in his stars but in his genes.

From the Talmud to Negritude

What could be the explanation both for the Jewish intellectual edge and for the black scientific marginality?

This is perhaps where the Talmudic tradition claims some degree of relevance. Over a period of time a people that was governed by codified laws and a covenant began to put a special premium on analytical, judicial, and speculative skills. A structure of motivation evolved among Jews which conferred social rewards on intellectual performance. This was inevitably accompanied by processes and structures of socialization which exposed a significant proportion of children to analytical and abstract aspects of Jewish culture.

Among the Jews in the Diaspora a reinforcing factor may have been some prior intellectual selection at the time of Jewish dispersal two millennia ago. Was the composition of the Jews who went into exile abroad disproportionately intellectual? C. D. Darlington has argued as follows in connection with one important part of the dispersal:

> The Jews who moved into the Western parts of the Persian Empire were . . . a highly selected remnant. . . . They were a group of skilled and partly intellectual classes differing from all other such classes in two vital respects. First, they were largely cut off from intermarriage with the other classes of the societies in which they lived. And, secondly, they were entirely liberated from the control of their own former military governing class. The Jewish intellectuals were thus free.[5]

Darlington suggests that a disproportionate number of intellectuals among those who fled from Palestine, combined with relatively strict endogamy, helped to maintain and accumulate a gene-pool of intellectual excellence.

This issue is also connected with the whole question of the relationship between professional specialization and intellectual performance. Partly because many alternative avenues of professional life were closed to Jews in Europe, the community began to specialize in commerce and later the liberal professions. The cumulative effect of specialization provided not a Darwinian natural selection, but a specialized cultural selection. Succeeding generations of Jewish intellectuals produced in turn children who were intellectually oriented. Specialization could provide the opportunity for the discovery of brilliance.

Also related as a factor is the whole tradition of Jewish prophets and of rules which are not only observed but continually enunciated and often intellectualized.

It might also be fortunate that Judaism does not demand celibacy of its rabbis. Had Jewish priests been expected to be celibate as Catholic priests, the Jewish intellectual contribution to world civilization might well have been significantly reduced. It has been estimated that many of the most impressive Jewish scholars have been sons or grandsons of rabbis. The tradition of the prophets has again helped to consolidate prior intellectual specialization.

With regard to black scientific marginality, there have been a number of different responses to the phenomenon. Among some black people, one response has been to deny that they have been scientifically marginal. Those who react in this way among black people then proceed to mention a number of famous black names in the intellectual history of the world. These would range from Aleksandr Pushkin, 'the father of Russian literature', to Alexandre Dumas, the French literary romantic. Both had the blood of black people in their ancestry, and many black men have taken pride in that.

The tendency to deny that there has been a black scientific marginality has been specially manifest among black Americans. It might well be that the precise nature of their humiliation from the slave days has created a resolve among their cultural nationalists to affirm black greatness in history.[6]

This kind of response is not unknown among black Africans either. In Ghana, while it was still under the presidency of Kwame Nkrumah, a number of postcards were issued with paintings depicting major achievements that had taken place in Africa. These included a painting with figures in the attire of ancient Egypt, showing the first paper to have been manufactured. The caption was 'Ancient African History: Paper was Originated in Africa'. Then there is a painting of 'Tyro,

African Secretary to Cicero, [who] Originated Shorthand Writing in 63 BC'. Then there are cards asserting that the science of chemistry originated in Africa, that Africans taught the Greeks mathematics and the alphabet. According to these postcards reproduced from 'the Archive of Accra, Ghana', many other scientific inventions also originated in Africa. The Ghanaian postcards under Nkrumah were in a way in the tradition of black American cultural assertiveness, but transposed to the African continent.[7]

An alternative response to black scientific marginality is not only to affirm it but also to take pride in it. Black countries ruled by France produced a whole movement called negritude, which revelled in the virtues of a non-technical civilization. In the words of the poet Aimé Césaire:

> Hooray for those who never invented anything
> Who never explored anything
> Who never discovered anything!
> Hooray for joy, hooray for love
> Hooray for the pain of incarnate tears.
> My négritude is no tower and no cathedral. . . .[8]

Clearly this response to scientific marginality is fundamentally different from the tendency to trace a black ancestry in the genealogy of Robert Browning, or of Pushkin or Alexandre Dumas.

The Black Studies movement in the United States has been influenced by both forms of response to black marginality. On the one hand, the movement asserts that too much distortion has taken place in the study of black history as a result of the white man's scholarship. Black contributions to world civilization have therefore been grossly underestimated. Only a Black Studies movement, controlled by blacks, can help to restore this balance.

On the other hand, the Black Studies movement has also been influenced by negritude with its emphasis on black cultural distinctiveness rather than black intellectual competitiveness. Let us now turn more fully to this linkage between the logic of negritude and the assumptions of the Black Studies movement.

Negritude and Negrology

It is with French-speaking Africa and with Martinique that the word 'négritude' is normally associated. And it is among French-speaking blacks at large that negritude as a movement has found its literary proponents. The term itself was to all intents and purposes virtually coined by Aimé Césaire, the poet of Martinique, as he affirmed:

> My négritude is no tower and no cathedral
> It dives into the red flesh of the soil.[9]

Césaire's poem was first published in a Parisian review in 1939. In Africa itself the movement's most distinguished literary proponent came to be Leopold Senghor, the poet-president of Senegal. It has been Senghor who has helped to give shape and definition to negritude as a general philosophical outlook. In his own words,

> Négritude is the whole complex of civilized values — cultural, economic, social and political — which characterize the black peoples or, more precisely, the Negro-African world. All these values are essentially informed by intuitive reason. . . . The sense of communion, the gift of

myth-making, the gift of rhythm, such are the essential elements of négritude, which you will find indelibly stamped on all the works and activities of the black man.[10]

Senghor's definition as given here, though illuminating, is not in fact complete. Negritude is not merely a description of the norms of traditional black Africa; it is also a capacity to be proud of those values even in the very process of abandoning them. Sometimes it is a determination to prevent too rapid an erosion of the traditional structure.

Whether we take Senghor's own definition, or give it greater precision, it is clear that a believer in negritude need not be a French-speaking literary figure. 'Negritude is the awareness, defence and development of African cultural values,' Senghor has said elsewhere.[11] Such awareness, defence, and development need not, of course, take the form of a poem in French. To limit the notion of negritude to a literary movement is to miss what the literary outburst has in common with other forms of black cultural revivalism. The word 'negritude' might indeed owe its origin to a literary figure, but the phenomenon which it purports to describe has more diverse manifestations. In any case the term negritude is too useful to be allowed to die with a literary movement.

Not that a romantic literary preoccupation with an idealized Africa is likely to come to an end all that soon. There will be black poems of such a romantic bias for at least another generation. What need to be defined now with a wider vision are the boundaries of the phenomenon as a whole.

If negritude is indeed 'the awareness, defence and development of African values', we could usefully divide it into two broad categories. We might designate one category as literary and the other as anthropological negritude. Literary negritude would include not only creative literature but also certain approaches in African historiography. An African historian who succumbs to methodological romanticism in his study of ancient African empires like Songhai and Mali is, in this sense, within the stream of literary negritude.

Anthropological negritude is on the whole more directly related to concrete cultural behaviour than literary negritude normally is. In its most literal form anthropological negritude is a romanticized study of an African 'tribal community' by an African ethnologist. The book *Facing Mount Kenya* by Jomo Kenyatta even on its own would have been enough to make young Kenyatta a proponent of anthropological negritude.

But there is more to this side of negritude than a formal study of a 'tribe'. There is a link between, say, Elijah Masinde, the prophet of *Dini ya Msambwa* in East Africa, and Aimé Césaire, the sophisticated poet of Martinique. At any rate, literary negritude and certain African messianic movements are different responses to one interrelated cultural phenomenon. Both the Greco-Roman aspect of European civilization and the Judeo-Christian side of it have sometimes forced the African into a position of cultural defensiveness. These two mystiques have come into Africa wrapped, to some extent, in Europe's cultural arrogance. The Greco-Roman mystique contributed to the birth of literary negritude as a reaction; the Judeo-Christian sense of sacred superiority contributed to the birth of Ethiopianism and African syncretic churches at large. The latter phenomena have intimate links with, or are themselves manifestations of, anthropological negritude.[12]

Sterling Stuckey has asserted persuasively that W. E. B. DuBois, the black American intellectual giant, was 'easily the most sophisticated proponent of negritude until the advent of Césaire and Senghor'. Stuckey has also recommended a study of DuBois's cultural views which should, *inter alia*, seek to determine how the DuBois variant of negritude differed from that projected by the Harlem Renaissance writers.[13]

It is right that the new wave of Black Studies in the United States should explore its links with the negritude movement, for those two waves of intellectualized black assertiveness have a good deal in common. Leopold Senghor, the chief of negritude in Africa, has argued that there is a fundamental difference between the white man's tools of intellectual analysis on the one hand and the black man's approach to intellectual perception on the other. Senghor has said: 'European reasoning is analytical, discursive by utilization; Negro-African reasoning is intuitive by participation.'[14]

Senghor, partly because of the complexity of his ideological position on culture, is not always consistent in his views on comparative epistemology as between European and Black-African modes of thought. But it is arguable that the logical conclusion of Senghor's position is that no European or white scholar can hope to understand fully the inner meaning of a black man's behaviour. This is the meeting point between negritude as the cultural essence of black civilization and negrology as the principles by which the black man was to be studied. For both Leopold Senghor and the militant wing of the Black Studies movement in the United States there are indeed certain socio-scientific principles of interpretation without which the black man cannot be adequately understood. The question is whether these principles can be mastered by a scholar who is not himself black. In his address to the Second International Congress of Africanists in Dakar in December 1967, President Senghor intimated that such principles of scholarly interpretation could be mastered by others if those scholars are sufficiently sensitive to the peculiar characteristics of the culture they are studying. Some of the advocates of Black Studies in the United States are more sceptical. For them only black scholars can fully command the principles of negrology.[15]

But if negrology is the science of studying the black man, should it not be sufficiently neutral to be accessible to diverse minds? Senghor would say that such a definition of 'science' is itself ethnocentric. He first quotes Jacques Monod, a Nobel Prize winner, who in his inaugural lecture at the Collège de France in 1967 asserted:

> The only aim, the supreme value, the 'sovereign good' in the ethics of Know-ledge is not, let us confess, the happiness of mankind, less so its temporal power, or its comfort, nor even the 'know thyself' of Socrates; it is the objective Knowledge of itself.

Senghor, after quoting this passage, says he disagrees with it fundamentally. With all due respect to those who hold this 'ultra-rationalist' position, knowledge for its own sake is 'alienated work'. For Senghor, as a child of African civilization, both art and science had a purpose — to serve man in his need for both creativity and love.[16]

Black Studies in the United States are of course also conceptualized in terms of purpose and social function. What about African studies in the United States? Should Americans study Africa for its own sake? Or should they study it in order to deepen the foundation of relations between Africa and the United States? Or should they study Africa in order to improve relations between whites and blacks within the United States? The second and third motives need not be mutually exclusive, but it may be necessary to decide on priorities and emphases.

There is a danger that if Africa is studied primarily in order to improve relations between whites and blacks within the United States, Africa itself might not be even remotely understood by either the blacks or whites in America. There may be a temptation to concentrate on only those aspects of African studies which are relevant to the domestic scene in America. African history might overshadow all other aspects of African studies. And with all due respect to Dr Stuckey, and to the importance of history, contemporary Africa cannot be understood simply by reference to its history. A preponderance of historians in African studies in the United States today would tend to distort American understanding of Africa as effectively as a preponderance of social anthropologists in African studies in Britain once distorted British understanding of the forces at work in Africa.

Studying Africa for the sake of black-white relations in America may also exaggerate the importance of white-black relations within Africa. Southern Africa might engage a disproportionate share of the attention of Americans studying Africa. White-black relations within Africa do indeed remain vitally important. But problems of black ethnicity north of the Limpopo, of the growth of new institutions in new African states, of economic development and changing cultural norms, are at least as deserving of scholarly attention. To study Africa primarily as a branch of American negrology may distort American understanding of Africa for generations to come.

If, as Senghor asserts, all science must be purposeful, American academics should be sure which purposes would be served by which branches of science. Black Studies should indeed be undertaken primarily to add rationality to relations between blacks and whites in the United States, and should therefore be accessible to both white and black students. But African studies in the United States should be undertaken primarily to add rationality to American understanding of Africa. The relevance of African studies for the domestic American scene should be indirect. By helping all Americans to understand Africa better, African studies should by extension also help white and black Americans to understand each other better.

The assumption of negritude and the principles of negrology might be correct in assuming that complete understanding between groups so deeply divided by history is impossible. The world of scholarship cannot afford to accept Alexander Pope's poetic assertion:

> A little learning is a dang'rous thing;
> Drink deep, or taste not the Pierian spring:
> There shallow draughts intoxicate the brain;
> And drinking largely sobers us again.[17]

Even a partial understanding of the black man in both Africa and the New World must be, from the point of view of white education, preferable to the ignorant intolerance of yesteryear. A little learning may be a dangerous thing, but a lot of prejudice might be worse.

More profound than any diplomatic disagreement about the place of African studies in relations between Africans and Americans is the continuing problem of comparative intellectual performance between whites and blacks. Among the whites the Jewish component at once sharpens the contrast with blacks and deepens the poignancy in their relations.

Black Power and Brain Power

Among sections of black Americans there is a view that 'the Jews are the brains of the white race'. They have been recognized as among the leading thinkers and writers, and they are suspected in such circles of being 'shrewd enough to manipulate the rest of the whites — to say nothing of the so-called Negroes'.[18]

It would also seem that the Jews are suspected among black militants of having a stranglehold on public opinion in the United States through their control of mass media. Either through outright ownership of radio and television stations, or through their massive advertising capability and power to withdraw advertisements, the Jews helped to 'dictate' the editorial policies of certain radio and television stations as well as magazines and newspapers:

> They hire Gentiles to 'front' for them so as not to antagonize the public; but on crucial issues, such as the Suez Canal, they control the thinking of the people.[19]

Then in 1968 and early 1969 the issue of the control of schools in New York City exploded into another area of Afro-Jewish antagonism. The black communities of New York City were agitating for the adoption of a system of education which would permit greater local controls of schools. The black community wanted a greater say in who taught in black schools and what was taught in them. In a sense it was a clash between Black Studies and the Talmudic tradition. Ultimately, however, local control of hiring and firing became the issue. This resulted in a head-on collision between black educational reformers and the teachers' union in New York City. Unionism of teachers in New York City happened to be dominated by the Jews, as many of the teachers in black schools were indeed Jewish. The idea of entrusting hiring and firing to local black communities was therefore a direct challenge to the security of tenure of Jewish teachers. The teachers' union won the first round of the tension, denying the local communities the demands they were making to control hiring and firing as well as curriculum. The issue brought to the fore once again the profound distrust by certain sections of black opinion of Jewish control of the educational system in some parts of the country. Open anti-Jewish speeches began to be heard more often from black militants. The so-called Jewish stranglehold on neighbourhood schools was sometimes linked to the disproportionate Jewish presence in the top sector of the American university system. The two levels of Jewish participation created an impression of a disproportionate intellectual influence upon the minds of others. The Talmudic tradition and its achievements in producing high-level intellectual quality was up against the Black Studies movement as a struggle to achieve educational and intellectual autonomy for black people.

John F. Hatchett, a black member of staff at New York University, was dismissed from his job for 'anti-Semitic' public statements. James Turner, the director-designate of the Black Studies Center at Cornell University, reportedly expressed a desire to have Hatchett on his staff. This in turn was taken on both sides of the Atlantic as further evidence of growing black anti-Semitism. Matthew Hodgart, professor of English at the University of Sussex, visited Cornell and wrote a report for *The Times* of London drawing attention to, among other things, these anti-Semitic tendencies. When challenged later in the correspondence columns of *The Times*, Hodgart emphasized afresh the signs of what he called 'black racism' in the United States.

The Black Liberation Front, which does *not* represent the majority of black students at Cornell, is racist: it practises a rigid segregation by refusing to allow its members to associate with white students. The black militant movement, with which the B.L.F. is in sympathy is openly anti-Semitic. James Turner, the Director-designate of the Cornell Afro Center, has reportedly expressed a desire to have on his staff John F. Hatchett, a black teacher who was dismissed from New York University for anti-Semitic public statements.[20]

Jewish synagogues were also included among the institutions from which black militants were demanding 'reparations' because of their part in the historical 'exploitation of blacks'. The idea of reparation emerged in Detroit in April 1969 at the black economic development conference. Mr James Forman, director of international affairs for the Student Non-violent Coordinating Committee, was addressing the all black audience when he suddenly read an unscheduled 'black manifesto' demanding 500 million dollars in reparations from white churches and synagogues. The manifesto called for a southern land bank, four major publishing and printing industries located in Detroit, Atlanta, Los Angeles, and New York, an audio-visual network based in Detroit, Chicago, Cleveland, and Washington DC, a research-skills centre on the problems of black people, a labour strike and defence fund, a black university, and an international black fund-raising effort.[21]

In the reparations issue the Christian churches have been at least as involved as the Jewish synagogues. The picture is part of increasing black pressure on certain aspects of Jewish life in the United States. By early 1969 it was already being suggested that while in Eastern Europe Jewish migrations to Israel, when permitted, were due to official pressure from the authorities there, in the United States Jewish migration to Israel was in part a response to black militancy and black pressures on the Jews. Speaking in March 1969 at a special conference on emigration to Israel attended by 700 people at the Park Sheraton Hotel, Jacques Torczyner, president of the Zionist Organization of America, said he knew of 'several instances in which Jewish merchants relinquished their businesses because of black extremists' pressure'.

Uzi Narkis, director-general of the Department of Immigration and Absorption of the Jewish Agency, reported at the meeting that 4,300 Jews from North America, including 500 Canadians, settled in Israel the previous year, the highest since the establishment of Israel as a nation in 1948. He added that 25,000 American Jews had settled in Israel since 1948 and predicted that 7,000 more would settle there by the end of 1969. There was clear feeling that one factor behind the renewed attraction of Israel for American Jews was the racial situation in the United States.[22]

Jews in New York were sensing this more immediately perhaps than Jews in many other centres, but then there were more Jews in New York than in the entire state of Israel. 20 April is Hitler's birthday, and so in April 1969 a whole page of the *New York Times* was taken over by a massive photograph of Hitler. The advertisement was from 'The Committee to Stop Hate', an inter-denominational organization. The caption under the massive picture of Hitler says 'April 20th is his birthday. Don't make it a happy one. Adolf Hitler would love New York City's latest crisis. Black against Jew. Jew against black. Neighbor against neighbor.'[23]

Whether the crisis over New York schools was an aspect of Jewish intellectual dominance or something simpler, the fact remains that it became an important contributory factor to the rise of Afro-Jewish tensions in the United States, as has affirmative action in most major universities in the United States, especially since Jews are often thought to be over represented and blacks to have less than their fair share.

The Foetus of the Future

From the 1840s onwards a man of Jewish extraction wrote or co-authored a number of historic publications. These included *The Manifesto of the Communist Party*. The man's name was Karl Marx. His Jewish father had converted to Christianity. A century later Marx was to capture the imagination of many black intellectuals struggling against the consequences of centuries of oppression.

There was one vital difference between the heritage of Marx and the heritage of black people. The majority of black people were heirs to an oral tradition, a transmission of song and oral wisdom ranging from Yoruba proverbs to black American blues. But Marx was at once a European and an heir to the Talmudic tradition, in spite of his father's opportunistic conversion to Christianity. Both the European and the Talmudic aspects of Marx put him within a vigorous stream of literary culture. The difference between Africa's oral tradition and the Euro-Talmudic literary tradition had immense relevance for the comparative performance of blacks and Diaspora Jews in recent history.

In the absence of the written word in most African cultures, many tentative innovations or experiments of a previous era were not transmitted to the next generation. The trouble with an oral tradition is that it transmits mainly what is accepted and respected. It does not normally transmit heresies of the previous age. A single African individual in the nineteenth century who might have put across important new ideas among the Nuer of the Sudan, but whose ideas were rejected by the consensus of his own age, is unlikely to be remembered today. Oral tradition is a tradition of conformity, rather than heresy, a transmission of consensus rather than dissidence.

Imagine what would have happened to the ideas of Karl Marx if in the nineteenth century Europe had been without the alphabet. If Karl Marx were simply propounding his ideas orally, from one platform to another, European oral tradition would have been insensitive to this revolutionary. After all, Karl Marx was not a particularly well-known figure in polite society in his own age. John Stuart Mill makes no reference to Marx in his own writings, betraying a total ignorance of Marx's contribution to the political economy of the nineteenth century.

Marx had many revolutionary followers, especially in continental Europe. He wrote interesting newspaper features for an American readership. Even that kind of effectiveness, however, presupposes the availability of an alphabet to get his ideas more widely publicized. In spite of that his fame for much of his own life was relatively modest. His fame by the second half of the twentieth century was greater than that of any other single figure in the nineteenth century. The fame that Karl Marx now enjoys, and the influence he has exerted on political, sociological, and economic thought in the twentieth century, would have been impossible had his ideas not been conserved by the written word and translated to a more receptive generation than his own.

The absence of the written word in large numbers of African societies was therefore bound to create a sense of isolation to some extent in a temporal sense, keeping one African century from another in terms of stimulation and interaction, suppressing innovative heresies, burying genius under the oblivion of the dominant consensus of a particular age.

In addition to the absence of literacy was the absence of numeracy. It was not simply the lack of the written word that delayed scientific flowering in Africa; it was also the lack of the written numeral. Jack Goody has drawn attention to the relationship between writing and mathematics, and the implications of the absence of both in some African societies. Goody draws attention to the fact that the development of Babylonian mathematics depended upon the prior development of a graphic system, though not necessarily an alphabetic one. And Goody then refers to the short time he spent in 1970 revisiting the Lo-Dagaa of Northern Ghana, 'whose main contact with literacy began with the opening of a primary school in Birifu in 1949'. Goody proceeded to investigate their mathematical operations. He discovered that while boys who had no special school background were efficient in counting a large number of cowries (shell money), and often did this faster and more accurately than Goody could, they were ineffective at multiplication.

> The concept of multiplication was not entirely lacking; they did think of four piles of five cowries as equalling twenty. But they had no ready-made table in their minds (the 'table' being essentially a written aid to 'oral' arithmetic) by which they could calculate more complex sums. The contrast was even more true of subtraction and division; the former can be worked by oral means (though the literate would certainly take to pencil and paper for the more complex sums), the latter is basically a literate technique. The difference is not so much one of thought or mind as of the mechanics of communicative acts.[24]

The absence of mathematics at the more elaborate level was bound to hamper considerably the black world's scientific development.

As for the more specific differences between blacks and Jews in intellectual history, part of the explanation may lie in the distinction between selective and comprehensive discrimination. When a people is suppressed in some fields and permitted to excel in others — as the Jews were in the last 600 years of Western history — they may attain striking achievements in those pursuits that are open to them. Certainly in the fields of 'money-lending' and commerce, fields which were deemed vulgar in polite European society at one time, the Jews in Europe acquired skills quite early. Shakespeare's Shylock was only a bizarre exaggeration of Jewish business acumen, caution and economic activism.

Selective discrimination against Jews had its ups and downs in Europe. Jews were allowed some professional avenues in some periods and lost them in other epochs. But on balance, selective discrimination against Jews in, say, politics contributed to Jewish excellence in the permitted professions of commerce, scholarship, and the arts. The Napoleonic legal code in the nineteenth century was among the milestones of fitful Jewish emancipation in modern Europe; it released once again Jewish energies as discrimination was relaxed. In the words of Isaiah Berlin:

> The Jews had every reason to feel grateful to Napoleon . . . [for] his newly promulgated legal code, which claimed as the source of its authority the principles of reason and human equality. This act, by opening to the Jews the doors of trades and professions which had hitherto remained rigidly barred to them, had the effect of releasing a mass of imprisoned energy and

ambition, and led to the enthusiastic — in some cases over-enthusiastic — acceptance of general European culture by a hitherto segregated community.[25]

But while fitful and selective discrimination against Jews released Jewish energies, comprehensive discrimination against blacks crippled the victims and stultified their innovative functions. It goes back to the slave trade.

A distinct factor worth bearing in mind when examining black intellectual marginality is indeed this impact of the slave trade, and later of imperialism, on the black world's capacity to innovate. The slave trade drained Africa of large numbers of its population. Those that reached the Americas, and survived to be effective slaves, were a fraction of those who were captured in the first instance for enslavement. The drastic depopulation of important parts of Africa was bound to have significant consequences on the continent's capacity to achieve major successes in the different branches of knowledge. Later, when Africa fell more directly under alien domination, imperialism once again delayed in at least some respects the capacity of Africa to attain new levels of scientific and technological initiatives.

Here the picture gets a little more complicated. It is possible to argue that while slavery did harm Africa's potential for scientific innovation, imperialism later on helped to create a new infrastructure for potential inventiveness. After all, imperialism, while it was indeed a form of humiliating political bondage, nevertheless proceeded to reduce the spatial, cultural, and temporal isolation which had previously been part of Africa's scientific marginality. European imperialism, almost by definition, ended for some societies that isolation in space and culture which had previously been an element of their very being. New values, as well as new modes of travel and mobility, created new intellectual possibilities. The arrival of the written word and of the numeral again began to establish a foundation for a new African entry into the mainstream of scientific civilization. Imperialism could be interpreted to be in part a mitigation of the consequences of the slave trade. Imperialism, by introducing new intellectual horizons, was inadvertently, and in spite of itself, laying the groundwork for a future intellectual liberation of the black man.

The final factor to be borne in mind in evaluating black scientific marginality is an exercise in humility — that is to say, that we might not know enough of the causes of intellectual flowering and maturation among human beings generally. It was Lévi-Strauss who reminded us how recent in absolute terms was the history of manifest human genius. The history of mankind is much older than the history of the revelation of major human intellects. Lévi-Strauss argued:

> I see no reason why mankind should have waited until recent times to produce minds of the caliber of a Plato or an Einstein. Already over two or three hundred thousand years ago, there were probably men of a similar capacity, who were of course not applying their intelligence to the solution of the same problems as these more recent thinkers; instead they were probably more interested in kinship![26]

Even if we reduce the life of mankind from Lévi-Strauss's 300,000 to 50,000 years, the question he raises is still significant. Why, out of the 50,000 years of the existence of the human race, do we have to look to the last 4,000 years for major indications of intellectual and scientific genius? The answer to that very question may have to await a future genius to unravel.

142

It was within those 4,000 years that the Talmudic tradition was born. Out of that tradition emerged a small segment of mankind, the Jews, destined to exert an unparalleled influence on the thinking processes of other men. From Jesus Christ to Karl Marx, from the Talmudic tradition to Einstein's theory of relativity, a Semitic heritage has manifested itself periodically in human genius.

The question which confronts us is whether within the next 4,000 years — and perhaps much sooner than that — another segment of the human race with a heritage of suffering, the blacks, will attain similar levels of intellectual performance and influence. For such a role the black people of both Africa and the black diaspora may have to shift from an oral tradition to a tradition of codified law, from a culture of consensus to a culture of prophecy, from a romanticization of a tribal past to an anticipation of a messianic future, from the chains of intellectual bondage to the ropes of intellectual mountaineering.

A black Talmudic tradition is needed, at once different in content from its Jewish counterpart and comparable in functions. The Black Studies movement may be the genesis of that black Talmudic tradition. In time the Black Studies movement may change beyond all recognition. It may become not merely a tolerated appendage in prestigious universities, not merely a cynical concession to black sensibilities in quality schools, not merely a forum of black rhetoric, but the beginnings of black intellectual independence which could spread from the ghetto. It could help to broaden still further the socialization processes to which the next generation of blacks would be exposed.

The black Muslim movement as a sacralization of black consciousness and the Black Studies movement as its intellectualization may indeed find that elusive point of fusion. On such a day a black prophecy would indeed be fulfilled, and a still Newer Testament would yet reveal even further the genius of Jehovah working itself out in man.

Notes

1. L. S. Senghor, *Négritude et Humanisme* (Paris: Seuil, 1964), p. 24, and *On African Socialism* (London: Pall Mall, 1964), p. 74.

2. Ibid.

3. Arthur R. Jensen, 'How Much Can We Boost I.Q. and Scholastic Achievement?' *Harvard Educational Review*, Vol. 39, No. 1, Winter 1969. See also the subsequent debate with J. S. Kagan, M. Hunt, J. F. Crow, Carl Beseiter, D. Elkind, Lee J. Cronback, W. R. Brazziel, Arthur Stinchcombe, and Martin Deutsch, *Harvard Educational Review*, Vol. 39, No. 2, Spring 1969, and Vol. 39, No. 3, Summer 1969. Similar debates have since occurred in the United States in response to the racist views of Nobel Prize winner W. Schockley of Stanford University in California.

4. *New York Times*, 1 April 1969.

5. C. D. Darlington, *The Evolution of Man and Society* (London: George Allen and Unwin, 1969), p. 188.

6. Consult, for example, J. A. Rogers, *World's Great Men of Color*, Vols 1 and 2, originally published in 1946. Reprinted in 1972 (New York: Collier Books, 1972).

7. These issues are discussed in a related context in Mazrui, *World Culture and the Black Experience* (Seattle, Washington: University of Washington Press, 1974). For information and illustration of the cards produced in Nkrumah's Ghana which emphasized African contributions to world civilization I am indebted to Mrs Simon Ottenberg, who later entrusted to my care her only set of those cards.

8. This rendering is from Gerald Moore (ed.), *Seven African Writers* (1962), p. viii.

9. Ibid.

10. Senghor, 'Négritude and African Socialism', in *St Anthony's Papers on African Affairs*, No. 2, edited by Kenneth Kirkwood (London: Chatto and Windus), p. 11.

11. *Chants pour Naëtt* (Senghor, 1950). This English rendering is from John Reed and Clive Wake (eds), *Senghor: Prose and Poetry* (London: Oxford University Press, 1965), p. 97.

12. The connection between literary negritude and separatist religious movements is discussed in a related context in my professorial inaugural lecture, 'Ancient Greece in African Political Thought', delivered at Makerere University College, Kampala, on 25 August 1966.

13. Stuckey, 'The Neglected Realm of African and Afro-American Relationships: Research Responsibilities for Historians', *Africa Today*, Vol. 16, No. 4, 1969, p. 4.

14. Senghor, *On African Socialism* (London: Pall Mall, 1964), p. 74.

15. See Senghor, 'The Study of African Man', *Mawazo* (Kampala), Vol. 1, No. 47, 1968, pp. 3—7.

16. Ibid., p. 7.

17. Alexander Pope, *Essay on Criticism*.

18. Cited by Eric Lincoln, *The Black Muslims in America* (Boston: Beacon Press, 1961), pp. 165—166.

19. Ibid., p. 166.

20. *The Times* (London), 23 and 26 May; and Miss J. Hodgart, 29 May 1969.

21. See *The Christian Science Monitor*, 10 May 1969.

22. 'Black Militants Seen as Factor in Migration to Israel', *New York Times*, 31 March 1962.

23. *New York Times*, 7 April 1969.

24. Jack Goody, 'Evolution and Communication: The Domestication of the Savage Mind', *The British Journal of Sociology*, Vol. 24, No. 1, March 1973, p. 7.

25. Berlin, *Karl Marx: His Life and Environment* (London and New York: Oxford University Press, 1972 edition), p. 25.

26. C. Lévi-Strauss, 'The Concept of Primitiveness', in R. B. Lee and I. DeVore (eds), *Man the Hunter* (Chicago: Aldine, 1968), p. 351.

8

On Race
& Conflict

Zionism
& Apartheid

Since the Middle East October War of 1973 Israel and the Republic of South Africa have been drawing close together. The interaction has ranged from cultural and sporting exchanges to the restoration of full ambassadorial relations, from consultations on techniques of counter-insurgency to cooperation in the production of steel and now even preliminary nuclear consultation. The visit of the South African premier to Israel in 1976 was symbolic of this new *entente cordiale* between Israel as a child of Zionism and South Africa as the father of apartheid.

By a curious historical destiny 1948 was a critical year for both Zionism and apartheid. In that year Israel was born, having previously won a majority in the United Nations in its favour. In that year also the National Party in South Africa was engaged in an electoral campaign on the policy of apartheid, defined as a rigorous, legalized separation of the races and cultures of South Africa. The National Party under Dr Malan captured power, and Afrikaner nationalism as an ideology began to be more systematically operated.

Is there much more between Israel and apartheid than the coincidence of a shared birthday in 1948 and a shared predicament since the 1970s? This chapter will focus especially on four factors: situational similarity between Israel and South Africa, normative congruence between Zionism and the ideology of apartheid, the trend towards greater economic cooperation between Israel and South Africa, and prospects for greater military consultations between the two.

This chapter accepts that the reasons behind the new *entente cordiale* between South Africa and Israel are indeed partly situational. We hope to demonstrate that this similarity in their situations has its roots in a prior ideological congruence between Zionism and apartheid. The sense of isolation which Israel now shares with South Africa is a consequence of parallel efforts to implement culturally separatist ideologies at the wrong time in history.

Let us therefore first examine these deeper normative similarities between Zionism and the ideology of apartheid before we turn to their political and structural consequences in the present day.

145

The Western Roots of Zionism and Apartheid

It is important to remember that apartheid as an ideology is not just another word for 'racism'. It is a philosophy which defines nationality in terms of cultural homogeneity and racial distinctiveness. As a policy, apartheid is committed to the separate development of different ethnic groups. It conceives of citizenship not as a legal contract between the individual and his state but ultimately as a cultural bond between the individual and his community.

There is little doubt that apartheid as an ideology is partly a child of nineteenth century European conceptions of nationality. Mazzini was not the only nationalist prophet who linked nationality to divine purpose. According to Mazzini, God 'divided Humanity into distinct groups upon the face of our globe, and thus planted the seeds of nations'.[1] In its alliance with the Dutch Reformed Churches of South Africa, Afrikaner nationalism embraced this linkage between national differentiation, ethnic separatism, and divine purpose.

The apartheid programme as a policy includes the ambition of macro-segregation, the creation of separate monoracial and unicultural 'homelands' for each group. The Transkei, given 'independence' in October 1976, was supposed to be the first of such Bantustans. The apartheid programme also includes micro-segregation, which has entailed such legislation as the Group Areas Act, committed to residential separation, the Bantu Education Act designed to arrest cultural convergence between blacks and whites, the Population Registration Act to control trans-ethnic movement, the Immorality Laws and Prohibition of Mixed Marriages Act, and many other pieces of legislation.

Apartheid was given a cosmetic face in the 1980s. Theatres and many cinemas were desegregated. In 1984 a new constitution was brought in, replacing the all-white parliament with a three-chamber legislature, one for whites, one for 'Coloureds' (the official government term for mixed-race people), and one for Indians, but the black majority remained excluded, and in any case the elections for the new parliament were widely boycotted by both 'Coloureds' and Indians. Two non-whites, Allan Hendrickse, leader of the Coloured Labour Party, and Amichand Rajbansi, an Indian, were made cabinet ministers, but they were given no departmental responsibilities and no white civil servants came under their authority. In 1985 the Mixed Marriages Act and part of the Immorality Act were repealed, but there are restrictions on where mixed couples can live because residential segregation remains, and children of mixed marriages still have to be officially racially classified. In July 1988 plans were announced to strengthen the Group Areas Act, making it easier to evict about 200,000 non-whites, living 'illegally' in white-owned areas of cities, to the rural 'homelands'. The amendments to the Act did include legal recognition of a few racially-mixed residential areas, but only if the whites in the area agreed. In practice, apartheid remains essentially unchanged (December 1989).

On the whole, Zionism has more in common with apartheid on the issue of macro-separation (separate homelands for culturally distinct groups) than on the issue of micro-segregation (racial separation within towns and localities). What is clear is that both Zionism and Afrikaner nationalism have borrowed from the anti-pluralistic and exclusivist tendencies of German nationalistic thought as a special case of European nationalism.

Theodor Herzl, the towering European founder of the Zionist movement, was an assimilated Jew. Born in Hungary, he later imbibed Germanic culture and many of its political postulates. From his professional base in Vienna he looked at European society through both liberal and nationalistic eyes. His liberalism inclined him towards pluralism and heterogeneity. His Jewish nationalism pulled him towards Zionism with all its potential exclusivity. Herzl never resolved the dilemma in his own sensitive mind, but the movement which he helped to create was to lean increasingly towards Germanic doctrines of 'the unified soul of the fatherland' and away from liberal diversity.

Herzl, in his original idea of a Jewish home, did indeed see a state populated almost only by Jews at first. His original solution involved the finding of vacant territory which the Jews could then populate — 'to give to the people without land a land without people'. These were the days when Herzl could allow of the possibility of an Israel in South America. By the time Britain's colonial secretary, Joseph Chamberlain, offered him Uganda, however, the lure of Palestine as the proper home for the Jews was too strong. Yet to Herzl himself the vision was that of a state where non-Jews might still live in an open society, and where the Jews and their religion would not constitute a privileged group:

> It would be immoral if we would exclude anyone, whatever his origin, his descent, or his religion, from participating in our achievements. For we stand on the shoulders of other civilized peoples. . . . What we own we owe to the preparatory work of other peoples. Therefore, we have to repay our debt. There is only one way to do it, the highest tolerance. Our motto must therefore be, now and ever: 'Man, you are my brother.'[2]

Herzl was more liberal but certainly less logical than the Zionists who later triumphed. The idea of having a Jewish home where everybody else was equal, and where others could be admitted even to the extent of tilting the balance of population, was to some extent a contradiction in terms. Morris R. Cohen captured this dilemma when he asked:

> Indeed, how could a Jewish Palestine allow complete religious freedom, intermarriage, and free non-Jewish immigration, without soon losing its very reason for existence? A national Jewish Palestine must necessarily mean a state founded on a peculiar race . . . a tribal religion, and a mystic belief in a peculiar soil.[3]

As Zionism gathered strength, a strong preference for a racially and religiously purist state for the Jews began to gain ascendancy, though this concept was up against considerable diplomatic difficulties in the international arena.

The Jewish Agency of Palestine, the shadow Jewish government before the creation of Israel, played down the notion of a racially and religiously purist state. The agency was even embarrassed during World War II when significant members of the Labour Party in Britain went to the extent of demanding that the Arabs should be forced to leave Palestine to make way for Jewish immigration.[4] Early discussions on the best solution for the Palestine problem sometimes envisaged a federation of Jewish and Arab states. This was deemed to be one realistic solution which would reconcile the interests of both groups, and fulfil the British Balfour Declaration of 1917, quoted on page 51.

> His Majesty's Government views with favour the establishment in Palestine of a national home for the Jewish people, and will use their best endeavours to facilitate the achievement of this object, it being clearly understood that nothing shall be done which may prejudice the civil rights of existing

non-Jewish communities in Palestine, or the rights and political status enjoyed by Jews in any other country.

At the diplomatic and international level a compromise seemed to be emerging. In 1947 a United Nations Special Committee on Palestine (UNSCOP) left to make a new study of the problems involved in Jewish-Arab relations and the conflicting ambitions involved. When UNSCOP completed its work, however, it was only the minority report which favoured a federation of Jewish and Arab states. On 3 September 1947, the majority report of UNSCOP recommended that the League of Nations mandate, initiated in 1919 after the Ottoman Empire lost control of its Arab territorial possessions, should now be terminated, and that Palestine should be partitioned into sovereign Arab and Jewish states. That school of Zionism which was militantly purist in its conception of a Jewish home had triumphed. On 29 November 1947, the General Assembly of the United Nations, by a vote of 33 to 13, with 10 abstentions, confirmed their vision. The state of Israel was given a global birth certificate in imminent anticipation. A new political community, explicitly defined in terms of race and biological descent from the ancient Hebrews, was about to enter world history.

What did this concept of an ethnically defined Jewish state have in common with Afrikaner nationalism in South Africa? Conceptions of citizenship under both ideologies were in an important sense anachronistic. C. G. Montefiore was surely right, in relation at least to Zionism, when he argued as long ago as 1899:

> There is no *a priori* reason why in any one state men of different races and creeds should not be ardent citizens living in peace and harmony with each other. The trend of modern thought, in spite of backwaters and counter currents, is surely in that direction. A Russia which must be purely Slav and of the orthodox Greek church strikes us as an anachronistic effort which in the long run will inevitably break down.[5]

Such a conception of citizenship is borrowed from tribal ideas of the past, as well as from German nationalism. Tribal polities were inseparable from kinship. A person could not belong to a social or even ceremonial collectivity if he did not have a kinship status. In many an indigenous society both in Africa and elsewhere 'there are no non-relatives'. All roles are allocated and activities organized in relation to kinship status broadly defined.

This pre-modern conception of citizenship is sometimes better illustrated in some South Pacific island societies and among aboriginal communities in Australia than in African political communities, but the element of similarity is strongly there all the same. Certainly many societies in southern Africa, before European settlement, organized themselves traditionally by kinship, either real or conferred. A new citizen became one either through complete cultural assimilation or through mixing his blood with members of the community concerned. What Meyer Fortes said of Kariera society is true of many traditional political communities in Africa as well:

> . . . outsiders can be incorporated into a society or a community or, more generally, brought into the ambit of sanctioned social relations, by having kinship status ascribed to them. Different communities, even those of different tribal or linguistic provenance, can exchange personnel by marriage, and can fuse for particular ceremonial occasions by, so to speak, intermeshing their kinship field. . . . Herein lies the essence of the kinship polity.[6]

Here an important difference does present itself between tribal society on the one hand, and Jewish and Afrikaner conceptions of citizenship on the other. For most African cultures readiness to intermarry is one approach to the forging of a shared community. The Zionist approach to citizenship is in some ways quite the reverse. The capacity of the Jews to see themselves as a group descended from the ancient Hebrews, and therefore as a group entitled to return to Palestine, was facilitated by a tradition of sexual exclusivity. When religion and ethnicity are so intertwined, both ethnic intermarriage and religious intermarriage become additionally constrained and inhibited. Again, Montefiore saw this as a problem for the modern Jew even by the nineteenth century

> I admit that in the case of the Jews religion and race are practically co-extensive. A Roman Catholic Czech of Bohemia may perhaps be united, so far as the Czech part of him goes, with his fellow Bohemian Protestant, and *qua* Catholic he will marry a German of the same religious denomination. Among the Jews, religion and race play into each other's hands, and the common refusal of intermarriage, however justified as the only means of maintaining the life of a tiny minority, preserves and strengthens the alleged isolation and difference.[7]

To some extent the Jewish tradition of sexual exclusivity has been undermined in the twentieth century. Out-marriage amongst British Jews is currently 35 per cent; amongst American Jews the figure is similar; amongst German Jews before Hitler's persecution it was higher. But the tradition survives strongly in Zionist Israel.

Today in Israel problems of defining the rights of Jews as against the rights of others have been bedevilled both by militarized nationalism and by Zionist Judaism's hostility to interreligious marriage. Cases have come before the courts in the last few years in Israel involving children of mixed descent. The political forces that are still capable of being mobilized against the liberalization of Israel's laws of descent remain significant. Both the government of Israel and the courts in Israel have felt the pressure of racial purity as a political force in the Jewish state. These pressures emanate in part from religion and in part from the psychology of the garrison state.

The orthodox Jewish concept of citizenship is no less purist than the Afrikaner approach. For both Jews and Afrikaners, kinship is ultimately designed to maintain internal cohesion. After all, had not the K'ai-feng Jews of China disappeared from the map of world Jewry mainly because they had permitted themselves to intermarry freely with the Chinese? And had not the Jews of Northern Ethiopia become so black that for centuries rabbis had found it difficult to accept them as Jews? It was not until 1972, the year of Idi Amin's expulsion of the Israelis and the Asians from Uganda, that the Sephardic Grand Rabbi Ovadia Yosseff decided to save the black Jews from the fate of the Chinese Jews — total disappearance. Recognition was at last reluctantly conceded to the 25,000 members of the Falashim tribe of Northern Ethiopia as a group biologically descended from 'genuine' Jews who went to Ethiopia centuries ago.[8] The Ethiopian famine of 1984–1985 caused Israel to launch 'Operation Moses', an airlift of Ethiopian Jews to Israel via the Sudan. By the end of 1984 about 13,500 Falasha Jews had settled in Israel. However, conservative rabbis treated the Falasha as 'impure' Jews and required them to undergo a 'purification' ceremony.

Did not German ideas of nationality and exclusivity also influence Arab nationalism? European nationalism generally has had a pervasive intellectual influence on much of the Third World, including the Arab world. And the German factor in global nationalist philosophy has been pronounced. It was not the Arabs, however, but the Jews who rejected the idea of Arabs and Jews living together in a united Palestine. It was not the Arabs but the Zionists and their supporters who insisted on partition. The principle of national exclusivity in the Middle East was much more a feature of Jewish nationalism than of Arab nationalism. Arab actions against their own Jewish citizens were a response to Zionist exclusivity rather than an independent doctrine within Arab ideologies.

We next turn to the role of religion in statecraft, from the Middle East to Southern Africa.

Religion, the State, and the Martyrdom Complex

A primordial feature of the normative convergence between Israel and South Africa lies in the impact of religion upon the ruling ideologies in the two societies. Zionism is the offspring of a marriage between Judaism and the legacy of the 1648 Peace of Westphalia; apartheid is the offspring of a marriage between the Dutch Reformed Churches and the legacy of race consciousness. Judaism in search of statehood resulted in the creation of Israel. The Dutch Reformed Churches in search of descendants of Ham and Shem as racial categories stumbled on the doctrine of apartheid.

The champions of both Zionism and apartheid have invoked the Old Testament as solemn witness to their doctrines. In the case of Israel the biblical influence is sometimes relatively mild, especially among the more secular citizens of the Jewish state. But the very notion of 'returning' to Israel, the fanatical commitment to the retention of Jerusalem as the capital, and the choice of the name Israel for a twentieth-century nation-state are all symptoms of an underlying merger between biblical nostalgia and Jewish nationalism within the ethos of Zionism. Not unexpectedly, given this framework, Prime Minister Begin invoked the Old Testament to justify Israel's territorial claims on the West Bank of the River Jordan and Gaza Strip.

Similarly, in the case of Afrikaner nationalism, the Old Testament has been used to validate racial segregation and white supremacy. In August 1982, at a meeting in Ottawa, Canada, the two Dutch Reformed Churches of South Africa (NGK and NHK churches) were at last suspended from the World Alliance of Reformed Churches on the grounds that apartheid as a religious doctrine was a heresy.[9] The stage was thus set for a more complete break between the Afrikaner churches and the international alliance of churches. In October 1986 the white Dutch Reformed Church at its synod defined racism as 'a sin which no person may defend or practise' and said apartheid 'cannot be accepted on Christian ethical grounds because it is in conflict with the principles of neighbourly love and justice'. But the synod rejected proposals to unite with the separate Dutch Reformed Churches set up to serve blacks, 'coloureds', and Asians and refused to condemn separate education or the Group Areas Act.

In addition to the doctrinal aspects of Afrikaner and Zionist fundamentalism, there is the common phenomenon of the martyrdom complex in both Boer and Jewish nationalism. The martyrdom complex in Jewish experience has had varied manifestations across the centuries, going back to the myth of the exodus from Egypt. It found a more compelling expression after the ghastly genocidal

150

horrors and obscenities of Hitler's concentration camps. Hitler was at once the greatest enemy of the Jews in history and the greatest (if unconscious) friend of the concept of Israel. The horrors he perpetrated resulted in a great boost for the Zionist movement. Western Jews who had previously had reservations about the movement were now more firmly converted. Western governments were now readier to ignore Arab wishes in favour of Zionist aims.

In the West, Hitler's holocaust created a pervasive sense of guilt which for a long time was used as a resource which the new Jewish state could draw upon. For two or three decades Western liberals were afraid of voicing reservations about Israel's behaviour lest this be interpreted as a form of anti-Semitism. American Jews committed themselves more firmly than ever to Israel, partly because of a sense of guilt arising out of their feeling that not enough had been done to save the Jews from Hitler's terror a few years earlier. Opposition to Zionism by a Jew was now interpreted as 'Jewish self-hate' and anti-Zionism in a gentile was interpreted as anti-Semitism, plain and simple.

In leaders like Menachem Begin the martyrdom complex of Jewish nationalism reached fanatical proportions. Heads of government of even friendly countries in Europe have been denounced in 'holocaust' terms if they showed any sign of deviating from policies preferred by Israel. And when the Pope agreed to give an audience to Yassir Arafat, the Vatican was denounced by Begin's government and accused of having failed to utter a word against the massacre of Jews in Europe under Hitler. The wording of the Vatican's rebuttal rejecting the Israeli charges showed signs of the Polish Pope's own hand:

> These comments are surprising, almost incredible. They overlook — possibly under the impact of an emotion which itself is hardly justified — all that the Pope and the Vatican have done to save thousands upon thousands of Jewish lives before and after the Second World War.[10]

The Vatican's strong reply not only emphasized the Church's role in saving Jews, but went on quietly to remind Israelis that it was not just Jews who were massacred by the Nazis.

Afrikaner nationalism has a martyrdom complex of its own with the British in the role of German Nazi. The Dutch had colonized South Africa before the British. British policies later caused Afrikaners to vacate some of their settlements and trek north in 1836. This trek was the equivalent of their exodus — a major symbolic event in Afrikaner mythology, as the migrants travelled north to create the Boer republics of the Orange Free State and the Transvaal.

By the turn of the century British-Boer relations had reached another point of supreme crisis. The Boer War broke out — a dirty war even by colonial standards. The British herded thousands of Afrikaner women and children into concentration camps, where it is estimated that 26,000 perished. There were no gas chambers, but there is evidence of widespread use of starvation as a military weapon. The Boer War left a deep martyrdom complex in the Afrikaner psyche.[11]

The British won the Boer War and maintained control until 1910: it was not until 1948 that Afrikaner nationalists at last captured political state power over South Africa as a whole. Unlike Zionism, however, Afrikaner nationalism did not have a fund of guilt-feelings even in Britain to draw upon for very long. The Afrikaner's new ideology of apartheid was less respectable than the ideology of the Zionists. Israelis could count on fellow Jews world-wide for moral and often material support; Afrikaners could not even count on fellow Dutch in the Netherlands for sympathy in their predicament. Jews outside Israel were among the vanguard defenders of Zionism; among the vanguard critics of apartheid were the Dutch outside South Africa. As a result, the martyrdom complex of Afrikaners found a new intensity arising from South Africa's increasing international isolation and its status as an ideological heretic.

The most frightening thing about the martyrdom complex is what it does to those who control the machinery of the state. The state is a principle of power and authority; the nation is a principle of identity. There is only one thing worse than the state, and that is a state which insists on becoming a 'pure' nation-state, which insists on attaining cultural or ethnic homogeneity within a single generation.

The martyrdom complex leads to a fortress mentality, which in turn reinforces ethnic exclusivity. Israel insists on its being a Jewish state; Afrikaners insist on creating tribal 'homelands' separate from 'white' South Africa. In pursuit of those aims both Israel and South Africa have been quite ruthless. Indeed, by the 1980s, Israel was on its way to becoming the most arrogant nation-state since Nazi Germany. Israel has frequently bombed or invaded Lebanon to attack Palestinian refugee camps and military bases there. In July 1981 Israeli air-raids on Palestinian-inhabited areas of Beirut killed over 300 Palestinians and Lebanese. The Israeli invasion of Lebanon in June 1982 left over 14,000 dead, about half of them Lebanese, and most of them civilians, in heavy air raids and artillery bombardments of Beirut, Sidon, and other cities and 600,000 people were made homeless. The Israelis, with their troops in the suburbs of Beirut, cynically used Christian right-wing militia to do the dirty work of clearing the Palestinian refugee camps of 'terrorists'. Hundreds of unarmed Palestinian men, women and children were duly massacred in the camps of Sabra and Chatila (September 1982). Hundreds more Palestinians and Lebanese were killed by Israeli forces in south Lebanon before Israel withdrew in 1985.

The Palestinian uprising against Israeli occupation in Gaza and the West Bank in 1987—1989 has seen the killing of 400 Palestinians, nearly all of them unarmed or armed only with stones, as against only eleven Israeli deaths, by the time of writing (August 1989).

These tragic events were all symptoms of the moral corrosion of the State of Israel under the control of rulers who were particularly haunted by the Jewish martyrdom complex. By 1982 Israel was ready to preside over a Palestinian holocaust in Lebanon. The wheel of genocide seemed to have come full circle — the victim was about to become the perpetrator.

On the issue of the value of human life, apartheid may have a more humane record than Zionism. Since 1948 far fewer civilians have died as a result of the implementation of apartheid than as a result of the defence of Zionism. This is not to underplay the degree of state terrorism displayed by the South African government towards black South Africans or in neighbouring states. The Sharpeville massacre of 1960 in South Africa was one of the most costly acts of barbarism in that country against unarmed civilians. The number of dead was put at 69, the number of wounded at over 150. The Soweto riots of 1976 were in fact more costly than Sharpeville, with nearly 600 dead. In South African state violence against unarmed civilians, the police have killed at least 3,400 people since 1975. They were shameless enough to shoot dead 20 Africans demonstrating peacefully in Uitenhage's Langa township in March 1985 to commemorate the twenty-fifth anniversary of the Sharpeville massacre.

South African raids against neighbouring states have led to considerable loss of life, notably at the Namibian refugee camp at Kassinga in Angola in 1978, when 867 people, most of them women and children, were slaughtered by the South African army.

So South African state violence has had truly devastating consequences. It is true, however, that since 1948 far more Palestinians have been killed by the State of Israel than black South Africans have been killed by the government of South Africa. Yet the population of Palestinians is only a fraction of the population of black South Africans.

In this respect, at least, the state has been even more cynically amoral in the bands of the Zionists than it has been in the hands of champions of apartheid.

Exporting Refugees and Importing Labour

The logic of ethnic exclusivity has had other profound consequences both for Zionism and apartheid. South Africa's solution to the problems of the plural society was an elaborate system of pass laws to discourage 'swamping' of white areas by blacks. Israel's solution to the 'threat' of cultural mixtures was even more drastic.

The ethnic 'purification' of Israel after its creation in 1948 was helped considerably by the military ineptness of the Arab states. The original Israeli boundaries as defined by the United Nations gave Israel 5,400 square miles with a population of 963,000, of whom 500,000 were Jewish. The Arab state partitioned out of Palestine had 4,500 square miles with a population of 814,000 of whom 10,000 were Jewish. Jerusalem, with a population of 206,000 had 100,000 Jews, and was turned into a separate body.

On 14 May 1948, the day on which the state of Israel was formally proclaimed, the Arabs launched a military attack. They were defeated before they could get near the controversial borders of partitioned Palestine. The Israelis had their first moment of triumphant expansion. They occupied more than half the territory allotted to the Arabs and increased the size of their state from 5,400 to 7,722 square miles.

Technically their territorial expansion should have resulted in a further dilution of the Jewish population of the new Israel. After all, little more than half of the original population of Israel was Jewish, while the new lands which were conquered had a preponderance of Arabs.

The Arabs of both the newly conquered territories and the original Israel were encouraged to flee. Who encouraged them to become refugees? The Israelis claim that Arab broadcasting stations instigated the flight of the Arab inhabitants within areas controlled by Israel. There is evidence, nevertheless, that the Arabs had begun to run before the fighting broke out, partly as a result of the conditions of terror deliberately created in some areas by Israeli militants. One of the most notorious of such operations of intimidation was the 'Deir Yassin Massacre', committed on 9 April 1948, which cost 245 lives, when dissident Jewish terrorists attacked an Arab village which had signed a non-belligerency pact with a neighbouring Jewish settlement.

One of the most thorough investigations into the alleged instigation to flight broadcast by Arab radio stations was undertaken by Irish journalist Erskine Childers. From the records in the British Museum, Childers examined and listened to all the tapes of Arab broadcasting stations monitored during the first Arab-Israeli war in 1948. Childers found nothing to substantiate the Israeli claim that the Palestinian refugee problem was created by Arab radio stations.

The Israeli government had promised Childers concrete proof of these broadcasting instigations. Childers visited Israel again in 1958, but was shown no proof of the point in dispute. On the contrary, he had found, upon listening to the broadcast tapes, evidence of appeals from Arab countries asking the Palestinians to stay put as a way of ensuring their claims.[12]

The number of refugees has swollen since 1948 to over two million. Technically some of these refugees should indeed be regarded as Israeli citizens, to the extent that they were part of the population of Israel on the day Israel was created and were deemed by the United Nations to be citizens of the country. The United Nations was the body which had brought the State of Israel into being. The Geneva Convention which Israel signed in 1949 recognized the rights of refugees to return to their homeland, whatever the reasons for which they originally fled.

But the doctrine of an Israel consisting of Jews was not easily compatible with the readmission of thousands of non-Jewish citizens. The Israeli immigration laws — especially from 1950 with the Law of Return — are prepared to admit large numbers of Jews from Russia, Eastern Europe, and elsewhere, and even complain that the Russian government makes it difficult for those Jews to get to Israel. And yet the same government, so keen on Jewish immigration, is militantly opposed to the resettlement of some of its own Arab citizens who fled in a moment of terror some three decades ago. The Jews of Russia had never known Israel, and would technically be alien to that part of the world, while the Arabs in camps next door to Israel were part of Palestine until Zionism triumphed and an ethnically exclusive state came into being. The Israeli government officials say they have no responsibility for the Arabs that had fled from Palestine, since Israel has replaced them with Sephardic Jews from Arab countries. The doctrine of ethnic purification continues to colour the ideological legitimation of the Jewish state.

Israel has continued to have its Enoch Powells, its defenders of an ethnically exclusive state, to the present day. There are strong voices not only defending permanent exclusion of those non-Jews that were terrorized into leaving the country in previous years, but also urging the further de-Arabization of Israel as it now exists. Life as a garrison state has taken its toll of Jewish tolerance. More than two decades of continuous military preparedness have sharpened Israeli chauvinism and Jewish consciousness.

Of the present population of three and a half million in Israel, ten per cent is Arab. An additional one and a half million Arabs have fallen under Israeli control as a result of the new lands conquered by Israel during the June 1967 war. The Jews still outnumber the Arabs almost two to one, even including the conquered territories. Many Israelis are nonetheless already worried about the survival of Israel's Jewishness. A survey commissioned by the Israeli government in 1972 pointed out that the Arab population was growing faster than the Jewish, and that by 1985, if present trends continued, the Arabs would constitute 40 per cent of the combined population of Israel and the occupied lands. This is what has come to be called 'the demographic nightmare'. In fact, by 1985 Arabs constituted as many as 37 per cent of the combined population.

Pinchas Sapir, Finance Minister under Golda Meir, represented an important school of thought among Israelis when he said that he would rather give up most of the territory now conquered since 1967 than see the Arab population of Israel come up to 40 per cent before the end of this century. In a television interview in 1972 he said: 'If I have to choose between a binational state which will include the town of Hebron, in the West Bank, and a Jewish state without Hebron, I shall prefer the latter.'[13]

Sapir has repeated that a binational state would be a 'tragedy'. The late Defence and Foreign Minister Moshe Dayan was less purist in his conception of Israel than are some of his compatriots. He would rather keep the conquered lands even if he had to put up with non-Jews. There was a time when Dayan believed that after ten years of economic union with Israel, the occupied Arab lands might prefer to remain part of the Israeli state. But even Dayan had to think in terms of a solution which would ensure a permanent Jewish majority in the Israeli state.

In reality Dayan's vision included a preference for the availability of cheap labour within Israel or the occupied territories in a manner fundamentally similar to the migration of cheap labour from Turkey into the Federal Republic of Germany. Currently, 75,000 labourers, or approximately one-third of the total Arab work force of the West Bank and Gaza Strip territories, commute to Israel. In some forms of unskilled labour, such as that found in the building trades and the service sector, Palestinians make up as much as 30 per cent of the work force. Within Israel itself, it is quite clear that these workers would be the first to be laid off should there be a major economic recession, for Palestinian wages are not covered by Israeli trade-union agreements. Nor are Palestinians eligible for the basic social welfare benefits given Israeli workers. Similarly, the Israeli National Insurance system does not include West Bank—Gaza residents. It is quite true, however, that the Arab workers are better off with the wages that they earn than they would be in their original areas, as employment in Israel accounts for 30 per cent of the total income of West Bank and Gaza Strip Palestinians. But the large number of workers who go into Israel also affects the local Palestinian economy; since most of these workers come from the agricultural sector, the area under cultivation in the occupied territories has been reduced by 35 per cent.[14]

Profound moral as well as economic problems are raised by a situation where cheap labour is imported on a temporary basis, and on the clear understanding that never would it be allowed to affect demographically the Jewish nature of the state. In this instance the Israelis want to have their cake and eat it. They want the availability of non-Jewish labour, on the one hand, and the guarantee of perpetual Jewishness of their state on the other. The dilemma has caused moral unease for many Israelis and humanitarians elsewhere.

The similarity with South Africa lies in South Africa's readiness to import personnel from other parts of Africa, on a temporary basis, provided the long-term white power in South Africa is not compromised.

But Israel and South Africa want to combine the economic blessing of alien personnel without compromising the ultimate racial principle of their own conceptions of statehood.

The Pretoria regime has at times sent recruiting agents to a number of different African countries, expressing a preference for imported labour but still unwilling to give up the basic assumptions of white supremacy. From time to time, black labour has poured into South Africa from Swaziland and Botswana, from Zambia and Namibia. Even Marxist Mozambique maintains a contract of cheap labour with South Africa in exchange for gold. After independence in 1975, Mozambique reduced the number of its miners in South Africa by two-thirds, but export of labour to South Africa is still (1989) Mozambique's most important source of foreign exchange. There is no doubt at all that South Africa excels in the arts of exporting refugees and importing cheaper labour than is locally available. More so even than those who enter South Africa, the foreigners Israel recruits constitute a pool of cheap labour.

> They come in the early morning, before most Israelis are awake, from the West Bank of the Jordan River and the Gaza Strip. Wearing Arab headdresses and work boots, they commute each day in overcrowded buses and taxis to construction sites and factories all over Israel. They are Israel's migrant workers — about 50,000 to 60,000 Arab labourers from the occupied territories who have come in steadily increasing numbers since the 1967 war to find jobs in Israel's overheated economy. In the last few years they have become an indispensable ingredient in Israel's economic boom — the cheap labour on which the economy has vaulted forward since the six-day war.[15]

The principle of the ethnic polity is up against the dictates of economic convenience in both Israel and South Africa. Economy and culture exert a mixed influence on these racial approaches to statecraft.

Militarized Zionism and Imperial Apartheid

The strategy of maintaining relative ethnic exclusivity with the assurance of relatively cheap labour has required policies which are both imperialist and militarist. South Africa and Israel have devised divergent policies but in pursuit of comparable goals. It is arguable that on the issue of territorial expansion since the Nationalists took over power in 1948, South Africa has been a more civilized country than Israel. Israel's territorial expansion started in the very year of its creation. With almost every new war with the Arabs, Israel has grown in size. In 1956 it was only because of the angry insistence of the United States under Eisenhower that Israel relinquished the large areas of the Sinai that it occupied as part of its conspiracy with Britain and France in the Suez War. In 1967 Israel got another chance to reconquer the Sinai. It took another war, in 1973, before Israel returned a little territory to Egypt. And after the Camp David Accords of 1978 the whole of the Sinai reverted to Egypt. On the other hand, since Camp David, the Golan Heights of Syria have been annexed by Israel, East Jerusalem incorporated, and Jewish settlements on the West Bank vastly expanded.

While Zionism has continued its hunger for more land, apartheid in its philosophy has envisaged surrendering land for the different 'Bantustans' and even land for neighbouring Swaziland.[16]

South Africa has indicated some readiness to give up direct occupation of territory, but without giving up indirect control over what goes on in that territory. South Africa's readiness to give 'independence' to Bantu 'homelands' is an assertion of this readiness to relinquish direct occupation. The Transkei's 'independence' in 1976 was the first of these moves. South Africa's Machiavellian plans for Namibia also include the prospect of a partial end to direct occupation.

And yet the kind of ethnic Balkanization envisaged for Namibia is bound to make a mockery of the country's prospective 'sovereignty'. South Africa intends to reduce occupation of Namibia, but without losing control.

As for the Transkei, its dependence on South Africa is well and truly assured by physical fragmentation of territory, combined with ethnic dispersal. As a British commentator put it:

> The Transkei, made up of three unconnected areas totalling the size of

Denmark, can never be economically independent of South Africa. Physically the least fragmented of South Africa's black homelands, it is the only one capable of achieving sufficient economic self-reliance to improve its economic relationship with the republic from one of complete subservience to self-respecting interdependence. However, the odds are stacked against it. . . . Vorster plans to give Transkei and other homelands a kind of freedom while tying them to the necessity to export their black workers to the white republic for jobs where they will have minimal rights. A quarter of a million Transkeians will have to go to white areas to work.[17]

In its more conciliatory moments, especially under American pressure, the Israeli Labour government also indicated periodically a readiness to give up part of the West Bank of the Jordan 'in the context of a general peace settlement'. But even the Israeli Labour government would still want to maintain control over the West Bank either through institutionalized arrangements or through the militarily weak government of Jordan. Israel under Labour would at times even consider a kind of 'Bantu homeland' for Palestinians, provided it was decidedly not a sovereign state, nor an autonomous political actor. Hence Israel's insistence that, even in peace negotiations, the Palestinians should somehow be represented as part of Jordan's delegation.

The paramount imperative of ethno-cultural exclusivity nevertheless continues to bring the ideology of apartheid closer to the ideology of Zionism in spite of divergent techniques of implementation. South Africa's 'homelands' policy seeks to strip South African citizenship from those deemed to be citizens of a Bantustan. Thus all Xhosa are declared to have ceased, or to be in the process of ceasing, to be South African now that the Transkei and, with even less credibility, the Ciskei, have attained 'independence'. This applies even to those Xhosa who are still living in the heartland of South Africa and have been outside the 'Bantustans' all their lives.

Thus the dream of apartheid is to have the heartland of South Africa 'white'. The richest and largest part of the country is to be reserved for the privileged immigrant Caucasian minorities.

Similarly, the logic of creating a Jewish state in Palestine has all along required that the great majority of citizens should be Jewish by one means or another.

There are two main approaches to such contrived ethnic preponderance. One is to increase the population of the privileged ethnic population. The other approach, as we indicated earlier, is somehow to reduce the population of the unwanted ethnic groups.

Both Israel and South Africa have devised ways of experimenting with the two approaches. On the strategy of increasing the population of the privileged group, both Israel and South Africa have had elaborate immigration laws which are ethnically discriminatory. As we argued before, that is what Israel's Law of Return is all about. Whether one defines Jewishness in religious or in ethnic terms, there is no doubt that Israeli immigration laws are comparable in their exclusivist implications to the old 'White Australia' policy. As we indicated, a Jew from, say, Eastern Europe who has had no connection with Palestine except for a tenuous myth two thousand years old has almost automatic access to Israel, whereas an Arab who was born in Palestine, and fled in 1948, can enjoy no right of literal return. The logic of the Jewish state has sanctioned the kind of discriminatory laws which the Jews themselves would condemn were they applied against them by some other state. If the United States Congress were to adopt immigration statutes for America which gave priority entry to white Anglo-Saxon Protestants, Jews all over the world would be among the first to protest. Yet Israel has laws which, by the very logic of creating a Jewish state, discriminate against both Christians and Muslims in favour of Jews.

The logic of white supremacy in South Africa has similarly resulted in immigration practices which encourage white settlers and discourage all other potential immigrants. Both Israel and South Africa have thus strongly promoted policies which aim to increase the population of the 'master race' within the total citizenry at the expense of other groups.

What about the parallel strategy of trying to reduce the population of the unwanted ethnic groups? Let us return to this theme in greater detail. On this issue, Israel has once again turned out to be as brutal as South Africa. Neither country has succeeded in 'purifying' itself ethnically. Apartheid has not managed to do without large numbers of black people in 'white' areas. And we know that Israel is still landed with a population which is one tenth Arab.

Yet white South Africa cannot be accused of the kind of tactics which Zionists used in 1948 to get as many Arab Palestinians as possible to flee for their lives. Those tactics ranged from threatening ghetto-dwellers in cities with 'the outbreak of cholera and typhus' to brutal intimidation by Jewish troops in the Lydda-Ramle. In such areas Arab Palestinians, all destitute, were given an hour to leave.

We have already referred to the worst single event in those early days, the notorious massacre of Arab villagers at Deir Yassin. Those who were killed by Jewish fanatics were old men, women and children. They were brutally and deliberately butchered. Many were stripped and sadistically mutilated. Some were thrown into a well in sheer random cruelty. Arthur Koestler described the Deir Yassin massacre as 'the psychologically decisive factor in this spectacular exodus'. It certainly contributed to the de-Arabization of Palestine as frightened inhabitants scrambled for refuge in neighbouring countries.

The Jewish state which was envisaged by the United Nations upon voting in favour of its creation in 1947 would have contained a 45 per cent Arab population. With a birth rate higher than that of the Jews, the Arabs in Israel might well have begun to equal if not outnumber the Jews by the 1970s, just as Muslims had begun to outnumber the Christians in Lebanon by the same period. But Zionist tactics in the early years of Israel's existence which led to the exodus of 700,000 Palestinians from their homes were so successful that a larger Israel in the 1980s has nevertheless a much smaller proportion of Arabs. South Africa under the Nationalist Party has embarked on a comparable brutal strategy of demographic manipulation. The regime in Pretoria since 1948 has often dreamt of the day when the heartland of South Africa would be completely white. The regime has tried to engineer a similar exodus of blacks by forced removals of 2,500,000 people to their 'homelands' between 1960 and 1983. On this issue of demographic manipulation there is little doubt that Zionism since 1948 has been as ruthless and cynical as apartheid.

Once the Israelis succeeded in reducing the Arab population of their country to less than a quarter of what it would otherwise have been, they could then simply take a stand against letting them come back to Israel. The Israelis have argued that it was up to other Arab countries to absorb these refugees. After all, they were fellow Arabs. Why should they go back to what was once Palestine? In the words of Abba Eban to the United Nations in 1957 on the issue of Palestinian refugees:

The responsibility of the Arab governments is threefold. Theirs is the initiative for its creation. Theirs is the onus for its endurance. Above all — theirs is the capacity for its solution.[18]

Abba Eban's assumption here is that because the Palestinians were Arabs, it was up to countries like Jordan, Syria, and Lebanon to absorb them into their own societies. It was like the government in Pretoria arguing that because a Xhosa or Zulu was an African, it was up to Angola, Mozambique, and Zambia to integrate them as fellow Africans. Xhosa and Zulu of South Africa are, of course, not merely black; they are also South Africans. Why should they be satisfied with being absorbed into Zambian or Angolan societies? Similarly, Palestinians were not merely Arab, they were also Palestinians. Why should they be satisfied with absorption into present-day Syrian, Lebanese, or Jordanian societies?

These Arabs, in short, are displaced persons in the fullest, most tragic meaning of the term. . . . Unlike other refugees, *these refuse to move, they insist on going home.*[19]

It is because of these factors that, strictly on the issue of displacement, the plight of Palestinians has been more tragic than that of the Zulu, Xhosa, and other South African blacks.

Yet the fate of these South African blacks is tragic enough. They may not have been induced to stream for safety to their 'homelands', but they have been made to feel humiliated, brutalized, and wantonly exploited. In the ultimate analysis the ideology of Zionism does converge with the philosophy of apartheid: both are discriminatory ideologies whose implementation inevitably and logically necessitated strategies of repression and ethnic exclusivity.

Yet internally, with their own societies, the privileged groups have been relatively humane. White South Africa within itself is one of the more liberal polities on the African continent. The white newspapers within South Africa are among the freest in the region; the judges are among the most independent; the white workers are among the most privileged.

Similarly, Israel within itself is the most liberal polity in the Middle East. Although both white South Africa and Israel score high in their treatment of their own 'kith and kin', the logic of their ethnic exclusivity prevents them from being humane to their own neighbours.

The result for each of them has been regional isolation. Sometimes they see this isolation in heroic terms. There is, for example, the image of Israel as a courageous immigrant community which has managed to defy a hostile environment and survive with honour. This hero-image of Israel has been important for white South Africans, as it was for white Rhodesians. *Die Burger*, for instance, draws inspiration from Israel's example of victorious loneliness in these words:

We in South Africa would be foolish if we did not at least take account of the possibility that we are destined to become a sort of Israel in a preponderantly hostile Africa, and that fact might become part of our national way of life.[20]

It is partly this sense of shared isolation that has led in the 1970s to a new *entente cordiale* between the land of apartheid and the land of Zionism. This has included reports that South Africa was prepared to finance 'an expansion of Israel's arms producing capacity', partly in exchange for South Africa's purchase of Israeli-built jet fighters.[21]

More immediately controversial in terms of Israeli—American relations was the news that Israel was building two missile boats for delivery to South Africa. American officials in the State Department were becoming concerned about aspects of Israeli—South African relations, according to 'usually reliable sources'.

The sources expect more US criticism of the links between Israel's state-owned Military Industry and South Africa.[22]

Israel is said to have been advised that deals like the missile boat arrangement with South Africa could hamper the efforts which Americans were making to help reduce Israel's international isolation. In some circles there has also been a fear that Israel's increasing friendship with South Africa could strain relations between American Jews and African-Americans.

Direct [US] aid to Israel would certainly be viewed by many black observers here as indirect aid to the hated South African regime. . . . [According to some blacks] pro-Israeli policies [could] become by extension pro-South African policies.[23]

Behind it all was the rapid evaporation of Israel's early idealism and moral fervour. Israel was becoming another paragon of commercialized warfare and arms trade. The little country was, *per capita*, trying to outstrip France as a cynical dealer in the arts of destruction. The main difference was that Israel's clients, unlike those of France, were disproportionately reactionary:

A list of [Israel's] clients that includes South Africa and Bolivia, and a sales catalogue with counter-insurgency weapons, does not sit too well with liberals anywhere.[24]

The most ominous of all the cynicism is the apparent nuclear collaboration between South Africa and Israel. Is Israel's technological expertise entering into an alliance with South Africa's financial power to create parallel nuclear capabilities in the two countries? Circumstantial evidence in support of the thesis that a joint military-industrial complex between Israel and South Africa is in the making has increased, especially since 1979.

The South African Iron and Steel Corporation is cooperating with Israel's Koor enterprise. Trade between the two countries has greatly increased since 1973. Alongside this industrial and commercial cooperation is the growing interaction in militarily relevant areas, from counter-insurgency to nuclear collaboration. In counter-insurgency, Israel has supplied military fencing equipment for use on the northern borders of South Africa against African National Congress (ANC) guerrillas. Israeli soldiers have from time to time acted as South African army instructors, have taken part in joint manoeuvres, and have engaged in operations against SWAPO, the Namibian freedom fighters.

In nuclear collaboration, it seems, from a leaked CIA report, that Israel and South Africa jointly tested a nuclear weapon at sea over the South Atlantic on 22 September 1979, a test that was monitored by a United States satellite. The explosion took place at a height of eight kilometers, which is commensurate with the performance of the G5 howitzer manufactured in South Africa or of Gabriel missiles fired from Reshef gunboats, both manufactured in Israel and both sold by Israel to South Africa. The nuclear bomb may have been produced at the Pelindaba nuclear reactor in South Africa but it is more likely to have been an Israeli bomb. The dissident Israeli nuclear technician Mordechai Vanunu revealed to the *Sunday*

Times of London in 1986 that Israel began developing nuclear weapons at its Dimona reactor in the Negev desert in the late 1960s and had produced 100 to 200 atomic warheads in twenty years.[25] Clearly, a possible motive for Israel to cooperate with South Africa in the military field would be to find friendly territory (the Kalahari desert) or friendly territorial waters where its nuclear technology could be tested.

In reality nuclear power may be more relevant for the survival of Zionism than for the survival of apartheid. Zionism's most dangerous adversary lies outside Israel — in the determination of the Palestinians and their prospective military and economic allies. Apartheid's most dangerous adversary is within South Africa in the form of internal black militancy. Israel could conceivably use military nuclear weapons against its external adversaries, but the architects of apartheid could hardly threaten nuclear annihilation against the restless masses of Soweto. In the ultimate analysis, apartheid is vulnerable from within where nuclear weapons are largely irrelevant. But Zionism is, in the first instance, vulnerable from without. In those circumstances a nuclear capability could at least delay the final day of reckoning for Jewish exclusivity.

Despite this assymetry in nuclear relevance between the techniques of Zionism and the strategies of apartheid, a momentous alliance has nevertheless emerged since the 1970s between Israel and Southern Africa.

Conclusion

When the Nazis asserted their control in Germany in the 1930s and proceeded to put their racist doctrines against the Jews into practice, the Nationalist Party in South Africa responded in sympathy. Dr Malan's Afrikaner Nationalist movement helped to work up an anti-Semitic hysteria in South Africa and provided an umbrella of semi-legitimacy to such fascist groups in the Union as the Greyshirts, the Blackshirts, and the Brownshirts. The centenary celebration of the Great Trek in 1938 aroused renewed racist fervour among Afrikaners, and Dr Malan appealed to 'the spirit of Blood River in a new Trek' in terms which were basically neo-Nazi.

Malan and his comrades were the architects of apartheid. These were the people who were trying to rally white South Africa behind the ideals of Nazism, urging South Africans at least to remain neutral in World War II. For a while Malan and his party lost — and Smuts carried white South Africa with him on the side of Britain. The vote in the South African parliament was relatively close. The outcome delayed the worst excesses of apartheid for another decade.

However, while Dr Malan and his fellow racial purists in South Africa awaited their chance to capture power, the Jews in Germany were suffering precisely from doctrines of racial purity and exclusiveness. In the words of Rupert Emerson of Harvard University:

> It is to Hitler and the Nazis that we are indebted for the full development of the appalling potentialities of the national concept in both its personal and its territorial aspects. . . . Under the spell of the Nazi racial doctrines, Germany moved to a ruthless implementation of the dogma that only the proper German was a member of the nation, entitled to an equal share in the state. . . . The Nazis likewise developed the fullest application of the idea that all persons whose origins were in the German community continued to be members of the *Volk* whatever their present residence and citizenship.[26]

What about all persons of Jewish origin regardless of their present residence and citizenship? On this issue Zionism had even more in common with pan-Germanism than does Afrikaner nationalism. The Jewish victims of Nazi exclusivity were driven to seek a new refuge in Palestine, based in turn on their own ethno-cultural exclusiveness. Those who ran away from the brutality of a 'pure Germany' sought to establish for themselves a 'pure Jewish State'.

On what principles could the Jews do this? Rupert Emerson answered in the following terms:

> The conception of creating a Jewish national home in Palestine could not possibly be squared with the principle of self-determination, or for that matter, of democracy, on the basis of any of the generally accepted criteria. The Arabs . . . received neutral support from the King-Crane Commission sent by President Wilson to ascertain the state of affairs in Syria and Palestine. Asserting that the Zionists looked to practically complete dispossession of the non-Jewish inhabitants of Palestine, this commission found nearly nine-tenths of the population to be non-Jewish and emphatically opposed to the entire Zionist program. . . . To the Arabs it [turned out to be] a prolonged and tragically successful invasion of an Arab country by an alien people under Western imperialist auspices, ending in the expulsion of most of the people whose country it was. No suggestion of a plebiscite accompanied the General Assembly's proposal that Palestine be partitioned.[27]

By the 1980s the logic of Zionism had come full-circle. The successors of Dr Malan in South Africa, once fervent in supporting Hitler's anti-Semitism, are now in alliance with the successors of Chaim Weizmann and Ben Gurion. The strategy of displacing Palestinians has found a point in common with the strategy of stripping black South Africans of their citizenship. The policy of opposing the creation in Palestine of a 'secular, democratic State in which Jews, Muslims, and Christians might live together' is now allied to a philosophy which opposed the creation of a diverse, democratic state in which Boer, Bantu, and Briton might live together. The anti-pluralist element in Zionism is now aligned with the anti-pluralist element in apartheid. Somehow the ghosts of Auschwitz in Germany, of Deir Yassin in Palestine, and of Sharpeville and Soweto in South Africa are suddenly in bewildered communion with each other. In the nightmare of historical change, those who might once have made strange bedfellows are now rudely transformed into natural if pathetic allies.

Notes

1. For further citations from Mazzini and other thinkers who relate nationality to divine purpose see Boyd C. Shafer, *Nationalism: Myth and Reality* (New York: Harcourt, Brace and Company, 1955), chapter 2.
2. Cited by Hans Kohn, 'Zion and the Jewish National Idea', the *Menorah Journal*, 46, 1 and 2, Autumn-Winter, 1958.
3. Morris R. Cohen, *The Faith of a Liberal* (New York: Holt, 1946).
4. Dan Kurzman, *Genesis 1948, the First Arab-Israeli War* (New York: The New American Library, 1970), p. 23.
5. See C. G. Montefiore, 'Nation or Religious Community?' reprinted in *Zionism Reconsidered*, edited by Michael Selzer (London: Macmillan, 1970), p. 61. Montefiore's discussion of these issues

originally appeared in *Transactions of the Jewish Historical Society of England*, 4, 1899—1901 (London, 1903).

6. Meyer Fortes, *Kinship and the Social Order* (Chicago: Aldine Publishing Company, 1969), p. 104.

7. C. G. Montefiore (note 5), p. 51.

8. See 'Israel Acknowledges Jewishness of Tribe of Northern Ethiopia', *The Washington Post*, 5 January 1973. For an alternative interpretation of why the K'ai-feng Jews were assimilated in China, consult Song Nai Rhee, 'Jewish Assimilation: The Case of Chinese Jews', *Comparative Studies in Society and History*, 15, 1, January 1983, pp. 115—126. On the question of the limits of the cultural assimilation of the Jews in foreign lands consult also Maurice Samuel, *I, The Jew* (1927) (Harcourt Brace, 1954 edition).

9. J. H. P. Serfontein, *Apartheid Change and the NG Kerk* (New York: Pilgrim Press, 1983).

10. *The Times* (London), 14 September 1982.

11. For a recent study of the Afrikaner mind, consult David Harrison, *The White Tribe of Africa* (London: BBC Publications, Los Angeles and Berkeley: University of California Press, 1982).

12. For a discussion of Childers's findings and their relevance for the present militancy of the Palestinian refugees consult the illuminating series of articles carried by *The Guardian* (London) in October 1972. See especially Paul Balta, 'Palestinian Refugees: A Growing National Consciousness', *The Guardian*, 21 October 1972.

13. See article by Yuval Elizur (*Washington Post* special), *Chicago Sun Times*, 16 August 1972.

14. American Friends Service Committee, *A Compassionate Peace: A Future for the Middle East* (New York: Hill and Wang, 1982), pp. 30—31.

15. Consult Terrance Smith, 'Israelis Debate Morality and Economics of Using Arab Laborers', *The New York Times*, 12 April 1972.

16. For some discussion of the principle of macro-segregation and its logic of repression see Pierre L. van den Berghe, *Race and Racism: A Comparative Perspective* (New York: John Wiley & Sons, 1967), pp. 108—110.

17. *The Sunday Times* (London), 15 August 1976. For a broader introduction see Ezekiel Mphahlele, 'South Africa: Two Communities and the Struggle for a Birthright', *Journal of African Studies*, 4, 1, Spring 1977, pp. 21—50.

18. Erskine Childers, 'The Other Exodus', *The Spectator* (London), 12 May 1961. For some of the wider moral issues touching on the issue of the Jewish conscience in relation to Israel consult Irving Louis Horowitz, *Israeli Ecstasies/Jewish Agonies* (New York: Oxford University Press, 1974).

19. Ibid. The emphasis is in the original.

20. *Die Burger*, 13 March 1962. Cited by Colin and Margaret Legum, *South Africa: Crisis for the West* (Pall Mall Press, 1964), pp. 107—108.

21. *New York Times*, 18 April 1976.

22. Jason Morris, 'Israel—South African Deal Stirs Debate', *Christian Science Monitor* (Washington), 12 August 1976.

23. *The Washington Post*, 21 April 1976.

24. *The Sun* (US), 18 August 1976.

25. Insight, 'Revealed: the secrets of Israel's nuclear arsenal', *The Sunday Times* (London), 5 October 1986, pp. 1, 4 and 5.

26. Emerson, *From Empire to Nation* (Cambridge: Harvard University Press, 1960), pp. 111—112.

27. Ibid., pp. 313—314.

9

On Youth
& Revolution

The Beijing Spring
& the Palestinian Intifadah

In December 1987 an uprising erupted in the Palestinian territories under Israeli occupation. It was a revolt against twenty years of Israeli military rule and a demand for Palestinian self-determination. A young generation of Palestinians found the will to sustain the revolt month after month — as hundreds of people were killed, maimed or detained.

In the spring of 1989 a pro-democracy movement started among students in Beijing. It was a revolt against corruption and dictatorship and a demand for a more open society. At first the demonstrations at Tiananmen Square in Beijing were given greater tolerance than anything ever extended to Palestinians in twenty years of Israeli occupation. The most important foreign visit to China since President Nixon's had to accommodate itself to the activities of the students. Gorbachev's visit to Beijing had to be relocated and rescheduled. But then in the first week of June 1989 the students' movement in Tiananmen Square was brutally crushed. Those hundred flowers were not allowed to bloom.

In this essay we seek to understand both the protesters and the suppressers, both the Palestinian uprising and the Israeli repression, both the pro-democracy students in Beijing and the hard-liners who crushed them. But we are approaching these phenomena of protest and power from a much wider perspective. We seek to explore the nature of historical change and the dynamic of civilization itself. Our focus is on a specific Sino-Semitic comparison in our own times.

Between the Exodus and the Long March

Purposeful nostalgia is one of the bonds linking the Semitic and Chinese people. Israel is after all a country which was born out of Jewish nostalgia — out of an effort to re-establish a Jewish state which had died two thousand years earlier.

Among the Jewish right-wing groups today, nostalgia has also been the inspiration for Israeli expansionism. Both Menachem Begin and Yitzhak Shamir as Prime Ministers were against exchanging territory for peace for reasons connected with a desire to recreate the past. The insistence on renaming the Palestinian occupied territories as 'Judaea' and 'Samaria' is part of that expansionist nostalgia. The Law

164

of Return is supposed to be the concluding chapter to a drama which began with the Mosaic Exodus from Egypt three millennia previously.

On the other hand, Communist China has at times experienced a profound desire to *destroy* nostalgia — resulting in what J. M. Roberts has described as 'extraordinary bursts of violent reaction against much of the Chinese past'.[1] The Cultural Revolution was a rebellion not only against ancient scholarship but also against ancestral family values:

> A quarter of mankind hurled itself (or was hurled) into the assault on tradition. The memorial stele of Confucius at Qufu still reveals . . . repaired cracks which record its deliberate shattering during the Cultural Revolution. This might be taken as an extreme symptom of the westernizing ethos, a brutal expression of the enthusiasm for modernization which many radicals felt. Religion was attacked whatever its origin, and so in China the militant secularism of nineteenth-century Europe won some of its last victories. . . .[2]

Such a revolt against nostalgia was quite the opposite of what Israel symbolized. The Chinese youth in the 1960s were in rebellion against custom and Confucius: Israeli youth continued to be inspired by the Judaic heritage even when they were secular in their own behaviour.

Since the mid-1970s China has moderated its rebellion against its ancient past, and initiated a partial retreat from its more immediate past. Confucius has retrieved some of his legitimacy — while Mao Tse-tung has lost some of his. Modernization under Deng Xiaoping was defined less as a rejection of ancient values and more as a renewed acceptance of market values without political pluralism.

In the case of Israel from the mid-1970s there was an even deeper return to ancestral values as right-wing and religious parties made significant gains in the political process. The heritage of Judaism was getting more deeply politicized.

What is not often realized is that China too had taken a stride *towards* Judaism when it went communist in the first place. Those two wars of 1948 — Jew versus Arab in the Middle East and Communist versus Nationalist in China — were both struggles over the Judaic heritage in varying degrees. This is partly because Marxism itself is not only a secular ideology — it is a creed which bears the marks of a rabbinic and Judaic impact. There is therefore some truth to the proposition that when China was moving towards a Marxist triumph in 1948–49, it was under the inspiration of a secular offshoot of Judaism.

Part of this cultural convergence arises out of the rabbinic background of Karl Marx's own heritage. Marx was not only ethnically of Jewish descent, but also descended from a long line of rabbis. In a metaphorical sense, and in spite of his own atheistic views, Marx unwittingly entered into the great tradition of Jewish prophets. He was a visionary seer, a moral sage and an impassioned oracle.

Mao Tse-tung in China was no Moses — though the Long March of Mao's movement enjoys almost the same heroic reverence in the history of Chinese communism that the original Jewish exodus from Egypt enjoys in biblical legend. The Chinese Long March covered 6,000 miles — while the Communists crossed eighteen mountains and valleys to reach the north-western province of Shensi. Both China's Long March and the original Hebrew exodus from Egypt were miraculous and heroic. For Mao and the Communist troops there was no equivalent to the Red Sea miraculously parting to let them pass. Yet the Chinese marchers did cross 24 rivers on the way — traversing jungles under fire. Out of 100,000 Communist troops who broke out of Kuomintang encirclement on 15

October 1934, only about 8,000 survived to arrive almost exactly a year later in Shensi in October 1935.

What should be borne in mind is that the Marxist inspiration of the Chinese Long Marchers and the Mosaic inspiration of the Jewish exodus were both off-springs of the same heritage. It is to this linkage between Marxism and Judaism that we must now turn.

A Marxist Debt to Judaism

The name Marx is a shortened form of Mordechai, later changed to Markus. Karl's father — Heinrich Marx — was born in 1782, the third son of Meier Halevi Marx — who became Rabbi of Trier. Karl Marx's paternal grandmother was also descended from Rabbis. As Davis McLellan put it in his biography of Karl Marx:

> In fact almost all the Rabbis of Trier from the sixteenth century onwards were ancestors of Marx.[3]

Marx's father converted to Protestantism for purely economic and professional reasons the year before Karl was born. When Karl was baptized in 1824, his mother Henrietta described herself as Jewish. Later on Karl Marx's youngest daughter, Eleanor, though only half-Jewish, said with defiant pride at a workers' meeting in the East End of London, 'I am a Jewess.'[4]

Marx himself showed signs of anti-Semitism — as in his pamphlet *On the Jewish Question*. But does Marx's whole system of ideas betray his rabbinic ancestry? Does his lifestyle lie in the prophetic tradition? Does his appearance affirm that prophetic credential?

Marx owed a lot to the German philosopher, Hegel. From Hegel Marx took the idea of the dialectic. According to Hegel, the evolutionary quest for greater unity and truth is achieved by the dialectic, positing something (a thesis), denying or opposing it (its antithesis), and combining the two half-truths (in a synthesis). Nachman Krochmal (1785—1849) — whose life overlapped with that of Marx — Hegelianized Jewish history. As a neo-Hegelian, Krochmal viewed the Jewish people as the bearer of the historical process. We are back to the concept of the chosen people. Krochmal added a cyclical dynamic to history. The Jews were the only nation to rise again and again, re-invigorated after every decline. The Jews alone had a direct link with the Absolute Spirit. It followed therefore that the Jews were a source of special creativity, for each new ascent brought a higher level of self-realization.

Karl Marx accepted Hegel's doctrine of the dialectic, of movement between thesis, antithesis and synthesis. But for Marx the cyclic movement of history was not to be given to a nation like the French or Germans (Hegel) or the Jews (Krochmal). For Karl Marx history will synthesise and culminate not in the triumph of a chosen nation or people but in the victory of an economic class. For Karl Marx the chosen people are not the Jews but the proletariat.

The idea that the Jews are the Elect of God has been recurrent in Jewish liturgy. 'For you are a people holy to the Lord your God, and the Lord has chosen you to be a people of his own possession, out of all the nations that are on the face of the earth' (Deuteronomy, 14:2).

For Karl Marx the proletariat was not the Elect of God but the Elect of History. And salvation is not for the individual (as in Christian liberalism or Reform Judaism) but for the whole of society. For Marx salvation is through revolution on this earth. Mao Tse-tung embraced this thesis — and translated it into the Long March right through into the cultural revolution.

There is the alternative interpretation that Marx's concept of the proletariat is *messianic*. For Jews 'the Messiah as envisioned by the prophets, transmitted by the tradition, and embraced by the consciousness of the Jewish people, is the capstone of Judaism'.[5] For Jews and Christians history will come to an end at the next appearance of the Messiah. For Karl Marx, politics and states will come to an end with the victory of the proletariat and the achievement of a classless society.

For Marx the messianic role is not to be played by an individual but by the supreme class of historical destiny — the proletariat. Mao Tse-tung re-defined the proletariat to encompass the masses of a rural country like China.

Although the idea of Divine Sadism is close to blasphemy, in the Old Testament God is often cruel in order to be kind. Noah had to have an ark to save only a fraction of God's creation. Sadistic or not, God elected not to preserve most people from His angry floods. For Karl Marx history (like God) has also been cruel in order to be kind. But for Marx the curse of history is not on the sexual sinners but on the economic exploiters. History's damnation is not upon the first born. History's curse is upon the privileged of each epoch of class struggle. Sodom and Gomorrah are re-created in each epoch and then destroyed. But the excesses are not of lust but greed.

Other aspects of Marx's prophetic tendencies are closer to Christianity than Judaism. In Karl Marx the Original Sin is indeed avarice. It was avarice which masochistically was responsible for:

— Causing class formation
— Causing class struggle
— Causing revolution
— Causing death

Marx then allowed a cycle of redemption before greed once again disrupted society. There is an underlying fatalism in Marx's theory of historical materialism. This is the inexorable march of class struggle. The 'march of class struggle' was part of the inspiration behind China's Long March.

The Hegelian aspects of Marxism are also partly biblical. The negation of the negation is a Hegelian principle. And the Bible says that out of death life often arises. Adam would have had eternal life but for his sin. Was it the sin of greed or disobedience? Jesus's death on the cross much later was the negation of Adam's death:

As by one sole man sin entered the world,
And death by sin.
And thus death passed to all men,
because all have sinned. . . .

As from one sole transgression
there followed condemnation for all,
So from one sole deed of justice,
there followed justification for life.[6]

In the Divine Dialectic Jesus and Adam become two Adams — two men who determined the whole course of human destiny. The fifteenth chapter of the First Corinthians is more explicit about this doctrine of the two Adams:

Thus is it written:
There was made the first man, Adam,
   living soul,
The last Adam,
   lifegiving spirit.

If therefore Marxism shows the impact of aspects of the Old Testament, and even of the New, to what extent did China turn its back on religion by going Marxist? By going Marxist the Chinese took two steps away from Confucius — and one step closer to the Judeo-Christian heritage. China without Marxism was an even more 'inscrutable' society than China under the influence of a renegade ethnic Jew of the nineteenth century, descended from a long line of rabbis from Trier.

The Chosen of God and the Elect of History

Theories abound about who are the decisive history-making groups in society. Social Darwinism created a human paradigm of the survival of the fittest — making the most enterprising groups the vanguard of fundamental change.

Racial Darwinism created a hierarchy of races — sometimes making the Anglo-Saxons the vanguard race of history. Under the Nazis racial Darwinism put the German people in the forefront of human destiny.

The Jewish concept of the 'chosen people' is a religious rather than a racial concept. It does not create a whole hierarchy of religious privilege — but it does separate out the Jews as an extra-special category of the human species.

As we indicated earlier, Marxism does not have a concept of 'the chosen people' but it does have a *de facto* concept of the chosen class. Marxism does not have a concept of the Elect of God, but it does indeed have a concept of the Elect of History. The chosen class is the proletariat — sometimes defined in China in terms which paradoxically encompass the peasantry.

Then there are the theories which entrust history to great personalities. In the nineteenth century the most honest of such theories in the English-speaking world was propounded by Thomas Carlyle in his works about Oliver Cromwell and Frederick the Great, and in his little book *On Heroes, Hero-Worship and the Heroic in History*. What we would now call charismatic figures capture the moment of destiny — and, according to Carlyle, push societies one more step forward.

All these concepts of the chosen people, the chosen race, the chosen class and the chosen personality may have contributed to our partial understanding of the historical process.

The big gap is perhaps an adequate theory of the chosen age-grade. Is the younger generation now destined to play a special role in human destiny? On the evidence so far, the historical role of the younger generation has been more convincingly demonstrated in the Third World than in the First and Second Worlds.

We define the First World of advanced capitalist countries — mostly North America, Western Europe and Japan. We define the Second World as that of advanced socialist countries — mainly the Soviet Union and its allies in Eastern Europe. We define the Third World as the universe of the technologically underdeveloped countries.

168

It is in this Third World that the younger generation has sometimes played a historic role. In Ethiopia in 1974 students played a part not only in overthrowing an ancient imperial dynasty under Haile Selassie — but they were also decisive in radicalizing the soldiers who captured power. In fact the students' role in pushing the military regime to the left was more fundamental than their role in toppling Haile Selassie.

In Iran under the Shah young people were part of the waves of demonstrators who gave up their lives in the streets of Teheran in 1978 and 1979 to bring down the Pahlavi dynasty. It was the most impressive non-violent demonstration since Mahatma Gandhi galvanized India some forty years earlier.

In the streets of Khartoum in 1985, young people protested against President Jaafar Nimeiry and forced the army to intervene and bring Nimeiry down after more than fifteen years in power. Civilian rule was later restored.

In South Korea students were the absolute vanguard of the struggle for democracy. From time to time large numbers of them were killed in the process of agitation for a more open society. In 1987 and 1988 they made major gains in the democratization of Korea.

And then came the Palestinian Intifadah — erupting in December 1987 in the occupied Arab territories. Since 1948 the Arabs had waged five major wars against Israel — and, basically, lost every one of them. The Intifadah was a brand new experience for the military might of Israel. For the first time the Israelis were confronting an adversary even weaker militarily than the Arab armies — but the younger adversary was endowed with a moral will which was of a different order. Month after month the casualties mounted — but the moral resolve of the young remained unshaken.

In far-away Beijing in the spring of 1989 another set of young people initiated their own Sino-Intifadah. For a while they retained a moral high ground of their own — as they turned the world's attention on the need for greater openness in the People's Republic of China. And then came the devastating first weekend of June 1989. Massive military power at Tiananmen Square crushed the democracy movement. The Chinese students had been a kind of collective Alexander Dubcek. Dubcek in Czechoslovakia in the spring of 1968 had attempted to give a human face to socialism. Then the tanks of the Warsaw Pact came rolling in in the name of Proletarian Internationalism. The Prague Spring of 1968 came to a brutal end.

Similarly the collective Dubcek of Beijing attempted to give to China a new socialism with a human face. The tanks of the 27th Army brought the Beijing Spring to a similarly brutal end.

The young people of both China and Palestine have attempted a fundamental vanguard role — not as a chosen people, or a chosen race, or a chosen class but as a chosen age-grade, the elect generation of history.

But it is worth remembering that young people sometimes play instrumental vanguard roles — rather than fundamental roles. When they play instrumental roles, it is to lead the implementation of a grand design chosen by others. From 1966 to 1969 students in China played a major role in implementing Mao Tse-tung's cultural revolution. The grand design was not of the youth. They were playing an instrumental role to implement policies made by others.

But the Palestinian Intifadah from 1987 onwards captured the initiative from the older generation. The demonstrators were playing a fundamental vanguard role, qualitatively different from that of the Palestine Liberation Organization.

Similarly the Sino-Intifadah of Beijing of 1989 — unlike the cultural revolution twenty years earlier — was an attempt by the young to play a fundamental, rather than an instrumental, vanguard role. In some sense, they saw themselves as the elect of history.

Between Masochism and Sadism

The Third World — most of Asia, Africa and Latin America — has a high propensity for collective masochism. The First World — Europe, the United States and Japan — has a long record of collective sadism.

Third World governments commit brutalities mainly against their own people (masochism). First World governments commit their worst brutalities against other people (sadism). Third World countries are victims of internal instability. First World countries are perpetrators of imperialism.

Where do China and Israel fit into this equation? China is ideologically part of the Second World of socialism. Technologically, however, it is part of the Third World of underdevelopment. China has a high propensity for collective masochism and continues to demonstrate tendencies of instability. The great Proletarian Cultural Revolution of the 1960s — especially from 1966 to 1969 — was one of the greatest eruptions of collective masochism even by Third World standards. Since Mao's death China has wanted to change itself technologically — to ease itself out of Third World realities. The quest for modernization is part of that desire.

But while technologically China has sought an exit out of Third World conditions, ideologically it has been reluctant to move too fast towards the First World. It has been reluctant to liberalize politically towards 'bourgeois democracy'. The student movement in the spring of 1989 was a declaration that modernization without democratization was not enough. Without saying so explicitly, the students were trying to nudge China towards the liberal paradigm of the First World. And then, all of a sudden, China's Third World collective masochism reasserted itself. The inherent Third World instability erupted. The human cost was heavy.

If China is still technologically Third World and ideologically Second World, what is the position of Israel? On the whole, Israel is both ideologically and technologically part of the First World — in spite of the fact that a large part of its population comes from Third World countries. Israel is a First World society not because 80 per cent of its population is Jewish but because 40 per cent is of Western and European extraction.

If the Third World is haunted by a tendency towards masochism, the First World has a record of sheer sadism against others. Part of the sadism has traditionally taken the form of imperialism.

Curiously enough, Israel started as a product of colonization rather than imperialism. Before 1948 deliberate Jewish settlement for Zionist reasons was indeed a case of colonization in the classical sense of the Pilgrim Fathers in America or the early Dutch settlers in South Africa. But it was not a case of imperialism in the sense of a powerful country dominating and exploiting a weaker society.

During the mandate period Palestine experienced both British imperialism and Jewish colonization. The British imperialist factor retreated in 1948. Jewish colonization became the Israeli state. One question which arose was whether the Jewish state would become an imperialist power in its own right. Would the chosen people become a chosen race?

A state created in the teeth of the opposition of indigenous people inevitably became a state surrounded by hostile neighbours. Could the collective sadism of the Western heritage be kept in check for very long? On the contrary, just as white Christians in Africa had used the Bible to justify imperialism, Jews in Palestine now used the Bible to justify Jewish expansion.

The expulsion of individual Palestinians, the shooting down of children, the bombing of Palestinian camps in Lebanon, and the detention of thousands of Arabs, are examples of official Israeli concessions to the country's own extremists. By the standards of German Nazism, these Israeli actions look benign. But by the standards of the Jewish dreams which accompanied the creation of Israel, something has gone seriously wrong. The dream of Israel is in danger of becoming a Jewish nightmare. Will Israel's collective sadism of today become Israel's collective masochism of tomorrow?

The Israelis thought that the Palestinian uprising was a threat to Israeli security. What the Israelis failed to realize was that the suppression of the Intifadah was a threat to Israeli democracy. If the whole of the Arab world had failed to defeat Israel in five and a half wars, how could a few thousand stone-throwing young Palestinians bring down the Israeli war machine?

The Intifadah itself is not 'a threat to Israeli security'. But the suppression of the Intifadah has been a threat to Israeli democracy. What form has that erosion of Israeli democracy taken? The impact has included, most immediately, the escalation of vigilante activities by Jewish settlers in the occupied territories. At a time when the United States is trying to recover from its old lynching tradition, Israeli citizens are learning the brutal tactics of lynch mobs and private executions.

Even Prime Minister Yitzhak Shamir is beginning to be alarmed that the Jewish settlers in the occupied territories have begun to take seriously his own proud proclamation that Jews can crush Palestinians like 'grasshoppers'.[7]

The second threat to Israeli democracy is the increased strength of the ultra-nationalist right wing in Israeli politics. The Jewish state has moved substantially to the right. Since the 1973 October War right-wing militancy carries both authoritarian and theocratic dangers in the Israeli context. Both the Israeli sense of fair play and the principle of the secular state have been at greater risk than ever since Menachem Begin inaugurated the era of right-wing militancy in Israeli politics.

The third threat to Israeli democracy is a new form of racism in Israeli thought. Within the wider move to the right in Israeli's political mood is the more ominous tendency of real nationalistic racism. The threat of Jewish racism is confronted honestly and frankly on campuses within the Jewish state itself. But on American campuses there is sometimes an attempt to silence voices which are prepared to say that Jews, too, can become racists, sometimes even fascists.

The worst threat to Israeli democracy is the widening of the moral gap between Israelis as victors and Jews as victims. What Jews suffered as victims, Israelis as victors are increasingly learning to practise. The 1989 decision to make Palestinians wear special badges correctly reminded many liberal Israelis of the yellow star that the Nazis had once forced Jews to wear.

Israelis as victors are diluting the moral standards that Jews as victims had originally set for themselves. The worst aspect concerns the spectre of fascist forms of arrogance and intolerance. Most Western countries encompass a fascist minority — the Ku Klux Klan (KKK) in the United States, the National Front in

France and Britain, and the residual Nazis in Germany. Fascism is one form of Western sadism. Has Israel caught up with the West in fascism, too?

'Judeo-Nazism': The Unthinkable?

Many friends of Israel are anxious that the repressive forces in the Jewish state are getting stronger — and a distinctly Israeli form of racism may be evolving. This is among a minority. But within that racist anti-Arab minority there may be a smaller and even more ominous sub-group.[8]

There is now a school of thought in Israel which is already becoming fascist. This issue is debated more frankly in Israel itself than in the United States. Lovers of democracy in Israel are alarmed by the fascist trend. There is even an Israeli term for this kind of Semitic fascism — Professor Yeshayahu Leibovitz of the Hebrew University has called it: Judeo-Nazism. As editor of *Encyclopaedia Hebraica*, Leibovitz has grappled with many trends in the Jewish experience. But he has now raised the issue of whether the concept of Judeo-Nazism is any longer a contradiction in terms.

Israelis are warning each other that the unthinkable is not necessarily impossible. Specific sociological conditions in inter-war Germany fostered right-wing extremism among the Germans. The history of German extremism started with a people who believed they had been humiliated and humbled.

The Treaty of Versailles which ended World War I created among many Germans a martyrdom complex which later favoured the rise of extreme nationalism. The martyrdom complex — strong among the Israelis today amd powerful among the Germans in the inter-war years — can degenerate into paranoia. We now know that lovers of democracy in the German population underestimated the danger. The whole world paid a heavy price for German paranoia.

Jews — like the Germans — have been impressive contributors to world civilization. But both people are human — and therefore psychologically vulnerable. The danger of extremism is real.

The stages of extremism through which the German psyche passed were as follows:

1. Martyrdom complex;
2. Paranoia;
3. Extreme nationalism;
4. Racial exclusivity;
5. Militarization and militarism;
6. Territorial expansionism.

It is very unlikely that Israelis will pass through similar stages. There are in any case major constraints to Israeli extremism. The question nevertheless remains whether the danger of fascism in Israel is real enough to alarm Israeli democrats themselves.

Israel was genuinely born out of the ashes and anguish of the holocaust. It was a more genuine martyrdom than was the Nazi sense of humiliation in the inter-war years.

But when does the martyrdom complex evolve into paranoia? In the case of the Jews, in two stages: (a) monopolizing the holocaust as an experience of the past; (b) pre-empting imaginary holocausts of the future.

A recent American immigrant into Israel from a religious family in New York prayed for a new persecution of Jews in the Diaspora so that they are forced to go to fortress Israel:

The hatred the Gentiles feel towards the Jews is eternal. There never was peace between us and them except when they totally beat us or when we shall totally beat them. Maybe if they will give someone like Sharon a chance to kill . . . until the Arabs will understand that we did them a favour letting them remain alive. . . . We are powerful now and power should talk now. The Gentiles only understand the language of power.[9]

Prime Minister Yitzhak Shamir declared in April 1988:

We say to them, from this hilltop and from the perspective of thousands of years of history, that in our eyes they are like grasshoppers.[10]

Menachem Begin's earlier denunciation of Palestinians as 'two-legged animals' has formed part of the same drift towards racist perceptions and perspectives in powerful Israeli circles.

Is Israeli nationalism stifling Israeli liberalism? Opinion polls of Israeli attitudes to the Palestinian uprising in the occupied territories is one measure. The death of over 500 Palestinians since the *Intifadah* began has not alarmed enough Israelis. Indeed, the majority of Israelis seem to want even stiffer measures against the Palestinians.

In its milder form, Israeli arrogance towards the Arabs is paternalistic. As an Israeli originally from Aden put it:

We know that the Arab is an obedient good creature as long as he is not incited . . . as no one puts ideas into his head. . . . He just has to be told exactly what his right place is. . . . They must understand who the master is. That's all.[11]

When united to fanaticism and nationalism, arrogance can take the form of neo-Nazi pronouncements. Take the case of the young rabbi who denounced the 'filth' of mixed marriages and the 'hybrid children' such marriages produce — 'a thorn in the flesh of the Jewish society in Israel'.[12] This particular rabbi even recommended school segregation and exclusion of Arabs from the universities. Echoes of apartheid are unmistakable.

As for the trend towards militarization, Israel has indeed become the most efficient war machine since Nazi Germany. In war after war the Jewish state has demonstrated staggering proficiency both in the air, on land and over water. The six-day war in June 1967 was its most dazzling military success. Did this military success increase territorial appetite?

In earlier years the Rabbinate had cited biblical authority to justify expulsion of the Arabs ('the foreign element') from the land, or simply their destruction, and religious law was invoked to justify killing of citizens in a war or raid.[13]

American rabbi Isaac Bernstein argued that religious law gives power and legitimacy to Israel to 'dispossess the Arabs of the conquered territories'.[14] Another rabbi, Rabbi Lubovitcher of New York, deplored Israel's failure to conquer Damascus during the 1973 October War.[15]

A doctrine emerged called 'secure and defensible borders'. After almost every war Israel has gained more territory. Because of Israel's military supremacy, only

Israel had such secure borders. The Arabs were easily penetrable by Israeli air and rocket power.

Rabbi Elazar Valdman of Gush Emunim wrote in the journal *Nekudah* about the West Bank settlers as follows:

> We will certainly establish order in the Middle East and in the world. And if we do not take this responsibility upon ourselves, we are sinners, not just towards ourselves but towards the entire world. For who can establish order in the world? All of those Western leaders of weak character?[16]

The small fascist minority in Israel is definitely succumbing to neo-Nazi proclivities. Among such extremists there is a search for a 'final solution' to the Palestinian problem. The Prime Minister's bravado was taken literally by extremists: 'We shall crush them like grasshoppers!'

It was only a matter of time before the moral cost had to be paid. The Director-General of Israel's Broadcasting Authority (radio and TV) in the 1970s was a 'long time admirer of South Africa and a frequent visitor there'. In 1974 he wrote an 'emotional article' expressing his preference for South Africa over black Africa, complete 'with citations of research proving genetic inferiority of blacks' — a view which 'seems to reflect the feelings of many in the Israeli elite'.[17]

The journal of Mapan (one wing of the Labour Alignment in Israel) published an explanation of the superiority of Israeli pilots. Blacks and Arabs were inferior in 'complex, cognitive intelligence'. That was why 'American Blacks succeed only in short distance running'.[18]

Israeli neo-Nazism reversed the scale of genetic values favoured by German Nazis. Both forms of extremism exaggerated the impact of the Jewish factor. The Nazi thought that the Jewish impact was negative. The Israeli extremists erred the other way.

Why has the United States outdistanced Europe in modern culture? The proportion of Jews in the American population has enhanced American creativity, according to this Israeli school of thought.[19] By implication German inventiveness before the holocaust was due to the Jewish creative infusion into the German population.

An Israeli labour party journal refers to 'genetic experiments' at Tel Aviv University — which have shown that 'Genetic differences among Jewish communities [Polish and Yemeni are cited] are smaller than those between Gentiles and Jews.'[20]

How have these minority factors influenced Israeli policies towards the Intifadah? How does Israel's performance in dealing with the Intifadah compare with the policies of the Chinese government towards the pro-democracy demonstrators in Beijing? Let us now return to this sub-theme in our Sino-Semitic comparison.

A Balance Sheet of Repression

It stands to the credit of the Israelis that over a period of eighteen months they have killed far fewer people than the Chinese seem to have done on a single weekend. That is a major difference between the 27th Army of China and the Israeli Defence Force. However, there is no room for complacency on either side.

To the credit of the Chinese is the fact that not a single student was hurt for some seven weeks while some of the highest Chinese leaders went to talk to them directly, face-to-face. The Israelis started killing Palestinians almost from the first day of the Intifadah. To the credit of the Chinese is the fact that the top leadership and the country as a whole have been deeply divided over the brutality — while Israeli public opinion seems to remain basically supportive of even harsher measures against the Palestinian uprising. To the credit of the Chinese is that the brutality against the students raised the spectre of armed conflict within the Chinese military itself.

In Israel, individual soldiers have spoken up at times against Israeli repression, and some other individual recruits have refused to serve. But the dissension within the Israeli army of occupation has not been deep enough to disturb overall military cohesion or threaten large-scale mutiny.

The Israelis have killed more than five hundred people in a Palestinian youth population of less than one million under their occupation. Let us assume that the Chinese army killed two thousand people in a Chinese youth population of approximately 400 million. In proportion to the number of young people under their respective jurisdictions (both within Israel and in the occupied territories) the Israeli army eliminated a far larger percentage of young people than has the Chinese army. Moreover, West Bank and Gaza demonstrations have never consisted of hundreds of thousands of people at a time. They have hardly ever consisted of tens of thousands.

The world has no idea how many people the Israeli Defence Force would kill at a time if confronted by the size of demonstrations which characterized the students' movement at Tiananmen Square in Beijing in May and early June 1989.

To the credit of the Chinese is that the suppression of students in Beijing has provoked student demonstrations in other Chinese cities. In Israel itself, there has been very little student agitation against the repression in Gaza and the West Bank. Even Israeli Arabs have been far more passive about repression in the occupied territories than Chinese students in Shanghai have been about repression in Beijing.

Comparative Western Reaction

As for the response of the outside world, the West's selective reaction to moral issues was worth noting. The United States imposed military sanctions against China's People's Liberation Army after one single weekend of chaos. But the United States continued to extend subsidies rather than sanctions in favour of the Israeli Defence Force after eighteen months of repression.

On 9 June 1989, the Australian Prime Minister, Robert Hawke, broke down in tears in public about the repression in Tiananmen Square. For an Anglo-Saxon leader such a tearful loss of control in public became world news. Even more remarkable was the fact that Mr Hawke was prime minister of a country which had long shut its doors against Chinese immigrants under its old 'white Australia' policy. And yet which Western leader ever shed tears for Palestinian casualties after a whole year and a half of the Intifadah?

Japan decided on tighter measures against the Beijing government after the brutal weekend of June 1989. And yet Japan had long been serenely relaxed about the brutal repression of the young in both Palestine and the Republic of South Africa over the years.

The question does indeed persist as to why the students' movement in China captured the imagination of Westerners more firmly in 1989 than had the Palestinian uprising in the Israeli-occupied territories. After all, the Palestinian youth had been in revolt from December 1987. The Chinese students' movement, on the other hand, lasted less than seven weeks in the spring of 1989. Yet both sets of young people were clamouring for freedom. Why the difference in Western response?

It would not be enough to say that China was a much bigger country than Israel plus the occupied territories added together. Size was relevant, but only marginally. Normally Israeli politics receive far more coverage in the American media than do the politics of China — size notwithstanding. And both China and the Middle East have a kind of fascination for the West.

In terms of international publicity the students' movement in China was indeed aided by Mikhail Gorbachev's visit to Beijing in May 1989. The visit was itself a momentous event in relations between the two communist giants after three decades of hostility. The Chinese students decided to regard Gorbachev as their *live* statue of liberty — before they later sculptured a more literal imitation of the New York statue. The disruptive impact of the students' movement on the ceremonies of Gorbachev's visit helped to attract spectacular international publicity. The Palestinian uprising had no equivalent media booster to intrigue Western journalists.

Were Western emotions engaged as a result of the brutal suppression of the Chinese student movement? As we indicated, the Israelis started shooting at Palestinians almost from the first day of the Intifadah — whereas the Chinese regime waited for more than six weeks before hurting any student's finger. We noted earlier that there were Chinese leaders like Zhao Ziyang who even treated the students' movement with respect at first — some of the leaders actually going personally to Tiananmen Square to beg the students to end the demonstrations and the hunger strike. The Israeli government at no stage treated the Palestinian protests with respect. We mentioned that Prime Minister Shamir even threatened to crush the protesters 'like grasshoppers'. It was not therefore brutality which engaged Western journalists. Israeli repression had started much earlier than the Chinese.

Part of the West's fascination with events in China was that there was a lot more at stake economically in China than on the West Bank. When I myself visited Tiananmen Square in 1987, it was as a participant at a massive international conference on a rather surprising subject for the People's Republic of China. Our conference in the Great Hall of the People was on *advertising*. There were about a thousand participants — including hundreds of Western businessmen. The whole mood of the conference concerned the economic opening up of China to external business interests. I was later singled out for special introduction to one or two Chinese leaders including the President. But that was window-dressing for Third World solidarity. The real focus of the conference concerned China's economic relations with the West. The Palestinian territories under Israeli occupation have had no comparable economic value for the West.

Yet another reason why Western sympathies were more dramatically engaged on the side of the Chinese youth was the fact that there were almost no conflicting Western emotions on the side of the oppressor. But in Gaza and the West Bank most Western observers were torn between friendly feelings towards Israel and revulsion at the shooting of children by Israeli security forces. A profound ambivalence affected even the emotions of American Jews, sympathetic as they are towards Israel. Indeed, many Israeli troops were themselves disturbed.

In fairness to the Israelis, their own excesses continued to be openly criticized at home. The Israeli leaders could get away with far less than could the Chinese leaders. Israel is a much more open society than China. What is more, Israeli law does not invoke the death sentence except in extremely rare cases (like the Nazi Eichmann).[21]

In fairness to the Western media, the Palestinian Intifadah had not been completely neglected. It received enough publicity to win for the Palestinian cause a lot more sympathy in the West in eighteen months than the Palestinian cause had received in the forty years since the creation of Israel.

Conclusion

1948 was the year in which Israel was created. 1948 was also the year in which the pro-apartheid National Party of South Africa came to power. Thirdly, 1948 was the year the communist Chinese began to turn the revolutionary tide against Chiang Kai Shek's nationalist movement. And fourthly, 1948 was the year of the United Nations' Universal Declaration of Human Rights. Momentous historical events converged on the year 1948. A stage was being set for both First World sadism and Third World masochism. And the Universal Declaration of Human Rights was helpless against those forces of cruelty and self-destruction — and impotent against the human hypocrisy which surrounded them.

The Chinese and the Jews are both heirs of great civilizations. They are both endowed with a *de facto* doctrine of the chosen people. There is a Chinese diaspora as well as a Jewish one. Both diasporas have been incredibly productive and energetic. Ethnic Chinese have been the Jews of Asia.

Both China and Israel have a kind of Law of Return. But not everybody in their diasporas wants to return. Will there be a return of Hong Kong to China in 1997 after a century of British rule? Will there be a return of Taiwan to China after half a century of Nationalist rule?

But although the Chinese and the Jews are among the greatest actors in the history of civilization, their role in the political drama of the twentieth century has ebbed between victim and victor, between martyr and master. The latest episodes in the drama have been acted out in Beijing, Gaza and the West Bank. And young people have been at the centre of these historical encounters.

When the Chinese students imitated the American statue of liberty and called it a Chinese goddess, the West was almost unanimous in recognizing the statue as a symbol of democracy for the students. But when young Palestinians wave the flag of the Palestinean Liberation Organization in defiance of Israeli laws, not enough Westerners recognize it as a symbol of self-determination for the Palestinians.

If Chinese students do not deserve to suffer for displaying the statue of liberty, surely Palestinian youth do not deserve to suffer for displaying the Palestinian flag. Both the statue and the flag are symbols of freedom. In the demonstrations in Tiananmen Square the students paraphrased a speech from Shakespeare's *Julius Caesar*. Brutus had assured his audience that it was necessary to kill Caesar for the sake of freedom in Rome:

Not that I loved Caesar less but that I loved Rome more. (Act III, Scene II).

The Chinese students in 1989 had a poster in Tiananmen Square saying 'Not that we love rice less, but that we love rights more.' The Palestinians in rebellion on the West Bank from December 1987 onwards and Gaza had a similar concern —

177

'Not that we love peace less but that we love justice more.'

Behind these great events in China and Palestine has been the role of young people in human destiny. The elect of history need not always be the chosen people like the Jews or the chosen class like the proletariat, or the chosen 'race' like the Germans, or the chosen personality like Confucius or Mao Tse-tung. The elect of history could be an age-grade, between the ages of fifteen and twenty-five, who manage to 'take at the flood' that momentous 'tide in the affairs of men' — and lead history onwards to fortune.

Notes

1. J. M. Roberts, *The Triumph of the West* (London: British Broadcasting Corporation, 1985), pp. 407–408.

2. Ibid.

3. D. McLellan, *Karl Marx: His Life and Thought* (New York: Harper & Row, 1973), p. 3.

4. Ibid., p. 5.

5. Heinrich Graetz, *The Structure of Jewish History*, translated by Ismar Schorsch (New York, 1975), p. 73. Consult also Shlomo Avineri, *The Making of Modern Zionism: The Intellectual Origins of the Jewish State* (New York: Basic Books, 1981), pp. 30–31.

6. Romans, 5: 18–19.

7. Consult Alfred Firmin Loisy, *The Birth of the Christian Religion and the Origins of the New Testament*, translated by L. P. Jacks (New York: University Books, 1962), p. 84.

8. See *New York Times*, 10 and 20 April 1988.

9. Cited by Noam Chomsky, *The Fateful Triangle: The United States, Israel and the Palestinians* (Boston: South End Press, 1983), p. 447.

10. Report by Israeli writer Amos Oz based on interviews and published in *Davar*. Noam Chomsky, *The Fateful Triangle*, pp. 446–447.

11. 'Search for Partners: Should the US Deal with the PLO?' *Time Magazine*, 11 April 1988. See 'What is a Grasshopper?', letter to *The New York Times*, 20 April 1988.

12. Report by Amos Oz in a series of articles in *Davar; ibid.*; Chomsky, *The Fateful Triangle*, p. 447.

13. Consult report by Eliahu Salpeter, *Ha'aretz*, No. 4, 1982.

14. Chomsky, *The Fateful Triangle*, p. 153; D. Astor, V. York, *Peace in the Middle East?* (London: Corgi, 1978), pp. 108–109; Shahak, *Begin and Co.*; E. W. Said, *The Question of Palestine* (New York: Times Books, 1979), p. 91.

15. Chomsky, *The Fateful Triangle*, p. 153; Bernstein, *Dialogue* (New York), Winter 1980.

16. *Al Hamishmar*, 4 January 1978.

17. Cited by Danny Rubenstein, *Davar*, 8 October 1982.

18. Benjamin Beit-Hallahmi, 'Israel and South Africa', *New Outlook*, March/April 1983; *Hotam*, 18 April 1975, 1 October 1982.

19. Chomsky, *The Fateful Triangle*, p. 152.

20. *Davar*, 8 September 1981, Chomsky, *The Fateful Triangle*, pp. 151–152.

21. Charles Hoffman, 'A Monkey Trial, Local Style', *Jerusalem Post*, 22 March 1983.

10
On Gender
& Power

A Post-Colonial Sexual Equation

Since the colonial period Africa and Asia have witnessed significant changes in the roles and functions of men and women. In many traditional cultures there has been a belief that God made woman the custodian of fire, water, and earth. God himself took charge of the fourth element of the universe — the omnipresent air.

Custody of fire entailed responsibility for making energy available. And the greatest source of energy in rural Africa and parts of Asia is firewood. The rural woman became disproportionately responsible for finding and carrying huge bundles of firewood, though quite often it was men who chopped down the big trees initially.

Custody of water involved a liquid which was a symbol of both survival and cleanliness. The rural woman became responsible for ensuring that this critical substance was available for the family. She has trekked long distances to fetch water. But where a well needed to be dug, it was often the men who did the digging.

The custody of earth has been part of a doctrine of dual fertility. Woman ensures the survival of this generation by maintaining a central role in cultivation — and preserving the fertility of the soil. Woman ensures the arrival of the next generation in her role as mother — the fertility of the womb. Dual fertility becomes an aspect of the triple custodial role of rural womanhood, though always in partnership with the rural man.[1]

What has happened to this doctrine of triple custody in the period since the 1930s? Different elements of the colonial experience affected the roles of men and women in Africa and Asia in different ways.

Gender Roles in Transition

In Africa among the factors which increased the woman's role on the land was wage labour for the men. Faced with an African population reluctant to work for low wages for somebody else, colonial rulers had already experimented with both forced labour and taxation as a way of inducing Africans (especially men) to join the colonial work force.

According to Margaret Jean Hay, wage labour for men took some time before it began to affect women's role on the land. Hay's own work was among Luo women in Kenya.

By 1930 a large number of men had left Kowe at least once for outside employment. . . . More than half of this group stayed away for periods of fifteen years or more. . . . This growing export of labour from the province might be thought to have increased the burden of agricultural work for women. . . . As early as 1910, administrators lamented the fact that Nyanza was becoming the labour pool of the entire colony. . . . Yet the short-term migrants of the 1920s were usually unmarried youths, who played a relatively minor role in the local economy beyond occasional herding and the conquest of cattle in war. Furthermore, the short-term labour migrants could and often did arrange to be away during the slack periods in the agricultural cycle. . . . Thus labour migration in the period before 1930 actually removed little labour from the local economy and did not significantly alter the sexual division of labour.[2]

Margaret Hay goes on to demonstrate how the Great Depression and World War II changed the situation as migrant labour and conscription of males took an increasing proportion of men away from the land. This was compounded by the growth of mining industries like the gold mining at Kowe from 1934 onwards:

The long-term absence of men had an impact on the sexual division of labour, with women and children assuming a greater share of agricultural work than ever before. . . . The thirties represent a transition with regard to the sexual division of labour, and it was clearly the women who bore the burden of the transition in rural areas.[3]

Women in this period, from the 1930s onwards, became more deeply involved as 'custodians of the earth'. In Southern Africa the migrations of men to the mines became even more dramatic. By the 1950s a remarkable bifurcation was taking place in some South African societies — a division between a male proletariat (industrial working class) and a female peasantry. South Africa's regulations against families joining their husbands on the mines exacerbated this tendency towards gender apartheid, the segregation of the sexes. Many women in the frontline states had to fulfil their triple custodial role of fire, water, and earth in greater isolation than ever.

The wars of liberation in Southern Africa from the 1960s took their own toll on family stability and traditional sexual division of labour. Some of the fighters did have their wives with them. Indeed, liberation armies like ZANLA and ZIPRA in Zimbabwe and FRELIMO in Mozambique included a few female fighters. But on the whole, the impact of the wars was disruptive of family life and of the traditional sexual division of labour.

After independence there were counter-revolutionary wars in some of the front-line states. The most artificial of the post-colonial wars was that initiated by the so-called Mozambique National Resistance (MNR or RENAMO). The movement was originally created by reactionary white Rhodesians to punish Samora Machel of Mozambique for his support of Robert Mugabe's forces in Zimbabwe. After Zimbabwe's independence the Mozambique National Resistance became a surrogate army for reactionary whites in the Republic of South Africa — committing a variety of acts of sabotage against the fragile post-colonial economy of distant villages of Mozambique.

It is not completely clear how this situation has affected the doctrine of 'dual fertility' in relation to the role of the African women. One possibility is that the extra-long absences of the husbands have reduced fertility rates in some communities like Mozambique. The other scenario is that the pattern of migrant labour in Southern Africa generally has initiated a tendency towards *de facto* polyandry. The woman who is left behind acquires over time a *de facto* extra husband. The two husbands take their turn over time with the woman. The migrant labourer from the mines has conjugal priority between mining contracts if he does manage to get to the village. He also has prior claim to the new babies unless agreed otherwise.[4]

If the more widespread pattern is that of declining fertility as a result of long absences of husbands, the principle of 'dual fertility' has reduced the social functions of the fertility of the womb and increased the woman's involvement in matters pertaining to the fertility of the soil.

On the other hand, if the more significant tendency in rural communities deprived of male migrant labour in Southern Africa is towards *de facto* polyandry, a whole new nexus of social relationships may be in the making in Southern Africa.[5]

Other changes in Africa during this period which affected relationships between men and women included the impact of new technologies on gender roles. Cultivation with the hoe still left the African woman centrally involved in agriculture. But cultivation with the tractor was often a prescription for male dominance:

> When you see a farmer
> on bended knee
> tilling land
> for the family
> The chances are
> It is a *she*

> When you see tractor
> Passing by
> And the driver
> Waves you 'Hi'
> The chancees are
> It is a *he*! [6]

Mechanization of agriculture in Africa and South Asia has tended to marginalize women. Their role as 'custodians of earth' is threatened by male prerogatives in new and more advanced technologies. It is true that greater male involvement in agriculture could help reduce the heavy burdens of work undertaken by women on the land. On the other hand, there is no reason why this relief in workload for women should not come through better technology. Tractors were not invented to be driven solely by men.

Another threat to the central role of Third World women in the economy in this period has come from the nature of Western education. It is true that the Westernized African woman is usually more mobile and with more freedom for her own interests than is her traditional sister. But a translation from custodian of fire, water, and earth to keeper of the typewriter is definitely a form of marginalization for African womanhood. Typing is less fundamental for survival than cultivation. The Westernized African woman in the second half of the twentieth century has tended to be more free but less important for African economies than the traditional woman in rural areas.

The third threat to the role of the African woman in this period came with the internationalization of African economies. When economic activity in Africa was more localized, woman had a decisive role in local markets and as traders. But the colonial and post-colonial tendencies towards enlargement of economic scale have increasingly pushed the women to the side in international decision-making. It is true that Nigerian women especially have refused to be completely marginalized even in international trade. But on the whole, the Africans who deal with international markets and sit on the Boards of transnational corporations are overwhelmingly men. At the meetings of the Organization of Petroleum Exporting Countries — where Muslims predominate — there are additional inhibitions about having even Nigeria represented by a female delegate.

But what is the future avenue which is likely to change the balance between men and women in public life in Asia and Africa? The reasons why women are politically subordinate are not to be sought in economic differentiation. Women in Africa are economically very active; women in Saudi Arabia are economically neutralized. And yet in both types of society women are politically subordinate. And so economic differences are not the real explanation of political subjection of womanhood.

What is indeed universal is not the economic role of women but their military role. All over Africa (and indeed all over the world) women are militarily marginalized. What will one day change the political balance between men and women is when the military machine becomes bisexual. The Somali army has started recruiting women. The Algerian air force has started recruiting women pilots. Both Muslim societies in Africa are beginning to give a military role to women. But the future needs more than tokenism in gender roles.

Such a gender revolution will of course take several generations to mature — preceded as it is by millennia of masculine specialization in the martial arts. What may come sooner to Africa than the gender revolution is the second major shift we have referred to — a more general transformation of Africa's level of expertise. While the continent may indeed be awaiting both a sexual revolution and a scientific one, prospects for the latter may be more imminent than for the former.

Gender, Religion and War

It has been said that war is the continuation of politics by other means. In traditional Africa war is sometimes the continuation of religion by other means. The same indigenous religion which has tended to be relatively unpoliticized in peacetime has sometimes been mobilized for combat purposes in war. Indigenous religions have been used in warfare not as part of a crusade to convert others but as sacred weapons for attack or sacred shields for defence. Indigenous religions have been a source of spiritual ammunition against 'the enemy' or part of the fortress of invincibility.

The most dramatic African Joan of Arc of the 1980s was Alice Lakwena of Uganda. She arose out of Northern Uganda's resistance to the rule of Yoweri Museveni. In 1987 she inspired thousands of Acholi and mobilized them for combat with very few weapons. Lakwena had visions and, like Joan of Arc before her, claimed to communicate with spiritual forces.

Religion has sometimes been the bridge between conventional feminine virtues and masculine roles in combat. In cultures which are otherwise vastly different from each other, the military profession has been a man's preserve. Women as a rule have not been expected to kill for their country. They have not even been expected to die for their country. Armed patriotism has usually been a masculine preserve.

But from time to time religion has played a part in militarizing women. In Uganda 1987 was such a year. In that year there arose the aforementioned phenomenon of Alice Lakwena as a female warrior with supernatural powers, engaged in combat against the forces of Yoweri Museveni. As an instance of using traditional religion for military purposes, Alice Lakwena's approach was often reminiscent of the Maji Maji war against German rule in Tanzania in 1904—5. Tanganyika warriors had immersed themselves in water in the expectation that sacred water was bullet-proof. Similarly Alice Lakwena convinced many Acholi warriors in 1987 that carrying a particular leaf or artefact would make them bullet-proof. Both in Tanganyika at the beginning of the twentieth century and in Uganda in 1987—1988 this faith in the protection of indigenous religion against bullets proved disastrous for the warriors. The faithful died in large numbers.

But Alice Lakwena's movement did not only illustrate a link between war and indigenous religion. It also illustrated how religion can make it possible for a woman to break the male monopoly of military command. At the beginning of this century a Muslim holy war in the Horn of Africa included women crusaders against European invaders and their local allies. Somalia produced its own Joan of Arc, another African 'Maid of Orleans'. A statue stands in her honour in today's Mogadishu. Hawo Osman Tako was pierced by an enemy's arrow and still continued to fight. Her statue symbolizes armed patriotism with a female face. But her valour also symbolized religious inspiration at work in re-militarizing women. Such historical figures have played a role in breaking the male monopoly in skills of combat and disciplines of war. France's Joan of Arc, Somalia's Hawo Osman Tako and Uganda's Alice Lakwena were all historic fusions of priestess and female warrior.

Religion elsewhere has fused priestess and politician from time to time. Another Alice, Alice Lenshina in Zambia, has been the leader of the Lumpa Church which clashed with government authorities and its supporters from time to time. Strictly speaking, the Lumpa Church was anti-political from the outset and did not want its members to join any political party. But to be anti-political was itself a political statement. The clashes between the Lumpa Church and the ruling party of Zambia in the mid-1960s resulted in President Kenneth Kaunda's authorization of the security forces to 'shoot to kill' in its efforts to control Lenshina's uprising of 1964—1965. The tradition of priestesses had in that period escalated into violence. And even a good Christian like Kaunda — self-consciously a disciple of Mahatma Gandhi — could be driven to a response of counter-violence ('shoot to kill').

But the confrontation between Alice Lenshina and Kenneth Kaunda had more symbolic contradictions as well. Alice was a woman who, by leading her men into violent political battle, seemed to have assumed a role normally associated with men. In his Gandhian days, on the other hand, Kenneth Kaunda was opposed to the use of violence in any of its forms — and seemed inclined towards the softer virtues of modesty and compassionate tears normally associated with women.

After all, Gandhi himself — Kaunda's guru — found himself torn between serving as a father figure and acting as a mother symbol. Gandhi's psychological biographer, Erik Erikson, has pointed to a 'persistent importance in Gandhi's life of the theme of motherhood, both in the sense of a need to be a perfect and pure mother, and in the sense of a much less acknowledged need to be held and reassured, especially at the time of his infinite loneliness'.[7]

A similar issue has arisen in the symbolism of Jesus and the meaning of Christianity. Is Christianity, in the ultimate analysis, a feminine religion? Does the centrality of forgiveness make the Christian God less 'manly' than the Jewish Jehovah? Is the transition from the Old Testament to the New Testament a process of the demasculation of God? Does the centrality of love as a divine attribute make the Christian God less 'masculine' than Islam's Allah?

'Turn the other cheek!' In Africa this could be viewed as the most feminine imperative of them all. Only a woman turned the other cheek upon being punished by her man. And even a submissive African woman attempted as a rule to shield herself with her arms. Yet the principle of 'turning the other cheek' was part of the feminine baggage that came with Christianity.

Kenneth Kaunda in his younger days was close to this kind of ethic. To his critics from within Africa's warrior tradition, young Kenneth exemplified how Christianity had softened Africa's masculinity. Brought up in a highly devout Christian home Kenneth exhibited early his abhorrence of physical fist fights and the nearness of his tears of compassion. Critics saw this as part of the process of demasculation under Christian missionary tutelage. Although as Head of State much later Kenneth Kaunda surrendered to Max Weber's definition of the state as institutionalized monopoly of physical force, Kaunda's tears of compassion persisted and came to embarrass many an international conference when (as president) he sometimes broke down in the middle of a speech.

Against this background Kaunda's confrontation with Alice Lenshina soon after independence was remarkable. Kaunda was a man with virtues normally associated with women. Alice was a woman with a leadership and combative role normally associated with men. In the mid-1960s either Alice had to retreat into feminine compassion and non-violence or Kaunda had to respond with *macho* toughness. Kaunda decided to be ruthless. He declared that he did not care if he was called a 'savage'. Alice Lenshina's followers had started killing innocent citizens of independent Zambia. Kaunda decided that only an order to the security forces to 'shoot to kill' would stop carnage by members of the Lumpa Church. Kaunda's Christian compassion had given way to the demands for 'toughness'. The exigencies of the state had remasculated him — to confront an Alice Lenshina already made 'masculine' and de-feminized by the exigencies of her own Lumpa Church. Kaunda's state machinery prevailed.

Gender, Race and Generation

In Southern Africa as a whole bridges need to be built not only between races, but also between genders and across generations. Relations between men and women have been disrupted by repression, by wars of liberation and by labour migration. And relations between the African youth and the older generations have been strained by the anger and radicalization generated by apartheid.

In the middle of these three sets of relations — gender, race and generation — came the crisis of Winnie Mandela late in the 1980s. As a woman whose husband (Nelson Mandela) had been in prison for more than a quarter of a century, Winnie Mandela had symbolized the strain of political struggle upon gender relations. As a woman who attempted to organize young activists for social roles, Winnie Mandela had been one of the bridge-builders across generations.

But in 1988 and 1989 things went seriously wrong for Winnie — partly because of the activities of those very young people that she had tried to organize. The woman who had been a martyr to apartheid since her husband was sentenced to life imprisonment in 1964, the woman who had herself suffered banning and restriction in a black ghetto for long periods of time, had now become a subject of denunciation and derision in some of the circles which once acclaimed her as 'mother of the nation'.

But her very status had been part of the wider saga concerning gender relations in Southern Africa. Repression and war have often created 'widows of the revolution' — widows of martyrs to the liberation struggle. There have also been 'cage widows' — wives of husbands put away in detention for life. Winnie Mandela had become the most internationally illustrious of the so-called 'cage widows'. But what was the Winnie Mandela crisis of 1989?

Mrs Mandela was accused of complicity in the abduction and assault of a 14-year-old black activist, Stompie Mokhetsi Seipei, whose decomposed body was found dumped in Soweto in January 1989.

Winnie vigorously denied being at home at all when the teenager and four others were abducted to her house on 19 December 1988 by members of her so-called soccer team of young activists, known as the Mandela United. The team acted as her bodyguard.

Behind it all were some hard sociological trends. For the black youth in Southern Africa, new forms of initiation into warriorhood had emerged. Many a teenager had been enlisted into the liberation armies. And in urban centres the new warriorhood sometimes took the form of confronting armed security forces in the streets of Soweto. Winnie Mandela's experiment of a youthful soccer team with additional responsibilities of guarding her could have been a pilot scheme worth emulating. But it became an experiment which had gone wrong. Her soccer team had degenerated into a gang fighting other young people. Youthful gang warfare caught up with Winnie Mandela's dreams.

Southern Africa has also created special kinds of divergence between gender and class. In South Africa's mining communities, men have not been allowed to live with their wives. Gender apartheid has been added to racial apartheid. Women have often remained on the land as subsistence farmers — while their men have trekked thousands of miles for wages. The result has been the creation of a migrant male proletariat and a secondary female peasantry. As a wife separated from her husband by an unjust system, Winnie Mandela became a role model for the rural peasant woman as well.

In the struggle to build bridges across races, South Africa has produced two black Nobel laureates for Peace — Albert Luthuli and Desmond Tutu. But there are no Nobel Prizes to be won in the struggle to build bridges between genders or bridges across generations. 'Peace' in terms of the Nobel Prize is not yet defined by the yardstick of either fighting sexism or moderating generational conflict. Winnie Mandela did not stand a chance of becoming the first black female to win the Nobel Prize even if her efforts across genders and generations had succeeded.

But if she was not a laureate was she at least a martyr to those causes? Since Winnie's political career is far from over, the final estimate of her contribution can only be computed by history itself in the fullness of time.

Women generally are martyrs to many types of pains, some biological, some cultural, some economic. Basically they are 'identity' martyrs. They are martyrs because of what they are, almost regardless of what they believe in. However, an interesting tendency has manifested itself in this last quarter of the twentieth century, which is only the beginning of what I hope will be something better. Sometimes women succeed to supreme office, not on their own credentials, which is what it should be, but because of the martyrdom of a related male — female succession to male martyrdom, usually a male 'belief' martyr, committed to a particular line of thought.

From Suttee to State House

Particularly startling is the cultural trend in South Asia. There has developed in the region the phenomenon of female succession to male martyrdom. A heroic male figure is killed, and out of the blood and anguish emerges a new political activist. It is a woman who is related to the deceased martyr.

This tendency has gone further in South Asia than in any other part of the world. It began in Sri Lanka (then Ceylon). Prime Minister Solomon W. R. D. Bandaranaike was killed in September 1959. Before long his widow, Sirimavo Bandaranaike, succeeded to the leadership of the party, the Sri Lanka Freedom Party. From then on Mrs Bandaranaike became a major political force in the country — serving at times as prime minister.

India, Sri Lanka's giant neighbour to the north, was also destined to be led by a woman. Indira Gandhi was the daughter of India's founding Prime Minister, Jawaharlal Nehru. After a brief interlude under the premiership of Lal Bahadur Shastri, the Congress Party in India looked to Nehru's daughter for at least formal leadership. The party pundits thought that the woman could be manipulated easily behind the scenes. That was one of their great miscalculations. Indira Gandhi turned out to be one of India's toughest leaders. When she finally became so tough as to take on the Sikhs militarily at the Golden Temple — ordering an invasion of the temple to clear it of 'terrorist fugitives' — she signed her own death warrant. She was subsequently assassinated by her own Sikh bodyguards in 1984.

We do not know yet whether another South Asian woman leader in neighbouring Pakistan will turn out to be as tough as Indira Gandhi. But at any rate Benazir Bhutto was elected leader of the largest party in Pakistan in 1988 — and soon became the Muslim world's first woman prime minister. She was successor to her own martyred father Zulfikar Ali Bhutto, who was executed under the regime of General Mohammad Zia-ul-Haq in 1977.

Bangladesh, another South Asian nation, has already produced major women opposition leaders, Begum Khalida Zia and Begum Hassina. It may be only a matter of time before Bangladesh in turn is officially led by a woman. It will probably be the second Muslim society in modern history to produce a female prime minister.

The Philippines is just outside South Asia proper. There too a female successor to a male martyr has emerged. Benigno Aquino, a dissident when the country was ruled by Ferdinand Marcos, was assassinated in 1983 as he disembarked from a plane on his return home from exile in the United States. The political shock of the assassination propelled his widow to national prominence. The momentum finally resulted in Corazon Aquino being swept into power as national president in 1986.

It is worth noting the different cultural backgrounds of these Asian women. Mrs

Bandaranaike was Buddhist; Mrs Indira Gandhi was Hindu; Ms Benazir Bhutto of Pakistan and the two Begums of Bangladesh are Muslims, and Mrs Aquino is Christian. There are significant cultural differences in their societies — and yet all of them are Asian countries in relative proximity to each other. Is there an underlying cultural bond between them which has nevertheless contributed to this female succession to male martyrdom?

There is a civilization in that part of Asia which is older than Christianity and Islam. It is the culture which produced concepts like reincarnation. In the relationship between husband and wife this sometimes took the form of co-incarnation — joint existence. In Hindu culture this resulted in the controversial institution of *suttee* (or *sati*). This was the custom of the widow burning herself on the husband's funeral pyre. Christians conceived of marriage as a pledge unto death; Hindus regarded marriage as a pledge *beyond* death. Christians affirmed 'till death do us part'. Hindus insisted that 'Not even in death will we part.'

Christians affirmed a continuing loyalty between husband and wife — 'in sickness and health'. Hindus extended the allegiance to apply 'in death as in life'. In reality the institution of *suttee* seemed to proclaim: 'What God has joined together let no Death put asunder.'

The question which arises is whether this underlying concept of co-incarnation in South Asian culture especially has now found a healthier resurgence in the phenomenon of female succession to male martyrdom. In the past the widow accompanied the husband in his death. Today the widow becomes a political incarnation of her martyred husband or, by extension, her martyred father.

Historically, the institution of *suttee* persisted in India even among converts to Islam. During much of the Moghul period in India *suttee* worried the rulers. In the eighteenth and nineteenth centuries there were reform movements among Muslims in India committed to 'purifying' Indian Islam and removing what were regarded as 'Hindu accretions and superstitions'. The Moghul rulers Humayun and his son Akbar took decisive steps to prohibit widow burning. But it was not until British rule that the custom was more effectively outlawed. *Suttee* was abolished by the British Raj in 1829.

In reality the custom of widow burning has not died out completely even in post-colonial India. Incidents of widow burning continued to be reported among Hindus in India right into the 1980s. But what particularly concerns us in this chapter is how the culture which produced the custom of a widow burning herself upon her husband's death was later inspired to produce a political culture of a widow rising from the ashes of her husband's martyrdom to assume supreme office. Were the two cultural tendencies related? Was political succession to a martyred father a mere refinement of political succession to a martyred husband?

A related aspect of Hindu culture is the tendency to narrow the gap between hard masculine virtues (physical courage, endurance, purposeful ruthlessness) and softer feminine virtues (humility, patience, modesty). The two most illustrious Gandhis in twentieth century India were Mahatma and Indira. Mahatma Gandhi was a man who behaved like a woman. Indira Gandhi was a woman who behaved like a man. Mahatma Gandhi revelled in the softer virtues of humility and patience. Indira Gandhi revelled in the harder virtues of power and ruthless courage. The Mahatma gave India the spiritual concept of 'soul force' (*satyagraha*). Indira gave India the military credentials of victory in war and nuclear status in regional politics. The Mahatma came close to echoing the Christian dictum of turning the other cheek. Indira initiated a *de facto* policy of *pax Indiana* — India's 'right' to intervene in other South Asian countries for the sake of regional peace.

The Mahatma was so keen to feminize himself that he behaved like a *mother* to a young woman relative. The young woman was later to write a book bearing the paradoxical title of *Bapu, My Mother* ('Bapu' being the affectionate title given to Gandhi as 'father' of the new India). The Mahatma even renounced sex with his wife in his quest for a truly androgynous existence. Erik Erikson, the psychiatrist, described Gandhi's quest as a case of 'sublimated maternalism'.[7]

Indira Gandhi, on the other hand, embodied sublimated patriarchy. The Soviets reserved for Mrs Margaret Thatcher the term 'the Iron Lady'. But the Soviet concept was equally applicable to Indira Gandhi. The inevitable jokes erupted during Mrs Gandhi's reign in power. Because of her toughness, it used to be said that 'Indira is the only man in the Cabinet!'

Yes — two people bearing the name of Gandhi have left their mark on twentieth-century India. One was indeed a man who aspired to female modesty; the other was indeed a woman who aspired to masculine ruthlessness.

Although South Asia is a unique region from the point of view of female succession to male martyrdom, it is by no means the only part of the world which has produced powerful women in the twentieth century. Nor was Indira Gandhi the only woman who presided over the nuclearization of her own country. Of all the over one hundred and sixty countries in the world it is astonishing that those which have gone nuclear include a disproportionate number of those which have produced female heads of government.

The Gender of Nuclear Power

Nuclear capability in the Third World has emerged disproportionately in countries which have also produced politically powerful women. Is there a link between the culture of potential nuclearization and a culture of political androgynization?

In China Mao's wife was powerful only while Mao lived. After Mao's death she was condemned as one of the 'Gang of Four'. Was China ready for nuclearization but not yet ready for androgynization?

In India both trends reinforced each other. Indira Gandhi was a symbol of both the nuclearization of India and a female conquest of supreme power.

Israel is in Asia but not of Asia. Israeli culture did, however, bring into being both Prime Minister Golda Meir and Israel's nuclear bombs. Although Israel's nuclear programme started long before Golda Meir's reign, there is no doubt that her years in supreme office (1969–1974) were crucial in making Israel more independent as a nuclear power.

In Latin America the two leading contenders for nuclear status are Brazil and Argentina. Both are very *macho* societies. Nevertheless, one of them — Argentina — has had one woman head of state, President Isabella Perón. Potential nuclearization and potential androgynization have once again coincided, though Perón herself was far from being an 'Iron Lady'.

Sri Lanka produced a female leader but did not become part of the nuclear vanguard. And yet this dissociation was probably an accident of history. Sri Lanka did stand a chance of becoming the scientific Israel of South Asia. It had become *per capita* the best educated country in South Asia — and stood a chance of a technological take-off.

But potential nuclearization was aborted by the schism between the Tamils and

Sinhalese. Civil conflict sucked away Sri Lanka's vigour both economically and in terms of education.

Whether Benazir Bhutto survives long as Pakistan's Prime Minister or not, Pakistan has already demonstrated that it is a culture which can produce a politically powerful woman. The world is also convinced that Pakistan is a culture which is capable of nuclear credentials. Pakistan: a culture capable of both nuclearization and androgynization. The Third World pattern of linkage between androgyny and the atom have at last come to the Muslim world.

Zulfikar Ali Bhutto was father not only of Benazir but also of nuclear Pakistan. Jawaharlal Nehru was not only father of Indira Gandhi, but also grandfather of nuclear India. Nehru presided over the Sino-Indian conflict — and the conflict was in turn the midwife of the nuclearization of India.

Prime Minister Zulfikar Ali Bhutto once said: 'There was a Christian bomb, a Jewish bomb and now a Hindu bomb. Why not an Islamic bomb?'

What Zulfikar did not live to say was the following: 'There has been a Hindu woman leader — Indira Gandhi. A Buddhist woman leader, Mrs Bandaranaike. A Jewish woman leader, Mrs Golda Meir. More than one Christian woman leader — Mrs Aquino and Mrs Isabella Perón. This is quite apart from Christian Margaret Thatcher. Surely there will one day be a Muslim woman leader — in Pakistan or Bangladesh?'

If Third World cultures which produce women leaders are also disproportionately cultures in the nuclear vanguard, are those cultures more militaristic?

Not necessarily. Less machismo in a society could mean less militarism. But those Third World societies which have produced female leaders have been androgynous enough to produce female kings but not genuine queens, female Rajas rather than genuine Ranis — a female pharaoh like Hatshepsut, Indira Gandhi, Golda Meir or Margaret Thatcher.

In other words, the women who succeed in those societies have been those who have demonstrated hard masculine virtues — toughness, courage, physical endurance and even ruthlessness. Only the pinnacle of the pyramid of power has been androgynized — the head of government. But the rest of the pyramid is still a monument to masculine supremacy.

Conclusion

In Asia the interaction between religion and colonialism is a major factor behind the changing role of women. In Africa it is the interaction between race and colonialism which has transformed gender roles.

South Asia has been an important arena of interplay between religion and the politics of imperial legacy. It seems almost certain that if British India had not been partitioned, the phenomenon of a female Muslim head of government in the world would have been delayed by at least a generation. If British India had remained intact, Indira Gandhi could still have become Prime Minister. But there would have been no Muslim state in South Asia east of Afghanistan. In the absence of either a Pakistan or a Bangladesh, the chances of female political succession to a male Muslim martyr anywhere in the world would have been drastically reduced. After all, nowhere else in the Muslim world but in South Asia have there been any indications of a woman assuming the supreme political authority of the state.

Theoretically, an unpartitioned Indian subcontinent, though preponderantly

Hindu, could one day have produced a Muslim woman prime minister. But that would have been most unlikely in the twentieth century. In any case, a Muslim female head of government of a preponderantly Hindu society would still not have been the same thing as a female premier in a preponderantly Muslim society. Benazir Bhutto as head of government is a product of many historical forces. But perhaps above all she is the product of the partition of British India.

Similarly there would have been no nuclear race in South Asia this century without that partition. India's decision to become a nuclear power was inspired at least as much by rivalry with China as by hostility towards Pakistan. But Zulfikar Ali Bhutto's initiative to nuclearize Pakistan was decidedly inspired by his country's adversarial relationship with India. The partition of the subcontinent must therefore be counted as one of the causes of both the androgynization and the nuclearization of Islam in South Asia.

Similarly, the partition of Palestine is one of the reasons why the region has already produced a woman prime minister. Had the Middle East remained almost exclusively Muslim, there would have been no equivalent of Golda Meir to assume the reins of any government in the region. It took the creation of Israel to introduce sufficient matriarchy in the region for the rise of Goldie Mabovitch to the position of Foreign Minister. Later (as Golda Meir), she rose to the rank of head of government (1969 to 1974).

Again, it was territorial partition which speeded up the nuclearization of the region. There is little doubt that Israel is already a nuclear power militarily. Without the creation of the Jewish state, and the political and military tensions caused by that development, nuclear weapons in the Middle East would probably have been delayed by at least a generation. Just as in South Asia territorial partition both androgynized and nuclearized Islam, so in the Middle East the partition of Palestine brought forward both the happy phenomenon of a woman prime minister in the region and the ominous phenomenon of nuclear arsenals in the Jewish state. In South Asia the tension was between Islamic nationalism and Hindu nationalism. In the Middle East the tension has been between Zionism and Arab nationalism. Religion and the politics of the post-imperial era have indeed profoundly affected both military developments and gender relations.

In Africa nationalism has been linked more to race than to religion. The continent has not yet produced a likely woman head of government. Perhaps the closest candidate, for a while, was Winnie Mandela, although she was indeed damaged in credibility by the events of 1988 and 1989. She was in any case more admired internationally than at home.

It was a different kind of 'partition' which produced Winnie Mandela. It was the ideology of 'separate development' and the white man's obsession with separate ethnic and racial 'homelands'. Apartheid as an ideology of partition was the mother of both a nuclear South Africa and a potentially androgynous black political movement. The white man's racial paranoia produced Africa's first nuclear power. The country's racism and gender apartheid in turn produced not only Winnie Mandela as a political figure but also the complex patterns of male labour migration and female peasants in the economies of Southern Africa.

The triple custodial role of the African woman is still socially alive in much of the continent. The female of the species remains a trustee of fire, water, and earth in most African villages. But the consequences of racism and of colonial rule have taken their toll. The African woman today is sometimes more socially free than she once was, but she often pays the price of being less economically central than the ancestors intended her to be. The custodian of fire, water and earth sometimes finds herself trustee of the filing cabinet. The struggle must, therefore, continue. Africa is still groping for the optimum balance between ancient roles and modern rights in the destiny of womanhood.

Notes

1. I am indebted to the late Okot p'Bitek, the Ugandan anthropologist and poet, for stimulation and information about myths of womanhood in northern Uganda. Okot and I also discussed similarities and differences between African concepts of matter and the ideas of Empedocles, the Greek philosopher of the 5th Century B.C. Consult also Okot p'Bitek, *African Religions in Western Scholarship* (Nairobi: East African Literature Bureau, 1971).
2. Margaret Jean Hay, 'Luo Women and Economic Change During the Colonial Period' in *Women in Africa: Studies in Social and Economic Change*, edited by Nancy J. Hafkin and Edna G. Bay (Stanford, California: Stanford University Press, 1976), pp. 98—99. For a feminist perspective consult also Maria Rosa Cutrufelli, *Women of Africa: Roots of Oppression* (London: Zed Press, 1983).
3. Hay, ibid., p. 105.
4. There is no doubt such arrangements occur in Mozambique. What is not clear is how widespread *de facto* polyandry is becoming in Southern Africa.
5. I am indebted to the field research and interviews in Southern Africa which accompanied the BBC/WETA television project, 'The Africans: A Triple Heritage' (1985—6). I am also grateful to the work associated with Vol. VIII of the UNESCO General History of Africa (edited by Ali A. Mazrui — forthcoming).
6. Ali A. Mazrui.
7. Erik Erikson, *Gandhi's Truth: On the Origins of Militant Non-violence* (New York: W. W. Norton and Company, 1969).
8. Ibid.

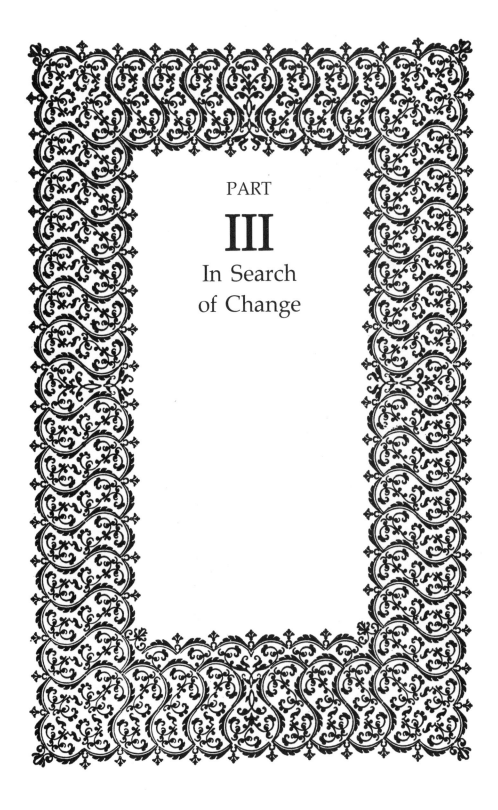

PART

III

In Search
of Change

11
On Culture
& Aid

Culture features in different stages and at different levels of the whole process through which foreign aid is either requested or transmitted.[1] In this chapter we shall deal first with the role of culture in motivating aid relations. Secondly, we shall address ourselves to the cultural content of aid. Thirdly, we shall examine the cultural constraints on aid. Fourthly, we shall turn to the rules and conditions which are supposed to regulate aid relations, and how culture affects these rules and conditions, and finally we hope to explore the general cultural consequences of foreign aid.

Values and Motives

Aid is given, and the recipients chosen, on the basis of a variety of considerations. But these multiple considerations might themselves be grouped under three general areas of motivation — charity, solidarity, and self-interest. Of these three, self-interest is constant, especially in relations between nation-states. But the balance between the other two — charity and solidarity — is culturally and ideologically relative.

The charitable impulse is perhaps particularly strong in liberal political cultures. After all, charity has for a long time been regarded as one of the answers to the kind of maldistribution brought about by capitalism. The system of private enterprise recognized that poverty existed and might even expand in scale. But, at least in its initial phases, modern capitalism coupled private enterprise with private charity as a mutually reinforcing system of values. Today the United States is the leading capitalist country in the world; it also has the most elaborate system of charitable foundations and institutions. Fund-raising for different causes has attained new levels of sophistication in American society. In the course of the twentieth century the state, even in the most doctrinaire capitalist societies, has had to undertake much of the burden of welfare, but for generations this approach was resisted in favour of reliance on the private conscience of the affluent. Even today a suspicion of government welfare schemes runs deep in many Western societies, and the habit of looking to private charity as the solution to poverty dies hard. It is because of these factors that liberal political culture appears to be particularly responsive to foreign aid as an area of charity.

In reality, especially in the case of official aid from one government to another, the charitable consideration is diluted by the other imperative of self-interest. Aid is often tied to make sure that it helps the trade of the donor, or serves other purposes favourable to the donor. But there is little doubt that charity as an idea plays a part in influencing liberals in Western societies in their dealings with the poorer countries of the world.

A major source of this sub-culture of private charity is, of course, Christianity itself. The notion of dying on the cross as a form of sacrifice, combined with the long tradition of Christian churches as havens for the poor and the desolate, has helped to condition at least some sectors of public opinion in the West in directions which are on occasion responsive to the policy of helping the poorer countries. It is not surprising that an ideology of private enterprise should interact with a Christian morality of charity.

Against the background of these normative antecedents, it is not surprising that Western aid — as compared with aid from other parts of the world — scores quite high on sheer charity and tolerance. Robert McNamara's call in June 1978 for aid to go to Vietnam was an evocative illustration of this line of thinking. Here was McNamara, who as US Defence Secretary had participated in the decision to bomb and devastate North Vietnam and greatly undermine its agricultural capacity, now, as head of the World Bank, become charitable enough and moderate enough to champion the cause of his former adversary. Enlightened self-interest in such situations reveals both a high level of calculating sophistication and a relatively low level of vendetta.

Also characteristic of the liberal political culture of the West is a relatively moderate commitment to solidarity. This is linked to the ideological toleration of plurality characteristic of liberalism at home. As Western motives for aid-giving have become more sophisticated, ideological divergence on the part of the potential recipient has become a less relevant factor in determining the transaction. McNamara's proclaimed aim to help Hanoi is therefore illustrative of this trend towards enlightened liberalism.

This is not to say that Western policy-makers are entirely indifferent to considerations of solidarity. The French, for example, are particularly susceptible to cultural solidarity with those who share with them the French language. France's readiness to extend support to President Mobutu Sese Seko was legitimized partly on the grounds that Zaire was nominally the second largest French-speaking nation in the world after France. French readiness to lend support to other French-speaking countries is also an aspect of this level of cultural solidarity. Considerations of cultural solidarity in British aid are less pronounced, though the idea of the Commonwealth as an organizing principle for certain forms of aid priority continues to have some relevance. Sweden's infatuation with Tanzania is also partly influenced by a moderate level of ideological solidarity. Many Swedes see Nyerere as a social democrat of a kind, seeking to achieve a humane society comparable to the accomplishments of the Swedes themselves. But Sweden is also very liberal in its toleration of plurality in the world, and has often given aid more for reasons of charity than for reasons of normative solidarity.

On the whole, then, we may conclude that Western aid scores high on charity, and also high on self-interest, but is only moderately influenced by motives of cultural or ideological comradeship.

What about aid from socialist countries like the Soviet Union, the German Democratic Republic, and Cuba?

Like Western aid, socialist aid includes a strong component of self-interest. Unlike Western aid, however, aid from socialist countries scores low on straight charity. This is partly because of a sociological distrust of charity as an answer to maldistribution. Some of the same considerations which have made charity so acceptable to capitalism have made it dubious to the socialists. This is certainly one major reason why Soviet economic aid to the Third World is strikingly more modest in volume than Western aid. A related consideration concerns the socialist worry that charity can be a form of hand-out that results in incorporation in the Establishment and deradicalization. Foreign aid in the economic domain must therefore not be allowed to become an obstacle to the emergence of revolutionary consciousness among the workers. Foreign aid even when given by a socialist country has to be handled carefully lest it become an ally of false consciousness and reaction.

While socialist aid scores low in terms of charity for reasons which make socialist sense, it scores high on the measurement of ideological solidarity. Whenever possible the aid is designed to help promote 'progressive change', defined in ideological terms. Of course, there have been times when Moscow has had to tolerate the repression of communists by someone like the late President Nasser, and still pour Soviet aid into Nasser's Egypt. The element of self-interest and higher political goals may all too often prevail against considerations of ideological solidarity with oppressed Egyptian leftists. But since aid policy is never determined on the level of one consideration alone, we have to allow for situations of contradiction and paradox. On balance, however, it is clear that the promotion of the interests of 'progressive forces' in Third World countries is one of the major manifestations of motives of solidarity in socialist aid.

Cuban aid to Africa has been more clearly committed to considerations of ideological solidarity than Soviet aid on its own. Soviet aid over the years has gone to a variety of regimes, some of which could by no stretch of the imagination be regarded as 'progressive'. There have been Soviet projects in countries ranging from Uganda to Sierra Leone, from Mozambique to Ghana. Because the degree of Russian involvement in Africa is more widespread than that of the Cubans, the pattern of Soviet aid is more complex. The theme of ideological solidarity is clear in the case of Cuba. Curiously enough it is clearer still in the case of the German Democratic Republic, whose economic involvement in Africa has been selectively and competently carried out in a manner which has combined high considerations of self-interest with high considerations of 'progressive comradeship'.

Aid from the Organization of Petroleum Exporting Countries has often had a marked component of cultural solidarity. The Arab members of OPEC tend to be particularly influenced by considerations of helping, first, fellow Arabs; secondly, fellow Muslims; and thirdly, other Third World countries provided there is some evidence of general sympathy with the 'Arab cause'.

The names of the different funds are themselves indicative of the salience of cultural solidarity. There is the Kuwait Fund for Arab Economic Development, established in 1961, with an authorized capital currently of $3.45 billion, and total potential lending resources estimated at approximately $11.5 billion. The Fund assists projects put forward by Arab governments. Then there is the Saudi Fund for Development, established in 1974, with an authorized capital of $2.9 billion and total potential lending resources of the same amount for the time being.

Although the Arab world still receives charity in effect under this Fund, its orientation is broader than that of the Kuwaitis. One example is the loan of $35 million for port development in South Korea. Thirdly, there is the Abu Dhabi Fund for Arab Economic Development, established in 1971 with an authorized capital of $512.8 million and potential lending resources estimated at approximately $1.93 billion. This fund has already broadened its concept of solidarity. Until 1974 its lending was limited to Arab countries, but it now extends to other developing countries in Asia and Africa and to all Islamic countries. It is still not permitted by its charter to lend to Latin America, however.[2]

It was not until 1976 that the first loans for non-Arab countries were made upon the conclusion of agreements with Bangladesh, Malaysia, India, Mali, and a few others. Aid to Africa gathered momentum in 1977. 21.4 per cent of Abu Dhabi loans approved during that year were for black Africa and 26.5 per cent for Arab Africa. Other Arab countries outside the African continent received an additional 37.8 per cent. The total which went to other parts of Asia accounted for 14.3 per cent. The relevance of the solidarity principle operates in clear terms, but there are different levels of solidarity important to policy-makers in Abu Dhabi. In three years since 1974 Arab countries received 71.7 per cent of its loans, followed by non-Arab African countries (10.9 per cent) and Asian countries (17.4 per cent). The same pattern of Abu Dhabi aid distribution has been maintained into the 1980s.

Then there is a whole area of multilateral lending where, once again, the principle of solidarity interacts with that of self-interest. The Arab Fund for Economic and Social Development, with an authorized capital of $1.3 billion and, at its foundation, potential lending resources of $4.14 billion, is the oldest, largest and busiest of all the multilateral development institutions based on the Arab world. It is also the only Fund which lends exclusively to Arab countries. There is also solidarity with black Africa in the more recent activities of Arab financial institutions. Especially noteworthy is the Arab Bank for Economic Development in Africa, with its headquarters in Khartoum. Established in 1974, with an authorized capital of $392.25 million and total potential lending resources authorized at $1 billion, this particular Arab Bank is the only Arab fund that concentrates entirely on Africa. It lends only to the non-Arab African countries, which makes it at the same time the only Arab fund that does no lending to Arab countries.

The Islamic Development Bank is, almost by definition, based on religious solidarity. It was established in 1975, and has its headquarters in Jeddah, Saudi Arabia. Its authorized capital is $2.4 billion, with potential lending resources authorized at approximately the same amount. In the case of this particular fund, the imperative of self-interest is diluted by that part of the *Shari'a* (Islamic Law), which prohibits the taking of interest. A formula has been devised to cover at least the cost of administering loans — 'loan charges' — but even this form of charging comes uncomfortably close to 'usury', according to some of the more orthodox Muslims. The membership of the Islamic Development Bank extends from Indonesia in the east to Senegal in the west, with voting power inevitably weighted in favour of those Muslim countries making the largest contributions.

A different basis of solidarity emerges from the OPEC Special Fund, established in Vienna with a subscribed capital of approximately $1.6 billion. The principle of solidarity operating here is that of Third World solidarity but there is the important additional consideration of self-interest because of OPEC's need for

Third World support at times of possible confrontation with Western consumers of oil. The fund draws most of its resources from Arab countries. It gives balance of payments support as well as project loans to Third World countries but requires those receiving such support to spend equal amounts of their own currencies on development projects.

We have discussed OPEC aid extensively partly because this kind of aid provides some of the clearest illustrations of the operation of the principle of solidarity in aid and loan transactions, as contrasted with the principle of straight charity, on the one hand, and straight self-interest, on the other. Cultural factors are particularly relevant in defining the basis of solidarity — be those factors shared religion, shared language, shared ideology, or shared class consciousness across international boundaries and in a global context. But culture also affects attitudes to questions of charity, and helps to condition one's view of self-interest.

The Cultural Content of Aid

Apart from the cultural impact on aid motivation, there is also the question of culture as embodied in aid itself. Here we shall address ourselves, first, to direct cultural aid; secondly, to the cultural content of economic aid; and thirdly, to the cultural content of military aid.

Direct cultural aid is in turn designed either to consolidate cultural solidarity or to expand that solidarity. For example, providing free copies of the Bible for a country which is already Christian is a case of consolidating Christian solidarity; but providing such literary aids to a country which has yet to be converted to Christianity is a case of aid motivated by evangelical expansionism. Free copies of the Qur'an from, say, the Arab world to an African country could either seek to consolidate an Islamic presence in the receiving country or to expand such a presence. Money transfers for the building of mosques or Qur'anic schools are usually cases of direct cultural aid.

Cultural aid need not be religious, however. On the contrary, it is often secular. What should be borne in mind is that there have been occasions when secular aid has been religiously motivated, as in the case of aid from the World Council of Churches to liberation movements in Southern Africa. There have also been occasions when not only have the motives been religious but even the primary intention of missionary secular aid has been oriented towards spreading the gospel. In the old days in Africa, missionary-built hospitals rendered secular medical services but also formed part of this grand design. We shall return to these themes of the consequences of aid in a later section of this chapter.

What should be emphasized is that cultural aid in more recent times has included a higher proportion of secular ideology than of religious creed. The embassy of every major power now includes a cultural arm of some kind, designed to promote the ideas and values of the country represented. Among Western countries, the French moved early in the direction of cultural diplomacy. The Alliance Française was founded in 1884. The Germans also entered early into cultural diplomacy with the establishment of the Verein für das Deutschtum im Ausland designed to promote and defend the ideals of Pan-Germanism through *Auslandsschulen*.

The British were at first rather suspicious of cultural diplomacy. Indeed, they remain suspicious about the term itself, although they have been engaged in it now for quite a time. It was not until November 1934 that the British Council for

Relations with Other Countries was founded, on the initiative of the Foreign Office. It was a milestone in Britain's realization of the value of propaganda, systematically undertaken for diplomatic ends:

> The British Council was itself created as a response to the malignant propaganda of the totalitarian regimes which had come into being following the Treaty of Versailles. . . . By expounding the wonders and marvels of British civilization, past and present, cultural publicity was used to illustrate that British society still had much to offer the world. Furthermore, this cultural projection was anything but a mass communication process. It was an attempt to influence those foreigners who were in a position to influence large numbers of their own people, and thus took an indirect route. Hence the emphasis was on cultural and educational, even 'intellectual', activity.[3]

With regard to socialist governments, cultural aid includes the provision of subsidized works of the great socialist masters, especially Marx, Engels, Lenin, and (in some cases) Mao Tse-tung.

A more disguised form of cultural aid is embodied in education and the provision of teachers. In most African countries the institution of the university itself is one large piece of Western culture transmitted to an alien society. Many African universities began as subsidiaries of Western academic bodies. A number of universities in former British Africa were initially overseas extensions of the University of London and awarded London University degrees. One or two universities in former French Africa are still, at least partially, part of the French university system. Louvanium University in what is now Zaire (Louvanium has become part of the University of Zaire) also began as an extension or subsidiary of Louvain in Belgium. It is in this sense that I have written about African universities as subsidiaries of multinational cultural corporations of the Western world.[4]

Some cultural policies pursued in the Third World may themselves affect the degree of cultural aid that is transmitted or accepted. For example, a change in the language policy of the Third World country would considerably modify the nature of technical assistance to that country. Thus, the promotion of Swahili in the Tanzanian educational system has reduced the relevance of English-speaking teachers from abroad for Tanzanian schools. Linguistic self-reliance in Tanzania has carried the implication of greater educational self-reliance, since Tanzania has to look primarily within its own borders for teachers knowledgeable and skilful in the Swahili language.

The greater utilization of Arabic in the educational system of Sudan has not necessarily broadened educational self-reliance but has changed the balance between the donors of technical assistance. Whereas the Sudanese educational system previously could absorb many teachers from the United Kingdom and other English-speaking countries, it is now in greater need of teachers from Arabic-speaking countries. Arabic was, of course, important in Sudan in any case, but it has now increased its role in education.

The cultural content of aid is not always direct, however, nor always transmitted within educational processes. It can sometimes be an element in a package of aid which is primarily economic. Certain forms of economic aid involve certain forms of production, and these in turn can have consequences for patterns of consumption. Some of the acculturation may have preceded the provision of the economic aid. For example, aid to increase a particular country's capacity to produce Western-style shirts and trousers, or American jeans, was preceded by the prior triumph of Western dress culture in the modern world as a whole. 'For the apparel oft proclaims the man' may have been true in Shakespeare's day, when a person's nationality or social class could be guessed from the way he dressed. But today, as we saw in Chapter 5, Western dress has become almost universal.

In view of this prior dress acculturation that has taken place all over the Third World, aid that helps to promote the production of Western style dress for local use does decidedly include both economic and cultural elements within it, and may at times help to consolidate the cultural conquest that had already begun.

As for cultural factors within military aid, these include technological elements and skills. The overwhelming proportion of military equipment in the Third World is a product of either Western or Soviet technology. Skills that are oriented towards the use of that equipment, or its maintenance, are skills which often have relevance beyond the immediate weapon or military vehicle. Transferred technical skills of this kind are part of both technology and culture. Indeed technology itself can be defined as applied science utilized in order to meet specific cultural ends. Military technology transferred from the Western world or the Soviet Union to a region like the African continent is a form of combat culture very different from the warrior traditions of many of those African societies. Some aspects of the original combat tradition may indeed persist in Africa in spite of the penetration of the alternative martial technology of the West. What is clear is that a clash of culture is involved in transactions which range from the arms trade to military training.[5]

Cultural Constraints on Aid

Culture does not merely play a role in motivating the giving or the receiving of aid; it also plays a role in inhibiting both. We might here look briefly at constraints on the giving of aid; secondly, constraints on the readiness to ask for aid or to receive it; and thirdly, constraints on a country's capacity to absorb aid or to use it effectively when it is given.

With regard to constraints on the giving of aid, these may sometimes be due to negative factors — like the absence of a tradition of charity, or the absence of the relevant basis of solidarity between the giver and the receiver. At least as fundamental would be the absence of a general cultural infrastructure necessary for evaluating projects or assessing proposals from prospective recipients of aid. A country like Abu Dhabi is hard put to it to decide between a road project in Bangladesh, a proposed irrigation scheme in Malaysia, a new industry in Burundi, or new schools in Uganda. One solution is to lean in favour of specialized criteria. As it happens, Abu Dhabi does tend to favour industrial projects, as against infrastructural or social service ones. It does not have the necessary administrative capacity and skill to evaluate systematically the coherence, viability, cost effectiveness, and developmental promise of many of the projects that come before it.

In the Western world one constraint on the giving of aid lies in electoral politics. The political culture puts a special premium on the month to month popularity of specific policies, and quite often foreign aid is simply not a vote-catcher. Also relevant is the stronger role of the principle of exchange in the capitalist ethos. While liberal culture may indeed, on the one hand, strongly champion the charitable instinct, it does also, on the other hand, favour the maximization of return. This second factor in liberal culture, when combined with the vagaries of electoral politics, results in all the contradictions of tied aid. Much of the transfer of capital to developing countries ends up by profiting the giver more than the receiver. Conditions are imposed on the receiver, designed to 'maximize returns' for the donor countries.

Just as some potential donors end up giving far less than their capacity, many potential recipients are often reluctant to ask for certain forms of aid or to absorb them. The reluctance to receive can occasionally be part of a general cultural autarky in that particular society. The voluntary isolation of Burma until relatively recently was a case of cultural and ideological withdrawal, and both resulted in reduced economic relations with others. China under Mao Tse-Tung also pursued self-reliance after the break with the Soviet Union in a style which included considerable cultural and economic autarky.

More common among Third World countries is not so much a reluctance to ask for or to accept aid as a relative incapacity to do full justice to what is received. Sometimes this may be due to the absence of an adequate culture of anticipation. Such a culture favours saving for tomorrow even if this involves sacrificing today. It is also important as part of the necessary infrastructure for effective planning.

Many traditional societies, almost by definition, are cultures of nostalgia rather than of anticipation. They value custom, ancestry, and tradition — rather than making preparations for the day after tomorrow. Cultures of nostalgia are also unlikely to monetize time as a commodity. Things move slowly, often very slowly. Cultures which love ancestry also tend to love kinship generally. It is not merely the great-grandfather that is revered; it is also often all the great-grandfathers, children, grandchildren, and great-grandchildren. Kinship solidarity has its effects on developmental capacity.

Cultures with pronounced kinship solidarity sometimes substitute the prestige motive for the profit motive among the drives of behaviour. The classical profit motives seek to promote investment while reducing consumption by the entrepreneur himself. The prestige motive, on the other hand, fosters social ostentation and conspicuous consumption as part of the struggle for status. Sometimes the status is among one's own kinsfolk. The status may even result in a combination of charity and solidarity with the poorer members of one's broad, extended family. But while the distribution of the new affluence may sometimes be impressive when judged by standards of charity and solidarity, productivity and effectiveness are less than optimal.

Cultural Rules and Conditions of Aid

The rules which are supposed to govern aid relations are themselves often culturally relative. When Jimmy Carter assumed the presidency of the United States the question of human rights became a governing factor in American aid policy. Human rights are often culturally relative. They can certainly be a form of moral imperialism when they motivate a powerful country to attempt to change the values of the weaker ones by means of sanctions.

The old British moralistic position of *Pax Britannica* pointed an accusing finger at weaker societies, reprimanded them for being incapable of maintaining peace and law and order, and then imposed a British presence upon them in pursuit of that alleged moral good. Carter's human rights crusade constituted not so much an imperialism of penetration, threatening to intervene if others did not adequately behave themselves, but more an imperialism of withdrawal, threatening to disengage if the target country persisted in its delinquency. Carter's administration warned the Third World not to carry repression too far — or America would pull out of their development projects and cut off the supply of dollars.

In reality, not all human rights are culturally relative. Let us illustrate this by the process by which a suspect ends up in jail. No one would disagree, surely, that trial by jury is culturally relative. It is limited mainly to countries of Anglo-Saxon tradition, or those influenced by that tradition. On the other hand, the principle that no one should be punished before receiving a fair trial is much less parochial. Anglo-Saxon tradition stipulates that the jury system is one way of assuring fairness, but there may be more than one way. What happens to the prisoner after he has been convicted and is languishing in jail is yet another area of differentiation. Most Third World cultures would probably agree that the torture of prisoners is morally wrong except in rather unusual circumstances, whereas contemporary liberal thought would insist that torturing prisoners is wrong under all circumstances. The behaviour of Third World governments may also often be out of line not only with liberal thought but also with the cultures of their own societies. Third World regimes are at times more repressive than would be defensible under any system of values, including their own. What all this means is that, whereas on one side of the process trial by jury is definitely thoroughly relative, on the other the principle of respecting the body of the prisoner and not torturing it is probably closer to universal acceptance.

As for basing aid on the principle of satisfying basic human needs, this is even more clearly universal than political human rights. The need for food, for clean water, for health and medical facilities, for shelter, is so clearly universal among human beings that it forms a less culturally relative basis of aid transaction than the need for political freedom.

Cultural Consequences of Aid

Finally, let us address ourselves to the general repercussions of aid. One area concerns the dilemma between cultural dependency and cultural self-reliance. Certain forms of aid, even if they are not directly cultural, have repercussions which increase the recipient's dependency upon the donor, and reduce the capacity of the receiving society to maintain its own authenticity. A related dialectic is that between national development and national decolonization. The pursuit of national development by Third World countries may reduce the pace of decolonization.

A third area of cultural consequences of aid is related to the urban bias in development. This urban bias is indeed often an economic curse, but it can be a cultural gain. If it means that the pace of Westernization in the rural countryside is arrested because development favours mainly the urban centres, this bias prolongs the survival of local culture, for better or for worse. On the negative side, rural culture may be in any case a culture of poverty and indigence. On the positive side, much of the countryside is the repository of what is authentic and distinctive in a particular society. If the 'modernization' of the countryside could be delayed for another generation or two, it could give the society as a whole a better chance to choose a path of 'modernization' which would not be excessively based on 'Westernization'.[6]

The fourth dialectic is that between capital-intensive and labour-intensive forms of aid and investment generally. Capital-intensiveness tends to require skill intensity. It therefore helps to promote technocracy and elitism. That itself could be a significant cultural modification in a given society. Labour-intensive aid projects, on the other hand, could help to democratize modernity. Such techniques would bring more people into the modern sector of production and increase effective economic participation in society as a whole. And yet, to the extent to which modernity as conceived in the third quarter of the twentieth century is still excessively Western-derived, it is possible to argue that labour-intensive aid projects are part of the process of spreading out Westernization broadly, whereas capital-intensive projects help to concentrate the technical impact of the West among a small elite.

The fifth area of the consequences of aid concerns stratification more broadly defined. Under this we are looking not merely at the narrow dichotomous distinction between the elite and the masses, but also at issues which decide who are the elite and from what their basis of privilege and power is derived.

In Africa, Western education helps to redefine even the concept of class. There was a shift from defining class in terms of who owns what to describing class in terms of who knows what. The Western-educated Africans attained levels of influence and power in their society out of all proportion to their numbers or indeed to their value for society. A whole generation of articulate intellectuals moved up to the commanding heights of their political system. Africans like Nkrumah, Nyerere, Azikiwe, Senghor, and that whole first wave of top political figures at independence got where they did partly because of the verbal and literary skills they had acquired from their foreign masters. Western education also helped to produce secondary levels of the elite, from bureaucrats like the late Frank Kalimuzo of Uganda to academics like Ali Mazrui of Kenya. The access to influence and sometimes power that this group had was intimately connected with the consequences of acculturation. Foreign aid which either maintains that situation, or consolidates it even further, is inevitably a form of aid with considerable consequences for class formation and class defence.

On the other hand, military technology when ingested into an underdeveloped society has resulted in re-stratification. The rise of the soldiers in modern Africa as they have captured power in one military coup after another is one political consequence of Western technological penetration. In a technologically underdeveloped society like, say, Uganda, power in its ultimate form is more likely to reside with those who control the means of destruction rather than with those in possession of the means of production. The infiltration of modern armaments in societies which are in other respects pre-modern has helped to construct new pyramids of power. To some extent this has inevitably been at the expense of the intelligentsia, especially in post-colonial Africa. Whereas those who imbibed Western culture were initially the beneficiaries of the transfer of power from the imperial rulers, those who inherited Western military weapons later challenged the credentials of the literati. Many of the soldiers were inadequately trained by Western standards, and their units were often disorganized. Large parts of Africa fell under the power of this *lumpen militariat*.[7]

Conclusion

Aid is only a small proportion of the capital flow of the world. Even the richest countries are still reluctant to make much more than a tiny proportion of their gross domestic product available for purposes of aid.

But our concern in this chapter has been less with the volume of aid than with the interplay between culture and aid transactions. We have sought to demonstrate how culture conditions the motives for giving aid and for wanting it. We have also explored the actual cultural content of different forms of aid, ranging from directly cultural projects involving the teaching of the French language or the promotion of Islam to indirectly cultural projects which embody culture in a particular kind of industry or military establishment.

Culture also plays a part in impeding aid transactions. Sometimes the giver becomes less willing to give as a result of some restraining normative elements, or the receiver becomes incapable of absorbing the aid because the society is still inspired by nostalgia and tradition rather than activated by anticipation.

The rules and conditions that aid givers impose also have cultural implications. We have explored elements of moral relativism in criteria of aid-giving based on human rights, but have discerned greater universalism in criteria founded on basic human needs.

We concluded with an exploration of the consequences of aid in terms of cultural variables. Problems of dependency and self-reliance, of development as against decolonization, often form a central feature of the dialectic. The urban bias in development is itself an economic curse but could be a cultural gain as it arrests the speed of Westernization. Capital-intensive as against labour-intensive techniques also have their cultural implications, ranging from promoting technocracy to democratizing modernity. As for stratification and its relationship to culture and aid, this is related partly to the whole process of acculturation in creating new social classes, and partly to the consequences of technological penetration.

Aid is itself a value. Culture is a system of interconnected values, perceptions, and modes of interaction. It is because aid itself is a normative concept that it has to be evaluated on the basis of a wider normative framework. Hence this essay as an exploration of the cultural ramifications of transactions between giver and receiver, between the affluent and the needy, between different socio-cultural systems.

Postscript: 1978—1989

The OPEC Special Fund has expanded considerably and continues to play a major role in building Third World solidarity by developing Third World economies. In its first ten years (1976—1986) the fund's resources grew from 800 million pounds to 4 billion pounds. By 1986, up to 83 non-OPEC countries had received assistance, the emphasis being on development projects in rural areas and reaching the 'poorest of the poor'. There have been imaginative and successful projects in agriculture, technical education, and health. Several OPEC loans have helped also to relieve balance-of-payments problems. Under two successive dynamic secretaries-general, Dr Ibrahim Shihata and Dr Seyyid Abdulai of Nigeria, the OPEC Fund has produced its own aid strategy for sub-Saharan Africa. The OPEC Fund is now self-sustaining, has not suffered from the collapse of oil prices since 1985, and will not need replenishment from member states until the twenty-first century.

OPEC's development aid continues to demonstrate the principle of solidarity as distinct from charity or self-interest in such transactions. The aid and loans policies of the major Western governments, in contrast, have been characterized increasingly by self-interest in the last decade or so.

In the United States, the Reagan Republican administration from 1981 abandoned not only Jimmy Carter's human rights policy but also his commitment to the New International Economic Order (NIEO). Reagan saw foreign aid largely in terms of increased US national security, not increased economic aid to the Third World. Reagan increased military and balance-of-payments assistance to pro-Western American allies in Latin America, Africa, and Asia. In 1986, US government contributions to food aid in Africa were cut. None of the starving countries of the Sahel or Central Africa were in the American orbit or of strategic military value. Under Reagan, the United States reduced multilateral aid through a variety of donors and increased bilateral aid from a single source, thus making it easier to manipulate aid for political and military purposes.

James Baker, the US Treasury Secretary, did launch a plan in October 1985 to help rescue Latin American debtor countries by increasing International Monetary Fund lending and long-term World Bank development planning. But the Baker Plan was not about ending world poverty. Its primary objective was to avert social and political revolution south of the Rio Grande.

The coincidence of Reagan's presidency with Margaret Thatcher's term as prime minister in Britain helped to ensure the failure of the work of the Brandt Commission and its proposals for world development. In the late 1970s, at the suggestion of the World Bank President Robert McNamara, former Chancellor of West Germany Willy Brandt chaired an Independent Commission on International Development Issues. Other members of the commission included experts and senior politicians from many countries — capitalist and socialist, rich and poor. The commission produced its report, *North-South — A Programme for Survival* (commonly known as the Brandt Report), in 1980. The report called for an emergency programme to help the world's poorest countries, especially in water and soil management, health care, solar energy development, mineral and oil exploration, and infrastructure for industry and transport. It also called for an end to mass hunger and malnutrition through increased food aid and food production, helped by agricultural research and land reform. The report proposed diversion of funds and skills from arms production to peaceful needs; a change in the pattern of world trade so that developing countries can have a bigger part in processing, marketing, and distributing their own commodities; an increase in international aid whether funds came from governments, international financial institutions, or private financial bodies; a strengthening of the United Nations system with a high-level advisory body to monitor various organizations and supervise a World Development Fund to spread wealth from the rich to the poor.

The Brandt Report also called for a summit of world leaders to take action to deal with the crisis of world development. Such a summit did take place at Cancun, Mexico, in October 1981. The Cancun meeting was a failure because Reagan and Thatcher were at odds with nearly all the other leaders present in their consistent rejection of the main proposals of the Brandt Report, which was not the official agenda but was brought up repeatedly by Indira Gandhi and by the Algerian delegation. The Reagan-Thatcher line was that fighting inflation in the First World was more important than development in the Third World, that such development in any case could only come about through freer trade and and increased Western private investment, and that market forces — not state regulation — provided the key for economic prosperity.

Two years after Cancun, worsening world economic conditions and the continuing lack of global cooperation impelled the Brandt Commission to prepare a new report, called *Common Crisis, North-South: Cooperation for World Recovery* (1983). *Common Crisis* called for the necessary steps to be taken in the fields of finance, trade, food, and energy to avert economic collapse and revive the world economy.

Both Prime Minister Thatcher (in 1983) and President Reagan (in 1984) were re-elected and once again the work of the Brandt Commission was ignored by the major Western governments. Willy Brandt, almost in despair, reiterated his arguments in a new book, *World Armament and World Hunger*, published in 1986, but the original Brandt Report was, by then, effectively a dead letter.

Yet another cut in the British overseas aid budget came in 1986, along with an increase in US aid but a cut in American *development* aid. Under Margaret Thatcher, British official aid declined from 0.52 per cent of Britain's economic wealth (Gross National Product) in 1979 when she first became prime minister to 0.33 per cent in 1984 and 0.28 per cent in 1987. The culture of charity has played little part in the overseas aid policies of Thatcher, who regards aid as a branch of commerce, with an increasing proportion of Britain's aid tied to the purchase of British exports.

Notes

1. This chapter deals with aid in its broadest sense and is not restricted to the customary definition of aid as 'official development assistance'.
2. The section of this chapter covering OPEC aid draws its material from John Law, *Arab Aid: Who Gets It, for What and How* (New York: Chase World Information, 1978).
3. Philip M. Taylor (University of Leeds), 'Cultural Diplomacy and the British Council 1934—1939' (mimeo). The paper is based upon a section of the author's doctoral thesis: 'The Projection of Britain: British Overseas Publicity and Propaganda 1914—1949, with particular reference to the work of the News Department of the Foreign Office' to be submitted to the University of Leeds. See also R. McMurray and M. Lee, *The Cultural Approach: Another Way in International Relations* (Chapel Hill, 1947). I am indebted to Philip M. Taylor for some bibliographical guidance on this question, and to his mimeographed paper for stimulation on the role of the British Council.
4. See Mazrui, 'The African University as a Multinational Corporation. Comparative Problems of Penetration and Dependency', *Harvard Educational Review*, Vol. 45, No. 2, Spring 1975. A version of the paper also appears as an Occasional Paper of the Institute of Development Studies, at the University of Sussex, England. See also Mazrui, *Political Values and the Educated Class in Africa* (London: Heinemann Educational Books and Berkeley: University of California Press, 1978).
5. For a collection of essays by different authors on these aspects of combat culture, see Mazrui (ed.), *The Warrior Tradition in Modern Africa* (Leiden: E.J. Brill, 1977).
6. For a brilliant and comprehensive study of the urban bias in development see Michael Lipton, *Why Poor People Stay Poor: The Urban Bias in World Development* (Temple Smith, 1977).
7. This concept is discussed more fully in Ali A. Mazrui, 'The Lumpen Proletariat and the Lumpen Militariat: African Soldiers as a New Political Class', *Political Studies*, Vol. 21, No. 1, March 1973, pp. 1—12. The article also forms the basis of a chapter in Mazrui, *Soldiers and Kinsmen in Uganda: The Making of a Military Ethnocracy* (Sage, 1975).

12

Changing the Guards from Hindus to Muslims

It is arguable that the most important post-colonial movements in the Third World are reducible to two struggles — first, the Southern movement to find the right military relationship with the Northern industrialized states; and second, the Southern movement to find the right economic relationship with the same states. The first quest has ranged from techniques of anti-colonial liberation to the principle of non-alignment, from *satyagraha* to nuclear proliferation. In this first movement for an appropriate military relationship between North and South, India, and possibly Hindu culture, have played a disproportionate role.

The second movement is economically oriented, in search of an appropriate economic balance between North and South. Among its latest manifestations is the quest for a New International Economic Order. In this second movement the torch may have been passed to the Muslim world. Let us examine these two basic trends in greater detail.

Rolling Back the Colonial Curtain

The most basic military issue which confronted the peoples of Asia and Africa at the beginning of the twentieth century concerned imperialism itself. In one sense imperialism could be defined as the monopoly stage of warfare. The imperialist powers in their colonization asserted a monopoly of the legitimate use of physical force. A basic preliminary aim was the so-called pacification of the natives. Wherever there was resistance to imperial annexation, force had to be used not only to end the resistance but to render the natives militarily harmless from then on. Hence the whole doctrine of *Pax Britannica* — asserting an imperial privilege to monopolize force and demilitarize local communities. One African ruler after another was made to sign a treaty which amounted, among other things, to a renunciation of the right to bear arms. The imperial power gradually asserted a monopoly of the legitimate use of physical force. To that extent, non-violence among the natives was used as a device for controlling the natives.

A great Hindu leader then emerged out of the womb of the imperial experience. His name was Mahatma Gandhi. He gradually evolved a philosophy of passive resistance and non-violent restraint. He inspired millions of his Hindu compatriots, and a minority of Muslims in India, to follow his banner of struggle against British rule in India. The doctrine of non-violence which the imperial power itself had encouraged and fostered as an instrument of pacification and control was now mobilized as an instrument of liberation and indigenous fulfilment. The Indian nationalist movement and its struggle for independence were now truly under way.

One question which arises is whether the use of Gandhian philosophy in the cause of India's independence was itself a perversion and betrayal of that very philosophy. After all, India's struggle was a knock on the door of the state system, asking for admission into that system of nation-states. The state is itself an instrument of structural violence, asserting, in Weber's terms, a monopoly of the legitimate use of physical force. The global system of nation-states has in turn been a structure of repressed international violence. State sovereignty has often been invoked to justify the most appalling brutalities. Under the global system of nation-states war itself as a historic human institution has attained new levels of sophistication, planning, and destructive power.

The Indian struggle for independence was a struggle to become a member of this system of nation-states. The prophet of non-violence, Mahatma Gandhi, helped to facilitate India's entry into a global structure of power and war.

In fairness to India and its leader, this struggle to enter the Westphalian state system (see Chapter 1), was virtually universal. One society after another in Asia, Africa, and elsewhere struggled for an entry visa into the nation-state system.

Nor was the paradox of using Gandhian non-violence in order to control the structure of state violence unique to India. Mahatma Gandhi influenced anti-colonial movements in other parts of the imperial order.

In June 1979 I had occasion to interview President Kenneth Kaunda of Zambia in Lusaka. Kaunda was a devout Gandhian in the 1950s and early 1960s. He regarded himself as a distant disciple of the Mahatma, and firmly subscribed to the principles of non-violence and *satyagraha*. He declared that he would fight the British only with agitation and peaceful campaigns, and not resort to armed struggle. 'I reject violence in all its forms as a solution to our problem,' Kaunda used to affirm.

And then the man received the keys of the kingdom of the state. He became leader of a newly independent African country. Almost immediately he was confronted with a threat to the state's monopoly of legitimate violence. A religious cult led by Alice Lenshina went on the rampage in Zambia, partly in rebellion against the efforts to force them to become members of a political party. Lenshina's followers killed and maimed other citizens in a fit of religious outrage. What was Kaunda to do? What guidance could Gandhian philosophy provide in such a situation?

Like Jawaharlal Nehru when he was confronted with the appalling slaughter between Muslims and Hindus at the time of India's independence, Kaunda's ethical theories seemed to disintegrate in the face of massive killing. As prime minister (soon to be president) he had to assert that old state monopoly of violence. In despair he virtually ordered his security forces to shoot to kill in the effort to stem the tide of violence by Lenshina's followers. Kaunda declared that if he had to be a savage to contain savagery, he was going to do it. The man who had tried so hard to refrain from violence while he struggled for entry into the global system of nation-states was now invoking violence as part of the logic of the nation-state.

209

In my conversations with him in 1979 I noticed that Kaunda was of course aware of the dilemma of trying to head a nation-state, on the one hand, and subscribe to the ethic of non-violence, on the other. He said he believed in world government as a solution to this dilemma. On the one hand, the human person as an individual had to learn the ethic of restraint and tame his nature; on the other hand, humanity as a collectivity had to devise global institutions of collective self-control and collective self-development. A marriage between the reformed individual and global structure seemed to Kaunda the only way forward in the struggle to resolve the dilemma posed by the incompatibility of nation-states and the ethic of non-violence. In some sense Kaunda still regarded himself as a distant disciple of Mahatma Gandhi but was caught up in the contradictions of statecraft.

Kenneth Kaunda was not the only African who was influenced by Gandhi during that period. In 1958, when the first all Africa Peoples Conference was held in Accra, Ghana, the Algerians had considerable difficulty persuading their fellow Africans to support their own armed insurrection against the French. Many African leaders still flirted with the ethic of non-violence, and felt unable at that stage to extend full sympathy to the Algerian revolution.

Even the host president, Kwame Nkrumah of Ghana, had still to 'outgrow' residual Gandhism. While he was struggling against British colonial rule he had himself championed Gandhian strategies for the Ghanaian freedom campaigns, calling Ghana's own techniques 'positive action' based on Gandhian methods.

How much of Gandhism was in fact a product of Hinduism? To what extent was his impact on parts of Asia and Africa a case of Hindu leadership of the Third World in a formative period of the anti-colonial struggle?

Certainly the Muslims of India, once they got converted to the idea of a separate state called 'Pakistan', substantially ceased to be part of India's leadership. By that period of the 1930s and early 1940s the Indian anti-colonial movement was in the main a Hindu anti-colonial movement. The Hindus were struggling against British rule; the Muslims were by then struggling against the prospect of Hindu domination.

Another Hindu factor behind the success of *satyagraha* was perhaps the so-called Yogi tradition — a capacity to sustain and transcend physical discomfort in a triumph of concentration and restraint. This aspect of the Hindu heritage lent familiarity to techniques like lying on a railway line to prevent a train moving, or embarking on a fast unto death. The latter strategy has come to be much used in other parts of the world, usually known as a 'hunger strike'. The Indian nationalist movement, and later aggrieved citizens of India after independence, learned to threaten fasting unto death as a political weapon. It is arguable that Hinduism as a culture was more congenial to these strategies of deprivation and immobility than other cultures might have been.

Gandhi himself was the very symbol of self-imposed deprivation — appearing everywhere as what Winston Churchill had called 'a half-naked fakir'. The emaciated little man gave up many of the material pleasures of life, from rich food to sexuality. His popularity in India had a good deal to do with this image of self-imposed renunciation.

It is true that the most important non-violent movement after Gandhi occurred without his inspiration or influence. This was the revolutionary and non-violent movement against the Shah of Iran, especially in 1978 and the beginning of 1979. The cultural factor at play in Iran at the time was of course not the Yogi tradition of India but the Kerbala tradition of Shiite Islam. It was at Kerbala that the Prophet

Muhammad's grandson was assassinated in the seventh century of the Christian era. This event profoundly influenced the nature of Shiite Islam in the centuries which followed, incorporating into this particular version of Islam a high veneration for both martyrdom and religious leadership. A combination of these two forces at a particular moment in Iran's time — a reactivation of the martyrdom complex and a reinvigoration of religious leadership — helped to make thousands of Iranians pour out into the streets of Teheran, sometimes to be killed in the hundreds, only for those who had survived to come out again the following day in relentless and heroic defiance.

Non-violence in Iran in rebellion against the Shah owed a good deal to the martyrdom legacy of Shiite Islam; non-violence of India in rebellion against the British owed a good deal to the Yogi and puritanical aspects of the Hindu heritage.

Gandhi had disciples in Africa, but without the underpinning of Hindu culture the African masses were seldom mobilized into passive resistance. The Yogi tradition could not easily be Africanized. It was hard to persuade Africans to lie across railway lines. It was unusual to arouse African interest in the technique of fasting unto death.

This did not of course mean that Africans did not make other sacrifices. In the twentieth century alone African resistance movements have ranged from the Maji Maji rebellion against the Germans in Tanganyika at the beginning of the century to the liberation movements in Zimbabwe and Namibia more recently, and from experiments in various forms of non-violent, unarmed resistance in South Africa from the 1950s to the 1980s, alongside growing armed resistance.

The most sustained forms of resistance in Africa have included fighting with weapons. And even the Maji Maji rebellion, though it involved the slaughter of hundreds of Africans confronting German gun power, was nevertheless a monumental mistake by the Africans as to the effectiveness of the guns against the protection of their own gods. This was not a case of martyrdom, as in Iran, where people genuinely expected to die for the greater glory of God. In the Maji Maji case the people did not expect to die. The massacre was a mistake.

What is important from the point of view of this chapter is that there was a Hindu factor in the legacy of Mahatma Gandhi, ranging from the Yogi tradition and its derivatives to the preponderance of Hindus among Gandhi's followers. The demonstration effect upon other parts of the Third World had a good deal to do with the Hindu response to Gandhi in India, rather than merely with the Indian response. The non-Hindus of India were more marginally involved in the Gandhi movement.

Hinduism and Non-alignment

While India's leadership of the Third World before independence was linked mainly to Mahatma Gandhi and his methods of liberation, India's leadership soon after independence was linked mainly to Jawaharlal Nehru and his methods of diplomacy. In many ways Nehru virtually invented the doctrine of non-alignment. It is true that Marshal Tito was an important co-founder of non-alignment, but Yugoslavia's influence on Asia and Africa was significantly more modest than India's influence. Non-alignment as a basis of the foreign policy of new states was fostered more effectively by India's demonstration effect than by Yugoslavia's.

It is true that Yugoslavia more dramatically demonstrated the efforts to create distance from both the Soviet Union and the Western powers. Tito's effort to prevent or avoid Soviet domination without falling into the Western embrace was a classic dramatization of sustained non-alignment.

In the final analysis, however, Yugoslavia was a European country, and this made it less of a model to Africans and Asians at that particular time of assertion of independence. Second, Yugoslavia is of course a significantly smaller country than India, however visible its geopolitical situation might be. Size is an important factor in international leadership. Third, Yugoslavia had little influence on its immediate neighbours, the countries which are usually the first circle of international influence. India, on the other hand, could wield considerable influence on the smaller Asian countries, apart from Pakistan.

Fourth, India had obtained independence from Great Britain, the country that had had the largest empire in Asia and Africa. Other former British territories regarded India's example as a demonstration of direct relevance to themselves since it symbolized a shared colonial predicament. Yugoslavia's experience, on the other hand, was almost unique in the modern period.

It is relevant that President Nasser of Egypt (United Arab Republic) had become a friend of Marshall Tito's, but Nasser was also influenced by Nehru and needed Nehru in the Suez crisis of 1956. Nehru's voice against the invasion of Egypt by Britain, France, and Israel was addressed both to the Commonwealth and to the emerging Third World. Nehru's voice in 1956 was a little more weighty than Tito's voice, especially since Tito was also anxiously looking at the Soviet invasion of Hungary, closer to his own borders.

As for non-alignment, the first great convert in black Africa was Kwame Nkrumah of Ghana. At the beginning he was, of course, less experienced in diplomacy and international affairs than the preceding giants of the non-aligned movement. To that extent, Nkrumah was for a while more susceptible to Nasser's influence than to Nehru's, and closer to Nehru than to Tito. He later became a non-aligned Titan in his own right, and indeed was one of the founding fathers of the movement.

The shaping of this new approach in foreign policy was thus considerably influenced by the stature and imagination of Pandit Jawaharlal Nehru. But to what extent was this even remotely a Hindu factor? After all, Nehru himself was hardly a classic case of devout Hinduism.

Part of the answer is to be sought in another question: to what extent was the Indian version of non-alignment itself a product of the Yogi aspects of the Hindu heritage? After all, non-alignment in this sense was a declaration of restraint and sobriety while the two ideological camps of East and West were shouting at and scheming against each other.

Second, the question persists as to whether non-alignment in the Indian context owed something to the preceding strategy of non-violence. After all, non-alignment was a disengagement from total war, though not necessarily from regional conflicts. The bipolar world of the Warsaw Pact pitted against the North Atlantic Treaty Organization was an effort to globalize war. Non-alignment as shaped by Nehru was a refusal to enter into alliances which implied this global military commitment. Nehru was prepared to go to war with Pakistan, and to conquer Goa by force. He was not prepared, however, to let India be part of the grand global strategy which could turn half the world into potential enemies.

Of course different countries had different reasons for moving in the direction of non-alignment. In the precise version which developed in Nehru's India the question persists whether the logic of *satyagraha* was part of the inspiration behind India's non-aligned stance.

Nehru formulated the link between non-alignment and the quest for peace forcefully in his speech at the Bandung Conference in 1955:

> I belong to neither bloc and I propose to belong to neither whatever happens in the world. . . . If all the world were to be divided up between those two blocs what would be the result? The inevitable result would be war. . . . It is an intolerable thought to me that the great countries of Asia and Africa should come out of bondage into freedom only to degrade and humiliate themselves in this way. . . . Every pact has brought insecurity and not security to those countries which have entered into them.[1]

Another Hindu aspect of non-alignment in that period was the composition of those who supported the stance within India itself. Some of Nehru's policies had at least as much support among India's Muslims as Hindus. Nehru's pro-Arab orientation on the Palestinian problem, for example, and his commitment to making India a secular state seemed to have been policies which were at least as popular among Muslims as among Hindus. It is less clear that non-alignment was among such policies. On the contrary, because of Pakistan's pro-Western alignment during that period, the Muslims of the Republic of India itself seemed to have been profoundly ambivalent about non-alignment as a doctrine. At the conference in Bandung Muhammad Ali of Pakistan asserted the right of all nations to self-defence collectively or individually, hoping that this formulation would help to legitimize Pakistan's membership of a Western-oriented pact. Pakistan was in disfavour among a number of newly emerging countries precisely because it was perceived as a military ally of one of the blocs in the Cold War.

This entire situation in those days of the Baghdad Pact helped to create a sense of profound ambivalence among Muslim citizens of India with regard to the doctrine of non-alignment. The general support that Nehru had was somewhat more purely Hindu than the support he received on his Middle Eastern policies or on policies concerning the secular state and democracy within India.

We should also remember that in the 1950s much of the Arab world was still conservative, and western military connections within the Middle East were more institutionalized than they have since become. A residual British military presence still remained in places like Aden, the Gulf, and even Suez in the first half of the decade. The real radicalization of President Nasser of Egypt did not get under way until the Western rebuff administered against him in 1956, which stung him into nationalizing the Suez Canal, and precipitated the crisis over Suez that year. On the whole, much of the Muslim world in the 1950s was in varying degrees aligned to the West, ranging from Turkey, which was an actual member of the North Atlantic Treaty Organization, to Iraq, after whose capital the Baghdad Pact was named.

Apart from Nasser's Egypt in the last years of that decade, the most important Muslim exception to pro-Western alignment was Indonesia under Sukarno. Indeed, Bandung in Indonesia had provided the setting for a particularly important and historic Afro-Asian conference which is now regarded as a milestone in the evolution of the non-aligned movement.

In view of this relatively low visibility of Muslim countries in the emerging non-aligned movement in the 1950s, India's stature within the movement was the more pronounced. The vocabulary of the day had not fully adopted the word 'non-alignment. Concepts like 'positive neutralism' were competing as alternatives in the late 1950s and early 1960s. The banner of this emerging movement was nevertheless decidedly carried by India under Nehru in the years before 1962. Tito could not feature in the parallel movement of Afro-Asianism since Yugoslavia was a European country; Nasser and Nkrumah were for a while inclined to defer to Nehru as the senior statesman from Hindustan.

Towards the Nuclearization of Non-alignment

And then came 1962. Two crises occurred in that year with implications for the future of non-alignment: China's invasion of India and, later in the year, the Soviet-American confrontation over Cuba. The crisis involving China and India seemed to strain the credibility of non-alignment as a viable strategy for Third World countries. The crisis over Soviet missiles in Cuba finally reestablished the credibility of non-alignment in the wake of the confrontation between the super-powers.

In addition to these implications for non-alignment implicit in the two crises of 1962 was the shadow of potential nuclear competition. The Cuban missile crisis was humanity's nearest point to a nuclear war, as the United States and the Soviet Union engaged in an eyeball-to-eyeball test of will. It is arguable that after the crisis was over, the very fact that these two super-powers were so near to a nuclear holocaust introduced a whole new element of caution in their subsequent relationships.

On the other hand, the two giants of Asia, namely China and India, had also engaged in a test of will. The fact that their relationship had experienced the strain of a border clash, with some humiliation of India by China, activated a new spirit of military competitiveness between them. Two years after China had inflicted a military setback on India with conventional weapons, China itself became a nuclear power. The stage was set, whether admitted by New Delhi or not, for an accelerated push by India towards a nuclear capability.

While the Cuban missile crisis between the global super-powers — the United States and the USSR — had resulted in a greater desire for arms control between them, the Sino-Indian conflict of the same year had resulted in a new spirit of military competitiveness between the giants of Asia.

Why was the Sino-Indian conflict a crisis for non-alignment? Because it was widely interpreted as a situation in which Nehru's faith in the goodwill of communist countries was proved to have been naive. Much of the international press seemed to take Nehru to task for having put too much trust in five principles of coexistence with China and other communist countries. Much of the Western world had been trying to convert Nehru to the proposition that communism was dangerous and expansionist. Nehru had resisted these sermons from John Foster Dulles and other Western policy makers and spokesmen.

And then, lo and behold, in 1962 the communist giant of Asia invaded India. The five principles of coexistence seemed to be compromised. Nehru's pet doctrine of non-alignment seemed to be in disgrace.

India needed friends in such a situation. Military and other support, though of a modest kind, came from the West. Britain's decision to provide military equipment to India was criticized by none other than Africa's leading spokesman on non-alignment, Kwame Nkrumah. Nkrumah argued that provisional support to one of the sides in this Sino-Indian conflict could soon result in competing support being given to the other side.

Prime Minister Harold Macmillan of Britain responded by arguing that if a member of the Commonwealth was attacked, it was right and proper that Britain should provide whatever help was possible. President Nkrumah's immediate rejoinder was that the Commonwealth, of which his own country was also a member, was not a military alliance and therefore membership laid no obligations on one member to go to the military aid of another when under attack. Nehru's own idea of non-alignment was being used by his African disciple against his receiving aid from the West at a time of military challenge from China. The principles of the most important founder of non-alignment, Jawaharlal Nehru, seemed suddenly to be in disarray. It was because of this that the first crisis of 1962, the Sino-Indian conflict, was in part a crisis of credibility for non-alignment.

Then came the Cuban missile crisis. Here was a small country allowing its territory to be used for establishing a missile base for one of the super-powers, the Soviet Union. The trend alarmed the United States, and President John F. Kennedy issued his ultimatum to the Soviet Union to remove the missiles from Cuba, and imposed a blockade around Cuba pending the removal of those missiles. The world waited with bated breath. A Soviet ship seemed to be approaching an American blockade. Would the Russians permit the Americans to interfere with their movement? If the Russians did not, was the world headed for the ultimate holocaust?

Nikita Khrushchev, the Soviet leader, had the good sense to step back from the nuclear brink. John F. Kennedy had in turn the good sense to protect Soviet pride by immediately congratulating the Soviet Union on its statesmanship. The super-powers then went into discussions about the aftermath of the crisis. The missile bases were to be dismantled, and the United Nations was involved in providing guidelines for the inspection of Cuba. And all this was happening without adequate consultation with Cuba's own leaders. In fact, so incomplete was the Soviet Union's consultation with Castro that Castro, incensed by being ignored, refused cooperation on some issues. On balance the government in Havana seemed to be humiliated by both super-powers as they stepped back from the nuclear abyss.

By permitting the Soviet Union to establish a missile base aimed at the United States, Cuba at that time had opted for alignment with the Soviet bloc. And yet this alignment had in turn resulted in a blockade of Cuba, a threat of nuclear war sparked near Cuba, and the subsequent humiliation of Cuba when its own super-power ally, the Soviet Union, regarded peace with the United States as more fundamental than respect for Havana.

It was this situation which re-validated non-alignment in 1962. If India's humiliation by China had dimmed the lustre of non-alignment, Cuba's humiliation by the global super-powers after Cuba had permitted itself to be aligned constituted a rekindling of non-alignment. Nehru's doctrine had found a new vindication in the wake of a colossal crisis in the Caribbean.

Did the Sino-Indian conflict, conversely, help to set the stage for nuclear proliferation in Asia, within the same year in which the Cuban missile crisis did so for nuclear arms control between the two global super-powers? It would be absurd to attribute India's and China's nuclear programmes entirely, or even primarily, to competition between them as the giants of Asia. In the case of China, there was, after all, the emerging conflict with the Soviet Union, which in time came to be an obsession in Peking. In the case of India, the preliminary military rivalry was with

Pakistan, rather than with China. Moreover, India had regarded itself as a potential major power since before independence. The attitude of India to nuclear energy and the rules of nuclear science within the International Atomic Energy Agency betrayed from the beginning a budding aspiration to participate in the nuclear age on a basis of equality with those who had already become nuclear powers. India was a major voice for equity and balance within the International Atomic Energy Agency almost from its inception.

It does nevertheless seem possible that India's humiliation at the hands of China in 1962 opened up a form of rivalry with China which had previously been disguised by Panch Sheel, or the five principles of coexistence. While before 1962 the most important rival to India seemed to be Pakistan, after 1962 the real contender for Asian preeminence emerged as the People's Republic of China.

As we indicated, in 1964 China became a nuclear power. At the tenth anniversary of the Bandung Conference in Bandung in 1965, President Sukarno of Indonesia could announce with pride: 'And now one of us is a nuclear power.'

It may be a while before our access to the confidential records of decision-making in the Indian government is adequate to estimate the impact of China's nuclear device on India's nuclear programme. There seems little doubt, however, that there was such an impact. If one of Asia's giants had gone nuclear, could the other be far behind?

It seems to have taken India a decade to cap China's nuclear achievement. In 1974 India exploded a nuclear device, ostensibly for peaceful purposes.

How much of the Hindu factor lay behind India's nuclear programme? Again this was an effort which had primarily Hindu support, backed by Sikh support, but was unlikely to enjoy the unqualified support of the Muslims of India. In other words, once again this was an issue which was specific to particular denominations within India. The Muslims of the Indian Republic had profound ambivalence about India's nuclear programme for reasons both obvious and subtle.

There was first the ambivalence of their own loyalties on issues of war and peace when India's adversary was Pakistan. The acquisition of a nuclear capability by the Republic of India was bound to create a qualitative difference in power between India and Pakistan. Supporters of such a qualitative difference within the Indian Republic itself were unlikely to include a majority of the Muslim citizens of the Indian Republic.

A similar ambivalence must have affected Muslim response to India's humiliation by China in 1962. Since India's previous conflicts with Pakistan had always ended in India's favour, and since India's retention of Kashmir was a measure of its ultimate triumph over Pakistan, it is unlikely that many tears were shed by Indian Muslims when the Republic of India sustained a kind of defeat from a blow inflicted by China. One might as well expect tears of anguish from Syrian Jews over the loss of the Golan Heights to Israel. China was now a potential ally of Pakistan.

What all this means is that India's nuclear programme was not simply a case of the government of a country opting for a particular policy. It was also a case of a particular cultural denomination within that society choosing a particular direction of effort. Hindus and Sikhs provided the ultimate moral support for New Delhi's decision to move in the direction of nuclear proliferation.

Of course, once India itself went nuclear, could Pakistan be very far behind? It took India a decade to catch up with China in nuclear status. Would it take Pakistan less than a decade to catch up with India in nuclear status? With

Pakistan's acquisition of that status, does Islam as a whole advance to a new arena of global competition? It is to these issues that we must now turn.

The Crescent: Between Petroleum and Plutonium

Three trends got under way in the 1970s in a manner profoundly affecting the crescent. The first concerned the rise of greater political consciousness in the Muslim world; the second concerned the emergence of petro-power as an important ingredient in the fortunes of Islam; and the third concerned the potentialities of Muslim nuclear power in the combat arena of world politics.

The politicization of Islam had Iran as its dramatic focus; the trend towards Islamic petro-power was centred upon the Arab world; and the nuclear issues came to the fore in Pakistan. These subdivisions are of course in many ways artificial. Politics, oil, and prospects for nuclear power have intermingled in the Muslim world especially from the early 1970s. The Shah of Iran was eager to establish his country as a major power, and his approach towards that goal included greater utilization of nuclear energy. Iran was itself also the second largest exporter of petroleum within the membership of the Organization of Petroleum Exporting Countries. That provided a link between petro-power and nuclear power. Yet Iran under the Shah was not eager to enter into the game of plutonium management. The quest was for a civilian nuclear capacity rather than for a military nuclear status. Yet the Shah also had military ambitions in the Gulf area and adjacent regions. The interplay between politics, petroleum, and the prospects for plutonium was certainly present in the fortunes of Iran under the Shah. What that demonstrated was the difficulty of disentangling the three concepts of politicization, petro-power and nuclear power within Islam. Nevertheless, for analytical purposes, we can indeed view Iran as a particularly dramatic focus of the politicization of Islam. Within that country the link between domestic discontent and international grievances became striking. The United States had been centrally involved in aborting the first modern Iranian revolution, that of Muhammad Mossadeq in the early 1950s. Mossadeq, an Iranian nationalist, had nationalized the Anglo-Iranian petroleum multinational. Mossadeq was eager to assert Iran's economic autonomy, and emphasize the right of those countries with economic resources to establish rules of their exploitation and utilization. The US Central Intelligence Agency entered Iran's conflict with Great Britain, and established conditions for Mossadeq's defeat. The first Iranian revolution, basically secular and in many ways modern, was thus aborted as a result of the intervention of the United States.

The Shah of Iran returned from exile as the government of Mossadeq collapsed. The Shah then reigned for another generation, a close friend of the United States, which had ensured his return to power.

As it happens, the Shah added another dimension to the politicization of Islam. He embarked on a policy of modernizing Iran, which in many respects simply signified the greater Westernization of Iran. In that particular country this resulted in a major cultural clash. Haphazard industrialization in Iran seemed to be undermining important aspects of the Islamic culture of the society. This, combined with the mechanisms of tyranny to which the Shah's regime increasingly resorted, created a growing response of rebellion against the Shah's structures of authority.

A combination of factors set the stage for the sustained defiance of 1978 and

217

early 1979 which led to the flight of the Shah, the collapse of the Pahlavi monarchy, and the settting up of the Islamic Republic in Iran. The Kerbala tradition of martyrdom in Shiite Islam, the Imam tradition of affirmative leadership in Shiite Islam, the cultural dislocations in the wake of industrial and economic Westernization under the Shah, and the general discontent arising from tyranny and dictatorship under the Shah and his machinery, all combined with a basic rebellion against the outside world and its penetrative and hegemonic power over Iran. The United States became the ultimate symbol of this fifth factor — external manipulative power over Iran. When combined with a spirit of martyrdom, a tradition of religious leadership, a rebellion against cultural Westernization, and defiance of political tyranny, the spirit of anti-imperialism in Iran created the drama of Islam's ultimate flirtation with politics in the global arena during the last quarter of the twentieth century.

In what way is this related to the rise of Islamic petro-power? The political revival of a religion usually comes when there are either forms of insecurity or a new level of self-confidence. In the case of the Islamic revival both factors were in play. The insecurity is long-standing and can ultimately be traced to the West's technological leadership of the world and its general economic and cultural hegemony. This insecurity may have taken new forms in recent times, but the basic foundation remains the general imbalance in power between the Muslim world on one side and countries that used to be referred to at one time as Christendom on the other. Muslims since the nineteenth century especially have been defensive about charges that their cultures, or the Shari'a, was 'pre-modern' or impossible to reconcile with modernity.

Along with this deep cultural insecurity in much of the Muslim world there has recently been, paradoxically, a resurgence of confidence. Suddenly the Muslim world has sensed that it has considerable power over the destiny of the world economy, as well as the fortunes of even the most powerful of the non-Muslim states. The basis of this new power is, of course, petroleum, and the new control which countries producing it have managed to assert over pricing and level of production.

The Organization of Petroleum Exporting Countries has become a major factor in the world economy. And the organization is overwhelmingly Muslim in composition. The largest oil-exporting country in the world is Saudi Arabia, the heartland of Sunni Islam and the custodian of the holy places of Mecca and Medina. Until the revolution the second largest exporter was Iran, the heartland of Shiite Islam. Iraq is emerging as a major oil power in its own right, and is of course also a Muslim country. The largest Muslim country in population is Indonesia, which is now also the fourth largest country in the world. Because its oil output is modest, and what it can afford to export even more modest, Indonesia's influence within OPEC is not commensurate with the size of the country. Indonesia is nevertheless part of the Muslim sector of OPEC, and responds to certain policy orientations.

Then there are the small countries of the Gulf, some of which have considerable surpluses in either oil or petro-dollars. Surplus in this area is, of course, power. To redirect the witticism, 'nothing succeeds like excess'. Abu Dhabi discovered additional reserves of oil in 1980. Other Gulf states like Bahrain and Oman have more modest oil reserves but are prospecting vigorously. Some might even have heard of a lesson which an old teacher of mine used to emphasize almost as a law of nature: 'Where there is desert, and there are Muslims, there may be oil!'

218

Within the African continent the leading oil producers are also disproportionately Muslim. These include Libya and Algeria in the north of the continent. Nigeria has more Muslims than Christians but it is much less of an Islamic state than north African countries are. Nigeria's Africanness is a more important part of its personality than any links with the Muslim world. Nor is the oil in Nigeria coming from Muslim areas.

As for Gabon, the fourth African member of OPEC, it has had a converted Muslim for president, but it is not itself a Muslim society. What could be argued is that conversions to Islam in places like Gabon and elsewhere in West Africa have themselves been partly due to the new self-confidence of the Muslim world and those who propagate the faith elsewhere.

More important for the world system is the increasing role of certain Muslim countries, especially Arab countries, in defining and shaping the agenda of world politics and North-South relations. The very slogan 'New International Economic Order' emerged out of the Algerian leadership before and during the special session of the General Assembly of the United Nations in 1974.[2] There was also vigorous Muslim leadership in the controversies and debates which culminated in the United Nations' charter of economic rights and duties.

Arab visibility in North-South relations became high from 1973 onwards, partly because of the impact of the Arab oil embargo of 1973 (as a response to the support of certain Western countries for Israel in the war with Egypt) and partly because of the continuing petro-power of certain members of the Arab world.

The Arab world has also succeeded in effectively isolating Israel within the United Nations and making it a pariah state. Much of the Third World has rallied behind the Palestinian cause. So might much of Western Europe, again in the wake of the new Arab oil power.

Meanwhile, Iran too has moved to the centre stage in high international visibility since its revolution of 1978 and 1979. The affirmation of Islam is more explicit in Iran as a foundation of policy. Revolutionary Iran's confrontation with the United States is partly a conflict between two nation-states, partly a conflict between the two civilizations of Islam and the West, and partly a confrontation between two hemispheres — the South represented by Iran against the North as represented by the United States. The issue of the American hostages in Teheran (1979–1981) and confrontation in the Gulf between Iran and the United States (1987–1989) became more symbolic of wider areas of political dissension, economic disparities, and moral differences between the industrialized North and the technologically underprivileged South.

Because the new self-confidence of the Muslim world has petroleum as its material foundation, and Muslim culture as its spiritual sustenance, insecurity among Muslims can sometimes lead to a spirit of 'petro-*jihad*', a readiness to use petro-power in defence of Muslim interests. A more relevant platform would be to use petro-power in defence of Third World interests more generally. One of the stumbling blocks is the conservatism of the ruling regime of Saudi Arabia and of the Sheikhdoms on the Gulf. A radicalization of Riyadh within the next decade cannot be ruled out. If that were to happen, and Riyadh went either the way of Teheran or the way of Tripoli, the use of oil power to enforce major adjustments in North-South relations would probably move closer to fulfilment.

What is clear is that since Nehru's death, and in spite of the new nuclear status of India since Nehru, much of the leadership of the Third World internationally has passed into Muslim hands. Global visibility in drafting the agenda of North-South relations has shifted — the limelight is focused more persistently now on Muslims and less on Hindus.

Does this new Muslim leadership of the Third World have any military relevance? Or will Islam itself have to go nuclear before it can play a major role in issues of war and peace at the global level? Let us now turn to these military aspects of the balance of influence between India and the Muslim world.

The Crescent over the Mushroom Cloud

If Islam goes nuclear within the 1990s, two regional rivalries are likely to have played an important part. One is the rivalry between India and Pakistan; the other is the rivalry between Israel and the Arabs.

India may have decided to speed up its nuclear programme more because of China than because of Pakistan; but Pakistan's decision to speed up its own programme was almost certainly influenced if not inspired by India's explosion of a nuclear device in 1974.

The cultural rivalry of Muslims versus Hindus is also more relevant in Pakistani attitudes than in Indian policies. The attitude of the Indian government towards Pakistan has relatively little to do with the fact that Pakistan is a Muslim country. The Indian government deals with a variety of other Muslim countries on an entirely different basis. In contrast, the attitude of the Pakistani government towards India is presumably often clouded by a historical rivalry with Hindus. India itself is of course a secular state; Pakistan is an Islamic republic. Perceptions of the state within Pakistan are conditioned by a cultural and religious self-consciousness. The pursuit of a new form of power like nuclear energy, and the quest for a new form of status as a member of the nuclear club, almost inevitably carries in Pakistan a sense of Muslim pride and cultural ambition. The basic dialectic in the Pakistani psyche between Islam as a religion in its own right and Islam as a negation of Hinduism is bound to have conditioned Pakistan's nuclear programme, as it has conditioned most other major directions of national, regional, and global policies adopted in Pakistan.

In reality Pakistan's nuclear ambitions go back to the late Prime Minister Zulfikar Ali Bhutto. In his case, as in the minds of subsequent leaders, nuclear capability was seen as part of cultural vindication. Prime Minister Bhutto was quoted as saying: 'There was a Christian bomb, a Jewish bomb, and now a Hindu bomb. Why not an Islamic bomb?'[3]

Pakistan's effort to match India's nuclear capability seems to have been considerably aided by the work of Dr Abdel Qader Khan, who worked for a while in a laboratory in Amsterdam and had access to a wide range of classified documents and scientific processes relevant to 'sensitive' nuclear research. According to reports he was even able to spend some time in Urenco Consortium's secret Uranium Enrichment Plant at Almelo near the border between the Federal Republic of Germany and the Netherlands. Dr Khan could thus observe the centrifuge process from close quarters.

It would seem that Khan originally accepted the job in the Netherlands purely as a means of livelihood prior to becoming a Dutch citizen (he was himself partly educated in Holland and was married to a Dutch woman) but reports imply that some time in 1974, presumably after India's explosion of its nuclear device and the impact this had on many Pakistanis still reeling from their defeat in the Indo-Pakistani war of 1971, Khan was persuaded to become a nuclear spy for Pakistan.

In 1975 he left Holland to go back to his native country, and became *in absentia* the most controversial Third World scientist in recent international history. Holland was taken to task by its Urenco partners, Britain and West Germany. The Israelis lodged a vigorous protest to the Netherlands. The United States for a time suspended most forms of aid to Pakistan; and much of the world speculated whether Libyan money and Pakistani know-how were together on their way towards nuclearizing Islam.

Then on 1 March 1987 the London newspaper the *Observer* in an exclusive report claimed that Pakistan had at last produced a nuclear bomb. The 'Islamic bomb' was a reality. It had been produced at the Kahuta uranium enrichment plant outside Rawalpindi, helped by the earlier purchase of and transport of 100 metric tons of Niger uranium by Libya, by the secret purchase of West German equipment to purify the uranium, and with some help in nuclear weapons technology from China. Arab — largely Libyan — financing of the Pakistani nuclear research programme was estimated at 5 billion dollars.

While Pakistan's nuclear ambitions have been conditioned by rivalry with India, Libya's military ambitions are connected with its bid for leadership in the Arab world and its hostility towards Israel.

A more likely Arab nuclear innovator than Libya at one time seemed to be Iraq. International controversy erupted in the summer of 1980 concerning a French nuclear deal with the government of Iraq. Reports had it that a hundred technicians of the French government company Technitome, an arm of France's Atomic Energy Commission, were already in Iraq to install a powerful Osiris resurge reactor and a smaller Isis reactor under a contract which included supplying enriched uranium. The technicians were also scheduled to train 600 Iraqis to run the reactors. Voices of protest were heard, especially from Israel, Britain, and the United States.

It was reported that the first shipment of approximately 33 pounds of highly enriched uranium (out of a total of some 158 pounds over three years) had left for Iraq in June 1980. Western scientists calculated that 158 pounds of the 93 per cent enriched uranium could enable Iraq to make between three and six nuclear bombs. It was estimated that it would take Iraq approximately five years to acquire this modest military nuclear capability.[4]

There was suspicion that the Israelis had attempted to abort the French-Iraqi deal even to the extent of committing murder and attempting sabotage. Important parts of one of the reactors were blown up near Toulon in France in 1979 in a commando-style operation. And an Egyptian nuclear expert working for Iraq was murdered in Paris in June 1979. The French authorities and others strongly suspected Israeli involvement. And in the course of the controversy of the summer of 1980 Western diplomats expressed fears about possible Israeli preemptive military action if and when intelligence revealed that Iraq was about to build nuclear weapons.

The anxieties expressed by the Israelis carried a certain historical cynicism. After all, France had sold Israel a reactor without any inspection safeguards in the 1960s. While Iraq has signed the Nuclear Nonproliferation Treaty, Israel has not done so.

Then in September 1980 the Israelis did launch an attack on the Daura nuclear research installation outside Baghdad. The two Phantom aircraft in the raid caused only superficial damage, however. But on 7 June 1981 the Israeli air force managed to destroy the Iraqi reactor. Three civilians including a French technician were killed. Israel publicly justified the raid on the grounds that Iraq was about to receive a consignment of enriched uranium from France which could have been enough to make an atom bomb. Israeli Prime Minister Menachem Begin also cited a statement published in the Baghdad newspaper *Al-Thawra* in October 1980 soon after the start of Iraq's war with Iran: 'The Iranian people should not fear the Iraqi nuclear reactor, which is not intended to be used against Iran, but against the Zionist enemy.'[5]

It has been reported that in the 1950s Israeli scientists at the Weizmann Institute perfected a new and cheaper way of making the heavy water that moderates the chain reaction in the nuclear reactor. Speculation has it that the Israelis sold their secrets to France in exchange for a reactor in a secret 1958 agreement. That reactor, situated at the secret Dimona Nuclear Plant, featured in a 1977 report of the United States Central Intelligence Agency to the effect that Israel already had between ten and twenty nuclear weapons.[6]

Eventually Mordechai Vanunu's evidence, released in 1986 (as we saw in Chapter 8), revealed that Israel had between 100 and 200 atomic warheads, and therefore ranked as the world's sixth nuclear power.

Whatever may be the extent of Israel's nuclear capability there is little doubt that the arms race in the Middle East, like the arms race between India and Pakistan, is a fundamental part of the background to Islam's forthcoming nuclear development. And even the peaceful uses of nuclear energy of the kind envisaged for Egypt by President Richard Nixon would, quite probably, be only a few years away from potential military uses accessible to a future government in Cairo.

How does all this relate to issues of leadership and politics at the global level? We should first note that the danger of nuclear war does come from two primary sources: vertical nuclear proliferation among the great powers and horizontal nuclear proliferation in the Third World. Vertical proliferation involves greater sophistication and diversification of nuclear options and nuclear technology in the arsenals of the great powers. The same nuclear powers increase and diversify their destructive capabilities.

Horizontal proliferation, on the other hand, involves new members of the nuclear club — more countries involved in the nuclear war game. The Nuclear Weapons Non-proliferation Treaty was in fact intended to deal with both the risk of vertical proliferation among the great powers and horizontal addition of new nuclear powers. The great powers were supposed to embark on effective steps towards disarmament, while at the same time helping to reduce the risk of more and more countries acquiring nuclear weapons. In reality, since 1968 when the treaty struggled to be born, both vertical and horizontal proliferation have taken place. And the vertical variety among the great powers has escalated faster than the horizontal addition of new members to the nuclear club.

What could effectively motivate the great powers not only to decelerate the arms race but also generally to declare nuclear weapons illegitimate, and subsequently to start the process of conventional disarmament? It would seem that vertical proliferation has sometimes motivated the great powers to seek ways of containing the arms race. The Strategic Arms Limitation Treaties were in part a response to the stresses of vertical nuclear proliferation, a search for ways of containing the competition. Yet for the time being vertical nuclear proliferation has not been adequate for the bigger goal of motivating the great powers to give up nuclear weapons altogether.

The question which arises is what sort of concern is likely to be effective enough to lead to world-wide nuclear disarmament. The accident at Three Mile Island in Pennsylvania in 1979 did more for the anti-nuclear movement in the United States than almost anything else. Had the accident gone further out of hand, and a meltdown resulted, the revulsion against nuclear energy would have been even more dramatic. Even so, in the wake of Three Mile Island, 66 projected nuclear plants have been cancelled and new ones in New Hampshire and New York have not been opened after completion.

The anti-nuclear movement in Europe received a boost from the world's worst nuclear accident to date, the meltdown and explosion at the Chernobyl reactor in the Ukraine on 26 March 1986. The radioactive cloud from Chernobyl spewed radiation over most of Europe, East and West (it refused to recognize the Iron Curtain), and over parts of North Africa and the Middle East. Surprisingly, Chernobyl has not produced a massive anti-nuclear reaction among the peoples of Europe. Perhaps the casualties were not high enough. Heroism by firemen and engineers at Chernobyl, and the mass evacuation of 135,000 people living close to the plant, kept the death toll down to 31. For the time being, that is. Dr Robert Gale, the American leukaemia specialist who went to the USSR and helped treat the injured, has estimated that eventually up to 75,000 people might develop cancer as a result of the accident.

In Britain, some parts of which received high doses of Chernobyl radiation, the Thatcher government has decided to go ahead with new nuclear power plants such as Sizewell B on the North Sea coast. Sweden was more heavily affected by fall-out from Chernobyl and has decided to phase out all its nuclear power stations — but that decision was taken long before the Chernobyl accident.

It seems as if only a second Chernobyl-like accident, or a major accidental nuclear catastrophe of a military kind, could provide enough of a shock to create an irresistible anti-nuclear movement among the populations of the great powers themselves.

One should under no circumstances pray for disasters, however accidental, of course. An alternative approach to shocking the world into nuclear renunciation is to take a risk with horizontal proliferation. There is still the possibility of a disaster, but at least not the certainty. The logic here is that a certain degree of nuclear proliferation in the world is bound to increase nuclear anxieties within the populations of the great powers themselves, and strengthen pressures for the total abandonment of nuclear weapons by everybody. The great powers do not trust Third World countries with those weapons. That distrust could become an asset if the threat of a nuclear spread through the Third World creates enough consternation in the Northern hemisphere to result in a massive international movement to declare nuclear weapons illegitimate for everybody, and to put an end to nuclear arsenals in every country that has them. What this means is that although the greatest risks of nuclear war come from vertical proliferation in the Northern hemisphere and, secondarily, horizontal proliferation in the Third World, the vertical variety in itself has not been enough to end this dangerous nuclear order. The 'vaccination' of horizontal nuclear proliferation might be needed to cure the world of this nuclear malaise; a dose of the disease becomes part of the necessary cure.

Here the Muslim world becomes relevant again. The most dangerous part of the Third World from the point of view of global war is the Middle East. Modest horizontal proliferation in the Middle East would be more dangerous in global terms than a slightly higher level of proliferation in Latin America or black Africa.

This is partly because a regional war in the Middle East carries a greater risk of escalating into a world war than does a regional war in Latin America or black Africa.

If, then, horizontal nuclear proliferation is a necessary vaccine against the existing nuclear order itself, proliferation in the heartland of the Muslim world should work faster than proliferation elsewhere. Although Brazil is much larger than Iraq, Brazil's nuclear capability would be less of a global shock than Iraqi nuclear bombs. Pakistan's explosion of a nuclear device would carry with it greater fears than a successful explosion by Argentina. Three nuclear powers in the Islamic world could be perceived as a greater threat to world peace than five nuclear powers in some other parts of the Third World. In the total struggle against nuclear weapons in the world as a whole the Islamic world might well play a decisive role in the years ahead.

In this instance Islam might at first be playing nuclear Russian roulette with two other civilizations — with Hinduism in South Asia and with Zionism and politicized Judaism in the Middle East. But out of the dangerous regional game might emerge an impetus for global reform; out of limited horizontal proliferation there might ultimately evolve global denuclearization.

When nuclear weapons are abandoned, and the dream of gradual global disarmament begins to come true, however, other sources of power and influence would emerge. It is to these dimensions that we should now turn.

Towards the Future

If the world does at long last begin to become demilitarized, the most important alternative forms of power are likely to be economic on one side and demographic on the other. How do these two forms of power even themselves out as between the world of Hinduism and the world of Islam?

By the end of this century there may well be almost as many Hindus in the world as there are Muslims. But Hindus are concentrated in one country, India, the second largest country on the globe; while Muslims control some three dozen nation-states. If the system of nation-states survives, and voting power in international organizations becomes even more significant, a relatively united Muslim world is bound to carry greater leverage in world politics than India on its own.

On the other hand, India is destined to be a super-power. The question which arises is whether the status of a super-power would count for less in a demilitarized world than it does now. If so, the fact that the Muslim population is multinational and widely spread out on the globe, while the Hindu population is on the whole concentrated in South Asia, would result in Islamic rather than Hindu leadership helping to set the agenda for North-South relations.

From a demographic point of view, there is also the question of Muslim minorities in otherwise non-Muslim societies. Muslim minorities tend to be particularly large, as contrasted certainly with Hindu minorities in otherwise non-Hindu societies. From that point of view, India itself may be the third largest Muslim country in the world, next only to Indonesia and possibly Bangladesh. In spite of the emergence of two separate Muslim countries out of the old British India, the Republic of India today still has a Muslim population which before long should reach 100 million.

Then there is the demographic Muslim bomb within the body politic of the Soviet Union. The Muslim population of the Soviet Union is currently estimated at

42 million, and is reportedly increasing at six times the rate of increase of European Russians. Second, the Muslim parts of the Soviet Union have so far been less subject to cultural Russification than have many other Soviet Republics.

The Russian composition of the Soviet Union is currently only a little more than half the population. The rate of increase in the Muslim Republics would help reduce the Russian population to a minority of the population of the Soviet Union within little more than a decade. If the proportion of the Russian population in the national composition declines much further, it could make a significant difference to the nature of the Soviet system in subsequent generations. From this point of view it could be argued that the greatest Muslim threat to the Soviet Union is primarily demographic, and not yet economic.

In contrast, the greatest Muslim threat to the Western world is primarily economic and not really demographic. The greatest exporters of petroleum continue to be, for the time being, Muslim countries; the greatest consumers of petroleum continue to be, for the time being, Western countries. A basic economic interdependence between Islam and the West, based in part on Muslim energy and Western technology, constitutes an aspect of the credentials of the Muslim world in setting the agenda in North-South relations in the decades which follow.

When all is said and done, India will continue to be a major part of the total global equation. Economically India may not produce enough oil to make other societies dependent upon it, but it has the industrial potentialities to be an economic super-power one day even if military super-powers are no longer in vogue. The huge domestic market, the considerable domestic human power, the evolving skills in the scientific field, and the natural resources of India should all guarantee a position of leadership in the years ahead even if that leadership becomes less clear-cut than was India's leadership under Mahatma Gandhi and his non-violence and under Jawaharlal Nehru and his non-alignment.

It remains true that in the South's struggle for a viable military relationship with the North, India has played a key role — from *satyagraha* through non-alignment to nuclear power status. In the South's struggle for a more equitable economic relationship with the North, the torch has indeed been passed to the Muslim world.

Would India under non-Hindu leadership have produced *satyagraha*? The answer is probably no. Would India under non-Hindu leadership have invented non-alignment? The answer is ambivalent. Would India under Muslim leadership have pursued a nuclear status? The answer is 'possibly sooner'.

Would the security situation in the Middle East have been different if the Arab world was Christian and Islam had never been born? The answer is probably yes, since the sensitivities of Iranians and Libyans are profoundly conditioned by Islam's cultural defensiveness in relation to the Western world.

Culture does indeed moderate perceptions of security, affect credentials of leadership, and help to define perimeters of power and influence. Within that context two civilizations have played a crucial role in the evolution of Third World security — Hinduism and Islam. In some sense they are guards on duty at the citadel of the Third World. A changing of the guards is under way: the Muslim shift is about to begin with the chimes of the hour. Responsibility for the citadel continues to be shared by all those with a stake in its security. Attention all guards!

Notes

1. G. H. Jansen, *Non-alignment Stakes* (New York & Washington: Praeger, 1966), p. 209. Whole speech — George T. Kahin, *Asian-African Conference* (Ithaca, New York: Cornell University Press, 1956), p. 64. I am grateful to Mr Darryl Thomas for bibliographical guidance.
2. The New International Economic Order, if ever implemented, will provide a better deal for the world's poorer nations, i.e., a transformation of the international trading system to ensure better prices and marketing opportunities for Third World producers of primary products and manufactures, and the use of interest-free loans or grants instead of loans as aid.
3. Cited by C. Smith and Shyam Bhatia, 'How Dr Khan Stole the Bomb for Islam', *The Observer* (London), 9 December 1979.
4. A United Press International report datelined Paris on some aspects of the French-Iraqi atomic deal was carried by newspapers, including the *Ann Arbor News* (Ann Arbor, Michigan), 9 August 1980.
5. Cited in the *Guardian*, London, 10 June 1981.
6. UPI report, ibid., and Smith and Bhatia, op. cit. Consult also Ryukichi Imai and Robert Press, *Nuclear Nonproliferation: Failures and Prospects*, A Report of the International Consultative Group on Nuclear Energy (New York and London: the Rockefeller Foundation and the Royal Institute of International Affairs, 1980).

226

13

The Third World & International Terrorism

Raymond Aron once analyzed contemporary warfare in terms of a triad of violence. The three types of warfare were symbolized by the hydrogen bomb, the tank, and the sten-gun. The most comprehensive of these three types of warfare was, of course, nuclear war, with its power of massive destruction and capacity to encompass widely dispersed areas. The age itself is called the nuclear age, and yet the warfare represented by it is the least experienced within that age. Numerous outbreaks of violence and a variety of battles have erupted in different parts of the globe since World War II. The range is from the Vietnam war in the Far East to the football war in Latin America early in 1970. Yet a nuclear war as such is still outside direct human experience. It is the fear of nuclear war, rather than its experience, which has affected the age.

By contrast, warfare symbolized by the tank and by the sten-gun has been very much part of the post-World War II period. The tank signified what is sometimes called conventional warfare, though what is conventional is itself subject to the mutations of time. The most important outbreaks of conventional war since World War II include the Korean War, the Suez adventure of 1956 when Israel, Britain, and France attacked Nasser's Egypt, the June war of 1967 between Israel and the Arabs, the more recent Iran-Iraqi conflict, the clashes between India and China and India and Pakistan, the Israeli intrusions into and invasions of Lebanon over the years, the Vietnamese occupation of Kampuchea, and the Soviet occupation of Afghanistan.

An even older form of conventional warfare is civil war. African experiences include Chad, Nigeria, Eritrea, Sudan, Angola, and others. Many of these are conventional both in being intra-territorial and in the armaments used.

A third type of warfare in Aron's triad of violence is that waged by guerrilla and terrorist movements. These are symbolized by the sten-gun, the stealthy steps in the stillness of the forest, the sudden spurt of fire on an unsuspecting target. Among the most notable guerrilla wars since 1945 have been anti-colonial wars of national liberation in south-east Asia (especially Indonesia and Vietnam) in the immediate post-World War II period, in Africa (especially Algeria, Kenya, and southern Africa) from the 1950s to the present time, and in Palestine especially since Israeli occupation in 1967. Then there have been revolutionary guerrilla wars

227

against corrupt elites, e.g., Castro's revolution against Batista in Cuba, the Sandinista revolution against Somoza in Nicaragua and the various uprisings against Mobutu in Zaire.

It should be noted from the start that the term 'terrorism' in this chapter is value-free in the same way as the term 'war' is. As far as this analysis is concerned, terrorism is a form of warfare and can be 'perpetrated' either by revolutionary movements or by governments. 'Terrorism' is the deliberate creation of specialized terror among civilians, through the use of violence, in order to promote political ends, whether it is revolutionary terrorism by opponents of governments or state terrorism by governments themselves. What are the purposes of politicized, conspicuous terrorism? Here we must distinguish between ultimate goals and immediate targets. The ultimate goals include an ambition to gain a hearing for causes which would otherwise go unheard, and to make a contribution towards the realization of those causes. The immediate target is the manipulation of fear as a mechanism of combat in the context of wide publicity. This is particularly so in the case of terrorism 'perpetrated' by revolutionaries instead of by governments.

It is not necessarily the purpose of terrorists to destroy society. Joseph Kechichian has highlighted the general objectives of revolutionary terrorists:

> Terrorism, broadly defined, is a form of political warfare by disenfranchised groups. What most terrorist organizations seem to want are rights which they are denied in the existing political order. By definition, such a quest indicates an awareness of power politics in the international system. It is precisely the lack of legitimacy that leads disenfranchised groups to the use of political violence in articulating their grievances. Thus, the ultimate purpose is not to destroy 'civilization' or democratic values but to participate as legitimate participants in the international system.[1]

Terror in the Skies: A Retrospect

Among the more sensational of terrorist initiatives by revolutionary movements is the use of the skies as a battlefield. A new version of this last type of warfare was initiated by the Palestine commandos in the 1970s. This was the tactic of attacking civil aircraft, sometimes on the ground, but more sensationally in mid-air. A more timid adventure tried in 1970 was that of planting bombs in aircraft. One blew up in mid-air, killing a number of people, many of whom had nothing to do with the issue of Palestine. But on 6 September 1970, Palestine commandos took this strategy a stage further. They hijacked four planes, two American, one Swiss, and one Israeli. According to some reports, the hijacking of the Israeli plane was thwarted by a somersault trick performed by the pilot, which threw the hijackers off balance, and by the intervention of the plane's steward, resulting in one hijacker being killed and the second wounded. One of the American aircraft was taken to Cairo, where, after the passengers had been permitted to disembark, it was blown up in one dramatic explosion.

The remaining two planes went to Beirut and Amman, and passengers were for a while held as hostages as demands were made for the release of other Palestinians held prisoner in different parts of the Western world. Three of these were being held in Switzerland, after being sentenced to serve seven years on charges of attacking an Israeli airliner at Zurich. The Swiss government, after urgent and decisive consultations domestically, agreed to release the three Palestinians in exchange for all the passengers from the Swiss airliner held by the terrorists.

For the remaining passengers, especially the male passengers from the United States, Britain, and West Germany, there were additional demands. Among stipulations reportedly made by the hijackers was the release of Sirhan Sirhan, under sentence of death in the United States for the murder of Robert Kennedy, though this demand was later withdrawn, if it was ever made.

What did these hijacks carried out by the Palestinians really mean in terms of the history of combat tactics? What the world was witnessing in September 1970 was guerrilla warfare transferred from the forests to the skies. The purpose of aerial terrorism is, of course, the same as guerrilla tactics on the ground, the manipulation of fear as a mechanism of combat. The grand design is to undermine morale, not only among the soldiers but also the civilian body. An atmosphere of general insecurity, promoted by spectacular acts of destruction or specially dramatized acts of brutality, is contrived in order to drive the enemy into a desperate readiness to seek a settlement. What the Palestinian commandos were doing in September 1970 was using the international skies as an arena for terrorist activities, since the streets of Israel were not accessible to them for domestic terrorism.

There is, however, an important difference between aerial terrorism and domestic guerrilla tactics. Aerial terrorism, as so far illustrated in its initial phases, is by the very nature of things international. Either the plane itself might be travelling across territorial boundaries, or the passengers on board might be nationally mixed, or both these international aspects might be present.

Aerial terrorism is in some important respects symbolic both of the communications revolution and of the conversion of the world into a global village. The communications revolution played its part in the degree to which a hijack attained spectacular publicity, and with regard to the very increase in air traffic and the greater reliance of influential sectors of humanity on air transport. The news aspect of the communications revolution has made aerial terrorism a useful device for attracting world attention to a particular grievance. The travelling aspect of the communications revolution meant heavy air traffic and therefore a wide choice of planes for hijacking. Among the passengers on such planes were men and women from influential countries of the world who were now forced to worry about the implications for their holidays or for their business of this whole new phenomenon in the skies.

The publicity side of aerial terrorism relied in part on the sensationalism of political piracy. By political piracy we mean the forceful takeover of a vessel at sea or in the air for such purposes as attracting publicity, carrying out political revenge, or preparing for a political deal. It had all started in 1961 when a Portuguese revolutionary captain, Henrique Galvao, seized control of a Portuguese ship, the *Santa Maria*, on the high seas in a dramatic assertion of solidarity with the colonized peoples of Angola and Mozambique. This was political piracy in the tradition of tactical publicity.

Will aerial terrorism increase since it is such a guaranteed way of getting international and media attention for otherwise obscure causes? Two trends are pulling in opposite directions. The fact that air traffic in the world will almost certainly continue to increase should expand opportunities for political piracy in the skies. Even more obscure causes may take to the skies, such as the grievances of North Yemenis against Saudi Arabia as manifested in the takeover of a Saudi plane by Yemenis in November 1984. The skyjackers were later overwhelmed by

Iranian troops with the help of passengers when the aircraft was at Teheran airport. The international obscurity of the cause was perhaps the most ominous aspect of the whole episode.

Although the expansion of air traffic in the world has increased opportunities for aerial piracy, there have also been simultaneous improvements in the technology of detecting metal weapons. There is thus a race between the opportunities provided by expanding air traffic and the controls afforded by improved technology.

Within the Third World it is the expansion of air traffic which is winning. Technological improvements are significantly slower than multiplication of air passengers and aircraft. At least in the immediate future, aerial terrorism is most likely to increase within the Third World or on aircraft which start in the Third World or pass through it.

There have, of course, always been Third World revolutionaries, including Palestinians, who have been opposed to hijacking. Some have felt that such tactics were bound to be counterproductive and to alienate international opinion. Those who have favoured such tactics have sometimes echoed Machiavelli's advice to the prince: 'It is better to be feared than to be loved.' The international community was more likely to want a problem resolved if it threatened its own safety and comfort. The international community might hate the terrorists — but it would still prefer a world without terrorism.

But if world opinion is a factor, is it really better to be feared than loved? Does aerial terrorism attract the right kind of publicity? Questions of this kind miss the whole point of the exercise. In a propaganda campaign to win sympathy in the more influential parts of the world, the Arabs are no match for the Jews. Quite apart from the greater sophistication of Jewish communities in the Western world, there is also the question of access to the influential media of the international system. One cannot escape the issue of comparative Jewish access to the media of communication. Indeed, without such access, Israel itself might never have been created. Any competition by Palestinian commandos for sympathy is handicapped from the start by the massive disproportion between them and Israel in terms of access to mass communications. To elements of the PLO, spectacularly bad publicity is better than no publicity.

For a time (1976–1985), the Palestinian movement seemed to have shelved the skyjacking option. It seems likely that three shocks helped to paralyze this particular arm of the Palestinian struggle. One was the shock of the Entebbe raid (1976) — a spectacular display of Israeli organizational superiority. Israel's reach exceeded its grasp — as the long arm of the Jewish state stretched itself from Jerusalem to the source of the Nile. The blow against Palestinian morale was devastating. The blow against the 'legitimacy' of skyjacking as a mode of Palestinian struggle was even more direct.

After the Entebbe raid, the second great shock for the Palestinian struggle was Anwar Sadat's visit to Jerusalem (1977) and the ensuing events which culminated in the Camp David Accords (1978). Again it was a major blow to Palestinian morale and inaugurated fundamental agonizing about priorities. Should the struggle redirect itself against 'the enemy within' the Arab nation (e.g., Sadat) or 'the enemy without', namely 'the Zionist entity'? Skyjacking was not appropriate as a method of inter-Arab infighting, so it was widely assumed among Palestinians. Skyjacking against 'the enemy without' was also suspended for the time being.

The third great shock for Palestinians, after Entebbe and the Sadat initiative, was of course Israel's brutal invasions of Lebanon, especially the devastating one of 1982. The invasion destroyed much of the military infrastructure of the Palestine Liberation Organization. But it did not destroy the PLO's capacity for skyjacking and other terrorist activities. Sometimes terrorism increases precisely because other military options have been weakened. About Israeli arrogance it may be true to say that 'power tends to corrupt and absolute power corrupts absolutely'. In the case of the Palestinians the fear is that they are forced to more extreme measures precisely because of weakness. It is after all equally true (in spite of Lord Acton) that *powerlessness* tends to corrupt − and absolute powerlessness corrupts absolutely. New levels of desperation, especially after the expulsion of the PLO army from Lebanon after the Israeli invasion of 1982, in fact forced segments of the Palestinian movement to return to the days prior to the Entebbe raid.

The first move, however, in a return to skyjacking as a revolutionary tactic came not from the PLO but from Islamic Jihad, a Shi'ite fundamentalist group in Lebanon. In June 1985 this group hijacked an American TWA plane and held 42 of its passengers and crew as hostages in Beirut for some weeks. One of the passengers, US Navy diver Robert Stethem, was shot dead. The other hostages and the plane were released after Syria arranged a deal and Israel released 735 Shi'a Lebanese prisoners being held in Israel (after Israel's occupation of half of Lebanon in 1982−1985).

Then in November 1985 a PLO splinter group opposed to PLO Chairman Yasser Arafat and apparently loyal to Arafat's rival, the Libyan-backed Abu Nidal, hijacked an Egyptian airliner and caused it to be flown to Malta. The Maltese government allowed Egyptian commandos to storm the plane but the operation was bungled and 60 passengers were killed.

On 27 December 1985, Palestinian gunmen, again apparently linked to Abu Nidal and Libya, opened fire on passengers at Israeli airline desks at Rome and Vienna airports, killing 14 people. These attacks were similar in style to the May 1972 massacre of 100 Christian pilgrims at Israel's Lydda airport by the pro-Palestinian Japanese 'Red Army'.

Another type of terrorist action which gained enormous publicity if not sympathy also reappeared in 1985. In October four Palestinians hijacked an Italian cruise liner, the *Achille Lauro*, in the Mediterranean. The group had originally intended not to seize the ship but to land at Ashdod in Israel and mount an attack there. But a ship's waiter spotted them cleaning their weapons in a cabin and, their cover blown, they seized the ship. The hijackers killed Leon Klinghoffer, an elderly wheelchair-bound American Jewish passenger. Syria refused to accede to the hijackers' request to allow the ship to enter one of its ports but the gunmen were able to surrender at Port Said with the promise of an Egyptian plane to take them from Cairo to Tunis, the PLO headquarters. The Egyptian plane was intercepted by US warplanes and forced to land at a US base in Sicily where the Americans handed over the terrorists to the Italian authorities. The hijackers had themselves been hijacked.

Political Kidnapping

Then there is the piracy involving the kidnapping of a specific individual or individuals. This is where political piracy ties in with the more recent phenomenon of political abduction, especially the abduction of foreign diplomats in Latin America. The abduction of foreign diplomats in Latin America involved the diversion not of airplanes in mid-air, but quite often of cars in the street. A car is stopped, and the victim is forced out and taken away in another car; or alternatively an uninvited passenger enters the victim's car, and at gunpoint hijacks the vehicle to another part of the city.

The kidnapping of diplomats of other powers is distinctive of recent times; but the kidnapping of specific individuals as a form of political vengeance or as a prelude to civic justice is part of an older tradition of political behaviour.

The kidnapping of Westerners in Lebanon by Islamic extremist groups such as the Hezb Allah (Party of God) since 1985, either for ransom or for political bargaining purposes, matches the similar pattern of kidnappings carried out in West Germany and Italy in the 1970s by left-wing terrorist groups. The kidnapping of the US embassy staff in Iran in 1979 by revolutionary students was undertaken partly as an act of revenge for American support for the Shah before and after his fall from power, and partly in an attempt to force President Carter to concede Iranian demands to return the Shah as a prisoner to Iran, together with all his wealth.

State Terrorism

Much terrorism is reactive, a violent response to violence. The attack on Israeli athletes at the Munich Olympic Games in 1972 was a response to Israeli occupation of the West Bank and Gaza five years earlier and harsh rule of these occupied territories. Israel's response to the Munich terrorism was to launch heavy air raids on Palestinian refugee camps and bases in Lebanon as a result of which hundreds of people were killed.

State terrorism is invariably more severe in its consequences than revolutionary terrorism because the state usually has greater force at its disposal than guerrilla forces. Also the purpose of state terrorism is to hit revolutionary terrorists exceptionally hard either to try to destroy them or to deter them from future operations. For example, when in 1978 Palestinian terrorists killed thirty Israeli civilians near Tel Aviv, Israel retaliated by sending 20,000 troops into Lebanon on a 'search and destroy' mission against Palestinian bases. In this operation several hundred unarmed people were killed. In 1981 the French ambassador to Lebanon was murdered by a pro-Syrian gunman and France retaliated by exploding a car bomb in Damascus which killed 110 people. In 1982 Palestinian gunmen shot and severely wounded the Israeli ambassador in London. Israel's reply was to launch a new invasion of Lebanon in which many thousands were killed (See Chapter 8).

In October and November 1983, Islamic Jihad suicide bombers destroyed the American, French, and Israeli military headquarters in Lebanon, killing over 340 soldiers. But an American naval bombardment of the Chouf mountains behind Beirut had already (in September) killed 200 Druze villagers. In March 1985 the CIA was linked to the car-bombing near the home of the militant Shi'ite cleric Shaikh Mohammed Hussein Fadlallah, leader of the Hezb Allah. That car bomb killed 60 people.

Two of the most spectacular examples of state counter-terrorism have been the Israeli attacks on Tunis, seat of the PLO headquarters after the PLO Army was forced out of Lebanon by the Israelis in 1982. In October 1985, after Palestinians killed three Israeli agents in Cyprus, Israeli planes destroyed the PLO buildings in Tunis, killing 45 Palestinians and 25 Tunisians. Then in April 1988 Israeli commandos assassinated the PLO's deputy leader Khalil Al-Wazir (known as Abu Jihad) in his Tunis home.

In matters of terrorism and counter-terrorism it is difficult to be objective. One person's terrorist is another person's freedom fighter. A president or prime minister may be a terrorist in his actions as much as any guerrilla or hijacker. Israeli prime ministers like Menachem Begin and Yitzhak Shamir were, as young men, revolutionary guerrilla terrorists against British rule in Palestine before they became 'state terrorists' in control of the Israeli armed forces.

So far, we have drawn many examples of terrorism from the Middle East. Neither Islamic fundamentalism nor Shi'a Islam has been specifically highlighted as a major source of terrorist violence, and for good reasons. First, the most fundamentalist regime among the Arab states is Saudi Arabia, which is not terrorist and is Sunni, not Shi'ite. Second, the main revolutionary terrorist force in the Middle East, the PLO, is neither fundamentalist nor even Islamic. Most of the Palestinians are Sunni, not Shi'a, Muslims and a sizeable minority are Christians, including many in the PLO. Thirdly, Shi'ite Iran is not quite the terrorist state portrayed by the Western media. Iran did hold embassy staff hostage for over a year but none of the hostages were killed and Iran has not significantly engaged in violence outside its own borders. The pro-Iranian Hezb Allah in Lebanon is not controlled by Iran. The Iranian disruption of the *hajj* at Mecca in 1987 was a demonstration, not terrorism. Iran's naval confrontation with the United States in the Gulf in 1987–1988 was not terrorism but conventional warfare — even if on a very limited scale. If Iran is a terrorist state at all, it is so at home, when the Islamic Republic is dealing with its own people, whether it is brutally persecuting the Bahai religious community or crushing internal opposition of all kinds.

If Iran is at present hostile to the United States, it is not necessarily terrorist in its relations with America. Iranian hostility may not even be based on 'religious fanaticism'. Louis René Béres has commented on the problems faced by the United States in its relations with Iran: 'Shi'ite hostility to the USA did not arise in a vacuum. It has its roots in the USA's prior embrace of the Shah, a geopolitical intervention that subordinated human rights in Iran to the present requirements of competition with the Soviet Union.'[2]

The main cause of revolutionary violence and conflict in the Middle East today is neither Islam nor the revival of Shi'a Islam: it is Israeli occupation of Palestine and the lack of any means other than terrorism for the Palestinians to present their case and make themselves heard.

There are other sources of conflict in the Middle East, such as Sunni-Shi'a rivalry, which has flared up in Saudi Arabia in 1979 (attempted Shi'a coup in Mecca) and 1987 (Iranian demonstrations), in the Iran-Iraq war since 1980 in which over half a million have been killed, and in Lebanon where Shi'a militia have fought with non-Shi'a Lebanese and Palestinians. This Sunni-Shi'a conflict, however, tends to be a problem internal to the Middle East and is rarely manifested in the form of international terrorism.

The major Western countries or their citizens seem to be fairly frequent targets of Middle Eastern terrorism because of their support for Israel and also because the Palestinians seem to believe that anti-Western terrorism can lead to the West putting pressure on Israel to grant Palestinian rights. Perhaps only the United States could bring Israel to the conference table with the PLO, in the course of time.

In Latin America and South Africa the United States could play a major role in reducing conflict but only if it abandons open or tacit support for state terrorism. In Latin America for several decades the United States has contributed to the conflicts and terrorism in that region rather than help reduce them.

In El Salvador the Reagan administration has backed government forces in what Archbishop Oscar Romero described as 'a war of extermination and genocide against a defenceless population'. Some 60,000 people have been killed in the 1980s in the counter-insurgency campaign in El Salvador, most of them being victims of an army organized, trained, and armed by Washington. Right-wing 'death squads', in practice police and army units, have played their part in this slaughter, one of their victims being Romero himself. The root of the problem in El Salvador is the ownership of most of the land by a few families while the mass of the people are landless peasants. Successive US administrations have opposed any significant measure of land reform as a solution. Hence the civil war and the terrorism and counter-terrorism.

Similarly in Guatemala the United States has (since 1954 when it backed a right-wing coup to overthrow President Arbenz who promised land reform) consistently supported the local security forces against left-wing guerrillas. It is estimated that over 200,000 Guatemalans have died in the long conflict since 1954.

In Nicaragua, most of the 45,000 people killed in the Sandinista revolution of 1978–1979 which overthrew the right-wing dictator Somoza were victims of atrocities carried out by Somoza's National Guard. President Jimmy Carter supported Somoza at first and then sat on the fence while Somoza was defeated. Reagan's support of the Contra terrorism against the Sandinista government resulted in the deaths of over 10,000 civilians, nearly all of them at the hands of the Contras.

In southern Africa, the Reagan administration followed a policy of 'constructive engagement', trying to get President Botha of South Africa to dilute apartheid. Reagan persistently opposed the armed struggle led by the ANC and regularly excused state violence. He insisted that opposition to apartheid must always be peaceful. In his notorious press conference on 21 March 1985, President Reagan said that the blacks recently shot by the South African police at Langa were excusable casualties of 'rioting'. Likewise Prime Minister Thatcher of Britain has opposed black violence but has been too ready to cast a blind eye over state violence.

Reagan and Thatcher did condemn South African army raids on ANC personnel in neighbouring Lesotho, Botswana, Mozambique, and Zimbabwe. But such raids have continued with impunity. South African state terrorism — outside South Africa itself, where over 3,700 people have been killed by the police since 1975 — is at its worst in Angola and Mozambique. Since Angolan independence in 1975 neither the United States nor South Africa has accepted the socialist MPLA in Luanda and they have assisted Jonas Savimbi and his rebel UNITA forces in a long civil war in the southern half of the country. Towards the end of 1988, however, American diplomacy was playing a major role in moves towards a comprehensive peace settlement for both Angola and Namibia, including a mutual withdrawal from Angola of South African and Cuban forces.

American influence over the South African government has not had any impact as far as Mozambique is concerned. Perhaps the United States is less interested in Mozambique because there are no Cuban troops there. However, it is probably in that East African coastal country that South African state terrorism can be observed at its most brutal and destructive.

Mozambique became independent in 1975 after a long guerrilla war and the guerrilla organization, FRELIMO came to power and implemented socialist policies. In 1976 Ian Smith, the leader of the illegal white settler regime in 'Rhodesia', set up RENAMO or MNR, the Mozambique National Resistance, out of former black soldiers of the Portuguese army. The MNR began to carry out acts of terrorism in Mozambique. In 1980 'Rhodesia' became Zimbabwe and the new Prime Minister Robert Mugabe expelled the MNR from Zimbabwe. However, Prime Minister Botha became the MNR's new patron and South Africa has given a great deal of assistance to the MNR to try to destabilize Mozambique. The MNR has received training, weapons, and supplies from the South African army. It has had few military successes but it is adept at sabotage and mindless destruction. The MNR has destroyed over a thousand schools and clinics, has killed many thousands of people, specializes in maiming people by hacking off limbs, and has caused 2 million to leave their homes. In late 1988, 1,600,000 were living in refugee camps in Mozambique itself and another 400,000 had taken refuge in Malawi or Zimbabwe.

In one massacre in July 1987, 420 people in the village of Homoine were killed by the MNR. In spite of South African government denials, there was clear evidence of its military assistance to the MNR in the second half of 1988.

State terrorism, according to our examples from the Middle East, Latin America, and southern Africa, is at least as serious a threat to peace as is guerrilla-style terrorism in these regions.

Is it time for the major Western democracies to recognize this dual nature of terrorism and to play their part in bringing both forms of it under control? Or will they continue to back state terrorism by propping up repressive and terrorist regimes as in South Africa?

Will the Western powers see both sides of the equation in the Middle East and, while supporting Israel's right to exist, join those over 100 states, including NATO members Greece and Spain, which have recognized the PLO as the official and legal representatives of the Palestinian people?

Will the major Western democracies ratify Protocol 1 of 1977, an addition to the Geneva Convention, which provides for the recognition of the role and status of, and protection for, liberation movements and their combatants fighting against colonial and alien occupation and against racist regimes? The United States, Britain, West Germany, and Israel are among the few states which have refused to sign the protocol. Will they undergo an imaginative change of heart or will they continue to reject the protocol as a 'charter for terrorism'?

Even if the leading Western democracies continue to have a one-sided approach to definitions of terrorism and regard the suppression of terrorism as purely or merely a law and order matter, can they fight terrorism fairly, without resorting to greater counter-terrorism? On this issue, Paul Wilkinson recently invoked the spirit of the great seventeenth-century Dutch jurist and founder of international law, Hugo Grotius:

> The true Grotian response by Western states to terrorism must combine firmness with a commitment to act within the framework of the rule of law. Heaven knows this rule of law internationally is pathetically weak. But it is all we have got. If powerful Western states disregard the inhibitions of international law and use means against terrorism which are totally disproportionate to the threat, they will risk increasing the very anarchy in which terrorists flourish.[3]

A further step would be to tackle some of the injustices which encourage terrorism, because that is the only long-term protection against terrorism. As Louis René Béres recently put it: 'To protect itself against terrorism, the USA will have to return to its own best traditions, reaffirming that human rights are valuable everywhere, and that they are valuable in themselves.'[4]

Notes

1. J. Kechichian, *Terrorism and the Search for Power*, in A. Gauhar (ed.), *Third World Affairs 1988* (London: Third World Foundation for Social and Economic Studies, 1988), p. 56.
2. Louis René Béres, *Understanding Terrorism*, in A. Gauhar (ed.), op. cit., p. 13.
3. From N. O'Sullivan (ed.), *Terrorism, Ideology and Revolution* (Brighton, England: Wheatsheaf Books), p. 222.
4. H. Béres, op cit., p. 13.

14

Exit Visa
from the World System

The twentieth century has witnessed two forms of international radicalism. One involves a knock from those who are left out in the cold. This is the radical knock of entry: the outsiders are clamouring for the right of participation. The other knock is from those who are already within the system. Some of them may be longstanding inmates; others could be newly admitted into the structure but have had a culture shock on seeing the inside. 'Knock! Knock! Knock! I want to get out. Stop the world — I want to get off!' This is the radical knock of exit, the urge to leave the system, the perceived imperative of disengagement.

The most important manifestation of the radical knock of entry has been the entire anticolonial movement. This movement, now in its last political stages, has often taken the form of demands for sovereign statehood of the kind already enjoyed by the Northern industrialized states. One society after another in Asia and Africa has demanded entry into the nation-state system, which started in Europe as a structure of diplomacy for European monarchs and princes and the new post-Westphalia European juridical entities. The first knock of exit for the United States came in 1776 as Britain's American colonies asserted their independence from Britain and seemed determined to seek fulfilment outside European quarrels.

It is arguable that another knock of exit, at least in part, the Monroe Doctrine, was contained in a message to the American Congress on 2 December 1823. The message was provoked by the threat of a new European intervention in the Spanish American colonies, which were in revolt. The United States perceived the threat of a European recolonization of Latin America.

The doctrine sought to prevent the reincorporation of Latin America into the new global system that Europe was bidding to create. President Monroe also declared the United States unwillingness to participate in European quarrels outside the Western hemisphere.

At least in appearance, the Monroe Doctrine might therefore be seen as a setback to the global structures that Europe was in the process of forging. The Latin American revolt against Spain and Portugal seemed for a while to be truly a collective knock of exit, cheered and morally supported by the United States.

Before long, the Monroe Doctrine became a device for justifying American intervention in Latin America, rather than a shield to safeguard Latin America from European intervention. In any case, the newly independent countries in the Western hemisphere were, in part, created in the image of the new territorial nation-state, and in time Europe's conception of this nation-state was largely embraced by these new extensions of Europe.

While the Western hemisphere was to some extent trying to disengage from the new European system, the Ottoman Empire became 'the sick man of Europe', ailing from crisis to crisis. The empire continued to decay until it finally collapsed in the wake of World War I.

After the Ottoman Empire, the second major non-Christian candidate for entry into the emerging global system was Japan. The Meiji Restoration of 1868 set the stage for Japan's modernization, its rise in global power and influence, its eagerness to participate in certain areas of European diplomacy, and finally, its determination to have a share in the spoils of imperialism.

There were other marginal participants in the new global system in the nineteenth century, including such peripheral states as Ethiopia, Liberia, and even fragmented China. On the whole, however, the persistent knock of entry into the European global system from among Asian and African societies only became truly loud and clear in the twentieth century. The early 'tribal revolts' in Africa, the primary resistance by proud communities who did not want to be dominated by outsiders, were instances of a quest for exit. The warriors of the nineteenth century and even early twentieth century were trying to prevent the incorporation of their societies into alien global structures.

In contrast, the African and Asian nationalists of the twentieth century have on the whole been demanding the right of entry into the international system originally created by the Western world. The Afro-Asian demands for sovereign statehood territorially defined, have now become even more fanatically possessive about state sovereignty than some of the older members of the world system. The paraphernalia of Western diplomacy were also adopted. Each new juridical entity had to have a flag with a design of its own, a national anthem with both words and music, a number of ambassadors scattered in different parts of the world with roles and functions meticulously copied from the Western model, a system of protocol embraced in entirety from that model, a seat in the League of Nations and later the United Nations, and general adherence to Western-derived international law and other rules of diplomatic conduct. Major figures in twentieth century Third World history — such as Nehru of India, Nasser of Egypt, Nkrumah of Ghana, Sukarno of Indonesia — were all champions of entry into the global system.

Even the policy of non-alignment was carefully distinguished from neutrality. Non-alignment was deemed to be the right to independent participation and independent judgement, without the entanglement of formal alliances with major powers. Had non-alignment been a form of passive neutrality, it might have been an aspect of Third World life which amounted to a kind of exit from the global war system. But in reality, the great architects of non-alignment — such as Nehru, Nasser, Nkrumah, and Tito — were all emphatic in describing non-alignment as positive participation without entanglement, rather than a withdrawal or passive neutrality.

The most important exception to this participatory trend in Asia was China under Mao Tse-tung. For nearly 30 years, China was relatively isolated, partly because it was ostracized and partly out of a growing ideological conviction. Its seat in the United Nations was given to a pretender, Taiwan under Chiang Kai

Shek. For a while, only a fraction of the nation-states of the world had diplomatic relations with China. A form of ideological autarky began to emerge in Mao's China, reinforced by the cultural revolution. Indeed, the cultural revolution was itself, in a fundamental sense, a knock of cultural exit.

Burma also experimented with an exit from the world economic system, though not from the political. Economic autarky prevailed for a while. Both in China since Mao and in Burma, however, the temptations of entry into the world system have once again reasserted themselves. Like everybody else in Asia, Africa, and Latin America, the pull of the Westphalia system continues to be for the time being irresistible.

And yet is that the whole story? Almost every country in existence seems to have accepted entry into the global political system and is not seeking an exit therefrom since Mao's death. But there are considerable variations between countries as to the balance between being in or out economically and culturally. In other words, political absorption into the international arena in terms of exchanging ambassadors, voting at the United Nations, expressing opinions on diplomatic issues of the day, is almost universal. How far a country permits itself to be absorbed into the world economy or to be conquered by the dominant culture nevertheless remains something which betrays considerable variation in the world.

These variations are to some extent ideologically relative. Third World radicalism takes a variety of forms, ranging from Marxist militancy to Islamic fundamentalism. How does this range relate to the tension between being in and being out? For example, does Marxism sound the knock of entry or the knock of exit from the global system?

It would seem that for Africans and Asians, going Marxist is a knock of exit from Western capitalism, but at the same time it is a knock of entry into Western culture and intellectual orientation.

Marxism: Exit or Entry?

Since the dominant global system is capitalist, and since Marxism is opposed to capitalism, it would seem that going Marxist is tantamount to giving notice that one needs an exit visa from the global system as it now exists. Since the dictatorship of the proletariat is not yet at hand, and might not be achieved on a global scale during one's own lifetime, why should one remain within a perverse and evil world arena? Would it not make better sense to withdraw from the evil and await revolutionary redemption?

Marxism is not merely a theory and a prophecy, however, it is also a commitment. On one side, there is the theory and prophecy of inevitable revolution; on the other there is the imperative of aiding history to speed up. At first glance, if a workers' revolution were inevitable, it would seem there would be no point in engaging in revolutionary activities to bring it about. On closer scrutiny, it would seem that Marxism asserts that the final outcome is inevitable but does not assert that its timing is also inevitable. In other words, a particular proletarian revolution in a particular society could take place this year or 50 years from now, depending upon the precise configuration of factors and the degree to which progressive groups are organized to frustrate it.

While one is awaiting the final outcome of history, how much of a participant in the existing order can one morally be? Marxism has historical precedents rather than adequate theoretical answers. We do know that Friedrich Engels continued to engage in capitalist activities in Manchester, while at the same time he was busy writing major drafts against capitalism. Engels was engaged in facilitating the operation of the profit motive, and denouncing it at the same time. We also know that Karl Marx depended on Engels a good deal for subsidies to enable him to maintain a tolerable standard of life in nineteenth-century England, while at the same time engaging his energies towards the long-term goal of destroying the system which fed him. Historically, we are therefore provided with examples of remaining inside a capitalist system while urging its annihilation. Theoretically, there has been no satisfying reconciliation between behaving like a capitalist, as Engels did, and writing like a revolutionary socialist, as Engels also did.

In reality, the economic exit from Western capitalism has become even harder to accomplish since Engels's days. Third World Marxist countries like Vietnam, Angola, Mozambique, and Cuba have managed to go socialist in their own domestic arrangements but are still prisoners of the capitalist system at the global and the non-global level. Internationally their products are still subject to market forces. The leading currencies of exchange remain, as they have discovered, the currencies of capitalist countries. The economies of fellow socialist countries are protectionist and difficult to penetrate; the other socialist countries themselves are beginning to seek new opportunities in the wider market of supply and demand regardless of ideology and class. The idea of maximization of return at the international level is often just another name for the profit motive. The socialist countries sell to each other with maximization of returns as an aim. In addition, they look around for foreign exchange rooted in capitalism, and for the global dynamic of supply and demand.

A country can thus be quite successful in creating within its own boundaries structures which discourage the profit motive, frustrate the bourgeoisie, enhance the efficacy of the proletariat, and increase the role of the state in the economy, and while experimenting with socialist structure internally, remain caged in by the market forces of world capitalism. The knock of economic exit from capitalism is domestically fulfilled but globally frustrated.

In what sense is going Marxist in the Third World a knock of cultural entry into Western intellectual civilization?

The Harvard University elder statesman, Carl Friedrich, once asserted that revolution was peculiarly a child of Western culture. He argued that other cultures might have produced coups and rebellions, revolts and insurrections, but only Western culture produced a capacity to challenge the existing order at its most fundamental and to redefine the ultimate directions of social change and moral purpose.

Why was Western culture predominantly qualified to achieve this transformation? According to Friedrich, the main reasons included the West's belief that man was in control of his own destiny. It was not Allah, or Kismet, or *karma* but the human person that shaped history and forged destiny. Since revolutions assumed a capacity to redesign the social universe, this faith in human potency was critical.

A related Western value of revolutionary potential is the principle of choice. Choice, to some extent, is at the heart of Western liberalism, and constitutes an aspect of consumer economy and a free enterprise system. Choice also relates in a stable liberal polity to competitive elections, multi-party systems, and a free market of ideas. In the ultimate analysis, liberal choice should presumably include the choice between whole systems, whole structures of government, whole universes of values. Revolutions are essentially concerned with choice between designs of alternative paradises. It is in this sense that Carl Fredrich regarded revolution as predominantly a Western concept.[1]

Another major Western scholar, the late Professor John Plamenatz of Oxford, used to argue that revolutionary theory, and indeed political theory as a whole, was also a child of Western culture. The tradition of social criticism and institutional analysis, the tradition of debate about fundamental political values, the tradition of defining and evaluating functions of government, and the relationship between authority and society all flowed out of the fountain of ancient Greece and its impact on Western intellectual history.

If we bring together Carl Friedrich's assertion that revolution is Western and John Plamenatz's assertion that political theorizing is also Western, we could indeed deduce that purposeful social and political engineering is itself also a child of Western thought and culture. Abstract theoretical design and practical revolutionary implementation are together what modern revolution has been all about.[2]

How valid is this approach which traces revolutions to the impact of Western culture? When revolutionary thought is interpreted in socialist terms, there does seem to be evidence in support of the Friedrich thesis that revolutionary socialism is indeed a child of Western culture. This need not mean that all revolutions emanate from Western culture. Neither need it mean that all forms of socialism are to be traced to the impact of Western civilization. It is a combination of two concepts — socialism and revolution — which is almost uniquely Western.

Revolutionary socialism is of course to be distinguished from primordial socialism. The latter has been discovered in many different cultures and societies. It usually is accompanied by simpler forms of technology, kinship, related collectivism, a greater egalitarianism than so far has been achieved in any modern revolutionary society, and communal forms of property and land tenure. In 1942, for example, the British Labour Party took stock of these elements of primordial collectivism and egalitarianism in the British African colonies. The Labour Party urged in its Report of the Forty-First Annual Congress as follows:

> In all colonial areas in Africa and elsewhere, where the primitive systems of communal land tenure exist, these systems should be maintained and land should be declared inalienable by private sale or purchase.[3]

Some African socialists after independence also moved in the direction of trying to marry traditional elements of collective life with modern socialist ideas. Not long after Tanganyika's independence, President Julius K. Nyerere drastically reduced the possibilities of freehold land ownership in his country on the argument that such a concept of property was alien to traditional cultures in Tanganyika. Much of the agricultural land was therefore deemed to be leasehold from the state on a collective basis. Traditional collectivism was now translated into ultimate state ownership.

One point of comparison between African socialists today and Russian socialists in the nineteenth century is precisely this concern with preserving what is traditionally collectivist. Indeed, African socialists today talk as if the African was almost unique in having the opportunity to begin with primordial socialism and extend it into modern socialist structures. Such ostensible uniqueness was, however, also planned by some Russian socialists in the nineteenth century. To such Russian plans, Karl Marx gave an emphatic retort. He said:

241

A ridiculous prejudice has recently obtained currency that common property in its primitive form is specifically a Slavonic, or even exclusively Russian, form. It is the primitive form that we can show to have existed among Romans, Teutons, and Celts, and even to this day we find numerous examples, ruins though they may be, in India.[4]

Was Marx saying that primordial socialism could not possibly lead to revolutionary socialism? To some extent he was indeed saying that. In subsequent formulations, however, Marx did allow for the possibility of 'primitive collectivism' skipping the bourgeois stage provided the less developed society is encircled by countries in the throes of socialist revolution.

In January 1982, Marx and Engels wrote a foreword to Plekhanov's Russian translation of the *Communist Manifesto*. This is what Marx and Engels argued in that foreword:

In Russia . . . we find that in contrast to the rapidly growing capitalist system and the emerging bourgeois system of landholding, more than half the land is owned in common by the peasantry. The crucial question now is: can the Russian *obsutchina* [village community], an already seriously undermined form of the age old communal property of the soil, become transformed directly into the superior form of communist ownership of land, or will it have to pass through the same process of decomposition which is evidenced by the historical evolution of the West? Today, only one answer is possible to this question. If the Russian revolution sounds the signal for a proletarian revolution in the West, so that each complements the other, the prevailing form of communal ownership of land in Russia may form a starting point for a communist course of development.[5]

If that did not happen, 'if Russia continued to move in the [capitalizing] path followed up to 1861, it will lose the finest occasion that history has ever offered a people not to undergo all the sudden turns of fortune of the capitalist system.'[6]

Much of this discussion concerns the possibility of primordial socialism becoming revolutionary socialism without the intermediate stage of bourgeois society and capitalist development. It can even be asked whether primordial socialism can become modern socialism without a revolution at all. At the very minimum, from the point of view of our analysis so far, is the simple proposition that not all forms of socialism are the offspring of Western culture.

Correspondingly, are all forms of revolution the offspring of Western culture? Here again the answer is decidedly no. The birth of Islam in the seventh century after Christ initiated an important revolution for the people of Arabia. Fundamental changes occurred to the belief systems and the political structures of the people of the Arabian peninsula. This transformation also included outward expansionism which resulted in major challenges to two of the apparently powerful empires of that period, Byzantium, which included Egypt, and the Persian Empire. The Islamic revolution in the Arabian peninsula soon gave rise to the dramatic Muslim conquests of the seventh century B C. The geography of the world underwent a change: the history of the world was never the same again. And yet that revolution of the seventh century had little to do with Western civilization as it later evolved. On the contrary, the Islamic revolution itself came to influence fairly profoundly the future course of Western culture and history.

The conclusions to be drawn from these observations are twofold — that not all forms of revolution are Western derived and that not all forms of socialism have

Western ancestry. What may be uniquely Western is the fusion between socialism and revolution.

A particularly striking illustration of this fusion between socialism and revolution is of course Marxism itself. Historical materialism is a long play in which every act, if not every scene, ends with a class revolution, and the curtain falls on a particular epoch.

But the playwright was a Westerner, and the drama is rooted in Western intellectual and economic culture.

It is partly because of these considerations that in Africa it is a socio-linguistic impossibility for a 'native' to be a sophisticated Marxist without being at the same time substantially Westernized. Access to the complex ideas of Marxism requires of an African for the time being a command of a major Western language. The works of Marx and Engels, let alone the hundreds of volumes of commentaries on these works, are not as yet available in Hausa Kidigo, Kiswahili, or Lunyoro-Lutoro.

Nor do Africans learn their first European language from a tourist phrase book. On the contrary, Africans in English-speaking African countries learn English as a whole process of socialization and acculturation; Africans in Francophone Africa learn French in the same manner. The cultural foundations of school children are profoundly altered in the process of acquiring command of the imperial language. By the time these young Africans are busy playing around with ideas of the dialectic and class struggle, with political economy and the negation of the negation, they are relatively immersed in Western intellectual gymnastics. The high road to Marxism for many an African intellectual is not only paved with Western stones, but very often requires to be traversed by a Western vehicle.

In spite of that, Carl Friedrich is wrong in the reasons he advances as to why revolutionary thought is a product of Western culture. We will remember that part of the reasoning concerned the belief in Western liberalism that man is in control of his own destiny. Yet the distinctive thing about Marxism as a Western heresy is precisely the Marxist belief in the inevitability of a socialist revolution. In this sense, man's destiny is not in his own hands, but lies in the hands of irresistible historical and social forces. On balance, historical materialism is the story of *Kismet* with a revolutionary face.

Nor is Marxism a product of Western belief in choice. Western liberalism might have been born out of that belief, but not Western Marxism. For the later tradition of thought, one point is clear: few things which matter are the outcome of personal choice. If the history of man is the history of his social class, and the history of his social class is preordained, it is not personal choice but historical commitment that lies at the heart of radicalism.

On Revolution and Nostalgia

Not all forms of radicalism amount to a commitment to an entirely new order, however. There can be forms of radicalism which aspire to reconstruct an old order. We must distinguish between revivalist and innovative radicalism.

Two of the most militant challenges to Western hegemony in the contemporary world are indeed Marxism and Islam. Marxism is innovative radicalism — seeking to forge an entirely new global order. Islam, for the time being, is, when militant, powered by revivalist radicalism: it seeks to regain its ancient vigour and distinctiveness.

While Marxism has sounded the knock of economic exit from the West, combined with the knock of cultural entry, contemporary Islam is reversing that order. Islam has sounded a knock of cultural exit from the West, but the legacy of oil maintains the momentum of economic entry into the inner recesses and structures of international capitalism.

Iran is of course a striking illustration of this particular dialectic. The rise of the Ayatollahs' power signifies a major application for an exit visa out of the Western cultural system that the Shah had attempted to transplant. Purely from a cultural perspective, the Ayatollahs have been screaming: 'Stop the world — we want to get off!'

Is Iran's attempted cultural exit from the west a case, then, of moving backwards? If so, is this pursuit of nostalgia a disastrous indulgence in the modern age? One answer would take us right back into fables of Arabia and Persia. Let us assume a caravan of Islamic culture peacefully meandering towards its own destination under the stars of history. Let us then assume a major interruption one night. The caravan is overcome and hijacked by Western highwaymen. These highwaymen divert it from its natural route, taking it into an alluring but alien destination. Then, many moons later, under the inspiration of the Ayatollah Khomeini, the original owners of the caravan succeed in overpowering their captors. At last the caravan is once again under indigenous control. The question arises as to whether the caravan should proceed. The robbers have brought it some considerable distance away from what seemed to be its natural route. Should the caravan continue along the path of diversion? Or should it seek to rediscover the precise point where it was hijacked and deflected, and from there seek once again its own destiny? The Ayatollahs of Iran have opted for a return to the historic point of deflection, a move backwards to transcend the diversion perpetrated by Western cultural hijackers. In this case, the quest is for a cultural re-entry into the original universe of Islam, as well as a cultural exit out of the Western diversionary maze.

At the present, Islam is the only major culture to rebel against the West. In reality, the West has diverted many other indigenous caravans. The cultures of India have taken new directions. Political and economic rebellion against the West is fairly strong in places like India, but so profound is the tradition of accommodation and synthesis in Indian culture that for the time being the rebellion against Western cultural penetration in India is definitely far weaker than it is in places like Iran, Libya, and even Pakistan.

China under Mao Tse-tung opted for economic exit from the Western dominated global system. Peking was also forced to accept political isolation. Culturally, however, Mao's China continued to apply for an entry into Western intellectual civilization. That, at least, is how the situation looked like when, on the one hand, Mao's China honoured and revered Marx, Lenin, and Stalin, and, on the other, it denounced the country's own paramount philosopher, Confucius.

In Africa, Western culture has been particularly triumphant against relatively small-scale African systems of values, beliefs, and institutions. Trans-Saharan African caravans have been diverted from their historic routes, but for the time being there is no determined African effort to overpower the hijackers and return the indigenous caravans to the point of original deflection, so that they might once again begin to find their own chosen destinations.

What all this means is that while the ultimate inspiration for economic revolutions in the modern world is a future-oriented ambition, the ultimate inspiration for cultural revolutions in the Third World must include a backward-oriented sense of restoration. Economic ambition is an effort to realize material well-being at a new level of efficiency; cultural ambition is the effort to realize spiritual well-being at the right depth of identity. Economic revolutions need to be effectively innovative; cultural revolutions must in part be, at least in the Third World, selectively revivalist. The latter is indeed a marriage between revolution and nostalgia.

Towards Strategies of Selective Entry

The most fundamental general question that finally arises is the following: What is the right balance between exit and entry for the Third World in relation to the Western-dominated global system?

Some things are surely clear. Complete exit from the global system is impossible in this day and age, partly because of the technological shrinkage of the world into a global village. The communications revolution has made it untenable to seek to isolate oneself from global perceptions, influences, expectations, and inspirations. Because every society is now subject to external stimulation of one kind or another, there are repercussions behaviourally and institutionally. No society is any longer impervious to exogenous conditioning.

Just as complete exit is impossible, so is it also undesirable. The Northern hemisphere has already the capacity to destroy the world either through depletion of resources, pollution and other ecological damage, or through a nuclear war. Since the North is so empowered to initiate, at its own discretion, the annihilation of the planet, the South cannot afford to turn the other way. Indeed, the South should seek to create instruments of leverage on the North. To disengage from the global system while the North enjoys this option of planetary destruction would, for the South, be tantamount to moral abdication. It would also be suicidal for the Third World.

A combination of strategies seems, therefore, to be the ultimate imperative — strategies for selective entry, selective participation. Unconditional entry into the global system, dominated as it is, would be a case of surrendering to Western hegemony. The decision either to enter or to remain within the system therefore requires carefully worked out principles of operation. After all, the entry should not be merely to rearrange the furniture within the system: it should ultimately be to renovate the structure of that system. To that extent, strategies of reconstruction and liberation are needed.

Within the Third World one relatively obvious strategy is that of indigenization. This involves the greater use of indigenous human power, natural and mineral resources, technologies and techniques, and principles of ownership and control. To some extent, indigenization is an exercise in self-reliance. And self-reliance is, on the whole, an exercise in selective exit.

A related strategy is that of domestication. While indigenization involves greater utilization of what is distinctively native, domestication is an effort to make what is foreign more relevant to local conditions and local needs. For example, there may be certain forms of technology that are distinctively imported. The question which would arise would be to make that technology more appropriate to the culture and material conditions of a given society. Another illustration concerns modern schools and universities. In Asia and Africa, some of these colleges and institutions are very distant from traditional modes of socialization and training. These imported colleges and universities could be made more responsive to local orientations and imperatives, more relevant to fulfilling local necessities. The imported wild animals could thus be domesticated. This is a form of partial entry into the wider global system of both production and training.

The third strategy is that of diversification. This could be wide-ranging. It might include diversifying what a society produces, or diversifying the trading partners, or the aid donors and benefactors, or the sources of raw materials and energy. Diversification is a visa for multiple entry — getting permission not only to move in and out of the global system as the national needs might require, but also to move into it at different points of entry. Single-entry exercises are subject to greater exploitation and harassment than forms of entry into the global system which permit a particular Third World society to experiment with different products, or experiment with different trading partners, or even to play one super-power off against another.

The fourth strategy is that of horizontal interpenetration among and between the underprivileged. If Tanzania needs computer experts, why seek them in Sweden or the United States; why not try India or Egypt? If Kenya needs new markets for its meat products, is it necessary to go to Brussels and negotiate for new import quotas? Is it not feasible that Kuwait or Libya might be more relevant markets? The strategy of horizontal interpenetration seems to facilitate greater interaction among Third World countries themselves, diplomatically, politically, economically, and culturally. Is this a case of entry into the global system or is it a case of exit therefrom? In reality, horizontal interpenetration is an effort to make the global system more truly global. It is a quest to maximize interactions between sectors which might otherwise have little contact with each other. Horizontal interpenetration is a method of internationalizing the globe.

The fifth strategy is that of vertical counterpenetration. This means enabling the underprivileged to find ways of penetrating and influencing the privileged. It means entering the corridors of power in the Northern hemisphere, seeking to exercise leverage at the centre of the world system. Just as the Third World has been subjected to Northern penetration, it is now necessary for the industrialized countries to be subjected to Southern penetration. Economically, this could take the form of Third World countries using their resources as political weapons or instruments of lobbying the North. Counterpenetration could also take the form of Third World countries acquiring banks in the Northern hemisphere, or buying up shares in major industries in Germany, Great Britain, or the United States. Culturally, counterpenetration could take the form of establishing Third World-oriented magazines or newspapers in the industrialized countries, or Third World teachers and professors transmitting Third World perspectives into the free market of ideas in parts of the industrialized North.

Is counterpenetration a case of entry or exit out of the global system? This is emphatically an entry visa, but there is a quest for symmetry involved in it. The strategy of counterpenetration accepts that a prior penetration of the South by the North was a case of absorption into the world capitalist system. The utilization of Southern power and resources to influence events and policies in the North is, by definition, an exercise in reciprocal visas. The South would be saying that it can no longer tolerate a situation in which the North can freely enter the South and affect its destiny without the South reciprocating by entering the North and helping to affect its direction.

Sixth, there is the strategy of Southern austerity, a quest for discipline in using

Northern resources. In this case, there is a link with the strategy of indigenization, but the two are different sides of the coin. Indigenization requires greater use of native resources, personnel, and techniques. Austerity requires reduced use of foreign resources, personnel, and techniques. In the latter case, the reduced use need not mean import substitution. It could merely mean import negation — a reduction of foreign luxuries without substituting them with indigenous indulgences. To some extent, this strategy of Southern austerity is an exercise in selective exit.

Then there is the seventh strategy of Northern extravagance. As a temporary measure it might well serve the Third World if the North continued to be relatively extravagant in its use of Southern resources. This could provide leverage for the Third World to induce the North to change the global system more fundamentally. A successful effort by the North to reduce its need of Southern oil would drastically reduce, in turn, Southern leverage upon the North. A resource-independent industrialized world is an industrialized world impervious to moral pressure from the South. The global system needs the cooperation of the North if it is to change in favour of the less privileged and more exploited sectors of humanity. That cooperation of industrialized nations is much less certain in conditions where the industrialized world does not need the South than in conditions where it is vulnerable to Southern turbulence and assertiveness. Excessive luxury in the Northern hemisphere becomes a necessary Achilles heel, a point of weakness that can be exploited to the greater advantage of equity and balance in the global scheme of things.

The strategy of Northern extravagance is a form of deepening entry into the world system. In this case, the South demands an entry visa with a work permit, an entry visa with an investment contract. The quest for symmetry in the game of entry and exit continues in the seven strategies of balanced merger.

The Nuclear Reactor: No Exit?

Relations between the Northern hemisphere and the Southern hemisphere are not merely political, economic, and cultural. They are also, of course, military and technological.

At the technological level, the dialectic has been between technology transfer and technology monopoly. Technology transfer has, in part, resulted in greater dependency on the part of the Third World upon the industrialized countries, a case of further penetration into the Southern hemisphere. Technology monopoly is an assertion by the Northern industrialized states of exclusivity in certain spheres of the Third World. Can the societies of the Southern hemisphere be trusted with certain branches of knowledge?

The most striking case of technology monopoly is in the nuclear field. There has grown, especially in the 1970s, a greater possessiveness on the part of the Northern hemisphere with regard to this particular form of technology. The major concern in Washington is certainly the fear of nuclear proliferation. There is anxiety that the dissemination of nuclear know-how would result in more and more Third World countries acquiring a nuclear capacity, and becoming nuclear powers in the military sense, with all the apparent consequences for world order. American presidents in recent times have therefore tended to display outside the gates of nuclear knowledge the unmistakable sign of 'No Entry'.

On balance, the champions of technological monopoly have overlooked one

247

fundamental dialectic. The pursuit of nuclear power can indeed radicalize but the acquisition of nuclear power tends to be deradicalizing in its consequences. The need to acquire a nuclear capacity increases militancy and deepens impatience for technological parity. To that extent, those countries that are near enough to nuclear power to seek it become eager and committed towards its realization unless they can empathize sufficiently with some other power that has already gone nuclear. Many Western countries do not need to acquire a nuclear military capability since they are already under an American nuclear umbrella and since their perceived adversaries, the Soviet Union and its allies, are already identified also as the adversaries of the United States. Such non-nuclear Western countries are not radicalized partly because they are not impelled by the need to pursue a nuclear capacity.

On the other hand, virtually all countries that do acquire that nuclear capacity have tended to subside in their radicalism. This includes the Soviet Union which has developed a greater vested interest in the status quo in proportion to its sense of nuclear credentials.

We can therefore sense why the pursuit of nuclear power in the military sense can be a radicalizing factor. But why should the acquisition of a nuclear military capacity tend to deradicalize?

One answer might be the increased sensitivity to the nearness of nuclear conflict. Countries that have acquired a nuclear capacity are, by definition, more sophisticated in the implications of nuclear war and, it may be hoped, more cautious in at least some of their military calculations.

Second, for the time being, countries which have acquired a nuclear capacity have acquired some kind of credentials for admission to the military establishment of the globe. The establishment of the globe, as indeed of national societies, tends to be conservative and inclined towards the preservation of the status quo. In this regard also, the acquisition of nuclear credentials has sociological propensities for deradicalization.

Third, the acquisition of a nuclear capacity should presumably mean increased influence of the culture of engineers and high technology in policy making. Engineers and high technologists are notoriously conservative in their political orientations. It might therefore seem that the deepening of technological sophistication in those branches of technology relevant to foreign policy making often results in declining commitment to fundamental transformations of the global system and declining commitment to globally oriented radicalism.

Is this a cry for every country to go nuclear? This would partly depend upon whether one is in favour of deradicalizing societies by making them part of the establishment. It would also depend upon whether one is adequately sanguine about the mathematical probabilities of a nuclear war as nuclear powers multiply.

What seems more persuasive as a strategy for the time being is a temporary overthrow of the 'No Entry' sign which the Western world has for the time being decided to hang across the gates of nuclear technology. Some degree of nuclear proliferation may be inevitable before enough anxiety is created in the world to induce more determined attempts to eliminate nuclear arsenals.

Nuclear weapons should be declared as illegitimate as germ warfare. *De facto*, there might still be efforts to develop or maintain a military nuclear capacity. Outlawing nuclear weapons might not mean the ending of nuclear weapons. On the other hand, outlawing murder has not meant the end of murder either. Humanity needs to reexamine its standards of legitimate conflict: nuclear conflict should not be included within that domain of legitimacy. How then should one arrive at that situation of total exit from the possibilities of nuclear war? Paradoxically, only by a temporary entry into a nuclear capacity by more and more countries could there be enough conviction for the need for a total nuclear exit by all the countries. The culture shocks of more and more Third World countries wielding nuclear devices might at last induce even the two super-powers to sit around the table, with many other countries, seeking a viable system of total nuclear renunciation.

It is as if there was one dangerous club called the nuclear club. It was comfortable as long as the members were only three, four, five, up to ten. But after a while, there was not enough room in the club for more members; the danger of suffocation increased, the risk of carelessness among cigarette smokers, the hazard of a possible explosion. As long as there were only up to ten members of the nuclear club, the club idea was viable. But there was a definite maximum limit of viable membership. When that limit was reached, even the founder members of the club might willingly agree, for the sake of basic survival, to estimate the assets as against the liabilities of the club, and take the decision to close down altogether.

Mere conferences on nuclear disarmament might not end the danger of war permanently. What needs to be examined once again is the sociology of war itself, which includes its persistent masculinity. In cultures which have otherwise been vastly different from each other, men have until now disproportionately mono-polized the war game. A major sociological experiment for the future is surely the need for the androgynization of the war machine — a sharing of the machine between men and women. Women should therefore sound the knock of entry into the war system — in the hope of transforming it, in the hope of taming it.

In the ultimate analysis, the world needs to feel two impacts: the strategy of normative transformation, with a knock of martial entry to be sounded by women. The world also needs the strategy of culture shock, with the knock of nuclear entry by the Third World. And yet both entries should amount to a knock of exit out of a culture of destruction and annihilation which has bedevilled the human predica-ment for millennia.

'Open sesame!', both Ali Baba and the forty thieves had occasion to pronounce. The world needs a secret password for opening and shutting the global gates with the right balance between equity and efficiency.

Notes

1. Carl Friedrich and I collaborated for nearly a decade in the affairs of the International Political Science Association (from 1967 to 1976).
2. cf. John Plamenatz on *Alien Rule and Self-Government* (London: Longman, 1960). Professor Plamenatz was the supervisor of my doctoral thesis at Oxford University in the early 1960s. He and I also discussed some of these ideas personally from time to time.
3. Cited in Louise W. Holbrun (ed.), *War and Peace Aims of the United Nations* (Boston: World Peace Foundation, 1943), p. 684.
4. *Kritik* (1859), p. 9, footnote 1.
5. Preface to the Russian edition of the Communist Manifesto, *Manifesto of the Communist Party* (1882) (Moscow: Foreign Languages Publishing House), p. 13.
6. Marx, *Das Kapital* (first German edition), volume 1, p. 763.

Towards
Cultural Realignment

A Conclusion

Power at the global level has been studied as a political, economic, and military phenomenon. This book has discussed power as a cultural reality. We have explored a hidden cultural agenda in international power struggles. We have noted that the world economy has been led by English-speaking countries in the last two centuries (England in the nineteenth and the United States in the twentieth). We have long suspected a link between the Protestant ethic and the rise of capitalism. We are faced with a world in which women have little say in decisions about war and peace. And is the pursuit of nuclear military status the latest version of the role of macho in world politics? All these are matters which begin by being deeply rooted in culture before they manifest themselves in political economy and military strategy. This book has addressed this cultural dimension in international affairs and world politics.

In March 1989 the Soviet Union declared its readiness to accept the jurisdiction of the International Court of Justice (World Court) on six treaties to do with human rights. The treaties included issues like torture, racial discrimination, sexual discrimination and genocide.

This was the latest in a series of moves by Mikhail Gorbachev — moves which implied the declining salience of ideology in relations between the Western world and the Soviet alliance.

We have to face some of the basic questions arising from these trends. What has this realignment meant for the rest of the world? If human beings stop quarrelling about secular ideology, will they find alternative arenas of conflict?

We have sought to demonstrate in this book that what we are witnessing may be the gradual unravelling of identities based on the state, a declining of identities based on political ideology — and the revival of identities based on culture.

As we indicated, it is not often realized that the people of Moscow have more in common with the people of New York than they have with fellow Soviet citizens in Uzbekistan and Azerbaijan. Ethnic Russians proper are more like West Europeans than they are like the citizens of Oriental parts of the Soviet Union.

We have to relate all this to the Gorbachev Revolution and the new rapprochement between the West and the Soviet alliance. We are confronted with a potential cultural realignment of forces in the wake of the decline of ideology. We have also

250

suggested that there has been a Jewish contribution to most movements of thought in the modern world — capitalist, Marxist, Christian, Muslim, as well as more directly Judaic.

George Bernard Shaw once said that the British and the Americans were a people divided by a common language. Is it conceivable that Eastern Europeans and Western Europeans are a people more genuinely divided by a common civilization?

We do know that liberal democracy in the West is partly a child of the Judeo-Christian tradition. But is communism in the Soviet alliance also partly a child of the Judeo-Marxist tradition? The genius of pluralism in western experience owes something to the heritage of the Jews as well as of Jesus. Does the conscience of equality in the Soviet world also owe something to the heritage of the Jews as well as Marx? As we tentatively suggested earlier, Karl Marx — like Jesus Christ — was a figure within the prophetic tradition of the Jews.

Among the Jews such questions set off alarm bells — a convergence of racism and potential anti-semitism. In extreme right-wing circles in the West Jews are sometimes hated for both their ancient religion and their modern liberal views. That may be one reason why the Jews themselves are sometimes nervous when Karl Marx is identified as an ethnic Jew.

And yet in order to understand what the West has in common with both Communist China and the Soviet Union, we have had to look at Marxism more closely. Marxism may be a heresy not just of Western civilization in the secular sense but also of the Judeo-Christian tradition as a sacred heritage. That Christianity began as an offshoot of Judaism is widely recognized in the history of religion. But is Marxism in turn an offshoot of the Judeo-Christian tradition? We have already argued that Marxism is indeed such an offshoot. What has been one of the great divisive factors between East and West in the twentieth century may conceivably become one of their unifying bonds in the twenty-first. After all, Christians and Jews were once a people divided by a shared religious heritage — more fundamentally than Americans and Britons have been divided by a common language. Will what Marxism has in common with the Judeo-Christian tradition one day be one of the unifying forces between East and West long after Gorbachev?

If therefore Marxism shows the influence of aspects of the Old Testament, and even of the New, to what extent did the Soviet Union turn its back on religion by going Marxist? And yet for a while Western and Soviet political cultures confronted each other — and militarized their rivalry to new levels of potential destructiveness.

Was it a Judeo-Christian Western alliance arming itself against a Judeo-Marxist Soviet bloc? Were two sister civilizations unnecessarily on a collision course?

The Politics of Cultural Realignment

European Soviet citizens may be in the process of being drawn closer and closer to the West — as Muslim Soviet citizens are drawn more and more towards the rest of the Muslim world. Is there a cultural realignment under way?

Soviet intervention in Afghanistan was partly motivated by a desire to prevent a cultural realignment between its own Muslim citizens and radicalized Islam elsewhere. Uzbekistan is the most populous of the five Muslim republics of Central Asia and Siberia. Families have an average of six or seven children. The

Uzbeks and other Soviet Muslims are increasing in number at a birth rate five times that of ethnic Russians. It has been estimated that at this rate of increase Muslims will constitute almost a quarter of the Soviet population by the turn of the century. Ethnic Russians will soon be less than half.[1] Can we entertain the possibility of a Muslim president in the Soviet Union early in the twenty-first century? Who will come first — a black president of the United States or a Muslim president of the USSR?

Three trends in the Soviet Union favour the prospect of a Muslim president sometime in the twenty-first century. One trend is the erosion of the power of the Communist Party. The second trend is the dramatic expansion of the Muslim population. The third factor is the declining official hostility to religion.

The power of the Soviet Communist Party seems to be decreasing partly because of changes in electoral politics. Membership of the Communist Party of the Soviet Union (CPSU) is no longer necessary for at least certain levels of the electoral process. While the Soviet Union — unlike some of its Eastern European allies — is not yet seriously discussing the possibility of a multi-party system, the Gorbachev revolution has already allowed for competitive elections between party candidates and non-party candidates in certain national bodies. Will these changes one day result in a Muslim head of state even if he or she is still answerable to the Communist Party of the Soviet Union?

The Muslim population of the Soviet Union is already fifty million strong — as large as the Muslim population of Egypt, the largest Arab country. The total population of Egypt is slightly over fifty million — but that includes some five to seven million Coptic Christians.[2]

The third factor in the USSR which favours a future Muslim President is declining hostility to religion on the part of the Soviet state. There is a kind of *perestroika* operating within the atheistic tendencies of Soviet political culture.

The USSR — once religiously intolerant, is it becoming less so?

The USA — once racially intolerant, is it becoming less so?

Declining atheistic militancy on the part of the Soviet state opens up the possibility of future black leadership.

Prejudice: Racial and Religious

There is little doubt that the United States since World War II has become a less racist society. The black underclass has remained large and a little overwhelming — but the black bourgeoisie has become larger and more influential.

Blacks as a whole have been promoted from being a lower caste (hereditary status) to being a lower class (with better prospects of social mobility than before). Afroamericans now have better access to the American economy, to American science and technology and to American politics. Jesse Jackson has knocked at the gates of ultimate political power — seeking no less than the presidency of the United States.

At the level of governorship, it is no longer unthinkable for Afroamericans to be serious candidates. The state of Michigan has shown the way of a Republican black candidate for the governorship. At the level of mayors of major cities Afroamericans have had a breakthrough. City after city has at least experimented with having 'black bosses'. Is the stage being set for an African-American president of the United States early in the twenty-first century?

But if Afroamericans are having more access to political power, is there a comparable opening up for Soviet Muslims? Because Soviet Muslims have republics of their own, they have always had the equivalent of state governorship in their own areas. They have also dominated the legislatures of their own republics. And on the Supreme Soviet of the USSR (the parliament) and the Congress of People's Deputies, Soviet Muslims have sometimes had representation closer to their numbers than Afroamericans have had.

Muslim geographical mobility is also increasing. And there have of course been Muslims on the Politburo of the Soviet Union — the supreme arm of the executive branch. On the other hand, relations between the West and the Muslim world are entering an uncertain period. There is a serious question whether the declining salience of secular ideology in the West's relations with the Soviet Bloc will result in expanding salience of culture conflict between the West and the World of Islam. Will Westerners be looking for other adversaries?

Even in the United States the question is already arising as to whether declining racial prejudice will be accompanied by increasing religious prejudice. If so this would be a return to things as they once were in Europe before Europeans became obsessed with skin colour.

In Shakespeare racism was more religious than pigmentational. *The Merchant of Venice* is a more racist play than *Othello*. Prejudice against Shylock as a Jew is stronger than prejudice against Othello as a black.

The two main arenas of prejudice are economics and sexuality. In *Othello* the arena is sexuality — a black man mates with a white woman. In the *Merchant of Venice* the arena is economics — Shylock's demand for his pound of flesh.

The Merchant of Venice deals with the issue of even racism more frontally than does *Othello*. That may be one reason why Julius Nyerere, when president of Tanzania, was tempted to translate *The Merchant of Venice* into Kiswahili more than he was tempted to translate, *Othello, the Moor of Venice*.

Even with the play *Othello* religious prejudice is stronger than racial prejudice. The Turks — who were of course Muslims — were viewed as circumcised barbarians. Othello's last words before he stabbed himself were the following:

> . . . in Aleppo once,
> where a malignant and turban'd Turk
> Beat a Venetian and traduced the State,
> I took by the throat the circumcised dog
> and smote him, thus. (*Stabs himself*)

But after Shakespeare the Western world got more secular but also more racist. Religious prejudice declined — and racial prejudice increased, until a real barbarian called Adolf Hitler combined both forms of of prejudice in his onslaught against the Jews.

In any case the nineteenth and twentieth centuries witnessed the rise of secular religion. A new kind of religious prejudice came into being — ideological prejudice. Here again racism and ideology sometimes intertwined.

A twentieth-century *Othello* came to symbolize this convergence of racism and ideological radicalism. This twentieth-century Othello was Paul Robeson.

Race and Political Realignment

African-Americans generally are often caught between Marx and the Messiah. They look to the Messiah for a sense of psychological security; they sometimes look towards Karl Marx for a sense of social security. Afroamericans look to Messianic figures like Marcus Garvey and Elijah Muhammed for psychic fulfilment. More rarely they look to Leninist figures like W. E. B. DuBois and Stokely Carmichael for proletarian redemption.

Paul Robeson looked to Marx himself for a sense of political direction and human orientation. But he did so at a time when the United States was obsessed with the presumed threats — the black peril of race and the Red peril of communism. By going Marxist, Paul Robeson fused the two presumed threats into one. In his powerful voice, Robeson stood up and sang — poised between the dark chasm of colour prejudice and the depths of ideological bigotry.

If there was an Iago in Paul Robeson's real life drama of *Othello*, the Iago was the McCarthyite tendency in American political culture — sowing the seeds of ideological hate. If there was a Desdemona, it was the American nation itself. But in this real life version of *Othello*, Desdemona was being made to resent Othello instead of the other way round. The Iagos of America were the McCarthyites — creating alarm, despondency and hatred. When the ideological McCarthyites joined forces with the racial conspirators, the martyrdom of Othello was assured.

Born in April 1898 in the United States, Paul Robeson was educated at Rutgers and was the first in his class. He emerged as the all-American sporting genius — all-American football player. Robeson went to Columbia University for legal training — but opportunities for blacks in the legal profession were at that time limited. He graduated as a lawyer in 1923. Robeson went to the stage instead.

Appearance in the title role of Eugene O'Neill's *Emperor Jones* caused a sensation in New York in 1924 and in London in 1925 (the film version of it came in 1933). Singing Negro spirituals in Greenwich Village won him new fame. Robeson became world famous as Joe in the musical play *Show Boat* with his version of 'Ol' Man River'.

Robeson then flirted with Shakespeare in his career. Robeson's *Othello* in London in 1930 was a new frontier. The Broadway production in 1943 set an all-time record run for a Shakespearean play on Broadway. Later Robeson flirted with Karl Marx. In 1934 Robeson visited the Soviet Union — and became increasingly identified with left-wing tendencies. The US State Department withdrew his passport in 1950 because he refused to sign an affidavit affirming that he was not a member of the Communist Party. He was ostracized in the United States for his political views. Ideology and racism once again converged.

In 1958 the Supreme Court overturned the affidavit ruling. He left the United States for Europe until 1963. Robeson died in 1976. Racial prejudice was declining in the United States. Were other prejudices on the rise?[3]

I make the following proposition for the future of the black experience as a whole: that in terms of technological skills, African Americans and black South Africans will become the vanguard of the black world in the twenty-first century. The case rests in part on the chemistry of skills. And here I pose the question once again in relation to two other cultural groups — the Japanese and the Jews. These two cultural groups are ancestrally non-European but they have beaten Europeans at their own game. What combination of elements created innovative Japanese? And how did the Jews become what Malcolm X called 'the brains of the white world?' Can black-ruled South Africa, in the future, develop into a kind of African Japan — beginning in the twenty-first century? And can African Americans develop into a kind of black intellectual Jew? The Jews have been compared with black people sometimes in being victims of discrimination. Jews are compared with African Americans in the impact on American foreign policy. But there has not been a sustained comparison of Jews and black people in terms of intellectual performance and intellectual goals.

We have noted earlier that the performance of the Jews in many creative fields has been fairly disproportionate with their numbers. For example, they have produced a disproportionate number of Nobel Prize winners. As we mentioned before, almost every year there is probably one Jewish name among Nobel Prize winners. They perform well in the arts and sciences, and have changed the way the modern person thinks. An earlier chapter demonstrated how Jewish thinkers have transformed the modern mind. The Jewish pool has produced Sigmund Freud, Karl Marx, and Albert Einstein, for instance. That is a staggering impact on intellectual history for a group so small. There are twice as many African Americans as there are Jews in the whole world added together. That is to say, the population of African Americans is almost twice the population of world Jewry. And yet we see the staggering difference in performance between the two groups.

What we have to bear in mind is that Jews have not only outperformed blacks; they have outperformed non-Jewish whites also. Jews have outperformed Western gentiles. And Western Jews have left Oriental Jews behind. What is this telling us? That it is not white gentiles who are at the top of the intellectual pyramid of the world. It is not even the eastern Jews, close to their own ancestry, who have outperformed everybody else. It is the intermediate family born out of the chemistry of acculturation. The geniuses are not the pure Jews of the Middle East, nor the Western or white gentiles. Genius lies in Western Jews. Something in the chemistry of cultural mixture.

Let us recall the story of Dr Jekyll and Mr Hyde by Robert Louis Stevenson, the saga of the gentleman who changes chemically from a sensible doctor into the villainous Mr Hyde. One day Dr Jekyll discovers he has lost control over the chemical process. Jekyll turns into Hyde without drinking the chemical of transformation. None of his friends know that he is two personalities in one. Jekyll in the reluctant body of Hyde keeps on trying the chemistry to recover his more respectable identity. He sends notes to the pharmacy for his original chemical. But every time it comes it does not work. It is only very late that he discovers that something in the original powder had been impure, that *unknown impurity* had made it possible for Dr Jekyll to turn into Mr Hyde and back. Since neither he nor the pharmacist know what that impurity was, and since he has run out of the original powder, he is now a person with an enforced new identity.

In the case of the performance of the Jews in intellectual history it may again be that unknown impurity. Not pure Jews from the Middle East, not pure whites from Europe, but the cultural combination of the two. Now the question which arises in the destiny of African Americans is whether they too have a potentially creative but unkown impurity which may have effects similar to the impurity of Western Jews. Will African Americans outperform the pure Africans from whom they descend? Will African Americans one day be more innovative than the Westerners by whom they were once subjugated? Let us not forget that the Jews too are ex-slaves. African Americans will one day be a transmission belt to Africa of scientific knowledge from the West, just as they have already been a cultural transmission belt to the West of rhythms from Africa. It all depends upon Afroamerican ability to effectively enter the technological world of the region to which they belong, and to develop the capacity to transmit and share those skills with the rest of the black world. Will they therefore become, in the intellectual sense, the Jews of the black world?

Let us now turn to the other half of the dual vanguard of the black world. Will South Africa become the Japan of the black world? Black South Africans are the least privileged blacks of the twentieth century. It is conceivable that these untouchables of the black world of today may become the Brahmins of the twenty-first century. These most underprivileged blacks of today will become among the more privileged ones of tomorrow. Black South Africans live in one of the richest parts of the world. So far they have not benefited very much by being there, but before the end of the century, they may inherit at last the land of their ancestors. The land has been subjected to forms of industrialization and exploitation. The blacks have built with their sweat, and the whites have come with their skills. Together they have built the biggest industrial powerhouse in the African continent. The whites have even come up with nuclear know-how, and are developing a nuclear infrastructure. I believe that all of these will be inherited by blacks in South Africa before the end of the century.

Will black-ruled South Africa therefore become a kind of Japan? Japan is the most technologically advanced country in Asia. Black-ruled South Africa will be the most technologically advanced country in Africa. Japan developed Western techniques, retained Japanese spirit. Black-ruled South Africa will develop Western technique, and, I hope, will retain African spirit. Japan has limited mineral resources but high levels of skills. South Africa has many mineral resources and already has intermediate skills. Japan is the most powerful country in Asia. South Africa is the most powerful country in Africa. Japan faces the temptations of exercising regional hegemony in Asia. South Africa will also have the temptation of regional hegemonic power in Southern Africa. Japan is the powerful trader in a world of commerce. South Africa is a powerful centre in a world of mining. The Japanese were the technological imitators of the West before they became technological innovators. Black South Africans may also have to be technological imitators before they finally establish themselves as technological innovators.

Conclusion

In this book we have brought cultural insights to bear on global concerns and broad historical trends. The range of issues treated is from sexism in world politics to the intellectual impact of the Jews on history, and from a comparison of Karl Marx and the Prophet Muhammad to the prospects of an African nuclear bomb before the end of the twentieth century.

But in recording these conflicting trends we may have to look more widely around the world for areas of cultural reconciliation and for creative opportunities. Cultural experiments may have to be conducted partly in Africa precisely because that is the one continent where the rival cultural forces of the human species have to learn the secrets of accommodation and synthesis.

North America has Christianity and liberal capitalism — but neither Marxism nor Islam are strong. Latin America has a bigger Marxist component as well as a Christian and capitalist presence. But Islam is a very modest force in this region. Europe has capitalism, Marxism and Christianity — but it has a very modest Islamic presence outside Turkey and the Balkans.

Asia, is, in a sense, the opposite of Europe. In Asia capitalism, Marxism, and Islam are well represented — what is modest is the Christian presence.

In geographical distribution, Islam is primarily an Afro-Asian religion. Christianity is primarily an Afro-Western religion in dispersal. The arena they share is the 'Afro' part. The two religions continue to compete for the soul of Africa. Africa is destined to be a laboratory of both religious ecumenicalism and ideological cooperation. Marxism, capitalism, Christianity and Islam are well represented in African conditions.

Senegal is an example of a Muslim society which accepted a Roman Catholic Head of State for 20 years. Leopold Sedar Senghor presided over the destiny of this Muslim country until he voluntarily retired of his own accord in 1980.

When will the United States have a Jewish president? Certainly much later than Muslim Senegal had a Christian president. When will the United States have a Muslim president? When you add up all Americans from the Arab world, Indonesia, Iran, Pakistan, Turkey and other parts of the Muslim world, there may already be as many Muslims as Jews in the United States. But a Muslim President in the White House remains remote in this land which separates church from state. And yet Africa has already set a precedent in presidential ecumenicalism.

Will southern Africa become the great laboratory of ideological ecumenicalism? Will Marxist-Leninist regimes in Mozambique and Angola coexist more fruitfully in the future with a liberated Republic of South Africa — a South Africa still fundamentally capitalist, but under African rule? Will there be a left—right rapprochement which is not based on the Nkomati Accord[4] of uneasy co-existence with apartheid but on a more enlightened accord between Africanized Marxism and Africanized capitalism?

While Africa plays this complex ecumenical role, the world may still be waiting to witness the first Muslim president of the Soviet Union and the first black president of the United States having their summit meeting either in a Jerusalem at peace with its neighbours, or in a Pretoria liberated from racial bigotry.

Amen.

Notes

1. For an early prediction of this trend see Seymour Topping, 'Soviet Moslems, Population Surging, Hope to Get a Bigger Piece of the Pie', *New York Times*, 16 November 1981.
2. It is hard to be sure of the exact number of the Copts since official statistics are reluctant to quantify by religion. But United States sources estimate seven million.
3. In 1958 Robeson published his book, *Here I Stand* (New York: Othello Associates, 1958). He argued that Booker T. Washington had put too much faith in the sympathy of Southern whites — while twentieth-century blacks had too much faith in Northern liberals.
4. The 1984 agreement between Mozambique and South Africa to end the civil war in Mozambique. South Africa promised to stop supporting the RENAMO guerrillas inside Mozambique fighting the FRELIMO government and in return Mozambique promised not to train ANC guerrillas to infiltrate South Africa.

INDEX

Index

Index

Index

Mecca, 81, 218
Medina, 77, 81, 218
Mein Kampf (Hitler), 95-6, 98
Meir, Golda, 59, 188, 189, 190
Melotti, Umberto, 70
Merchant of Venice (Shakespeare), 54, 253
Mexico, 104, 108
Milan, Edict of (313), 33
Mill, John Stuart, 19, 21, 27, 140
Milton, John, 14-15, 29, 35-6, 86
Mobutu, President, 103, 196, 228
Monde, Le, 120
Monod, Jacques, 136
monotheism, 13-28, 35-7
Monroe Doctrine, 44, 237-8
Montefiore, C. G., 148, 149
Mosaic Law, 85
Mossadeq, Muhammad, 217
Mozambique, 78, 155, 159, 180-1, 197, 229, 234-5, 240, 257, 257n
Mozambique National Resistance Movement, 180, 235, 257n
MPLA, 111, 234
Mugabe, Robert, 180, 235
Muhammad (Prophet), 15, 34, 61, 67, 69, 73, 94, 96, 99, 256; and advertising, 78; and Jews, 76, 77; and merchant class, 74-5; and price control, 76; and Qur'an, 85-7; and *riba*, 76-7; and wage labour, 80; wives, 74-5, 88-9
Muhammad Ali (boxer), 127
Muhammad Ali (Egypt), 4-5
Muhammad Ali (Pakistan), 213
Munich Olympic Games (1972), 232
Museveni, Yoweri, 182, 183
music, American influence on, 120
Muslims, see Islam
Mwinyi, Ali Hassan, 103

Nabar, Vrinda, 94
Namibia, 3, 109, 155, 156, 160, 211, 234
Nandy, Vaskar, 94
Napoleonic legal code, 141-2
Narkis, Uzi, 139
Nasser, President, 197, 212, 213, 214, 238
Nation of Islam, 130
nationalism, Third World, 110
Nazis, see Germany
negritude, 129-37
Nehru, Jawaharlal, 52, 186, 189, 209, 211, 212, 213, 214, 215, 219, 225, 238
Nekudah, 174

Neo-Colonialism (Nkrumah), 110
Netherlands, 151-2
New International Economic Order, 206, 208, 219, 226n
New Testament, 36, 73
New York Times, 120, 139
New York University, 138
New Zealand, 92
newspapers, American influence on, 119-20
Newsweek, 119
Newton, Isaac, 37, 131
Nicaragua, 7, 107, 109, 112, 116, 117, 228, 234
Nigeria, 182, 219, 227
Nimeiry, President Jaafar, 169
Nixon, President Richard, 35, 164, 222
Nkomati Accord (1984), 257
Nkrumah, Kwame, 41, 110, 204, 210, 212, 214-5, 238
Noah (Bible), 167
Nobel Prize, 132, 185, 255
non-alignment, 208, 210, 211-7, 225, 238

North Atlantic Treaty Organization, 212, 213
North Korea, see Korea
North-South, dependency relationship, 6; technological gap, 1
Northern Ireland, 89-90
nuclear accidents, 113, 223
nuclear weapons, 9-10, 44, 111, 112-4, 117, 125, 160-1, 188-9, 214-7, 220-4, 227, 247-9, 256
Nuclear Weapons Non-Proliferation Treaty, 112-3, 221, 222
Nuer people, 140
Nyerere, President Julius K., 29, 103, 196, 204, 241, 253

October War (1973), 145, 171, 173
oil industry, see petroleum industry
Okigbo, Christopher (*Trial of Christopher Okigbo*), 98
Old Testament, 36, 73, 150, 167
Oman, 52, 218
O'Neill, Eugene, 254
O'Neill, 'Tip', 107
On Heroes. . .' (Carlyle), 168
On the Jewish Question (Marx), 166
Operation Moses, 149
Organization of Petroleum Exporting Countries, 26, 182, 197, 217, 218; special fund, 198-9, 205-6
Othello (Shakespeare), 54, 253, 254
Ottenberg, Mrs Simon, 143n
Ottoman Empire, 51-2, 238
OXFAM, 105

Pakistan, 51, 117, 210, 212, 213, 215, 227, 244; and Islam, 51; and *Satanic Verses*, 94; nuclear weapons, 190, 216-7, 220, 221, 224; woman leader of, 186, 189
Palestine, see Israel
Palestine Liberation Organization, 3, 169, 177, 230, 231, 232-3, 235
Palestinians, 7, 57, 152, 153-4, 155; 156, 157, 158-9; 164, 227, 233; Intifadah, 169, 171, 173, 174, 175-8; skyjacking, 228-9, 230
Pan-African Congress, 3
pantheism, 37
Papacy, 49-50, 74
Paradise Lost (Milton), 14-15, 35-6, 86, 87
Pastora, Eden, 107
Paul, St, 32
Peking, see China (Beijing)
perestroika, 1-4, 252
Perón, President Isabella, 188, 189
Persian Empire, 34, 242
Peru, 103, 104
Petrarch, 37
petroleum industry, 72, 124, 217-20, 225, 247
Philippines, 108, 186
piracy, political, 229, 231
Plamenatz, Professor John, 241
Plekhanov, Georgy, 71-2, 242
Poland, 55, 117
polytheism, 13-14, 37
Pope, Alexander, 137
Portugal, 237
Potter, Barnett, 131-2
Protestantism (Christian), 25, 38-9, 49-51, 67, 74, 75; see also Islam
Puerto Rico, 108
Puritans, 25
Pushkin, Aleksandr, 133

Qur'an, 85-7, 95, 98, 99-100

racism, 40, 41, 42, 52, 96, 98, 121, 131-2, 138-9
Rainbow Warrior, 92-3
Rajbansi, Amichand, 146
Ramadhan, 79
Raman, V., 94
Reagan, President Ronald, 92, 106-7, 112, 206, 207, 234
Reformation, 37-9, 49, 67
Renaissance, 37-8
RENAMO, see Mozambique National Resistance Movement
revolution and Western culture, 240-3
Rhodesia, see Zimbabwe
riba (interest), 76-7, 79
Ricardo, David, 47
Roberts, J. M., 165
Robeson, Paul, 253, 254
Rockefeller Foundation, 105
Roderick, King of the Visigoths, 34
Rodinson, Maxime, 82n
Roling, B. V. A., 17-18
Roman Catholicism, 50-1
Roman Empire, 32, 33
Romero, Archbishop Oscar, 234
Roosevelt, Franklin D., 21, 47
Roots (Haley), 52, 96, 98
Rosenberg, Julius and Ethel, 84
Rousseau, Jean Jacques, 37
Roy, Ashim, 94
Royal Society, 25
Rushdie, Salman, 83-101
Russia, see Soviet Union

Sadat, Anwar, 230
Sandinistas, 107, 228, 234
Santa Maria, 229
Sapir, Pinchas, 154-5
Satan, 14, 35-6, 87
Satanic Verses, The (Rushdie), 83-101
sati see suttee
satyagraha, 208, 209, 210, 213, 225
Saudi Arabia, 4, 26, 52, 182, 198, 218, 219, 229-30, 233
Saudi Fund for Development, 197-8
Savimbi, Jonas, 112, 234
Schelling, Thomas C., 111
Schockley, W., 143n
science, rise of, 25
Scotland, blasphemy laws, 85
secularism, 19-21
Seipei, Stompie Mokhetsi, 185
Semitic peoples, 29-37, 61-3
Senegal, 198, 257
Senghor, Leopold Sedar, 129, 134-5, 136, 204, 257
Shah of Iran, see Iran
Shakespeare, William, 18, 53-4, 85-6, 122, 131, 141, 177, 201, 253, 254
Shame (Rushdie), 99
Shamir, Yitzhak, 164, 171, 173, 176, 233
Shapiro, Harold, 91
Sharpeville Massacre, 152
Shastri, Lal Bahadur, 186
Shaw, George Bernard, 251
Sheel, Panch, 216
Shihata, Dr Ibrahim, 205
Show Boat, 254
Sicily, 34-5
Sierre Leone, 53, 197
Sikhs, 186, 216
Singh, Kushwant, 94
Sinn Fein, 89-90
Sirhan Sirhan, 229
Six-Day War (1967), 173, 227
skyjacking, 228-31

Index